MW00999312

Previous victims of the congressional hearing root canal will ask themselves, "Where was this invaluable book when I needed it?"

Mitch Daniels, Governor, Indiana

Testifying before Congress isn't a fair fight, and there are few rules to protect you. Bill LaForge has packed years of experience, seeing congressional hearings done well and done very badly, into this practical book, *Testifying Before Congress*.

If you are a corporate leader summoned to testify before Congress and you want to survive what could be one of the most horrible, and dangerous, experiences of your career, you must read this extremely valuable book. If you are a lobbyist or government affairs professional advising a client who will be testifying before a congressional committee, you must give them this book before they dig whatever hole they are in even deeper.

If you want to make the fight fair, prepare yourself and read this book.

Charlie Cook, Editor and Publisher of *The Cook Political Report*,
Political Analyst for the National Journal Group

Bill LaForge has written a thoughtful guide for those who are called to testify before the House or Senate. His insights are right on target.

Thad Cochran, United States Senate

Testifying before Congress is a critical opportunity to tell your organization's story, but to do it effectively, it pays to have the advice of an old pro. Bill LaForge's excellent how-to guide to the hearings process and preparation of witnesses is a "must-read" for any executive called to testify on Capitol Hill.

Susan Neely, President & CEO, American Beverage Association

Bill LaForge has written the perfect resource for anyone who wants to understand the congressional hearings process or who is preparing to testify before Congress. This book opens the door to the world of congressional hearings, and lays out a path to excellence for witnesses testifying on Capitol Hill.

Charles A. Bowsher, Comptroller General of the United States (Retired)

Being called to testify on Capitol Hill can be a career high point or a disaster. Whether your organization is a not-for-profit or a Fortune 100 company, you will want this practical guide by Bill LaForge at the ready when you face one of the most important moments in the life of a citizen.

Dan Perry, President & CEO, Alliance for Aging Research

Testifying before Congress is a new but increasingly necessary experience for most business leaders. Bill LaForge's book, *Testifying Before Congress*, is a practical and comprehensive how-to guide that should be required reading before your first experience on the "hot seat" in front of a congressional committee.

Chad Holliday, Chairman, Bank of America

Testifying Before Congress by Bill LaForge is a gold mine for anyone engaging in the congressional hearings process.

Richard E. Wiley, Managing Partner, Wiley Rein LLP

Testifying Before Congress is the "bible" for anyone engaging in the congressional hearings process and the preeminent guide for any witness preparing to testify before Congress. This deskbook "picks the lock" of the congressional hearings process and the preparation of witnesses. Everything you want to know to prepare your client or the head of a federal agency to testify before Congress is thoroughly discussed in this exceptional guidebook. This informative "how-to" guide should be required reading for every new congressional staffer and for the congressional relations staff of every federal department and agency.

Bill LaForge's book is a very useful, one-of-a-kind, comprehensive treatise that provides an excellent road map. Private and government practitioners—and their clients—will be well-served by consulting this valuable guide before going to testify on Capitol Hill.

Lawrence Baca, President, Federal Bar Association, and Deputy Director of the Office of Tribal Justice in the Department of Justice (Retired)

This insightful and instructive treatise is ideal for mayors and other municipal officials who deal with the U.S. Congress and its committees, and it provides excellent background and preparatory guidance for those testifying or preparing witnesses for testimony before Congress.

Susan Narvaiz, Mayor, City of San Marcos, Texas

I wish I had a book like Bill LaForge has produced when I first testified before Congress. The year was 1958; I was testifying on behalf of the Methodist Student Movement; and Bill was still in short pants. Now LaForge is sharing his years of experience with us, and he has turned out a unique manual for anyone who wants to, or must, appear before a congressional committee, from ordinary citizen to experienced advocate. This book can become for congressional testimony what Robert's Rules of Order has become for legislative procedure.

Richard F. Celeste, President, Colorado College; Former Governor of Ohio, Peace Corps Director, and Ambassador to India

Bill LaForge's excellent treatise, *Testifying Before Congress*, is the ideal "one-stop-shopping," easy-to-use reference for any witness preparing to testify before Congress. For example, Chapter Four focuses on the details of preparing the witness to testify. It discusses in practical detail the use of prepared materials and witness preparation, including making certain the witness knows what to expect. Every corporate and association executive should have this valuable resource tool available before venturing into the congressional hearings process.

Larry D. Thompson, Senior Vice-President for Government Affairs and General Counsel, PepsiCo; former Deputy Attorney General of the United States

Testifying Before Congress is a superlative work. The book has the depth of background and the precision of practicality to make it a helpful treatise for the practitioner as well as a thoughtful textbook for use by professors in classes on Public Policy or Congressional Oversight. It should be on the bookshelf of anyone who follows the business of Congress.

Jim Rosenblatt, Dean, Mississippi College School of Law

With *Testifying Before Congress*, Bill LaForge has provided an invaluable and comprehensive resource for law school faculty, students, and researchers interested in gaining an in-depth understanding of how congressional committees organize hearings and how witnesses prepare for testimony.

Judith Areen, Paul Regis Dean Professor of Law and Dean Emeritus, Georgetown Law

The congressional hearings process with its tough questions, full media coverage and complicated array of participants has become a bewildering spectacle. In this book, Bill LaForge draws on his experience as a congressional staff member as well as a lobbyist to bring coherence to the process and much-needed advice for those charged with providing testimony. He sets these hearings nicely within the legislative process to highlight their importance for the development of public policy. He is an excellent coach for witnesses in preparing effective testimony, delivering it successfully and responding to difficult questions.

His experience as an adjunct professor in the School of Business at George Washington University has broadened the targeted audiences to include faculty and students involved in courses in the American legislative process, business and government relations and business representation and lobbying. Both practitioners and academics will find this book enlightening.

It is an enjoyable read as LaForge includes examples throughout to bring the congressional committee rooms to life with conflicting interests often waging heated battles in shaping public policy.

D. Jeffrey Lenn, Associate Vice President for Academic Operations and
Professor of Strategic Management & Public Policy, The George Washington University

Testifying Before Congress should be on the desk of every government relations professional in the corporate, association, agency and private firm arenas.

Jack Gerard, President and CEO, American Petroleum Institute (API)

This is a time when the interest in understanding the workings of Congress is particularly acute. For those of us who have spent time in the halls of the House and Senate and now have an interest in helping others understand how these institutions function, their relationship to the other branches of government and the changing patterns of power, this book could not come at a better time. Bill LaForge has given us a new tool to use in helping students truly understand the greatest deliberative body in the world.

Sheila Burke, Kennedy School of Government, Harvard University

Bill LaForge has written an important treatise on congressional investigations and the legislative process. It blends a thorough understanding of the purpose of congressional investigations in gathering and evaluating information on a wide range of issues with an informative and practical guide to the preparation for and participation in the hearing process. With its step-by-step approach to dealing with the preliminary fact-finding process, the committee hearing and the legislative report, including the nuances of an uneven playing field, it is must reading for lawyers and witnesses involved in this critical governmental function.

Mark H. Tuohey III, Partner, Brown Rudnick

I wish I had this book before I testified in front of a Senate committee examining eye safety and computer use. I sat at a table with two academicians and peered at a group of senators sitting above us—quite an intimidating experience. What you see on the evening news or C-SPAN doesn't reflect the reality of testifying before Congress. As physicians we were prepared with the facts but totally unprepared for dealing with the process. A must reference for associations or NGOs!

William L. Rich III, MD, FACS, Medical Director of Health Policy,
American Academy of Ophthalmology

Testifying Before Congress is the best "how to" resource that I have seen—it is well-researched, experience-based, and thoughtfully written, with a dash of humor added for good measure.

Samuel M. Davis, Dean of the School of Law, The University of Mississippi

For anyone or any group delivering testimony to Congress, Bill LaForge's book should serve as the Bible for preparation and delivery of the message. It is a must for those who approach this sometimes intimidating experience.

David Pryor, Former U.S. Senator (D-AR), Dean of The University of Arkansas Clinton School of Public Service and Director of The Institute of Politics, Harvard University

Bill LaForge has penned the definitive treatise on the preparation and delivery of congressional testimony, and a valuable resource for scholars, researchers and staffers. Packed with how-to insight, it's leavened with humor.

Charles Babington, Congressional Reporter, The Associated Press

Testifying Before Congress captures the magic formula for successful advocacy inside the Beltway. Bill LaForge provides a masterful road map to help you navigate the congressional testifying process and identifies every opportunity to make concise and compelling arguments to achieve your desired result.

Catherine Reheis-Boyd, President, Western States Petroleum Association

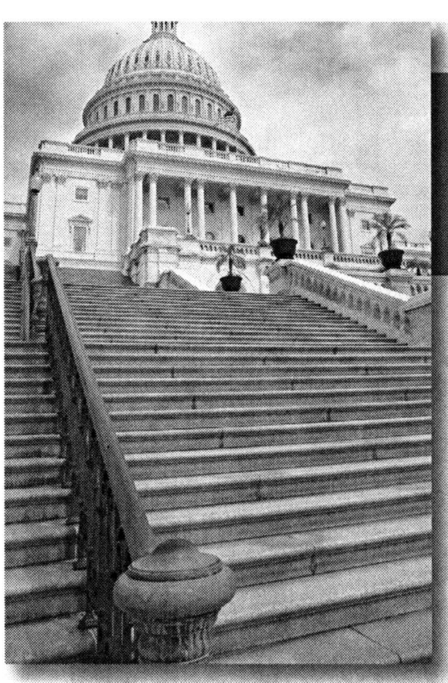

A Practical Guide to Preparing and Delivering Testimony Before Congress and Congressional Hearings for Agencies, Associations, Corporations, Military, NGOs, and State and Local Officials

By William N. LaForge

Testifying Before Congress

For over 30 years, TheCapitol.Net and its predecessor, Congressional Quarterly Executive Conferences, have been training professionals from government, military, business, and NGOs on the dynamics and operations of the legislative and executive branches and how to work with them.

Our training and publications include congressional operations, legislative and budget process, communication and advocacy, media and public relations, research, business etiquette, and more.

TheCapitol.Net is a non-partisan firm.

Our publications and courses, written and taught by *current* Washington insiders who are all independent subject matter experts, show how Washington works.™ Our products and services can be found on our web site at <*www.TheCapitol.Net*>.

Additional copies of *Testifying Before Congress* can be ordered from your favorite bookseller or online: <*www.TestifyingBeforeCongress.com*>.

Design and production by Zaccarine Design, Inc., Evanston, IL; 847-864-3994.

∞ The paper used in this publication exceeds the requirements of the American National Standard for Information Sciences—Permanence of Paper for Printed Library Materials, ANSI Z39.48-1992.

PO Box 25706
Alexandria, VA 22313-5706
703-739-3790 Toll free: 1-877-228-5086
<*www.TheCapitol.Net*>

v 1

Testifying Before Congress
Softcover: ISBN: 158733-163-2 Hardbound: ISBN: 158733-172-1
ISBN 13: 978-1-58733-163-3 ISBN 13: 978-1-58733-172-5

To my family—
Nancy, Caroline, and Clayton

Summary Table of Contents

Table of Contents

Chapter Two:
Congressional Hearing Organization, Planning, and Preparation 65

Chapter Five:
Presentation and Delivery of Oral Testimony ... 261

Acknowledgments

For his guidance, assistance, and support in the writing and production of this deskbook, I extend my deepest appreciation to my editor and publisher, Chug Roberts of TheCapitol.Net, who had the vision for this book and the confidence in me to write it.

Friends and colleagues who contributed perspectives, critique, quotations, ideas, suggestions, and occasional research and technical assistance include Cathi Henderson, Chuck Bowsher, Brenda Becker, Nancy Perry, Jim Bayless, Monte Lake, Bruce Moyer, Walt Oleszek, Cordia Strom, Bruce Evans, Galen Fountain, Jim Morhard, Fred Pagan, Ed Pease, and Doug Todd.

I am particularly grateful to the government relations professionals at the Government Accountability Office who were helpful in sharing information about GAO's excellent internal training programs on preparing and delivering congressional testimony, and to the experts at the Congressional Research Service of the Library of Congress who have produced excellent written materials and have been superb authorities and resources on the subject of congressional testimony for many years. I am also appreciative to the congressional relations offices of a number of federal departments and agencies, and to the government relations offices of numerous corporations, associations, nonprofits and public interest organizations, for the information they provided about their hearing preparation procedures and operations.

Finally, I thank my principal mentors during fourteen years of government service —Senator Thad Cochran (R-MS), former Peace Corps Director Richard Celeste (D-OH), and former Congressman David Bowen (D-MS), who provided me with opportunities to learn and participate in the congressional hearings process—as well as the numerous clients during twenty years in the private sector who have afforded me the privilege of representing them in the processes of government.

About the Author

William N. LaForge is an attorney, Washington office managing shareholder, and government relations practice group chair with the Winstead law firm. A registered lobbyist, he specializes in federal government relations and public policy advocacy, and he represents businesses and other organizations with public policy interests before the United States Congress and federal executive branch agencies. For more than thirty years, he has been involved with federal public policy in all three branches of government, and from the perspectives of both a government professional and a private practitioner.

On Capitol Hill, Bill served as senior legislative counsel to Republican and Democratic lawmakers in both houses of Congress. He was chief counsel of the U.S. Senate Appropriations Subcommittee on Agriculture, and culminated his government career as chief legislative counsel and chief of staff to United States Senator Thad Cochran (R-MS). Previously he served as congressional liaison for the Peace Corps and as a legislative assistant to Congressman David Bowen (D-MS).

As a U.S. Senate committee staff professional, Bill organized and helped conduct numerous congressional hearings. In the private sector, he has prepared a wide array of written testimony for clients, advised and trained witnesses appearing before congressional committees, and served as a hearing witness himself.

Bill is a member of the bars of The District of Columbia and Mississippi, and he is past national president of the Federal Bar Association. He is a frequent speaker on the topics of government and congressional relations, communicating with Congress, the congressional hearings process, and the congressional appropriations process. He holds an academic appointment as an adjunct professor at George Washington University, where he has taught courses in the fields of commercial law, public policy, lobbying, and business-government relations for more than 25 years. He also served as an adjunct professor at Georgetown University, and he has been a visiting professor of law at universities in Russia, Poland, and Bulgaria.

Bill graduated with honors from Delta State University, earned his J.D. from the University of Mississippi School of Law, received an LL.M. in international law from Georgetown University, and studied international law at Cambridge University. He received fellowships to study government and public policy in the European Union and at the Kennedy School of Government at Harvard University, and he is the recipient of an honorary doctorate of laws from the Stetson University College of Law. An avid runner and a triathlete, he has completed sixty-one marathons, including twenty-four Boston Marathons, and he has logged more than 66,000 miles running. He plays guitar in an oldies rock-and-roll band.

To contact Bill, please go to <*BillLaForge.com*>.

Introduction

Every year the United States Congress conducts hundreds of hearings on every conceivable topic involving public policy, regulation of business and industry, the operations of government itself, and myriad other issues affecting the country at large and the lives and fortunes of individual American citizens.

As a key historical and institutional component of the congressional process, hearings provide a "pipeline" of information to assist Congress in carrying out its responsibilities. Throughout the year, congressional committees hear from a wide array of witnesses called to testify about the most important issues of the day. Through congressional committee hearings, and on behalf of the good of the nation and the home-state constituencies that elected them, members of Congress explore virtually every aspect of American life, and beyond, in an effort to help ensure that fair and effective laws are passed, and that the best interests of the American people are served.

Testifying before Congress entails for a witness a variety of preparatory activities and the need to execute numerous tasks effectively, especially the crafting of written testimony, the delivery of oral testimony, and the presentation of answers to questions asked by a committee. Congressional hearings, and the process of receiving testimony from witnesses who appear before committees, are very important enterprises in the U.S. systems of legislating, law-making, and governance generally.

As a practical guide to assist witnesses and their organizations in preparing and delivering congressional testimony, this desk reference is intended for use by anyone or any organization called upon to testify before a committee of the United States Congress, and for those who are providing assistance in preparing the testimony and the witness. This book can serve as a guide through the unique maze of the congressional hearings process for virtually any witness or organization, including especially federal departments and agencies, the federal judiciary, members and staff of the legislative branch itself, associations, corporations, the military service branches, non-governmental organizations (NGOs), private and voluntary organizations (PVOs), public interest entities, state and local governmental officials and institutions, and individuals who are chosen to appear as a witness before Congress for any reason on any topic.

Similarly, in the world of academics and scholarship, this reference work can be helpful to scholars and writers in think-tanks and research organizations, as well as to faculty, researchers and students engaged in the study of law, business, government, politics, political science, and the legislative processes of government. This deskbook can also serve as a reliable reference source and helpful tool for law, lobbying, government relations, accounting, and other public policy-related service industry professionals who are involved with the congressional hearings process on behalf of their clients', their customers' and their own public policy, legislative, and government relations interests.

This book is organized in such a way that it can be utilized as a ready-reference and easy-to-use guide section by section, or it can be used to obtain information and understanding about the various aspects of preparing and delivering congressional testimony through a review of the book in its entirety or its individual chapters. As a desk reference, the treatise lays out for the reader's use and guidance the various processes and stages of proper hearing, witness and statement preparation, as well as the best practices involved in delivering testimony and answering committee questions. The text addresses the key aspects of a congressional hearing and its preparation from the perspectives of both a committee and a witness. At the end of each chapter is a bullet-item summary cross-referenced with pertinent sections in the text. To a great extent, the principles in this book may also be used by those preparing for hearings before federal agencies and international tribunals, as well as state and local governmental bodies. However, the major thrust of this work focuses on the distinct congressional hearings process and its major elements.

Congressional testimony is a key institutional element of the legislative processes of government. More precisely, testimony is an important ingredient in the congressional committee system employed in the development of legislation and funding measures, the education of Congress and its committees, and the oversight, evaluation, and investigation of government programs and virtually any issue of importance to the American public and its governance.

For purposes of a working definition, congressional testimony is a vital means through which congressional committees become knowledgeable about issues that are before them for discussion, debate, and the development of legislative remedies. It is a method of collecting data and gathering intelligence through an open and public forum and dialogue that utilizes personal appearances and presentations by witnesses who testify, as well as the submission of written statements for the record, from organizations both inside and outside of government.

These organizations typically are stakeholders in the issues before the committee holding the hearing. Congressional testimony is also an opportunity for those who wish to influence the decisions and actions of Congress to make their views known directly to the decision makers. Thus, congressional testimony serves a valuable purpose from the perspectives of both the Congress as decision makers and lawmakers, and those individuals and entities who appear before them and have a vital interest in the issues of the day and the outcome of any congressional action that might be taken.

The setting and platform for congressional testimony are committee hearings that are rather structured and formal, as are many aspects of congressional committee work. But if approached and used properly and effectively by both the committee holding the hearing and by the organizations whose witnesses testify before the committee, the enterprise of congressional testimony can be a productive, educational, enlightening, and legitimate exercise in two-way communication.

Congressional testimony and the hearing process are as American as apple pie. For the Congress, it represents the openness of our government and the opportunity afforded to business, nonprofit organizations, interest groups, and individual citizens, as well as federal, state, and local governmental entities, to participate in their national government first-hand and to help influence government decision-making. It is an institutionalized delivery system for hearing views and perspectives on pending legislation and the operations of government.

For the witness and the organization providing testimony, a congressional hearing offers the opportunity to express and advocate views and opinions, and especially "... to petition the government for redress of grievances"—an important right guaranteed by the First Amendment to the U.S. Constitution. For those in the executive and judicial branches of the federal government, it is a formalized method of "cross-branch" communication within the uniquely American scheme of shared governance.

The larger context for congressional testimony is its place in the universe of public policy development and government decision-making. Effective public policy advocacy and lobbying often include the use of congressional testimony to make the record and inform law makers on a particular issue. Consequently, congressional testimony is a frequently used strategy in government relations and public policy advocacy. In a broad sense, testimony provides a multifaceted strategy because it conveys important information and messages to a committee, produces a public record, and engages a committee and a witness in questions and answers, as well as in other follow-up and related communications and activities. In these ways, testimony complements and supports other congressional and government relations strategies such as direct lobbying (from outside government), cross-branch and intra-branch education and advocacy (from within government—the executive, legislative, and judicial branches), media and communications activities, grassroots and grasstops initiatives, and coalition efforts.

Another contextual consideration is congressional testimony's role in the doctrine of separation of powers among the three branches of government generally, and the development and oversight of federal laws and programs more specifically. Congressional testimony is an important tool used by Congress both to "check and balance" the other two branches of government, as well as to elucidate issues and actions that may need review and reform through a legislative response or remedy. In its simplest form, congressional testimony facilitates communications with Congress by the other branches of government and with U.S. business, public interest organizations and private citizens. It institutionalizes a method for an ongoing or episodic dialogue at the prerogative of the Congress.

This reference work is intended to provide the reader with a user-friendly treatise on the "who, what, where, when, why and how"—especially the "how to" aspect—as applied to the congressional hearings process, the development and delivery of testimony, and the preparation and role of witnesses. While most people might associate the terms "hearing," "testimony," and "witness" with legal or court proceedings, each term actually has a special meaning and application in the context of the congressional committee hearings process. These terms are explained and expanded throughout the text.

Webster defines a hearing variously as "an opportunity to speak, a chance to be heard" in general terms, and, more specifically as "a formal meeting, as of an investigative body or legislative committee, before which evidence is presented, testimony is given . . ." The committee hearing is *the* forum for congressional testimony, and, consequently, those involved in the enterprise of testifying should have a keen understanding of how congressional committees operate and how hearings are conducted. While formal in nature, congressional hearings are quite different in structure, content and purpose from those activities conducted in the judicial process. But the general outcome and goal are similar—good, sound decisions based on accurate facts.

To testify, says Webster, means to "make a serious declaration to substantiate a fact; bear witness or give evidence, especially under oath in court." Testimony is essentially verbal or written factual evidence provided for consideration by a decision maker, whether in the judicial, legislative, or executive branches of government. Testimony provided in the congressional hearings context provides congressional committees, and the Senate and House at large, with important information that serves as a foundational basis for making decisions, formulating legislation, and dealing with federal programs and the issues of the day. It is critical that written and oral testimony delivered in the congressional process be well-crafted, accurate, reliable, and presented in the appropriate manner, and that witnesses who appear before hearings of congressional committees be well-prepared.

With a final reference to Webster, a witness is defined as "an attesting of a fact, statement, etc; evidence; testimony . . ." and "a person who saw, or can give a firsthand account of, something; a person who testifies in court." Again, the analogy to a court hearing is similar in some respects, but the witness in the congressional committee hearings process appears before the committee to proffer a statement in support of or opposition to an issue, a bill, a program or a policy that is the topic of the hearing, and to answer questions asked by the committee.

What follows in this deskbook are both an overview and explanation of the context for congressional hearings, how hearings are organized and conducted, how to prepare testimony and a witness, how to make an effective oral presentation as a witness, and how to respond to hearing questions. Post-hearing follow-up activities are also discussed, and a number of sample documents and hearing examples are provided throughout the text.

- **Chapter 1** sets the stage for the legislative process and the context for congressional hearings. It explains how hearings fit into the legislative scheme and how they provide value and meaning to the process. The opening chapter provides an overview of the environment surrounding congressional hearings and of the legislative committee system itself, and it describes the types, purposes, missions, and results of congressional hearings.

- **Chapter 2** explains what is entailed in organizing and conducting a hearing by the committee, and what is involved in preparing for a hearing on the part of a witness. It describes committee rules and logistics, the hearing "players," the types of witnesses and their selection, and the conduct of a hearing. It also outlines the important formulas for effective congressional testimony and a successful hearing.
- **Chapter 3** takes the reader through all the vital aspects of preparing effective written testimony, and explains the nature, differences and importance of both written and oral testimony. It also provides suggestions for building a strong substantive case and developing compelling arguments in both written and oral testimony.
- **Chapter 4** focuses on the importance of preparing the witness who will deliver the testimony. It discusses the use of prepared materials and witness rehearsals, and it outlines what a witness should expect in a congressional hearing.
- **Chapter 5** lays out the major concepts of superior witness performance in presenting and delivering congressional testimony. It discusses speaking format and presentation style, use of supporting materials, and the order and method of delivering a concise and compelling statement to a committee. It also provides a number of special "tips" for a witness.
- **Chapter 6** instructs a witness on handling and being responsive to committee questions after the testimony is complete. It describes how to field and respond to questions, and how to engage the committee to enhance the presentation.
- **Chapter 7** outlines post-hearing activities and follow-up for which a committee and a witness are responsible.

At the conclusion of the deskbook, for the reader's use, is a quick-reference "back-of-the-book" section containing additional information on useful web sites; congressional committee contact and hearing schedule information; media and webcast contacts; resources for sample documents; a bibliography; a section on FAQs (frequently asked questions); and further contact information about *Testifying Before Congress*, followed by an index.

It is the purpose and intention of *Testifying Before Congress* to help demystify the congressional hearings process, and to assist witnesses and their organizations to be well-prepared when appearing before a congressional committee to testify.

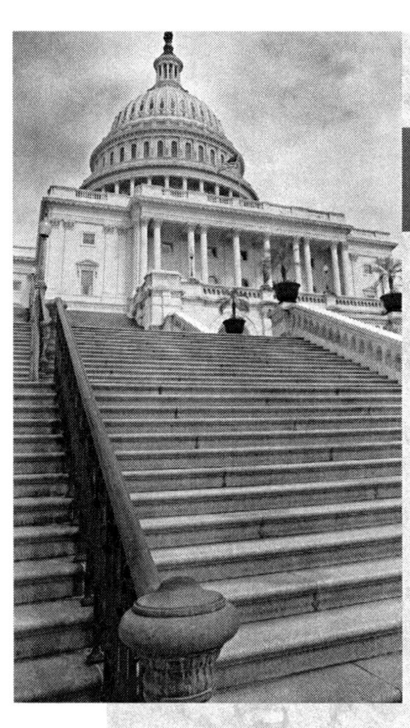

Chapter One

The Context for Congressional Hearings and Testimony

Chapter One

Section

1.0 Introduction and Overview: The Authority and Foundation for Testimony before Congress and Congressional Committee Hearings

1.1 What is a Hearing?

1.2 Source of Committee Rules

1.3 Official Rules of the United States Senate and the United States House of Representatives

1.4 Congressional Committee Web Sites that Include Hearing Guidelines

1.5 Congressional Hearing Information Sources: Web Sites and Links

1.6 Access to Congressional Committee Hearing Transcripts

1.10 Congressional Hearings Process in a Nutshell

1.20 The Use, Importance, and Value of Congressional Hearings

1.21 Testimonial of a Senate Committee Staff Director on the Value of Congressional Hearings and the Importance of a Witness's Role

1.22 Contrary Perspectives on the Value of Hearings

1.30 The Dynamics and Environment of Congressional Hearings

1.31 Making the Record

1.32 Partisanship and Political Analysis: Where Policy and Politics Converge

1.40 Understanding the Congressional Committee System: The Hearing as a Vital Step in the Legislative Process

1.50 The Purposes and Types of Congressional Hearings

1.51 Legislative Hearings

1.52 Sample Notification of a Legislative Hearing

1.53 Budget and Appropriations Hearings

1.54 Sample of Appropriations Committee Hearing Notice

1.55 Sample Appropriations Hearing Transcript

1.56 Oversight and Investigative Hearings

1.57 Sample Oversight Hearing Transcript: Opening Sections of House Oversight and Government Reform Committee Hearing on Treatment of U.S. Troops at Walter Reed Hospital and Other Medical Facilities

1.58 Senate Advice and Consent: Hearings to Consider Nominations, Confirmations, and Treaties

1.59 Sample Confirmation Hearing Opening Statement: Opening Segment of Senate Judiciary Committee's Hearing on the Nomination of Judge John Roberts to Become Chief Justice of the United States

1.60 Field Hearings

Summary Table of Contents

§ 1.0 Introduction and Overview: The Authority and Foundation for Testimony before Congress and Congressional Committee Hearings

Welcome to the unique world of congressional witnesses, testimony, and committee hearings, major components in the processes of public policy review, formulation and development, and the delivery system for providing Congress with important information and perspectives that help shape public policy decisions.

Three basic components combine to form the heart and soul of the congressional hearings and testimony scenario:

1) **The Witness**—the individuals who appear before a committee to present testimony as experts or knowledgeable sources;

2) **The Testimony**—the written and oral statements presented to a committee by witnesses that help provide the rationale and substantiation of a policy issue, deliver the message of the witnesses, and make the case for the witnesses' positions; and,

3) **The Congressional Committee**—the panel of congressional committee members who conduct the hearing, receive the testimony of the witness, and question the witness with respect to the topic of the hearing and within the committee's specific portfolio of public policy issues.

Congressional testimony is a key institutional component of the legislative processes of government. The presentation and reception of testimony are important elements in the congressional committee system employed in the development of legislation and funding measures, the education of Congress and its committees, and the oversight, evaluation, and investigation of government programs and virtually any issue of importance to the American public and its governance.

Congressional testimony and the committee hearings process represent the openness of our government and the opportunity afforded to business, nonprofit organizations, interest groups, individual citizens, and government itself to participate in informing Congress about public policy priorities and helping to influence government decision-making. This integral and democratic process utilized by congressional committees is an institutionalized delivery system for hearing views and perspectives on pending legislation, the operations of government, and important public policy matters. Indeed, committee hearings are perhaps the most visible of all congressional actions and procedures.

For the nonfederal government witness, state and local governmental entities, commercial enterprise or private organization providing testimony, the congressional hearings process provides the opportunity to express views and offer information to Congress on which important policy decisions can be based, and especially "... to petition the government for redress of grievances ...," an important right guaranteed by the First Amendment to the U.S. Constitution. For those in the executive and judicial branches of the federal government, the congressional hearings process is a formalized method of communicating to the legislative branch the policy and spending priorities of the other two branches under the aegis of the American scheme of shared governance and separation of powers.

Among the roles of congressional committees is their responsibility to review proposals for legislation, conduct and develop research and background for study and decision-making, consider bills under their jurisdiction that have been introduced by members of Congress, produce and advance legislative proposals under their purview, and approve, report, and recommend legislation for consideration by the committee's respective chamber.

As committees carry out their responsibilities, especially in conducting and providing research and background on issues that come before them for review, they frequently rely on the hearings process to solicit relevant information, collect pertinent data on specific topics, make the record for further consideration, hear from witnesses who bring expertise to the subject under review, and help create and provide a body of knowledge and information on which the committees can rely in their decision-making regarding legislation and other functions of the committee system.

A committee's overall agenda typically focuses on achieving these objectives generally, and its agenda for any given hearing is to accomplish these goals for specific topics proactively in order to accomplish substantive results in the form of legislative measures that can be embraced and reported further in the legislative process.

Because congressional hearings provide Congress and its committees with vital information needed to carry out institutional, legislative, and oversight responsibilities, written and oral testimony is important to the process. Consequently, testimony, both written and oral, should be carefully and thoughtfully prepared and effectively delivered by a witness who is likewise well-prepared for the role of testifying. (For more information about these three key topics, see Chapter 3, "Preparation of Written Testimony"; Chapter 4, "Preparation of the Witness"; and Chapter 5, "Presentation and Delivery of Oral Testimony.")

The basic authority for conducting hearings and calling witnesses to testify before committees of Congress lies in the official rules and guidelines of the United States House of Representatives and of the United States Senate and their various committees. Citations for the rules of both houses of Congress are included in § 1.3 below, but it is highly suggested that witnesses and those preparing for a hearing also consult each committee for specific rules that are written in conformity with the overarching House or Senate rules. Congressional committee citations are provided in § 1.4.

For more information and an overview of congressional testimony and the hearings process, as well as standard definitions of the terms "hearing," "testimony," and "witness," see the Introduction.

§1.1 What is a Hearing?

"A hearing is a meeting or session of a Senate, House, joint, or special committee of Congress, usually open to the public, to obtain information and opinions on proposed legislation, conduct an investigation, or evaluate/oversee the activities of a government department or the implementation of a Federal law. In addition, hearings may also be purely exploratory in nature, providing testimony and data about topics of current interest. Most congressional hearings are published two months to two years after they are held."

Source: U.S. Government Printing Office <*www.gpoaccess.gov/chearings/index.html*>.

§1.2 Source of Committee Rules

"The Rules of the House are the rules of its committees and subcommittees as far as applicable."

Source: Rule XI of the Rules of the House of Representatives.

This chapter sets the stage for the legislative process, and explains the basic context for congressional hearings and testimony. It describes how hearings fit into the legislative scheme and how they provide value and meaning to the process. It outlines and discusses the various authorities and rules affecting the conduct of hearings, and provides an overview of the environment surrounding congressional hearings and of the legislative committee system itself. The chapter outlines the basic components of a hearing (see § 1.10, Congressional Hearings Process in a Nutshell), as well as the types, purposes, missions, and results of congressional hearings, and also includes numerous samples of hearing testimony that is illustrative of the diverse nature of the world of the congressional committee hearing.

§ 1.3 Official Rules of the United States Senate and the United States House of Representatives

Included in the Rules of the United States Senate and the Rules of the United States House of Representatives are many rules and guidelines that affect the conduct and organization of congressional committee hearings. To access the official rules of the United States Senate and the United States House of Representatives, go to:

- **Senate:** <*rules.Senate.gov*>
- **House:** <*rules.House.gov*>

§1.4 Congressional Committee Web Sites that Include Hearing Guidelines

Specific rules and guidelines for each congressional committee regarding committee hearings can be found in the general rules and guidelines of each individual committee. Committee links are accessible through the Senate and House web sites.

For United States Senate committee links, go to <*www.Senate.gov*>, and click on the relevant committee.

Standing Committees

- Agriculture, Nutrition, and Forestry
- Appropriations
- Armed Services
- Banking, Housing, and Urban Affairs
- Budget
- Commerce, Science, and Transportation
- Energy and Natural Resources
- Environment and Public Works
- Finance
- Foreign Relations
- Health, Education, Labor, and Pensions
- Homeland Security and Governmental Affairs
- Judiciary
- Rules and Administration
- Small Business and Entrepreneurship
- Veterans' Affairs

Special, Select, and Other Committees

- Indian Affairs
- Select Committee on Ethics
- Select Committee on Intelligence
- Special Committee on Aging

Joint Committees

- Joint Committee on Printing
- Joint Committee on Taxation
- Joint Committee on the Library
- Joint Economic Committee

For United States House of Representatives committee links, go to <*www.House.gov*>, and click on the relevant committee.

- Committee on Agriculture
- Committee on Appropriations
- Committee on Armed Services
- Committee on the Budget
- Committee on Education and Labor
- Committee on Energy and Commerce
- Committee on Financial Services
- Committee on Foreign Affairs
- Committee on Homeland Security
- Committee on House Administration
- Committee on the Judiciary
- Committee on Natural Resources
- Committee on Oversight and Government Reform
- Committee on Rules
- Committee on Science and Technology
- Committee on Small Business
- Committee on Standards of Official Conduct
- Committee on Transportation and Infrastructure
- Committee on Veterans' Affairs
- Committee on Ways and Means
- Joint Economic Committee
- Joint Committee on Printing
- Joint Committee on Taxation
- House Permanent Select Committee on Intelligence
- House Select Committee on Energy Independence and Global Warming

§1.5 Congressional Hearing Information Sources: Web Sites and Links

To access an excellent source of congressional hearing transcripts (and other valuable government information) that have been posted by the Government Printing Office, go to: <*www.gpoaccess.gov/chearings/index.html*>.

Other sources of congressional hearing information, schedules, and transcripts may be found at:

- <*www.thomas.gov*> (Library of Congress legislative information source)
- <*www.capitolhearings.org*> (provided as a public service by C-SPAN)
- <*www.loc.gov/law/find/hearings.html*> (Library of Congress Law Library site)
- <*www.lexisnexis.com/infopro/zimmerman/disp.aspx?z=1324*> (LexisNexis)
- <*www.gpoaccess.gov/congress*> (GPO Access—Government Printing Office)
- <*www.gao.gov*> (Government Accountability Office—GAO)

To determine the schedule, topic, date, time, and location of congressional hearings in the U.S. Senate and U.S. House of Representatives, contact the relevant committee directly by telephone via the U.S. Capitol switchboard at 202-224-3121, or via the committee's web site, which can be found as an electronic link by committee name at <*www.Senate.gov*> and <*www.House.gov*>.

Schedules of committee hearings are usually available through these resources:

- <*www.Senate.gov*> (Click on "Committees," and then on "Hearings and Meetings" to access the Daily Digest Committee Meetings/Hearings Schedule)
- <*www.House.gov*> (Click on "committee hearings" under "Currently on the House Floor")
- Individual committee web sites accessed through committee name links at <*www.Senate.gov*> and <*www.House.gov*>
- Individual committee offices by telephone via the U.S. Capitol switchboard at 202-224-3121
- <*www.Thomas.gov*> (Library of Congress legislative information source; see Senate and House hearing schedules under Congressional Schedules, Calendars)
- <*www.capitolhearings.org*> (provided as a public service by C-SPAN)
- <*www.gpoaccess.gov/congress/index.html*> (GPO Access—Government Printing Office)
- *CQ Today*, the Legislative News-Daily from *Congressional Quarterly*
- *Congressional Daily*, a *National Journal* Group Publication
- *The Washington Post*
- *The Washington Times*

Committees in both the House and Senate have access to video broadcasting and taping technologies for their hearings on committee cable channels administered by their respective chambers. Many committees post live and archived webcasts of their hearings on their respective committee web sites. To see the webcasts of numerous hearings available for viewing, go to the individual committee sites accessible through *<www.House.gov>* and *<www.Senate.gov>*, and proceed to the links for menus of webcasts. See the Back of the Book for more information on this source.

§1.6 Access to Congressional Committee Hearing Transcripts

Published hearings are available online via the U.S. Government Printing Office at: *<www.gpoaccess.gov/chearings>*, and, to a limited extent, through the relevant committees, accessed through committee links at *<www.Senate.gov>* and at *<www.House.gov>*.

How to Find Committee Hearings

Published hearing transcripts contain all witness testimony, the question-and-answer portion of the hearing, and any other material requested of the witness by the committee. It takes several months, or even years, for a hearing to be published. Unlike most other congressional documents, hearings are not available from the Senate or House Document Rooms. You may be able to locate a hearing from the Government Printing Office, from a committee web site, or from a federal depository library.

Web Access

Many committees post witness testimony on their web sites shortly after a hearing takes place. However, the transcripts are generally the prepared statements submitted by each witness, so they will not contain the question-and-answer portion. You can find committee web pages through the main Senate and House web sites and on THOMAS. Most committees organize their hearing transcripts by date, and sometimes by subcommittee. Generally, testimony is only available for witnesses who submitted their statements electronically. A limited number of published hearings since 1995 are available in full text on the Government Printing Office (GPO) web site.

Libraries

Published hearings may be available in a federal depository library. The federal depository library program is made up of over 1,300 libraries that collect government documents and make them available to the public for borrowing or reading. A list of depository libraries is on the GPO web site. Most depository libraries are within a university or state library, so sometimes borrowing privileges are restricted.

Purchasing from GPO

Published hearings may be available for sale from the Government Printing Office (GPO), although it is often difficult to locate them in GPO's *Catalog of U.S. Government Publications*. More information is available from GPO by calling 202-512-1800 or writing to the Superintendent of Documents, P.O. Box 371954, Pittsburgh, PA 15250-7954.

Source: United States Senate <*www.Senate.gov/reference/common/faq/how_to_committe_hrg.htm*>.

§ 1.10 Congressional Hearings Process in a Nutshell

While there are many intricate and arcane aspects to the congressional hearings process, many of which are discussed in other chapters, this deskbook attempts to examine and demystify the process so that those preparing testimony and witnesses will have as complete an understanding as possible of the enterprise with which they are engaged.

In a nutshell, here is how the congressional hearings process works:

- As the major formalized method within the legislative branch for gathering, analyzing, and critiquing information from a wide array of sources, public and private, congressional hearings help provide Congress with important rationale and data that underpin policy decisions and priorities.
- While there are many different types of congressional hearings, such as legislative, appropriations, oversight, investigative, and confirmation (Senate only), all hearings share common traits regarding preparation, planning, participants, purpose, conduct, and operation. Anyone testifying before a committee should contact and work with the professional staff of that committee to ensure compliance with committee policies and rules regarding witnesses, testimony, and hearing logistics.
- The chair of a committee, under the relevant Senate, House and committee rules and guidelines, calls a hearing of the committee to hear presentations that are known as testimony. Written testimony, usually submitted in advance of the hearing, and oral testimony presented in real time by a witness before the committee, are key components in any congressional hearing.
- Witnesses are selected and invited to testify based on the agenda of the committee and its need to collect information, as well as with an eye on ensuring that key and relevant stakeholders have an opportunity to be heard. The *hearing* is just that—an opportunity for an issue to "have a hearing." After making their own opening statements, members of the committee hear from witnesses who are experts or knowledgeable about the issue, and the witnesses presenting testimony have the opportunity to educate the committee members and advocate a particular position.

- After the formal presentation of testimony by a witness, the committee members may engage the witness in a question-and-answer period to elucidate the issue further.
- At the conclusion of the hearing, the proceedings may be published and, in any case, provide a record of the various positions announced by those testifying, upon which the committee can rely during its deliberation over policy matters that come before the committee for action. There may also be follow-up questions posed to witnesses to provide the committee and the hearing record with additional and more specific information needed by the committee for future deliberation.

§1.20 The Use, Importance, and Value of Congressional Hearings

Congressional hearings are important early steps in the legislative process and in the path of a bill on its way to congressional passage and ultimately becoming law. In many cases, hearings are one of the first major steps in the formation of a consensus in support of a measure and can be considered one of Congress's primary fact-gathering systems, somewhat akin to the scientific process of gathering data prior to making assumptions or decisions.

Once a bill has been introduced in either house of Congress and has been assigned to the proper committee or committees (or when an issue is properly before a committee for oversight purposes), the next logical step in the committee process is to conduct a hearing to expand the committee's knowledge and understanding of the issue or the bill's purpose. When an issue or bill reaches the hearing phase of the committee process, it can be said to have achieved a certain amount of traction and credibility that are necessary for the committee to give it additional attention, to make it the subject of a possible "markup," and generally to garner political support for the issue or bill, first within the committee, and then throughout the full chamber.

Hearings and the testimony offered by witnesses provide considerable value to the committee conducting the hearing and its parent chamber, as well as to those participating as witnesses. Committees use hearings to gather valuable information and to develop political support concerning legislative and other measures being considered by Congress. The hearings system depends on input from witnesses who are knowledgeable about, or have a stake in, the issues before the committee. In some cases, committees strive to include witnesses from a broad array of backgrounds and experiences to ensure consideration of many perspectives and a balanced presentation. In other cases, committees have a narrow agenda in mind and invite only witnesses expressing a decided point of view.

Committee hearings also notably provide a forum, widely used as a matter of practice, for members of the committee to make opening statements that are sometimes speeches or monologues in disguise. By using their committee statements to announce their positions on a particular issue and to add to the official record with their views, inform their colleagues, educate anyone listening, and sometimes even lecture a witness, committee members take full advantage of their leadership role in the legislative process.

Congressional hearings also take on a special importance as a central clearinghouse or focal point for information that is being directed to Congress. Because of the availability of so much information today through contemporary technology and other sources, Congress faces the challenges associated with "data overload"—on what sources to depend, how to get timely and reliable information, how to separate relevant data from tangential information, and how to know the most accurate and reliable basic sources of information. Committee hearings provide an institutionalized, recognized, and accepted means for information to be provided to Congress that is needed as the basis for decision-making. This official clearinghouse function allows congressional hearings to enjoy an elevated status as a source of input and data that helps separate focused, relevant communications and information from the randomness of mass information. Hearings also assist Congress with time management challenges. Each member and committee of Congress has only a limited amount of time to devote to a certain issue or activity. Congressional hearings provide a structured, well-timed, and dependable forum for the delivery and reception of information that is vital to congressional decision-making.

The records of congressional hearings are also a treasure trove for researchers and anyone interested in U.S. government, the Congress, and public policy development. Hearing records are excellent sources for researching, tracing, and understanding lawmaking, legislative history, issue development, and policy formulation. Hearing transcripts tell real stories through testimony and interrogation, and put on public display the key issues, players, and strategies of a particular moment in history.

From the perspective of a witness and organizations that testify, hearings provide a valuable means to communicate viewpoints on a matter of public policy directly to congressional decision-makers. Hearings are important to both private and public institutions in communicating their policy positions on issues of importance to them. Organizations, ranging from federal executive and judicial branch officials and national associations to state and local governments, private businesses, and nonprofits, use congressional hearings to "have their say" in the national debate and formulation of federal laws, and to make the record clear on policy subjects near and dear to their hearts.

From an internal practical perspective, committees use witness statements and testimony, as well as other information in the record of hearings, to support and substantiate decisions made by the committee going forward, including the "markup" (committee writing) of bills, priorities for federal spending, changes in federal law, confirmation of presidential nominees (Senate only), and oversight and investigatory follow-up. The transcript of congressional hearings *is* the record of the committee during the fact-gathering phase, and committees have a vested interest in having as complete a record as possible. Likewise, organizations providing witnesses and testimony for the hearing process wish to make the record as complete as possible through the prism of their own organization and perspectives.

From an external political and practical point of view, petitioners who expect their views to be heard, taken seriously, and understood by Congress, whether or not the action ultimately taken by decision-makers is favorable to them, should engage fully in the hearings process to ensure that the record includes their statement and policy position. Making the record is a key component in persuading Congress of the validity of a particular position. Participating in the process not only provides valuable information, it also sends the message that the petitioner is serious and engaged.

Conversely, not engaging and not providing testimony can send the signal to Congress that a party is not interested enough to participate in the hearings process, and may, in some cases, give the committee reason to ignore the petitioner's point of view or take an action that is adverse to the petitioner. In short, to be safe, interested parties should participate in the process as much as possible, including testifying in person, filing a written statement, and working with committee staff to ensure that the record is accurate and complete. Doing so can be very helpful to a cause and can hardly ever be seen as harmful, except possibly in some investigative situations in which criminal liability or individual constitutional rights are in play.

To glean a larger and clearer picture of the use, importance, and value of congressional hearings, one should also approach the process with a good understanding of, and healthy respect for, the U.S. system of government, the legislative process, the congressional committee system, and the professionals involved. (For more information on these major themes, go to the following sites: <*www.TheCapitol.Net*>; <*www.usa.gov*>; <*www.Senate.gov*>; <*www.House.gov*>; and <*www.thomas.gov*>. For information on congressional testimony as a lobbying strategy, and for additional perspectives on effective congressional testimony, see Chapter 10, *Lobbying and Advocacy*, Deanna Gelak, TheCapitol.Net. Also see the *Congressional Deskbook*, Michael L. Koempel and Judy Schneider, TheCapitol.Net; the *Congressional Directory*, for sale by the Superintendent of Documents, U.S. Government Printing Office <*www.bookstore.gpo.gov*>; the *Congressional Staff Directory*, CQ Press <*www.cqpress.com*>; and *The United States Government Manual*, for sale by the Superintendent of Documents, U.S. Government Printing Office <*www.bookstore.gpo.gov*>.)

§1.21 Testimonial of a Senate Committee Staff Director on the Value of Congressional Hearings and the Importance of a Witness's Role

"Without question there are 'check the box' hearings in any given week, with Members, staff and witnesses all sort of going through the motions. But a well-constructed and well-timed hearing can be a powerful tool. A cogent, concise witness can lodge arguments or facts in a Member's brain and directly impact legislation. A well-conceived series of questions—coupled with a Member's ability to follow up—can establish a record in support of a bill, or help stop one in its tracks. On the other hand, a long-winded or unresponsive witness can be terminal to the cause being advocated.

"Solid preparation on both sides of the dais doesn't ensure a successful hearing; there are too many other variables in an average Congressional day. Lack of preparation, however, nearly guarantees a forgettable result."

Source: Bruce Evans, Minority Staff Director, Committee on Appropriations, United States Senate.

§1.22 Contrary Perspectives on the Value of Hearings

While a compelling case can be made for engaging in the congressional hearings process, some observers, including an occasional committee staff professional, might suggest that committee hearings, witness statements and testifying before committees are relatively meaningless activities that produce little in the way of substantive results and a document that is destined to sit on a shelf and collect dust, never to be used for any productive purpose. In some cases, the hearing exercise may seem to fit this description, but it is always better to err on the side of doing more rather than less to influence the legislative process.

Some organizations, such as federal departments and agencies, are expected, even compelled, to testify to justify their budget requests and to explain the meaning of proposed changes in the law or how laws are being enforced. But others who might appear before congressional hearings voluntarily are served well by making their best case to the committee through both oral and written testimony. To do otherwise is to miss an opportunity in the legislative process to educate, advocate, and persuade, and that missed opportunity just might invite the committee to ignore a particular viewpoint or position simply because it is not included in the hearing record.

§1.30 The Dynamics and Environment of Congressional Hearings

Congressional hearings are an everyday occurrence in the life of a congressional committee. When a hearing is announced by a committee, it means that a bill, issue, or problem has risen to the level of gaining the attention of the Congress through its relevant committee so that it is scheduled for a public airing to hear and consider the expression of various viewpoints. The environment for congressional hearings is the committee system itself, wherein Congress does most of the work in preparing legislation and other matters for final consideration and possible passage by the full House or Senate.

Committees in both houses of Congress have the authority to conduct hearings on any subject under their respective jurisdictions. Many hearings, especially those dealing with the federal budget and appropriations, are conducted early each year, while others dealing with legislation, nominations, and oversight are scheduled as necessary throughout the year whenever bills, nominations, or issues "ripen" for consideration and review, and the committee chair feels it is timely and wise to hold a hearing.

The dynamics of congressional hearings entail all the various constructs and activities of a committee rolled into a single, sometimes multi-day, event that brings the committee members together to hear witnesses and consider wide-ranging perspectives relative to a timely issue or proposed legislative matter. The chair of the committee calls and conducts the hearing, and designated committee professional staff members take care of all the preparation and arrangements.

Under the direction of the committee chair, committee staff handle all aspects of the planning and execution of the hearing, ranging from the communications with all participants, the collection of advanced copies of statements, and the issuance of invitations to witnesses to testify, to the briefing of committee members, preparation of questions to be asked, organization of the hearing room, the editing and printing of the record, and the follow-up with witnesses and members of the committee after the hearing.

Unofficial statistics from the CQ.com committee database and the Congressional Research Service of the Library of Congress indicate that there are hundreds of hearings a year—an average annual number of Senate hearings for years 2006–2008 of 782, and an average annual number of House hearings for years 2006–2008 of 1,266.

For additional information, see § 8.40, Committee Hearings, in the *Congressional Deskbook*, by Michael L. Koempel and Judy Schneider.

§1.31 Making the Record

The congressional hearing provides a formalized setting for making the record for an issue, bill, or candidate under consideration. A formal transcript is taken or recorded by an official reporter in most cases, and later transcribed as a permanent record for the committee to use as a reference source. These hearing records include the opening statements of committee members made at the hearing, oral and written testimony of witnesses who appear before the committee, "outside witness statements" from those who submit written testimony in lieu of an appearance, the actual hearing and follow-up questions and answers between the committee and witnesses, and any other information, evidence, statements, or documents deemed relevant by the chair and the committee members. Whatever the type, focus, purpose, and direction of a congressional hearing, one of its primary missions is making the record.

§1.32 Partisanship and Political Analysis: Where Policy and Politics Converge

In committee hearings, much like Congress and its committees generally, policy and politics converge. Consequently, congressional hearings often take on a politically partisan nature. Partisanship can exist within a committee and can also be associated with issues under consideration by a committee.

Under the principle of majority rule, congressional committees are controlled by the party with the majority in that particular chamber of Congress. Thus, traditional partisan differences between the political parties can color or influence a hearing, and partisanship can often play itself out vividly in the statements made by committee members and in their questioning of witnesses. Although the majority rules in the hearing setting, the minority party's representation and voice in committees are protected by rules in both chambers. House, Senate, and various committee rules guarantee that the minority party members of a committee have opportunities to make statements and call and question witnesses in a fair and orderly process. However, with the majority party wielding the gavel in the chair, there is ample opportunity for the majority party to control the direction, flow, and tone of a congressional hearing.

Some of the most partisan viewpoints are expressed when committees engage witnesses from the incumbent administration. Quite often, members of the committee of the same party as the president become advocates for administration witnesses, help to ensure fairness and balance in the committee's dealings with witnesses, and are even known to lob "softball questions" or offer flattering or complimentary remarks in the direction of an administration witness, all presumably intended to balance real or perceived opposition or hostilities by the other party. In fact, committee hearings provide a ripe and lively forum for the expression of policy differences between the two major political parties, including occasional high-drama sparring. Hearings offer committee members and witnesses a high-stakes venue for debate, argumentation, and lectures on virtually any topical subject, and the result quite often is the illumination of partisan viewpoints that challenge the position or actions of others in government or the private sector.

Issues that come before a committee in a hearing setting also get caught up in partisanship in ways other than political party differences, most notably on the basis of ideology and the personal experiences of members. Members of committees often formulate positions on a given issue based on other information provided through briefings; personal research and professional experience; the stated positions of other branches of government, special interest groups, and targeted industries or business sectors; think tanks and research institutions; and information resulting from public debate, media coverage, and home state or district constituent interests.

Individual members of a committee have their own personal, professional, and ideological views and concerns that quite often influence their partisan leanings in a hearing setting and in decision-making, especially when contrasted with differing viewpoints of their colleagues. These views manifest themselves in hearings in the form of opening and position statements, comments for the record, colloquies with colleagues, and questioning of witnesses. Members of Congress are heavily influenced by constituent concerns, political considerations, media coverage, and personal experiences.

In the extreme, partisanship sometimes leads to inefficiencies and ineffectiveness in a hearing setting. Committee members can have such strong partisan views and positions on an issue, legislative measure, nominee, or agency action under review that they focus only on their own agenda and may have minimal interest in other information, however valuable it might be, that emanates from a hearing. On occasion a particularly controversial or sensitive issue that is fraught with partisanship can even dominate a hearing to the extent that the hearing's or committee's original purpose is lost in the partisan rhetoric and klieg lights. Increased partisanship can lead to a decrease in civility in both the House and Senate, with the result in the committee hearings process often being very one-sided presentations, ideologically driven agendas and testimony, and less tolerance for balanced presentations and discussion.

Those preparing testimony and witnesses for congressional hearings should conduct a political analysis of the relevant issues, committee, timing, and other related circumstances to ensure a thorough understanding of the political landscape and the potential opportunity for, and role of, partisanship in the hearing process.

For more information on political analyses, see § 3.9, Political Analysis and Landscape; § 5.11, Recognizing and Understanding Partisanship; and § 6.25, Dealing with Partisanship and Political or Policy Agendas.

§ 1.40 Understanding the Congressional Committee System: The Hearing as a Vital Step in the Legislative Process

When it comes to the development of legislation and the detailed consideration of policy issues in the U.S. Congress, the predominant action is in the committee system. The numerous standing, special, and select committees in each house of Congress conduct the majority of work on legislation, including the preparation of a bill leading up to floor consideration. It is to congressional committees that bills are referred for any further action. If the committee decides a bill or issue has merit, it can so recommend to the full chamber. But committees are also a place where many bills go to die. The committee decides whether a bill or issue has life, whether it will be considered further, and whether it merits the attention of the committee as it turns ideas into laws and other results.

The entire scope of the legislative process itself—essentially how a bill becomes law—is integrally tied to the congressional committee system. Members of a committee focus on a dedicated portfolio of issues and federal jurisdiction, and are in a position to review and dispose of proposals for changes in the law. Committees revolve around the formulation of legislation and other measures that require congressional approval.

When an issue or bill is referred to the committee, the committee must decide whether to devote resources that will advance the measure. If the decision is to move ahead, quite often the first major endeavor is conducting a congressional hearing. If the hearing phase of the process produces sufficient results and the issue or bill remains alive, the committee may move to a "markup" (committee drafting) of a bill that is then reported, or recommended, to the respective full chamber. From there the measure is taken up by the full House or Senate, and, if passed, referred to the other chamber. If both houses act favorably on the measure, a conference committee meets to resolve any difference in the two versions before a final version is put to a final vote in each chamber, and, if approved by both houses, subsequently sent to the president for signature or veto.

The committee hearing is one of the initial staging grounds and laboratories in the development of legislation. As committee members express themselves on certain issues through their opening statements at a hearing, and as information is elicited from witnesses through testimony and questioning, members of the committee not only become educated about an issue, they also begin formulating their own policy positions and sharpening their political views on an issue. This is an important dynamic in the hearings process because political support is necessary for an issue or bill to proceed to further committee and congressional consideration.

Although a measure does not absolutely have to have been the subject of a hearing before it is considered further by a committee and its parent chamber, most important measures and issues certainly receive a full vetting through the hearings process. In fact, when a measure or amendment has not been the subject of a hearing, a typical ploy of its opponents both in committee and on the floor is to argue that the issue should not proceed or be approved *because* it was not considered in the hearings process. Thus, the congressional hearing is critical in most cases to the activities and successes of a committee as it shepherds a measure through the maze of the legislative process, and particularly as it lays the foundation for the committee's decision-making regarding priorities and the making of sound public policy.

For more discussion of the legislative process, see Chapter 8, "Legislating in Congress," in the *Congressional Deskbook*, by Michael L. Koempel and Judy Schneider.

§1.50 The Purposes and Types of Congressional Hearings

The major overall purpose of any congressional hearing is to elicit information from witnesses that will be helpful to the committee in its work on legislation and other matters that come before the committee. There are several different types of congressional hearings categorized and defined either by their specific purpose or committee venue or both.

There are seven major types of congressional hearings:

- Legislative Hearings (see § 1.51)
- Budget and Appropriations Hearings (see § 1.53)
- Oversight and Investigative Hearings (see § 1.56)
- Senate Advice and Consent Hearings:
  Nominations, Confirmations, and Treaties (see § 1.58)
- Field Hearings (see § 1.60)
- Showcasing, Publicity, Celebrity, and Grandstanding Hearings (see § 1.63)
- Public or Open Hearings and Closed or Classified Hearings (see § 1.65)

Most congressional hearings are conducted within the U.S. Capitol complex, which includes the Capitol building and the adjacent Senate and House office buildings. Each committee has one or more assigned committee rooms where it meets to conduct business, including the staging of hearings. There are hundreds of hearings a year in each chamber of Congress. The number and purpose of individual hearings are the prerogative of an individual committee. Hearings may be subtle and relatively quiet, or they can take on theatrical characteristics—even a circus-like atmosphere on occasion—especially in situations when the subject of the hearing is controversial or a major curiosity of the media and the public.

For a detailed discussion of congressional committees, see § 7.50, Committees and Subcommittees, in the *Congressional Deskbook*, by Michael L. Koempel and Judy Schneider.

§1.51 Legislative Hearings

Hearings that are intended to help a committee review a legislative proposal and possibly produce a bill that will create new law or add to or modify the United States Code are known as legislative or authorizing hearings. While the terms "legislative" and "legislation" are used in a generic sense in connection with the movement of many types of legislative measures generally, their more precise usage means a bill or resolution that is on the track of congressional consideration and possible approval, and that will, if passed by both chambers of Congress, potentially become federal law. The subject and purpose of a legislative hearing can focus on a pending measure under review and consideration by a committee, or on the enterprise of collecting information from witnesses that will be used by the committee in drafting or initiating a legislative measure.

Most legislative committees of Congress are authorizing committees in nature based on their responsibility for developing legislation that focuses on certain portfolios of federal laws, policy, programs, departments, agencies, subject matter, and issues. Authorizing language in a legislative measure typically leads to changes in or additions to federal law embodied in the United States Code. By way of example, the House and Senate Judiciary Committees have, among their many responsibilities, authorizing jurisdiction for most Justice Department programs, intellectual property law, and many of the criminal statutes in the United States Code. The House and Senate Agriculture Committees are responsible for, among other things, writing the federal Farm Bill every few years.

Legislative committee hearings are conducted whenever a committee deems them necessary to gather data in preparation for committee consideration of a measure, including the writing of new or revised legislation affecting the laws of the land.

§1.52 Sample Notification of a Legislative Hearing

H.R. 547, THE ADVANCED FUELS INFRASTRUCTURE RESEARCH AND DEVELOPMENT ACT

(selected opening sections)

TUESDAY, JANUARY 30, 2007

House of Representatives, Subcommittee on Energy and Environment,
Committee on Science and Technology, Washington, DC.

The Subcommittee met, pursuant to call, at 2:10 p.m.,
in Room 2318 of the Rayburn House Office Building,
Hon. Nick Lampson [Chairman of the Subcommittee] presiding.

Hearing Charter

SUBCOMMITTEE ON ENERGY AND ENVIRONMENT
COMMITTEE ON SCIENCE AND TECHNOLOGY
U.S. HOUSE OF REPRESENTATIVES
H.R. 547, the Advanced Fuels Infrastructure
Research and Development Act
Tuesday, January 30, 2007
2:00 p.m. – 4:00 p.m.
318 Rayburn House Office Building

Purpose

On Tuesday, January 30, 2007 the Subcommittee on Energy and Environment of the Committee on Science and Technology will hold a hearing to receive testimony on H.R. 547, the Advanced Fuels Infrastructure Research and Development Act.

H.R. 547 directs the Department of Energy (DOE) and the National Institute of Standards and Technology (NIST) to initiate a research, development, and demonstration program to make alternative bio-based fuels more compatible with present-day infrastructure. H.R. 547 also directs these agencies to develop technologies and methods to provide low-cost, portable, and accurate measurements of sulfur in fuels, and to develop a physical properties database and Standards Reference Materials for alternative fuels.

Science and Technology Committee Chairman Bart Gordon introduced H.R. 547 on January 18, 2007. This bill was originally introduced in the 109th Congress as H.R. 5658. The language from H.R. 5658 was included as Section 17 of H.R. 5656, the Energy Research, Development, Demonstration and Commercial Application Act of 2006, which was later passed by the House under suspension of the rules as H.R. 6203.

To date, H.R. 547 is expressly endorsed by the following organizations:

- National Association of Convenience Stores (NACS)
- Renewable Fuels Association (RFA)
- Society of Independent Gas Marketers of America (SIGMA)
- National Association of Truck Stop Owners (NATSO)
- Coalition of E-85 Retailers
- Petroleum Marketers of America (PMAA)

The hearing will seek to address the following questions related to H.R. 547:

1. What infrastructure challenges currently hinder wide scale marketplace distribution of alternative fuels?
2. What are the limitations in the current testing equipment and protocols for verification of the sulfur content of diesel fuel?

Witnesses

- Mr. John Eichberger is the Vice President of the National Association of Convenience Stores (NACS) and will also testify on behalf of the Society of Independent Gasoline Marketers of America (SIGMA).
- Mr. Bob Dinneen is the President and CEO of the Renewable Fuels Association, the trade association for the U.S. ethanol industry and advocate for the increased production and use of fuel ethanol.
- Mr. Richard Kassel is the Senior Attorney and Director of the Clean Fuels and Vehicles Project at the Natural Resources Defense Council which advocates for cleaner diesel fuels and increased use of bio-based alternative fuels.

Source: Subcommittee on Energy and Environment, Committee on Science and Technology, U.S. House of Representatives, Washington, DC.

For the full transcript of the hearing online, perform an Internet search for "f:32612.wais", including the quotation marks.

§1.53 Budget and Appropriations Hearings

Budget and appropriations hearings are types of legislative hearings, and are typically conducted in the late winter and spring of each year following the submission of the president's annual budget to Congress in January or February.

Budget hearings are conducted by the House and Senate Budget Committees to review the president's budget requests prior to preparation and decisions relating to the First Concurrent Budget Resolution, a nonbinding "road map" or blueprint used to establish appropriations allocations and to set spending and revenue targets for the government's next fiscal year in the budget process. In analyzing the upcoming fiscal year, the House and Senate Budget Committees review the government's financial planning from a "top-down" perspective using major funding categories called "functions." They do not make specific spending decisions, which are the prerogative of the appropriations process and authorization committees.

The budget committees may also conduct hearings as necessary at mid-year in conjunction with the process known as "budget reconciliation," in which a "snapshot" of federal revenues and expenditures is taken, and adjustments are made in the budget via instructions to the standing committees of Congress, the results of which appear in the Second Concurrent Budget Resolution, which has the force of law as the nation's budget when passed and signed into law.

Appropriations hearings typically begin in February each year and run through late April or early May, and they are conducted by the various appropriations subcommittees in each chamber. The House and Senate full appropriations committees conduct large comprehensive hearings from time to time to consider major budget revisions or supplemental requests, or to engage top officials from the White House, the Office of Management and Budget (OMB), or other departments of government.

In the regular order of annual appropriations business, each appropriations subcommittee conducts a number of hearings relating to its areas of funding jurisdiction in its respective bill. Each subcommittee is responsible for a specific portfolio or grouping of federal departments, agencies, and programs, and representatives from those entities are requested and expected to appear before their respective subcommittee of jurisdiction each year in the hearings process to explain, defend, and support their portion of the president's overall budget request. For example, the Senate Appropriations Subcommittee on Interior, the Environment and Related Agencies will conduct hearings that will include the Secretary of Interior and other individuals from the subcabinet, budget, and program offices, as well as the administrator of the Environmental Protection Agency (EPA) and many of that agency's subordinate program officers.

The number of hearings, the witnesses invited, and the programs reviewed are up to the subcommittees to decide. Witnesses from nonfederal organizations, such as businesses, trade associations, private and voluntary organizations, educational institutions, state and local governments, program benefit recipients, and ordinary citizens, may also be called to testify or may submit an "outside witness statement" that is made part of the hearing record.

For a more detailed discussion of the federal budget process, see Chapter 9, "Legislating in Congress: Federal Budget Process," in the *Congressional Deskbook*, by Michael L. Koempel and Judy Schneider.

§1.54 Sample of Appropriations Committee Hearing Notice

APPROPRIATIONS COMMITTEE HEARING NOTICE

Tuesday, May 10, 2005

10:00 a.m.—The Subcommittee on Defense will meet in Room 192 of the Dirksen Senate Office Building. The program includes a review of the FY 2006 Defense Medical Health Program

Witnesses:

Panel 1—
LTG Kevin C. Kiley, M.D., Surgeon General of the Army
VADM Donald C. Arthur, Surgeon General of the Navy
Lt. General George Peach Taylor, Jr., M.D., Surgeon General of the Air Force

Panel 2—
COL Barbara J. Bruno, Deputy Chief, Army Nurse
RADM Nancy J. Lescavage, Director, Navy Nurse Corps
Major General Barbara C. Brannon, Assistant Air Force Surgeon General, Nursing Services

2:30 p.m.—The Subcommittee on Military Construction and Veterans Affairs will meet in Room 138 of the Dirksen Senate Office Building. The program includes a review of the Overseas Basing Mission Report.

Witnesses:

Honorable Al Cornella, Chairman
Major General Lewis E. Curtis III, USAF (Ret)
Vice Admiral Anthony A. Less, USN (Ret)
Brigadier General Keith Martin, Pennsylvania ARNG (Ret)
Lieutenant General H. G. Taylor, USA (Ret)

Wednesday, May 11, 2005

10:00 a.m.—The Subcommittee on Defense will meet in Room 192 of the Dirksen Senate Office Building. The program includes a review of the FY 2006 Missile Defense Program.

Witness: Lt. General Henry A. "Trey" Obering, III,
Director of the Missile Defense Agency

10:00 a.m.—The Subcommittee on Labor, Health and Human Services, Education, and Related Agencies will meet in Room G-50 of the Dirksen Senate Office Building. The program includes a hearing on ALS (Lou Gehrig's Disease)

Witnesses:

Panel 1—
Story Landis, Ph.D.,
Director, National Institute of Neurological Disorders and Stroke

Panel 2—
Lucie Bruijn, Ph.D. Science Director and Vice President, The ALS Association
Mr. Eric Obermann, Huntsville, Alabama
Mr. Rob Borsellino, Columnist, The Des Moines Register

Panel 3—
Mr. Tommy John, Former Major League Baseball Player
Mr. David Cone, Former Major League Baseball Player
Ms. Kate Linder, Actress

10:30 a.m.—The Subcommittee on Labor, Health and Human Services, Education and Related Agencies will meet in Room G-50 of the Dirksen Senate Office Building. The program includes a hearing on the Gynecologic Cancer Education and Awareness Act of 2003.

Witnesses:

Andrew von Eschenbach, M.D., Director, National Cancer Institute
Ms. Fran Drescher
Ms. Sheryl Silver

10:30 a.m.—The Subcommittee on the Legislative Branch will meet in Room 116 of the Dirksen Senate Office Building. The program includes an overview of the FY 2006 Budgets for the Government Printing Office, the Congressional Budget Office, and the Office of Compliance.

Witnesses:

Mr. Bruce James, Public Printer, Government Printing
Dr. Douglas Holtz-Eakin, Director, Congressional Budget
Mr. William Thompson, Executive Director, Office of Compliance
Ms. Susan Robfogel, Chair of the Board, Office of Compliance

Thursday, May 12, 2005

9:30 a.m.—The Subcommittee on Transportation, Treasury, the Judiciary, Housing and Urban Development, and Related Agencies will meet in Room 138 of the Dirksen Senate Office Building. The program includes an overview of the FY 2006 Budget for the National Railroad Passenger Corporation (Amtrak).

Witnesses:

Mr. David L. Gunn, President and CEO, Amtrak
Mr. David M. Laney, Chairman of the Board, Amtrak
Mr. Jeffrey A. Rosen, General Counsel, Department of Transportation
Mr. Kenneth M. Mead, Inspector General, Department of Transportation

2:00 p.m.—The Subcommittee on Commerce, Justice and Science will meet in Room 192 of the Dirksen Senate Office Building. The program includes an overview of the FY 2006 budget for the National Aeronautics and Space Administration (NASA).

Witness: Mr. Michael Griffin, Administrator, NASA

2:00 p.m.—The Subcommittee on State, Foreign Operations and Related Programs will meet in Room 124 of the Dirksen Senate Office Building. The program includes an overview of the FY 2006 Budget request for the Department of State and Foreign Operations.

Witness: The Honorable Condoleezza Rice, Secretary of State

Source: Committee on Appropriations, United States Senate

§1.55 Sample Appropriations Hearing Transcript

Opening sections of hearing transcript of the Senate Appropriations Subcommittee on Commerce, Justice, Science and Related Agencies

THURSDAY, MARCH 1, 2007

U.S. Senate, Subcommittee of the Committee on Appropriations, Washington, DC.

The subcommittee met at 10 a.m., in room SD-192, Dirksen Senate Office Building, Hon. Barbara A. Mikulski (chairman) presiding.

Present: Senators Mikulski, Kohl, Reed, Shelby, and Alexander.

DEPARTMENT OF COMMERCE

Office of the Secretary

STATEMENT OF THE HONORABLE CARLOS M. GUTIERREZ, SECRETARY

Opening statement of Senator Barbara A. Mikulski:

Senator Mikulski. Good morning, the Subcommittee on Commerce, Justice, Science, and Related Agencies will come to order. This is the first time in 13 years that I assume the chair of this subcommittee, and it's a great honor, and it's a bit of an emotional moment.

In 1994, the power transferred to the other party, and in those 13 years, much has changed. Our economy has certainly changed, the challenges to our country have certainly changed, the jurisdiction and scope of this subcommittee has expanded.

The one thing that will not change, is the enduring spirit of bipartisanship that has always been characteristic of this subcommittee, working as I did at VA/HUD, with Senator Bond, and last year with my esteemed colleague, Senator Shelby. We see ourselves as a partnership, on promoting what is right, and so this sense of cordiality, consultation, and civility will continue to be an enduring principle of this subcommittee.

Just to outline a few of the priorities for this year, this subcommittee will focus on innovation, security, and accountability. When I look at the agencies in our jurisdiction, I see tremendous opportunities to promote innovation that creates jobs in our own country, makes our community more secure, while assuring accountability for the stewardship of the taxpayers.

The funding that this subcommittee puts in the Federal checkbook, must meet the mission and mandate of each agency, and make a down payment on its priorities. The Commerce, Justice, Science Subcommittee is the innovation subcommittee. If America is going to be more competitive, we need to focus on funding and policies to develop new technologies, that lead to new products and new industries that create new jobs.

It is not the role of this subcommittee to pick winners and losers. We are not an industry-controlled society. But it is to provide the basic and applied research that results in these new products and technology, and our agencies set the policies that will make sure that we have an innovation-friendly government.

Over the next several weeks, we will initially focus on innovation. Then we will go to both Federal Bureau of Investigation (FBI) and law enforcement to focus on security. Underlying in all of the hearings will be questions related to accountability, and our stewardship of taxpayers dollars.

We're looking at the National Science Foundation (NSF) that funds promising research and cultivates the next generation of science and engineers, particularly at the graduate level. The National Institute of Standards and Technology (NIST), that we're going to hear from later today, that funds new technologies, to make us more competitive. And, by the way, they win Nobel Prizes, too.

The science at the National Aeronautics and Space Administration (NASA) and the National Oceanic and Atmospheric Administration (NOAA) help us better understand our planet and provides the scientific building blocks for innovation. Nothing gets kids more interested in science, like exploration and discovery in outer space, and the inner space in the ocean.

We want to make sure, though, this—we have an innovation-friendly government. NIST sets measurements and standards that the private sector can rely on, and the world counts on. The U.S. Patent and Trademark Office protects our intellectual property, and the International Trade Administration (ITA) enforces our trade agreements.

We also will be focusing on security, but that's for another day. This subcommittee will also be looking at accountability in terms of the expenditure of taxpayers dollars, and to make sure that, whether it's waste, or abuse, or poor performance, will not be tolerated. But today, we're going to kick off our innovation hearing with the Secretary of the Commerce Department, a long-advocate for America's role in international trade, promoting competitiveness, and encouraging innovation and technology.

Later on, in the second panel, we'll be hearing from the Director of the National Institute of Standards and Technology and also the Director of the Patent Office.

Today, I will want to know how the budget meets the Department of Commerce mission to foster, serve, and promote the Nation's economy, which is a little bit rockin' and rollin' today, but again, you know, we're a country of institutions, and innovation. I want to know how the budget will promote the mission, and how the Commerce Department will improve accountability.

In the accountability areas, the three flashing lights we have are, the NOAA satellite program, also some issues that—the Patent Office, that I will raise from there, and also the managing of the 2010 census.

But, today, we're very pleased to have the Secretary of Commerce, we want to hear what he has to say, we've enjoyed such a cordial relationship. He has been the President's link to the business community here, and to the growing international markets. So, we welcome him, and with that statement, I turn to my colleague, ranking member and, essentially, vice chairman, Senator Shelby.

****

Senator Mikulski. Thank you very much, Senator Shelby.

Just in terms of the rules of the subcommittee, we're going to recognize people in their order of arrival. And, if they have opening statements, we will put them in the record, or we ask that they incorporate them in their early questions, so we can move to the Secretary, and move to your questions.

****

Mr. Secretary, would you proceed, and then we'll go to questions?

Mr. Gutierrez. Thank you.

Madam Chairman, and Senator Shelby and members of the subcommittee, I'm pleased to present President Bush's fiscal 2008 $6.55 billion budget request for the Commerce Department. With your permission, I'd like to briefly discuss some key elements of our budget and programs, and submit my written testimony for the record.

Source: S. Hrg. 110-329, U.S. Senate Appropriations Subcommittee on Commerce, Justice, Science and Related Agencies, Mar. 1, 2007; DOCID: f:59104239.wais.

§1.56 Oversight and Investigative Hearings

In addition to legislative, budget, and appropriations functions and responsibilities, committees of Congress also have oversight and investigatory responsibilities. Congressional hearings are primary ingredients and tools in the process of legislative and program oversight and investigations. These types of hearings may be conducted by congressional committees whenever a committee chooses, usually in connection with a timely public policy question, cutting-edge issue, or question of government action or accountability. However, committee oversight hearings may also be combined with legislative or authorization hearings (see § 1.51), especially in the context of a routine review and analysis of a federal program and its implementation prior to reauthorization.

Akin to a quality control study, the oversight function of Congress and its committees involves selective or periodic reviews of federal departments and agencies and their activities, federal policies and programs, and especially the way federal laws, regulations and programs are administered, executed, enforced, and applied. Oversight hearings focus on the quality of federal programs, measure the implementation of federal laws against legislative intent, hold executive branch policies and actions up to the test of public interest and value, and evaluate the performance of both government officials and the programs they administer.

The goals of these oversight hearings usually are to ensure that executive branch agencies are carrying out federal programs the way Congress and the enabling statutes intended, and to attempt to correct or alter executive branch behavior or to lay the foundation for corrective legislation. Through oversight hearings, Congress attempts to enhance the efficacy, economy, efficiency, effectiveness, and responsiveness of federal government programs and operations, as well as to identify and ferret out waste, fraud, and abuse in government programs. Oversight hearings provide a congressional committee with an effective tool to apply the scrutiny of Congress to the executive branch's implementation of federal laws and programs.

Investigative hearings typically focus on the suggestion or suspicion of wrongdoing, perhaps even criminal in nature, within the ranks of government or concerning public policy issues subject to federal laws and regulations. While investigative hearings are similar in many ways to oversight and even legislative hearings in style and format (see § 1.51), the major distinction is the focus on an allegation of wrongdoing or a breach of governmental or personal responsibility. Congress and its committees have broad authority to conduct investigatory hearings on virtually any subject, especially in connection with suspected wrongdoing by a government official or institution, or even a private sector individual or institution when there may be a need or possibility for legislation or a change in federal law.

Investigative hearings usually are not connected with legislation per se, but serve the purpose of probing a subject matter of interest to the committee and under its proper jurisdiction. Wrongdoing or problems that are discovered during hearings quite often lead to new or remedial legislation or other actions dealing with federal funding, and sometimes they result in referrals to the federal or state court systems. However, investigatory hearings conducted by the legislative branch of government are separate and distinct by nature and by law from judicial inquiries and proceedings that may be conducted by state or federal judicial systems.

There are many examples of congressional investigations, some quite high-profile, that utilized hearings as their primary activity, including the Titanic investigation (1912), the Teapot Dome scandal (1923-24), the Kefauver Committee Hearings on Organized Crime (1950-51), the Army-McCarthy Hearings (1954), the Watergate investigation (1973-74), and the Iran-Contra investigation (1987).

§1.57 Sample Oversight Hearing Transcript: Opening Sections of House Oversight and Government Reform Committee Hearing on Treatment of U.S. Troops at Walter Reed Hospital and Other Medical Facilities

IS THIS ANY WAY TO TREAT OUR TROOPS?

PART II: FOLLOW-UP ON CORRECTIVE MEASURES TAKEN AT WALTER REED AND OTHER MEDICAL FACILITIES CARING FOR WOUNDED SOLDIERS

****

TUESDAY, APRIL 17, 2007

House of Representatives,
Subcommittee on National Security and Foreign Affairs,
Committee on Oversight and Government Reform, Washington, DC.

The subcommittee met, pursuant to notice, at 10:05 a.m. in room 2154, Rayburn House Office Building, Hon. John F. Tierney (chairman of the subcommittee) presiding.

Present: Representatives Tierney, Yarmuth, Braley, McCollum, Cooper, Van Hollen, Hodes, Welch, Shays, Burton, Turner, and Foxx.

Also present: Representative Cummings and Delegate Norton.

****

Mr. Tierney. Good morning, everyone.

A quorum being present, the Subcommittee on National Security and Foreign Affairs' hearing entitled, "Is This Any Way to Treat Our Troops? Part II," will come to order.

I ask unanimous consent that only the chairman and ranking member of the subcommittee make opening statements. Without objection, so ordered.

I ask unanimous consent that the hearing record be kept open for 5 business days so that all members of the subcommittee will be allowed to submit a written statement for the record. Without objection, so ordered.

I ask unanimous consent that the following written statements be placed on the hearing record: Dr. Allen Glass, a military physician who has worked at Walter Reed for 20 years; Gary Knight, a former patient at Walter Reed; Patrick Hayes, a police officer who has worked at Walter Reed for almost 20 years; Dr. Richard Gardner, who worked at Winn Army Community Hospital at Fort Stewart in Georgia; Specialist Stephen Jones, an Iraqi veteran; and Corporal Steve Schultz and his wife, Debbie. Without objection, so ordered.

I ask unanimous consent that the gentleman from Maryland, Representative Cummings, and the Delegate from the District of Columbia, Representative Eleanor Holmes Norton, members of the full Oversight and Government Reform Committee, be permitted to participate in the hearing. In accordance with our committee practices, they will be recognized after members of the subcommittee. Without objection, so ordered.

We will proceed to opening statements.

I want to just say good morning to everybody here on the panel and all of our witnesses on both panels here today. On March 5th, you will recall that this subcommittee convened our first ever hearing on the care of wounded soldiers at Walter Reed Army Medical Center. I think it is fair to say that all of us were appalled by the heart-wrenching stories from Staff Sergeant Dan Shannon, Annette McCleod, and Specialist Jeremy Duncan. They spoke of living with mold, being lost in the bureaucratic abyss, and being treated with a shameful lack of respect.

But their stories are not, unfortunately, isolated incidents. After our first hearing, we created a special hotline, an e-hotline. We heard from hundreds of people, and the problems went well beyond Walter Reed.

A doctor who had come out of retirement to help out at Winn Army Community Hospital at Fort Stewart, GA, said that there they were understaffed, overextended, and "much worse than at Walter Reed."

A soldier who fought in both Gulf wars spoke of cuts in the soldier advocate program at Darnall Army Medical Center in Fort Hood, Texas, and that traumatic brain injury patients were being un- or under-diagnosed.

Someone at 29 Palms Marine Base witnessed examples of post traumatic stress disorder going undiagnosed, untreated, and purposefully ignored to return soldiers to active duty. She told us about one navy psychiatrist who said "clearly he did not believe in PTSD."

We also, unfortunately, heard additional troubling stories about Walter Reed.

A 20-year police veteran there wrote of cockroaches and mice at their police station. He also wrote, "The [police] station is not handicapped accessible, which is ironic considering we have a large number of handicapped veterans here that may need to come to our station for police services."

A Walter Reed JAG lawyer spoke of a broken disability review process that under-rates wounded soldiers, a system in which there were only three JAG officers and one civilian counselor available to represent all wounded soldiers at Walter Reed; a system so overburdened there was no time to get an outside medical opinion or to adequately prepare for these absolutely vital hearings.

We also heard in the media about computer programs that can't talk to each other, a growing backlog of VA disability claims, and egregious allegations of still-injured soldiers being returned into battle.

At our March hearing, with the committee's support, I made the commitment that this subcommittee would perform sustained and aggressive oversight, and as a first step we would follow up with a hearing in 45 days.

Today marks the 43rd day, and I hope we will hear across the board from our witnesses that the Department of Defense acknowledges the seriousness and pervasiveness of these problems; that we are rapidly fixing the broken bureaucracy, knocking down the institutional walls across the services and with the VA Administration, and ensuring that each soldier and his or her family is treated with the utmost respect. That is what we hope we can hear.

We will hear today from the Independent Review Group, led by distinguished former Army Secretaries Togo West and Jack Marsh. Their report, released yesterday, examines the problems at Walter Reed and elsewhere and offers a series of recommendations.

Source: H. Hrg. 110-16, Committee on Oversight and Government Reform, U.S. House of Representatives, April 17, 2007.

For the complete transcript of the hearing online, perform an Internet search for "f:36999.wais", including the quotation marks.

§1.58 Senate Advice and Consent: Hearings to Consider Nominations, Confirmations, and Treaties

Under the "advice and consent" clause of the United States Constitution, Article II, Section 2, Paragraph 2, the United States Senate has the responsibility for considering and passing judgment on presidential nominations for cabinet positions and other executive branch political offices, U.S. diplomatic posts, and federal judges, as well as on treaties with foreign countries and international organizations. Called when necessary and when circumstances dictate, congressional hearings are utilized in all these instances by the relevant committee of jurisdiction to bring information into the public domain for consideration by the committee and the full Senate. Witnesses typically include the individuals nominated and others who are in a position to provide information about the nominee's credentials, qualifications, experience, character, and general fitness for service, or, in the case of a treaty, government officials and others who can testify about the content, purpose, and wisdom of the proposed treaty.

Confirmation hearings are conducted by Senate committees regarding executive and judicial branch nominations that come within their respective jurisdictions. Examples would include Senate Armed Services Committee hearings to consider the nomination of an individual to serve as Secretary of Defense, and Senate Energy and Natural Resources Committee hearings to consider the nomination of someone to serve as Secretary of Energy. The Senate Judiciary Committee conducts hearings to review the nominations of federal district and appellate court judges and Supreme Court justices (see § 1.59). Typically there are a large number of confirmation hearings in the weeks and months immediately following the inauguration of a new president, but confirmation hearings are routinely scheduled by committees whenever presidential nominations occur.

A similar committee hearing function applies to consideration of treaties proposed by the president. Senate committees, most notably Foreign Relations and Armed Services, conduct hearings to review treaty proposals before making decisions whether to recommend ratification of a treaty to the full Senate, which must give its consent before a treaty can be implemented. Examples of treaty ratification hearings include multiple hearings conducted in conjunction with the Senate's approval of the North American Free Trade Act (NAFTA) (1993) and the Comprehensive Nuclear Test Ban Treaty (1996).

§ 1.59 Sample Confirmation Hearing Opening Statement: Opening Segment of Senate Judiciary Committee's Hearing on the Nomination of Judge John Roberts to Become Chief Justice of the United States

S. HRG. 109–158

CONFIRMATION HEARING ON THE NOMINATION OF JOHN G. ROBERTS, JR. TO BE CHIEF JUSTICE OF THE UNITED STATES

HEARING BEFORE THE COMMITTEE ON THE JUDICIARY
UNITED STATES SENATE
ONE HUNDRED NINTH CONGRESS
FIRST SESSION

SEPTEMBER 12–15, 2005
Serial No. J–109–37

Printed for the use of the Committee on the Judiciary

****

OPENING STATEMENT OF HON. ARLEN SPECTER, A U.S. SENATOR FROM THE STATE OF PENNSYLVANIA

Chairman SPECTER. Thank you very much, Senator Leahy. And now we will begin the opening statements, as I have said, of 10 minutes' duration.

This hearing, Judge Roberts, is being held in the Senate Caucus Room, which has been the site of many historic hearings, going back to 1912 with the sinking of the Titanic; 1923, Teapot Dome; 1954, Army-McCarthy; 1973, Watergate; 1987, Iran-contra; and this chamber still reverberates with the testimony of Judge Bork in 1987, and it still reverberates with the testimony of Justice Clarence Thomas and Professor Anita Hill in 1991.

This is a very unique hearing—the first one in 11 years in the Senate for a Supreme Court Justice, and the first one in 19 years for a Chief Justice. And you would be, if confirmed, the 17th Chief Justice in the history of the country and the second youngest since Chief Justice Marshall was sworn in, in 1800.

Your prospective stewardship of the Court, which could last until the year 2040, or longer—the senior Justice now is Justice Stevens, who is 85, and projecting ahead 35 years, that would take us to the year 2040 and would present a very unique opportunity for a new Chief Justice to rebuild the image of the Court away from what many believe it has become, a super-legislature, and to bring consensus to the Court with the hallmark of the Court being 5–4 decisions—a 5–4 decision this year allowing Texas to display the Ten Commandments, and a 5–4 decision turning Kentucky down from displaying the Ten Commandments; a 5–4 decision 4 years ago striking down a section of the Americans With Disabilities Act; and last year, a 5–4 decision upholding the Americans With Disabilities Act on the same Congressional record.

Beyond your potential voice for change and consensus, your vote will be critical on many, many key issues, such as Congressional power, Presidential authority, civil rights, including voting rights and affirmative action, defendants' rights, prayer, many decisions for the future, and perhaps institutional changes in the Court, looking for the day when the Court may be televised.

This hearing comes at a time of turbulent partisanship in the United States Senate. Turbulent partisanship. Earlier this year, the Senate faced the possibility of a virtual meltdown, with filibusters on one side of the aisle and on the other side of the aisle the threat of the constitutional or nuclear confrontation. This Committee, with the leadership of Senator Leahy, has moved to a bipartisan approach. We had a prompt confirmation of the Attorney General. We reported out bills which have become legislation, after being stalled for many years, on bankruptcy reform and class action. We have confirmed contentious circuit court nominees. We have reported out unanimously the PATRIOT Act and, after very deliberate and complex hearings, reported out asbestos reform. So it has been quite a period for this Committee.

And now we face the biggest challenge of the year, perhaps the biggest challenge of the decade, in this confirmation proceeding. I have reserved my own judgment on your nomination until the hearings are concluded, and it is my firm view that there ought not to be a political tilt to the confirmation of a Supreme Court Justice, thought to be Republican or Democratic. We all have a responsibility to ask probing questions to determine qualification beyond academic and professional standing.

These hearings, in my judgment, ought to be in substantive fact and in perception for all Americans, that all Americans can feel confident that the Committee and the full Senate has done its job.

There are no firmly established rules for questions and answers. I have expressed my personal view that it is not appropriate to ask a question about how the nominee would vote on a specific case, and I take that position because of the key importance of independence, that there ought not to be commitments or promises made by a nominee to secure confirmation. But Senators have the right to ask whatever questions they choose, and you, Judge Roberts, have the prerogative to answer the questions as you see fit or not to answer them as you see fit.

It has been my judgment, after participating in nine—this will be the tenth for me personally—that nominees answer about as many questions as they think they have to in order to be confirmed. It is a subtle minuet, and it will be always a matter of great interest as to how we proceed.

I do not intend to ask you whether you will overrule *Roe* v. *Wade*. I will ask you whether you think the Constitution has a right of privacy, and I will ask questions about precedents as they bear on *Roe* v. *Wade*. I am very much concerned about what I conceive to be an imbalance in the separation of powers between the Congress and the Court. I am concerned about what I bluntly say is the denigration by the Court of Congressional authority. When the Supreme Court of the United States struck down a portion of the legislation to protect women against violence, the Court did so because of our "method of reasoning." And the dissent noted that that had carried the implication of judicial competence, and the inverse of that is Congressional incompetence. And after 25 years in this body, on fact finding—and there was an extensive record made in the case, in the legislation to protect women against violence, the Court simply disregarded it.

And then the issue of States' rights, the Supreme Court of the United States has elevated States' rights, but in a context that it is impossible to figure out what the law is. The Americans With Disabilities Act had a very extensive record, but when the case came up in 2001, Garrett, a woman who had breast cancer, the Supreme Court said that the section of the Act was unconstitutional. Four years later, in *Lane* v. *Tennessee*, you had a paraplegic crawling up the steps access to a courtroom. The Court said that that was constitutional, again 5–4, on what really turned out to be inexplicable decisions.

You have a very extensive paper trail, and there will obviously be questions on that subject, and we will be concerned about what your views are today contrasted with what your views may have been in the past. Phyllis Schlafly, the president of the Eagles Forum, said that they were smart-alecky comments by a bachelor who did not have a whole lot of experience. So she is putting on an understandable gloss on that subject. But I know that will be a matter of considerable interest.

In one of your earlier memoranda, you came forward with an intriguing thought, one of many in those early memoranda, as your conceptualization power was evident, that Justices ought to be limited to a 15-year term. And with that idea in play, if time permits, it is something I would like to explore, voluntary action on the part of a Justice or perhaps the President could make that a condition.

Between now and the year 2040, or in the intervening years, technology will present many, many novel issues, and there, again, if time permits, I would like to explore that.

I am down to 10 seconds, and I intend to stop precisely on time, and this Committee has a record for maintaining that time. That is it.

[Laughter.]

Judge ROBERTS. Thank you, Mr. Chairman.

Chairman SPECTER. I now yield to my distinguished colleague, Senator Leahy.

Source: S. Hrg. 109-158, Confirmation Hearing on the Nomination of John G. Roberts, Jr. to be Chief Justice of the United States, Committee on the Judiciary, U.S. Senate, September 12-15, 2005.

For the complete transcript of the hearing online, perform an Internet search for "sh109-158", including the quotation marks.

§1.60 Field Hearings

Congressional hearings that are conducted outside Washington are known as field hearings. The rules, procedures and format of field hearings are basically the same as for those hearings conducted on Capitol Hill. Committees in both the House of Representatives and the Senate utilize field hearings to complement the hearings conducted in

Washington, quite often with a focus on a specific regional concern over the topic of the hearing. The rules of both chambers provide or allow for field hearings as deemed necessary and relevant by their respective committees.

Field hearings are frequently used in an effort to respond to a crisis or emergency, such as a crop pest infestation that is the subject of field hearings conducted in California by the agriculture committees. As an illustration of another valuable use of field hearings, those same agriculture committees also utilize field hearings around the country to gather valuable information prior to the writing of federal farm legislation. Field hearings are also a method for "bringing government to the people" since the hearings are conducted in a locale that is more widely accessible for attendance and participation by some who otherwise might not be able to take part in or attend Washington hearings.

§1.61 Sample of a Field Hearing Announcement

December 12, 2003
For Immediate Release

Contact: Robert Reilly
Deputy Chief of Staff
Office: (717) 600-1919

Platts to Co-Chair Field Hearing on Coordinating the Government's Attack on Terrorist Financing

Committees Seek to Identify, Disrupt and Dismantle a Constantly Evolving Threat to National Security

Tampa, Florida—Congressman Todd Russell Platts (PA-19), chairman of the Subcommittee on Government Efficiency and Financial Management, will be co-chairing a field hearing at the Tampa Port Authority on Monday, December 15, 2003, to assess the federal government's response to terrorist financing.

Congressman Platts' subcommittee will be joined by members of the Subcommittee on Technology, Information Policy, Intergovernmental Affairs and the Census, chaired by Rep. Adam Putnam (FL-12). Members of these two Government Reform Subcommittees will hear testimony from employees of the State Department, the Federal Bureau of Investigation, the Treasury Department, the Department of Homeland Security and the U.S. Secret Service.

Financial crimes provide the functional equivalent of a war industry for terrorists. Since the 1980s the federal government has targeted money laundering—the disguising of profits from illegal activities such as drug sales, smuggling, or piracy. These illicit funds can and do provide a ready source of money for terrorists. The full scope of terrorist financing, however, is much larger.

Legitimate charities, non-profit corporations, and think tanks funneled millions of dollars through the U.S. banking system to fund terrorist organizations, including al-Qaeda, Palestinian Islamic Jihad, and HAMAS. Many of these organizations earned tax-exempt status from the IRS. The complexity of targeting these types of entities required a new focus in the war on financial crime.

"Rooting out the perpetrators of such financial crimes can expose the infrastructure of criminal organizations and provide a roadmap to those who facilitate criminal activities and terrorist acts," Congressman Platts said. "Effectively leveraging all available resources and technology is perhaps our best protection against future attacks."

While the source and destination of funding may differ, the mechanisms used to disguise funds for terrorist organizations are similar to those used by drug traffickers and criminal organizations. With tools provided by the USA PATRIOT Act and the strategic efforts that had been in play to fight drug cartels, the federal government has sharpened its focus and has striven for unprecedented coordination among law enforcement entities and foreign governments.

The witnesses will testify on the 2003 National Money Laundering Strategy, issued last November, and their efforts to leverage resources and utilize information technology effectively and efficiently.

Tampa, Florida, is home to University of South Florida Professor Sami Al-Arian, who was indicted on February 19, 2003. A federal grand jury indicted Al-Arian, three foreign nationals who served as leaders of Palestinian Islamic Jihad, and four members of the Tampa PIJ cell with 50 counts, including conspiracy to commit racketeering, murder, and material support of terrorism. PIJ, a designated foreign terrorist organization under Executive Order 13224, is a Syrian-based organization that has engaged in a campaign of suicide bombings and attacks that have killed hundreds—including American tourists traveling in Israel.

Sami Al-Arian and his co-conspirators used facilities in the U.S., including the University of South Florida and affiliated non-profit research foundations, to serve as the North American base of PIJ. Eight years of intercepted wire conversations and faxes demonstrated the defendants' active involvement in the worldwide operations of PIJ.

Witnesses

Jeff Ross, Senior Advisor, Executive Office for Terrorist Financing/Financial Crimes, Department of the Treasury

George A. Glass, Director, Office of Economic Sanctions Policy, Bureau of Economic and Business Affairs, Department of State

Carl Whitehead, Special Agent in Charge, Tampa Office, Federal Bureau of Investigation, Department of Justice

Marcy M. Forman, Deputy Assistant Director, Financial Investigations Division, U.S. Immigration & Customs Enforcement, Department of Homeland Security

Bruce Townsend, Deputy Assistant Director, Office of Investigations, U.S. Secret Service, Department of Homeland Security

Source: § 8.45, Field Hearing Announcement, the *Congressional Deskbook*, by Michael L. Koempel and Judy Schneider

§1.62 Example of a Field Hearing Transcript and Proceedings

Opening segment of OVERSIGHT FIELD HEARING
before the COMMITTEE ON NATURAL RESOURCES,
U.S. HOUSE OF REPRESENTATIVES

OVERSIGHT FIELD HEARING ON "THE NEEDS AND CHALLENGES OF TRIBAL LAW ENFORCEMENT ON INDIAN RESERVATIONS"

****

Friday, June 1, 2007
U.S. House of Representatives
Committee on Natural Resources
Lower Brule, South Dakota

****

The Committee met, pursuant to call, at 12:15 p.m., at the Lower Brule Tribal Headquarters, 187 Oyate Circle, Lower Brule, South Dakota, Hon. Stephanie Herseth Sandlin presiding.

Members Present: Representative Herseth Sandlin.

Staff Present: Cynthia L. Freeman, Clerk, Office of Indian Affairs; Janet Erickson, Counsel; Chris Fluhr, Staff Director; and Phil Asmus, Legislative Assistant to Ms. Herseth Sandlin.

STATEMENT OF THE HON. STEPHANIE HERSETH SANDLIN,
A REPRESENTATIVE IN CONGRESS FROM THE
STATE OF SOUTH DAKOTA

Ms. Herseth Sandlin. The House Natural Resources Committee field hearing will now come to order.

Good afternoon to all of you. I'm very pleased to be here today to convene this field hearing which follows a string of Natural Resources Committee oversight hearings in Washington, D.C., but has the important distinction of being the Committee's first Native American focused field hearing in the 110th Congress.

Though he isn't here today, I would like to extend a word of thanks to Chairman Nick Rahall for his leadership in this Congress and his willingness to support this.

I also want to extend my appreciation to Ranking Member Don Young of Alaska, who has a long record of service to his state, to Alaska Natives, and to all Native Americans.

Additional thanks are certainly due to the Natural Resources Committee staff who worked with my office to schedule, organize, and prepare for this hearing. And I want to introduce them, Janet Erickson, Cynthia Freeman, Chris Fluhr, and certainly to the Lower Brule Sioux Tribe and all of those who worked with us and have graciously offered to host this hearing in the beautiful tribal headquarters.

I want to thank each of our witnesses who have taken the time to travel here today and who have such important leadership roles within their communities and within the administration.

I want to acknowledge and thank Tonya Peterson from Senator Johnson's office as well as Jeannie Faber from Senator Thune's office and both of our senators for their interest and their dedication to these issues as well.

The focus of today's hearing is law enforcement in Indian Country and this oversight opportunity is long overdue. I've been repeatedly alarmed by reports from tribal leaders across South Dakota both during meetings in Washington and through my own travels back in the state.

****

Following Mr. Ragsdale's comments we'll hear from two distinguished and passionate tribal leaders who will certainly have much to say about the state of law enforcement services for the tribal members and communities they represent. I've greatly appreciated both Chairman Jandreau's and Chairman Thompson's strong leadership and advocacy on behalf of their tribes and look forward to hearing from them as well.

So let's begin with the first testimony today on the first panel, Mr. Ragsdale, please.

Source: H. Hrg. 110-28, Oversight Field Hearing on the Needs and Challenges of Tribal Law Enforcement on Indian Reservations, Committee on Natural Resources, U.S. House of Representatives, June 1, 2007.

For the complete transcript of the hearing online, perform an Internet search for "f:36020.wais", including the quotation marks.

§1.63 Showcasing, Publicity, Celebrity, and Grandstanding Hearings

Congressional hearings occasionally take on a theatrical aspect beyond the normal give-and-take of a hearing format. Known by various terms, and somewhat overlapping in meaning, these hearings often tend to center around controversial or unique issues, and they are utilized by committees or members of Congress, and, through them, outside interests as well, to highlight or draw notoriety to a particular issue. Hearings of this nature tend to be rather narrowly focused or even one-sided. They can occur in the context of virtually any of the other types of hearings, and they are usually focused on high-profile, high-stakes, and "hot-button" issues. These categories of hearings tend to be hyped by the participants and the media more than run-of-the-mill hearings, and media coverage—for purposes of entertainment and reporting value—quite often exceeds that of a routine hearing. Multiple cameras, media crews, klieg lights, and reporters are the norm at these types of hearings.

Showcasing and publicity hearings are those that are primarily intended to hold up an issue or situation for congressional and public review, and to establish some special notoriety and attention, perhaps to advance a legislative agenda or merely to educate the public. The hearing underscores a particular position held or advanced by the proponents of the hearing. One example would be a hearing that supports a political and legislative agenda of a cleaner environment by showcasing a new higher efficiency automobile engine.

Celebrity hearings involve an appearance and testimony by a celebrity witness such as a Hollywood performer, musical entertainer, or other well-known individual who typically has championed a cause or issue and is willing to add his or her credibility to the cause by testifying. The celebrity status of the witness draws unique and additional attention to the issue, and the occasion of the celebrity testimony often takes on many of the attributes of a Hollywood premiere, with lights, cameras, the media, and rubber-necking fans (including members of Congress). An example of an effective celebrity witness appearance at a congressional hearing would be Michael J. Fox's testimony before the Senate Appropriations Subcommittee on Labor, Health and Human Services, Education and Related Agencies in 1999 on the need for additional federal research funding for Parkinson's disease (see § 1.64 below).

For more examples of celebrity hearings, see § 8.44, Celebrity Witnesses, the *Congressional Deskbook*, by Michael L. Koempel and Judy Schneider.

Grandstanding hearings are more or less extreme forms of publicity or showcasing hearings, in which the proponent members of Congress, and outside sources through the members, utilize the committee hearing process either to support or oppose an issue in a grandiose manner, often with extremely one-sided testimony. Examples include a 2006 House Judiciary Committee hearing bashing Senate bill 2611 on immigration reform, in which the committee lined up witness after witness to oppose the measure in a very scripted way, and a 1992 hearing before the House Judiciary Committee, in which citizens groups opposed to the opening of a hazardous waste incineration plant in Ohio were successful in obtaining the committee's support during a raucous hearing to expose alleged irregularities in the Environmental Protection Agency's permitting process.

§1.64 Sample Celebrity Testimony: Michael J. Fox's Testimony before the Senate Appropriations Subcommittee on Labor, Health and Human Services, Education and Related Agencies in 1999 on the Need for Additional Federal Research Funding for Parkinson's Disease

TUESDAY, SEPTEMBER 28, 1999

U.S. SENATE, SUBCOMMITTEE ON LABOR, HEALTH AND HUMAN SERVICES, AND EDUCATION, AND RELATED AGENCIES, COMMITTEE ON APPROPRIATIONS

Washington, DC. The subcommittee met at 9:40 a.m., in room SH–216, Hart Senate Office Building, Hon. Arlen Specter (chairman) presiding.

Present: Senators Specter, Cochran, Gorton, and Murray.

Also present: Senator Wellstone.

****

OPENING STATEMENT OF SENATOR ARLEN SPECTER

Senator SPECTER. Good morning, ladies and gentlemen. The hearing of the Appropriations Subcommittee on Labor, Health and Human Services, and Education will now proceed.

We have a hearing today which focuses on Parkinson's Disease. This is a medical problem of enormous impact. We have with us today a very distinguished panel, including Mr. Michael J. Fox.

One of the issues of developing public concern, public support, for research occurs in a very natural way, when someone of the prominence of Michael J. Fox comes forward and talks about his own situation. Senator Cochran, who has been the originator of the idea for this specialized hearing, and I, were just talking to Mr. Fox, who told us about his own personal reaction on going public, so to speak, of how he felt good this morning, with a sense of purpose, in coming to this hearing. Mr. Fox is one of thousands, tens of thousands, hundreds of thousands, of people in America who suffer from Parkinson's.

****

Senator SPECTER. OK, thank you very much, Dr. Fischbach. We turn now to our second panel, Mr. Michael J. Fox, Mr. James Cordy, Dr. J. William Langston, and Ms. Joan Samuelson. If you, lady and gentlemen, would step forward, we will proceed with your testimony.

We welcome you all here. Ms. Samuelson is president of the Parkinson's Action Network and has been very active in promoting funding. Dr. Langston is the president of the Parkinson's Institute and a renowned expert in the field. Mr. James Cordy—where is your hourglass, Jim? OK—has been an extraordinarily effective advocate in this field.

As I noted earlier, we have with us today Mr. Michael J. Fox, a successful actor for many years. First, as Alex P. Keaton, on the television series "Family Ties." You always work with a middle initial, do not you Mr. Fox? Later in many movies, including "Back to the Future," and, most recently, on television again in the highly acclaimed "Spin City." Michael was diagnosed with Parkinson's in 1991, at the age of 30.

He has become very, very active in Parkinson's advocacy. One of the facts of life is that when someone like Michael J. Fox steps forward, it very heavily personalizes the problem, focuses a lot of public attention on it, and has the public understanding of the need for doing whatever we can as a country to conquer this disease and many, many others. So we thank you for being here, Michael J. Fox, and look forward to your testimony.

Again, we will put the lights on, for 5 minutes, on testimony. Mr. Fox, we are going to start with you.

****

STATEMENT OF MICHAEL J. FOX, ACTOR

Mr. FOX. Mr. Chairman and members of the subcommittee, thank you for inviting me to testify today about the need for greater Federal investment in Parkinson's research.

Some, or perhaps all, of you, most of you, are familiar with me from my work in film and television. What I wish to speak to you about today has little or nothing to do with celebrity save for this brief reference. When I first spoke publicly about my 8 years of experience as a person with Parkinson's, many were surprised, in part, because of my age. Although 30 percent of all Parkinson's patients are under 50, and 20 percent are under 40, and that number is growing.

I had hidden my symptoms and struggles very well, through increasing amounts of medication, through surgery, and by employing the hundreds of little tricks and techniques a person with Parkinson's learns to mask his or her condition for as long as possible. While the changes in my life were profound and progress, I kept them to myself for a number of reasons—fear, denial for sure, but I also felt that it was important for me to quietly just soldier on.

When I did share my story, the response was overwhelming and deeply inspiring. I heard from thousands of Americans affected by Parkinson's, writing and calling to offer encouragement and to tell me of their experience. They spoke of pain, frustration, fear, and hope. Always hope.

What I understood very clearly is that the time for quietly soldiering on is through. The war against Parkinson's is a winnable war, and I have resolved to play a role in that victory. What celebrity has given me is the opportunity to raise the visibility of Parkinson's Disease and focus attention on the desperate need for more research dollars. While I am able, for the time being, to continue doing what I love best, others are not so fortunate.

These are doctors, teachers, policemen, nurses, and, as you had indicated earlier, legislators, and parents who are no longer able to work to provide for their families or to live out their dreams. The 1 million Americans living with Parkinson's want to beat this disease. So do the millions more Americans who have family members suffering from Parkinson's. But it will not happen until Congress adequately funds Parkinson's research.

For many people with Parkinson's, managing their disease is a full-time job. It is a constant balancing act. Too little medicine causes tremors and stiffness. Too much medicine produces uncontrollable movement and slurring. And far too often, Parkinson's patients wait and wait—as I am right now—for the medicines to kick in.

New investigational therapies have helped some people like me control symptoms but, in the end, we all face the same reality— the medicine stops working. For people living with Parkinson's, the status quo is not good enough. As I began to understand what research might promise for the future, I became hopeful that I would not face the terrible suffering so many with Parkinson's endure. But I was shocked and frustrated to learn the amount of funding for Parkinson's research is so meager.

Compared to the amount of Federal funding going to other diseases, research funding for Parkinson's lags far behind. In a country with a $15 billion investment in medical research, we can and must do better.

At present, Parkinson's is inadequately funded, no matter how one cares to spend it. Meager funding means a continued lack of effective treatments, slower progress in understanding the cause of the disease, and little chance that a cure will come in time.

I applaud the steps you are taking to fulfill the promise of the Udall Parkinson's Research Act. But, we must be clear, we are not there yet.

If, however, an adequate investment is made, there is much to be hopeful for. We have a tremendous opportunity to close the gap for Parkinson's. We are learning more and more about this disease. The scientific community believes that with a significant investment into Parkinson's research, new discoveries and improved treatment strategies are close at hand. Many have called Parkinson's the most curable neurological disorder and the one expected to produce a breakthrough first.

Scientists tell me that a cure is possible—some say even by the end of the next decade—if the research dollars match the research opportunity.

Mr. Chairman, you and the members of the subcommittee have done so much to increase the investment in medical research in this country. I thank you for your vision. Most people do not know just how important this research is until they or someone in their family faces a serious illness. I know I did not.

The Parkinson's community strongly supports your efforts to double medical research funding. At the same time, I implore you to do more for people with Parkinson's. Take up Parkinson's as if your life depended on it. Increase funding for Parkinson's research by $75 million over the current levels for the coming fiscal year. Make this a down payment for a fully funded Parkinson's research agenda. It will make Parkinson's nothing more than a footnote in medical textbooks.

I would like to close on a personal note. Today you will hear from, or have already heard from, more than a few experts in the fields of science, bookkeeping and other areas. I am an expert on only one—what it is like to be a young man, husband and father, with Parkinson's Disease.

With the help of daily medications and selective exertion, I can still perform my job, in my case, in a very public arena. I can still help out with the daily tasks and rituals involved in home life. But I do not kid myself—that will change. Physical and mental exhaustion will become more and more of a factor, as will increased rigidity, tremor and dyskinesia.

I can expect, in my forties, to face challenges most will not expect until their seventies or eighties, if ever. But with your help, and if we all do everything we can to eradicate this disease, in my fifties, I will be dancing at my children's weddings, and mine will be one of millions of happy stories.

Thank you for your time and attention.

Senator SPECTER. Thank you very much, Mr. Fox, for those very profound and moving words.

Source: S. Hrg. 106-373, Special Hearing Before the Committee on Appropriations, Subcommittee on Labor, Health and Human Services, and Education, and Related Agencies, U.S. Senate, Sept. 28, 1999.

For the complete transcript of the hearing online, perform an Internet search for "f:59959.wais", including the quotation marks.

§1.65 Public or Open Hearings and Closed or Classified Hearings

Open or public hearings are just that—open to the public to attend. Most congressional hearings, by nature, practice and rule, are open hearings, in concert with the democratic notion of a "public hearing." In fact, each congressional hearing must be open to anyone, unless specifically deemed a closed hearing by the committee, in open session, under the rules of the Senate or House and the relevant committee. Hearings that are closed to the public include those concerning certain aspects of national security and defense, select foreign policy and energy policy matters, sensitive homeland security and law enforcement information, and intelligence matters, as well as when a rule of the House or Senate might otherwise be violated. In cases where hearing testimony might be degrading, defamatory, or incriminating, a committee will typically close the session with a majority vote, which is also required to release testimony to the public that is taken in closed session. Examples of closed hearings would include House or Senate Armed Service Committee hearings to review a proposed new weapons system, and a Senate or House Intelligence Committee hearing to review covert operations in a foreign country.

Closed or classified hearings are accessible only to those deemed necessary to the proceedings by a committee, and typically may include committee members and select staff, House and Senate colleagues if invited, and other invited and screened witnesses and officials from government agencies or the private sector. Those participating in closed hearings are sometimes required to have a certain level of security clearance, and the hearing rooms may be "swept" to guard against the possibility of surveillance or listening devices. Occasionally an otherwise open or public hearing will be closed at a point in the proceedings when sensitive matters come under review. Committees normally give advance notice of the possibility of a closed hearing, or they conduct a vote in advance in open session to close a future session as may be appropriate.

For more information, see § 2.99, Regular Order and Format of Proceedings: The Normal Procedural Conduct of a Hearing—Open and Closed Hearings.

For a sample notice of an open and closed hearing, see § 1.66 below.

§ 1.66 Sample of Open and Closed Hearings: Notices from the Senate Armed Services Committee

UNITED STATES SENATE COMMITTEE ON ARMED SERVICES
Sir/Madam: There will be a meeting of the Committee on ARMED SERVICES Room S-407 of the Capitol Thursday, January 18, 2007 ~ 2:30 p.m.

CLOSED

To receive a briefing on intelligence assessments on the situation in Iraq.

Witnesses:

Dr. David F. Gordon, Vice Chairman, National Intelligence Council

Lieutenant General Michael D. Maples, USA, Director, Defense Intelligence Agency

Honorable Randall M. Fort, Assistant Secretary for Intelligence and Research, Department of State

UNITED STATES SENATE COMMITTEE ON ARMED SERVICES
Sir/Madam: There will be a meeting of the Committee on ARMED SERVICES Room SH-216 Hart Senate Office Building Tuesday, February 27, 2007 ~ 9:30 a.m.

OPEN*

To receive testimony on current and future worldwide threats to the national security of the United States.

Witnesses:

Vice Admiral John M. McConnell, USN (Ret.), Director, National Intelligence

Lieutenant General Michael D. Maples, USA, Director, Defense Intelligence Agency

Dr. Thomas Fingar, Deputy Director of National Intelligence for Analysis, and Chairman, National Intelligence Council

There is a possibility of a CLOSED session in S-407 of the Capitol, following the OPEN session.

UNITED STATES SENATE COMMITTEE ON ARMED SERVICES
Sir/Madam: There will be a meeting of the SUBCOMMITTEE ON READINESS AND MANAGEMENT SUPPORT Room S-407, The Capitol Tuesday, April 17, 2007 ~ 3:00 p.m.

CLOSED

To receive a briefing on the current readiness of U.S. ground forces in review of the Defense Authorization Request for Fiscal Year 2008 and the Future Years Defense Program.

Witnesses:

Lieutenant General James J. Lovelace, Jr., USA, Deputy Chief of Staff, G-3/5/7, Headquarters, Department of the Army

Lieutenant General Richard F. Natonski, USMC, Deputy Commandant for Plans, Policies, and Operations, Headquarters, United States Marine Corps

Source: Committee on Armed Services, United States Senate.

§1.70 The Psychology and Culture of Congressional Hearings: Mission, Education, Information, and Advocacy

The psychology of a congressional hearing varies significantly based on a committee's jurisdiction, its culture and membership, and on the type, purpose and mission of the hearing. Generally committees conduct well-organized, thorough and usually fair hearings that sufficiently produce useful information, elicited from the testimony of witnesses and from the answers to questions posed to witnesses, that educates the committee members and is helpful in the conduct of their work. In conducting a hearing around a certain topic or issue, the committee seeks to afford those on the outside, with expertise or knowledge about an issue, the opportunity to provide helpful testimony to the committee upon which it can rely in making decisions about legislative, funding, or oversight matters.

At the same time, the committee culture provides for the time-honored practice of allowing members of the committee to make opening or even extended statements that sometimes precede a question and other times are expounded as remarks for the record or offered up for the purpose of educating the committee or public, persuading their colleagues, or lecturing a witness.

Through its hearings, a committee is undertaking a form of research and is making a record of its findings. Its primary mission is to gather accurate and timely information that can advise the deliberations of the committee, and, in this sense, committees utilize hearings to lay the foundation for future actions such as the introduction of bills and the markup of legislation. The committee is seeking information and engages witnesses through testimony and questions to learn about issues.

From the witness's perspective, the hearing provides an opportunity to advise the committee, provide information, educate the members and advocate a specific position on a public policy issue. The culture and mission of a congressional hearing can certainly be colored by partisanship and political brinksmanship, with the result of such influence being good or bad, productive or unproductive, depending on one's perspective.

§1.80 Results and Outcomes of Hearings: Legislative and Regulatory Actions and Remedies

Hearings can produce a wide array of results, intended or unintended, and are used broadly in support of various outcomes, including making a complete record of the hearing proceedings, educating and informing the committee and the public, adding value and advocacy to a public policy debate, influencing legislation or executive branch actions, and fueling public interest and discussion. Hearings are also used as a strategy to stimulate media coverage that, in turn, feeds public opinion, as well as the perspectives of lawmakers. For a discussion of various results and outcomes of hearings, see § 1.81 through § 1.92 below.

§ 1.81 Results and Outcomes of Hearings: Legislative and Regulatory Actions and Remedies—Published for Public Record

Congressional committees are authorized to publish and have printed a written transcript of a hearing that is bound and distributed to a limited audience, mainly the committee itself. A limited number of copies is sometimes made available to the public, but access to the committee's official record is always available to the public, either by inspection of the actual bound document or through access provided by postings on the committee's web site (with the obvious exception of closed hearings). Making the record—a published record—is an important step in underscoring the importance of the committee's work in deliberating on the subject matter within its purview. The hearing record provides a compendium of testimony, committee members' statements, and questions and answers between the committee and witnesses, all of which, taken together, establishes a resource for the committee and others to utilize in further actions and deliberations. The hearing record is a valuable source of information, a recognized resource of authority on a subject matter, and an official reference that can be cited in other writings and in public discourse.

For information on a committee's role in reviewing and editing hearings transcripts, see § 7.7, Committee Follow-Up Activities and Responsibilities—Review and Editing of the Hearings Transcript.

For information on a witness's role in reviewing and editing a hearing transcript, see § 7.26, Follow-Up Activities and Responsibilities of a Witness—A Witness's Review and Editing of Hearings Transcripts.

§ 1.82 Results and Outcomes of Hearings: Legislative and Regulatory Actions and Remedies—Committee Hearing Transcripts as Published Documents for the Committee and Public Record

Hearings

Witnesses present oral and written testimony at hearings, and are questioned by committee members and, occasionally, by committee staff. Statistical data, correspondence, written answers to questions, and other information can also be submitted by committee members and witnesses for inclusion in the hearing record. Hearings might be broadcast or webcast. Stenographers are always present at committee and subcommittee hearings. They record transcripts of all the proceedings. The transcripts are then edited by committee staff. Hearing records are generally published by committees, but they are often not available until months after a hearing or series of hearings is held. However, committees maintain transcripts of hearings in the committee offices. The transcripts are usually available for inspection, often the day following a hearing.

Many committees put witness testimony on their web sites soon after a hearing. Many committees are posting transcripts as well, and some make audio or video recordings available online. Although most witnesses provide written testimony to a committee, printed copies may be difficult to obtain before a hearing transcript is printed (unless one attends the hearing). However, for executive branch witnesses, the respective agency web site, or the Office of Management and Budget web site, often provides the full text of agency witnesses' testimony. If a witness is representing a private organization, testimony may be posted on that organization's web site.

House committees use House stenographers. Transcripts may be purchased when committees grant sale permission. Availability and cost information may be obtained from the Office of Official Reporters, at 202-225-2627.

Senate committees make use of reporting services to transcribe their hearings. Copies may be purchased directly from reporting services, when committees grant sale permission. Individual committees can provide information on the reporting services. If printed, hearings are available from the respective committee. However, they are generally printed in limited quantities.

Printed hearings are also often available online at GPO Access, at: <*www.gpoaccess.gov/chearings/index.html*>. (Congressional Information Service is a source for nearly all committee documents. Information can be found at the Lexis-Nexis web site, <*www.lexisnexis.com/academic*>).

Source: § 12.10, Committee Documents/Hearings, the *Congressional Deskbook*, by Michael L. Koempel and Judy Schneider.

For more information about congressional committee documents, see Chapter 12, "Congressional Documents: Committee, Chamber, Party and Administrative Publications," the *Congressional Deskbook*, by Michael L. Koempel and Judy Schneider.

§1.83 Results and Outcomes of Hearings: Legislative and Regulatory Actions and Remedies—Education and Information

One of the obvious yet classic results and outcomes of congressional hearings is the valuable information gathered by the committee in the context of its mission to become more educated about a particular issue. Through the data gathering produced by a hearing, the committee benefits from the input provided by key sources, constituencies and stakeholders—those with expertise or special knowledge—who actually testify or who are represented by those who do testify. This fresh information provides the committee with a body of knowledge that serves as a factual basis both for an enhanced understanding of the issue at hand and for decision-making by the committee regarding further committee and congressional action.

§ 1.84 Results and Outcomes of Hearings: Legislative and Regulatory Actions and Remedies—Public Policy Advocacy and Debate

Congressional hearings provide a front-line forum for discussion and debate about the issues of the day and an opportunity for these issues to be aired publicly in the context of policy advocacy. Hearings offer Congress and all interested parties the chance to explore an issue in a public setting through the testimony of witnesses and the "give-and-take" of the questions and answers between the committee and witnesses. Committees are able to dig deeply into the "pros and cons" of national policies, federal programs, spending priorities, agency regulatory matters and the administration of federal laws and policy across the board. Congress benefits from the discourse, but the media, the general public and any interested parties also have the opportunity to learn from and, in most cases, participate in the hearing process. High-profile issues are usually widely covered by the media, which further stimulates public interest and discourse. Congressional hearings are often used strategically to stimulate or increase media coverage of an issue in order to heighten public opinion and advise informed decision-makers, or they have those effects in many cases even if unintended. Examples that are noted in following sections demonstrate the effect of the media's coverage of congressional hearings. (See § 1.85, § 1.87, § 1.89, § 1.91 and § 1.92.)

§ 1.85 Example of a High-Profile Hearing: The Senate Watergate Hearings that Led to the Resignation of a President

WATERGATE

"Watergate" is synonymous with a series of events that began with a botched burglary and ended with the resignation of a U.S. President. The term itself formally derives from the Watergate building in Washington, DC, where, on the night of 17 June 1972, five burglars were arrested in the Democratic National Committee offices. Newspaper reports from that point began revealing bits and pieces of details that linked the Watergate burglars with President Richard Nixon's 1972 re-election campaign. The president and his chief assistants denied involvement, but as evidence of White House complicity continued to grow, the U.S. Congress was compelled to investigate what role the Watergate matter might have played in subverting or attempting to subvert the electoral process.

The U.S. Senate, by a 77-to-0 vote, approved a resolution on 7 February 1973, to impanel the Senate Select Committee on Presidential Campaign Activities to investigate Watergate. Known as the Ervin Committee for its Chairperson, Senator Sam Ervin, the Committee began public hearings on 17 May 1973, that shortly came to be known as the "Watergate Hearings."

Television cameras covered the Watergate hearings gavel-to-gavel, from day one until 7 August. 319 hours of television were amassed, a record covering a single event. All three commercial television networks then in existence—NBC, CBS, and ABC—devoted an average of five hours per day covering the Watergate hearings for their first five days.

The networks devised a rotation plan that, beginning on the hearing's sixth day, shifted coverage responsibility from one network to another every third day. Any of the three networks remained free to cover more of the hearings than required by their rotation agreement, but only once did the networks choose to exercise their option. All three networks elected to carry the nearly 30 hours of testimony by key witness and former White House counsel John Dean.

The non-commercial Public Broadcasting Service (PBS) aired the videotaped version of each day's Watergate hearing testimony during the evening. Many PBS station managers who were initially reluctant to carry such programming found that as a result of the carriage, station ratings as well as financial contributions increased.

The decision to televise Judiciary Committee meetings was not immediate nor did it meet with overwhelming approval. Only after several impassioned pleas from the floor of the U.S. House that such an extraordinary event should be televised to the fullest extent did the House approve a resolution to allow telecast of the Judiciary Committee's impeachment deliberations. The Committee itself had final say on the matter and voted 31-to-7 to concur with the decision of their House colleagues. One major requirement of the Judiciary Committee was that television networks covering the committee not be allowed to break for a commercial message during deliberations.

The Judiciary Committee began its televised public debate on the evening of 24 July. The commercial networks chose to rotate their coverage in the same manner as utilized during the Senate Watergate hearings. What's more, the commercial networks telecast only the evening portions of Judiciary Committee deliberations, while PBS chose to telecast the morning and afternoon sessions as well. As a result, television viewers were provided nearly 13 hours of coverage for each of the six days of Judiciary Committee public deliberations.

Eventually, the full House and Senate voted to allow television coverage of impeachment proceedings in their respective chambers, once assurances were made that the presence of television cameras and lights would not interfere with the president's due process rights. Final ground rules were being laid and technical preparations for the coverage were underway when President Nixon's resignation on 9 August 1974, brought the impeachment episode to an end.

As the Ervin Committee concluded its initial phase of Watergate hearings on 7 August 1973, the hearing's television audience had waned somewhat, but a majority of viewers continued to indicate a preference that the next hearing phase, scheduled to begin on 24 September, also be televised. The networks, however, felt otherwise. The Ervin Committee continued the Watergate hearings until February 1974 but with only scant television coverage.

Television viewers were attracted to the Watergate hearings in impressive numbers. One survey found that 85% of all U.S. households had tuned in to at least some portion of the hearings. Such interest was not universal, however. In fact, Special Prosecutor Archibald Cox had argued that television's widespread coverage of Watergate testimony could endanger the rights of witnesses to a fair trial and in doing so, could deprive Americans of ever hearing the full story of Watergate. The Ervin Committee refused Cox's request to curtail coverage, saying that it was important that television be allowed to carry Watergate testimony to the American public firsthand.

On 6 February 1974, a new phase of Watergate began when the U.S. House of Representatives voted 410-to-4 to authorize the House Judiciary Committee to investigate whether sufficient grounds existed to impeach President Nixon. If so, the Committee was authorized to report necessary articles of impeachment to the full House.

The Judiciary Committee spent late February to mid-July 1974 examining documents and testimony accumulated during the Senate's Watergate hearings. When this investigatory phase ended, the Judiciary Committee scheduled public deliberations for 24-27, 29 and 30 July to debate what, if any, impeachment recommendations it would make to the House. Three articles of impeachment eventually were approved by the Committee, recommending that the House begin formal impeachment proceedings against President Richard Nixon.

Source: "Watergate," Ronald Garay, *Encyclopedia of Television*, Museum of Broadcast Communications, Chicago, IL. Reprinted with permission from the Museum of Broadcast Communications, Chicago, IL.

§ 1.86 Results and Outcomes of Hearings: Legislative and Regulatory Actions and Remedies—Influence on Legislation and Other Committee Action

One of the major reasons and purposes for congressional hearings is to provide a committee—and ultimately the full House or Senate—with the factual basis, knowledge and basic understanding of an issue that will inform the committee's legislative, oversight or confirmation role. The nature, substance, usefulness, and timing of the information gathered in the hearing stage can greatly influence whether an issue advances in the committee process and ultimately in one or both chambers of Congress. For an issue under consideration as a legislative initiative, whether as a stand-alone bill or an amendment, a hearing can provide not only the factual foundation needed, but it can also serve as a platform of momentum, inspiration, and political support for the issue to move ahead to markup and approval. For a proposed funding issue in the appropriations process, a hearing on the intended use, purpose, and direction of the federal dollars involved can make or break the request, and influence the committee accordingly to approve or disapprove the matter. In the confirmation process, there are numerous examples of how the substance, optics, and outcomes of a congressional hearing affected the decision of a committee and the Senate to confirm or reject a presidential nominee. (For an example of the influence of a hearing on committee and congressional action, see § 1.87 below.)

§1.87 Example of the Influence of Hearings on Committee Action: The Senate Judiciary Committee Supreme Court Confirmation Hearings that Led to the Defeat of Judge Robert Bork

One of the highest-profile and most significant congressional hearing dramas in U.S. history involved the Senate Judiciary Committee's scrutiny of Judge Robert Bork, who was nominated in 1987 by President Reagan to be an associate justice on the United States Supreme Court. With Reagan appointees Sandra Day O'Connor and Antonin Scalia already in place as associate justices, and with the elevation of Associate Justice William Rehnquist to be chief justice, the proposed addition of Bork to the highest court seemed to many to tip the ideological and philosophical balance of the Court to the conservative side of the political ledger. A huge battle over the Bork nomination ensued, with an outpouring of support from the political right and opposition from the political left being played out in media headlines and on Capitol Hill, especially throughout the confirmation hearings, from the moment the nomination was announced. The confirmation fight in the Senate Judiciary Committee was one of President Reagan's biggest challenges of his second term, and he was committed to the fight that would likely be his last chance to change the makeup of the nation's highest court. In the end, he lost that battle. Without question and by all accounts, the drama that unfolded in the Senate Judiciary Committee hearings had a great deal to do with the defeat of the Bork nomination.

At the time of his nomination to the Supreme Court, Judge Bork was a member of the U.S. Court of Appeals for the District of Columbia Circuit. As a possible replacement for retiring Associate Justice Lewis Powell, part of the so-called liberal voting bloc on the Court, Bork represented the antithesis to the type of nominee many Democrats, then in control of the Senate, had hoped and advised Reagan would name. Judge Bork was a scholarly and highly educated jurist with a distinguished career in the private sector, as a Yale Law School professor, and as solicitor general of the United States, the chief advocate for the federal government at the Department of Justice. He had been on the firing line in 1973 as the number-three in command at the Department of Justice when President Nixon ordered him to dismiss Watergate Special Prosecutor Archibald Cox in the aftermath of Attorney General Elliot Richardson's and Deputy Attorney General William Ruckelshaus' refusal to do so.

Judge Bork's conservative credentials made him a target for many senators, the media, and the public to criticize his positions and decisions, and to urge his defeat by the Senate. He was highly critical of judicial activism, and he proclaimed himself a strict constructionist and champion of judicial restraint with respect to interpreting the U.S. Constitution and the laws of the land. His performance in the hearings showcasing his brilliance and understanding of jurisprudence, along with the fact that the

American Bar Association rated him "exceptionally well-qualified," made him an even more dangerous candidate for the Court in the eyes of liberal activists and lawmakers.

Activist groups of both liberal and conservative persuasions spent millions of dollars in public and media campaigns to generate support for, or opposition to, Judge Bork. Some senators even announced their opposition to Bork long before the hearings began and the committee's vote on the nomination was scheduled. The Senate Judiciary Committee conducted twelve days of hearings, and Judge Bork himself testified for an unprecedented five of those days. During his testimony, the judge unexpectedly modified many of his conservative and controversial views, a result that did not resonate well with anyone, supporter or opponent. He quite often sparred with senators during questioning, and he seemed to want to leave the impression that he was the smartest person in the room. Whether he was or not did not matter in the end. What mattered was the performance that he turned in when under fire by the Judiciary Committee, coupled with his long record of decisions and opinions—all exploited by opponents who were able to rally a significant majority of senators to deny Judge Bork a seat on the United States Supreme Court. A hundred witnesses appeared before the committee to support or oppose the nomination. The Judiciary Committee voted 9-5 against confirming Judge Bork, but he announced he wanted to proceed with a Senate floor vote, railing against what he called a "campaign of distortion." The full Senate voted against confirmation by a vote of 58-42.

Source: S. Hrg. 100-1011, Hearings on the Nomination of Robert Bork to be an Associate Justice of the Supreme Court of the United States, Committee on the Judiciary, U.S. Senate, Sept. 15, 16, 17, 18, 19, 21, 22, 23, 25, 28, 29, 30, 1987.

Note: The complete multi-volume printed transcripts of the Bork hearings are not online, but are available through the library of the United States Senate Committee on the Judiciary, the Library of Congress, and most repository libraries. For more information on the Bork hearings, see "The Bork Nomination," Jason Manning, Material Things (The Eighties Club: eightiesclub.tripod.com/id320.htm), and "Bork's Nomination Is Rejected, 58:42; Reagan 'Saddened,'" Linda Greenhouse, *New York Times*, Oct. 24, 1987 <*www.nytimes.com/1987/10/24/politics/24REAG.html*>.

§1.88 Results and Outcomes of Hearings: Legislative and Regulatory Actions and Remedies—Influence and Pressure on the Executive Branch and Federal Regulatory Process

One of the useful purposes of congressional hearings is to focus on an issue or problem that Congress believes might deserve attention or correction by an executive branch department or agency. By making an issue the subject of a hearing and, thus, potentially a household name within Congress and perhaps in the eyes of the public as well, a congressional committee can exert influence or pressure on an agency that in many cases can lead to results that include changes Congress wants the agency to make in a policy or program, or in the way a policy or program is administered. The overriding message to the agency in the hearing takes on the not-so-subtle sound of "fix or change it," or Congress will be forced to legislate on the matter or revisit your funding.

The outcomes of such hearings can lead an agency to alter its views or actions on matters of importance to the committee and to Congress in general. Hearing scenarios such as this often take the form of committee oversight regarding an agency regulation and its application to end-users of a program or policy. The hearing process provides a congressional committee a "bully pulpit" and allows Congress the opportunity to influence the federal regulatory process in an informal, but usually direct and unmistakable, way. The agency involved is typically willing to engage in the possibility of a change or correction because it is always "owing" to Congress under the aegis of "the power of the purse."

§1.89 Example of a Congressional Hearing concerning Executive Branch Agency Activities: Opening Statement of OSHA Hearing

HAVE OSHA STANDARDS KEPT UP WITH WORKPLACE HAZARDS?

****

Tuesday, April 24, 2007, U.S. House of Representatives Subcommittee on Workforce Protections Committee on Education and Labor Washington, DC

The subcommittee met, pursuant to call, at 1:37 p.m., in Room 2175, Rayburn House Office Building, Hon. Lynn Woolsey [chairwoman of the subcommittee] presiding.

Present: Representatives Woolsey, Payne, Bishop of New York, Hare, Wilson, Price, and Kline.

****

Chairwoman Woolsey [presiding]. The hearing of the Workforce Protection Subcommittee on `Have OSHA Standards Kept Up With Workplace Hazards?" will come to order.

Pursuant to Committee Rule 12(a), any member may submit an opening statement in writing which will be made part of the permanent record.

I now recognize myself, followed by Ranking Member Joe Wilson, who is running over here as we speak, for an opening statement.

In 1970, the United States Congress passed the Occupational Safety and Health Act, OSHA, to provide every working man and woman in the nation a safe and healthful workplace. One of the most important roles that it gave the new agency was to develop safety and health standards.

The standards that OSHA has established have saved literally thousands of lives. For example, in 1978, when OSHA's cotton dust standard was adopted, there were 40,000 cases of brown lung disease annually. Twelve percent of all textile workers suffered from this deadly disease. By the year 2000, and because of the OSHA standard, brown lung had virtually been eliminated. OSHA's 1978 standard on lead dramatically reduced lead poisoning. And the 1989 evacuation standard, designed to protect workers from trench collapse, has reduced deaths by more than 20 percent, while construction activity has actually increased by 20 percent.

OSHA has made an enormous difference in workers' lives, but sadly many workers are still at risk from unsafe conditions in their workplaces. The Bureau of Labor Statistics reported that in the year 2005 there were over 5,700 workers, or 16 workers a day, killed in the workplace.

In addition to terrible fatalities, there are millions more workers like Mr. Peoples, who is here to speak with us today as a witness, who suffer from injuries and illnesses based on their working conditions.

This is not a time to slow down on protecting worker safety. But yet that is what the administration has done. There are various areas where OSHA has failed to do its job, and over the coming months, this committee will look into those failures.

Today's hearing will focus on standard setting. And in this arena, the administration has the worst record on standard setting of any administration in the history of the law.

The administration began on a tragic note for American workers with the shameful repeal of OSHA's ergonomic standards. That was followed by the removal of dozens of rules from the regulatory agenda, including the standard to protect health care workers against tuberculosis.

I pray that we don't live to regret this when extremely drug-resistant T.B., which is killing two-thirds of those who get it in South Africa, arrives. If that reaches this nation in significant numbers, we don't have any standards. We don't know what to do about it in our workplace.

To date, this administration has issued only one significant health standard protecting workers against a cancer-causing chemical called chemical hexavalent chromium. And that standard was issued under court order; it was not done voluntarily.

One of the worst failures of this administration is its failure to issue a rule that requires employers to pay for employees' personal protection equipment. This rule was almost finished during the Clinton administration. Seven years later, OSHA has finally agreed to issue this standard, again under the threat of a court order.

Today we will hear the tragic story of Eric Peoples, who has popcorn lung disease and has lost much of his lung capacity. He faces, because of his exposure to a chemical, possibly a shorter life than others his age.

Source: H. Hrg. 110-25, Committee on Education and Labor, Subcommittee on Workforce Protection, U.S. House of Representatives, April 24, 2007.

For the complete transcript of the hearing online, perform an Internet search for "f:34633.wais", including the quotation marks.

§1.90 Results and Outcomes of Hearings: Legislative and Regulatory Actions and Remedies—Influence on Public Knowledge and Actions of Public and Non-Governmental Entities

Congressional committee hearings also produce results that amplify, inform, advise and influence public knowledge and understanding of public policy issues, as well as exert influence on non-governmental organizations (NGOs) to correct a problem or to take a particular course of action on their own. Hearings and their attendant publicity serve as a means of drawing public and media attention to an issue that can be translated into grassroots, lobbying, media or other strategies in support of, or in opposition to, a particular issue or measure. For example, the public may become outraged at information emanating from a congressional hearing on a controversial subject, such as accusations of mismanagement and financial irregularities at the American Red Cross in 2001, and may, in turn, put additional pressure on Congress to remedy the situation (see § 1.91). Another example is the outcome of hearings, such as those conducted in 2005 to investigate the use of steroids in professional baseball, being used to persuade organizations—in this case Major League Baseball and the players' union—to develop policies and procedures to address a major problem (see § 1.92).

§1.91 Example of Congressional Hearing on Public and Non-Governmental Entities: Press Coverage of Red Cross Financial Hearings of 2001

THE CHRONICLE OF PHILANTHROPY

UPDATE

November 6, 2001

Red Cross's Spending Attacked at House Hearing

By Ian Wilhelm Washington

Members of Congress Tuesday condemned the American Red Cross's plans to spend donations received after the September 11 attacks on causes other than direct aid to families of those harmed or killed.

The Red Cross has said it planned to reserve \$264-million of the \$564-million it raised to deal with future terrorist acts, such as the anthrax contamination, building a strategic blood supply, and other needs. At a Congressional hearing to examine how good a job charities are doing distributing funds raised after September 11, members of a subcommittee of the House Commerce Committee criticized the organization's decision, saying the charity was ignoring the intent of its donors.

Helping the Red Cross prepare for future threats was "not what the people opened their hearts and their wallets for," Rep. Bart Stupak, a Michigan Democrat, told Bernadine P. Healy, the departing president of the Red Cross, after she defended her organization's choice to use its Liberty Disaster Fund, created soon after the September 11 attacks, in part to cover what she called "emerging needs."

Dr. Healy said the Red Cross had repeatedly told donors and the general public in television ads and other solicitations that donations would be used to meet needs beyond those that resulted from the September 11 attacks. Members of the House committee asked to see transcripts of public service announcements, radio shows where Dr. Healy asked for funds, and other donor solicitations to verify her statements.

Even if the Red Cross did say it would use funds for additional purposes, it still misled Americans, said one congressman.

"I don't care what it says on the back of an envelope or in a P.S.A. or so forth, you know that if you asked Americans where they thought the money was going when it was to the Liberty Fund, they thought it was going to victims of the disaster," Rep. Charles F. Bass, a New Hampshire Republican, told Dr. Healy.

The hearing was the first of two to be held this week by House members examining the distribution of charitable funds. A subcommittee of the House Ways and Means Committee has scheduled hearings for Thursday.

Dr. Healy resigned as the charity's president on October 26 after the board voted that it had no confidence in her ability to manage the Red Cross, in part because of her decision to separate the Liberty Fund from the group's general disaster-relief fund. Dr. Healy will continue to serve as president until December 31, but she put distance between herself and the Red Cross during the hearing, saying it was not her choice to stop soliciting donations for the Liberty Fund, which the organization did October 30.

Worries About Congressional Pressure

After the hearing, Dr. Healy said she was worried that Congress would pressure the Red Cross into spending the money solely for families of victims. "There's a movement afoot to take that $550-million and divide it by 5,000 [victims]," she said.

Earlier in the day, the Red Cross detailed how it would spend the money collected in the Liberty Fund. It said that the Red Cross Board of Governors was considering extending benefits for victims' families from three months to six months or longer. The organization said it had given $121-million in direct cash assistance to victims and their families. It has also spent $6-million on administrative costs and plans to spend $50-million from the fund to set up a strategic blood reserve. An additional $15-million has been spent to produce brochures with information on anthrax and mental-health counseling.

At Tuesday's Congressional hearing, members of the House subcommittee focused on Dr. Healy, but also heard testimony from women who lost their husbands in the World Trade Center attack. Elizabeth McLaughlin, of Pelham, N.Y., said she had to create an 18-page spreadsheet to keep track of the funds she had applied for. Russa Steiner, of New Hope, Pa., said she had not received any cash assistance from the Red Cross until the day of the hearing, when she said the charity gave her a check for $27,000. Dr. Healy called the amount of time Mrs. Steiner had to wait for cash assistance a mistake by her organization.

The lawmakers urged New York State Attorney General Eliot Spitzer, who testified before the subcommittee, to speed up his coordination of the roughly 200 charities helping families and victims of the terrorist attack. Mr. Spitzer promised to build a database of aid recipients in three weeks. The database would help charities identify what victims are not being assisted, Mr. Spitzer said. He added that he understood how serious it would be if charities did not distribute money quickly and fairly. "The public could lose faith in the entire not-for-profit sector," he warned.

Source: *The Chronicle of Philanthropy*, Nov. 6, 2001; *<http://philanthropy.com/free/update/2001/11/2001110601.htm>*.

Reprinted with permission from *The Chronicle of Philanthropy*.

§1.92 Example of Congressional Hearing on Public and Non-Governmental Entities: The Use of Steroids in Major League Baseball

RESTORING FAITH IN AMERICA'S PASTIME: EVALUATING MAJOR LEAGUE BASEBALL'S EFFORTS TO ERADICATE STEROID USE

HEARING before the COMMITTEE ON GOVERNMENT REFORM, HOUSE OF REPRESENTATIVES, ONE HUNDRED NINTH CONGRESS, FIRST SESSION

****

MARCH 17, 2005

Washington, DC.

The committee met, pursuant to notice, at 10 a.m., in room 2154, Rayburn House Office Building, Hon. Tom Davis (chairman of the committee) presiding.

****

Chairman Tom Davis. Good morning. The committee will come to order, and welcome to the Committee on Government Reform's hearing on Major League Baseball and the use of performance enhancing drugs. Fourteen years ago, anabolic steroids were added to the Control Substance Act as a Schedule III drug, making it illegal to possess or sell them without a valid prescription. Today, however, evidence strongly suggests that steroid use among teenagers, especially aspiring athletes, is a large and growing problem. The Centers for Disease Control and Prevention tells us that more than 500,000 high school students have tried steroids, nearly triple the number just 10 years ago.

A second national survey conducted in 2004 by the National Institute on Drug Abuse and the University of Michigan found that over 40 percent of 12th graders describe steroids as fairly easy or very easy to obtain. And the perception among high school students that steroids are harmful has dropped from 71 percent in 1992 to 56 percent in 2004. This is but a snapshot of the startling data that we face.

Today, we take the committee's first steps toward understanding how we got here and how we begin turning those numbers around. Down the road, we need to look at whether and how Congress should exercise its legislative powers to further restrict the use and distribution of these substances.

Our specific purpose today is to consider Major League Baseball's recently negotiated drug policy, how the testing policy will be implemented, how it will effectively address the use of prohibitive drugs by players and most importantly, the larger societal and public health ramifications of steroid use.

Yesterday, USA Today reported that 79 percent of Major League players surveyed believed steroids played a role in record-breaking performances by some high profile players. While our focus is not on the impact of steroids on Major League Baseball records, the survey does underscore the importance of our inquiry. A majority of the 568 players in this survey think steroids are influencing individual achievements. That's exactly our point. We need to recognize the dangerous vicious cycle that perception creates.

Too many college athletes believe they have to consider steroids if they are going to make it to the pros. High school athletes, in turn, think steroids may be the key to getting a scholarship.

It is time to break that cycle and it needs to happen from the top down. You can't do this by just sending people into the high school classrooms talking about it. It hasn't worked. It has to start from the top. When I go to Little League opening games these days, kids aren't just talking about their favorite teams' chances in the pennant race, they're talking about which pro players are on the "juice." After the 1994 Major League Baseball strike, rumors and allegations of steroid use in the league began to surface. Since then, longstanding records were broken. Along with these broken records came allegations of steroid use among Major League Baseball players. Despite the circulating rumors of illegal drug use, Major League Baseball and the Players Association didn't respond to ban the use of steroids, which were illegal until 2002.

The result was an almost decade-long question mark as to not only the validity of the new records, but also the credibility of the game itself. In February of this year, former Major League Baseball all star Jose Canseco released a book that not only alleges steroid use by well-known Major League players, but discusses the prevalence of steroids in baseball during his 17-year career. After hearing Commissioner Bud Selig's public statements that Major League Baseball would not launch an investigation into his allegations, my ranking member, Henry Waxman, wrote to me asking for a committee hearing to "find out what really happened and to get at the bottom of this growing scandal." I was initially reluctant to hold such an investigation because Major League Baseball assured us they had the problem under control.

However, a cursory investigation raised more questions than it answered and we decided to proceed. Major League Baseball and the Players Association greeted the word of inquiry first as a nuisance, then as a negotiation replete with misstatements about the scope of the documents and information we had sought and inaccurate legalese about the committee's authority and jurisdiction. Fine. I understand their desire to avoid the public's prying eye. I understand this is not their preference.

I understand that they just wish it would go away. But I think they misjudged the seriousness of our purpose. I think they misjudged the will of the American public. I think they mistakenly believed we got into this on a whim. We did not. We gave this serious, serious consideration. And we decided it was time to break the code of silence that has enveloped the game.

I'm a baseball fan and always have been. I didn't become a political junkie until the Senators left town and I needed something to replace my near daily routine of memorizing box scores. And I'm not looking forward to being relegated to the nose bleed sections in the next few years. But there is a cloud over the game that I love. Maybe we're late in the game in recognizing it. Maybe we're partly to blame implicitly and wrongly sending the message that baseball's anti-trust exemption is also a public accountability exemption. But the cloud hovers over us nonetheless and our hope is that a public discussion of the issues with witnesses testifying under oath can provide a glimpse of sunlight.

Why? Because more than just the reputation of baseball is at risk. Our primary focus remains on the message being sent to the 500,000 steroid users in America's high schools, children who play baseball, children who idolize and emulate professional baseball players. I still have faith in Major League Baseball and a lot of players, managers, trainers and fans want to join us in helping kids understand this. Steroids aren't cool. Our responsibility is to help make sure Major League Baseball strategy, particularly its new testing program, gets the job done. We need to know if the policy is adequate in terms of how the tests are done and the punishments and the scope. As Mr. Waxman and I wrote to Major League Baseball and the Players Association yesterday, there are real doubts about this new policy and all that it's cracked up to be. The same USA Today survey I referenced earlier found that 69 percent of players believe the new policy is strict enough. Frankly, I'm surprised the number isn't higher. That's like asking trial lawyers if we need more tort reform. The answer is going to be no. Over the years, there have been a consistent drip, drip, drip of information about steroids in baseball with not much of a response from Major League Baseball. After all, it was, in large part, due to congressional pressure that the current policy took shape. Now we have not only the BALCO case, but a book by a former big league star naming names. We don't know if the allegations are accurate, but the truth needs to come out, however ugly the truth might be. Baseball can't simply turn its back on recent history, pronounce that the new testing policy will solve everything and move on. You can't look forward without looking back. I would hope that baseball would see this hearing as an opportunity to talk about the steps it is taking to get a handle on the situation. That's what we are interested in. We're not interested in embarrassing anybody, ruining careers or grandstanding.

This is not a witch hunt. We're not asking for witnesses to name names. Furthermore, today's hearing will not be the end of our inquiry. Far from it. Nor will

Major League Baseball be our sole or even primary focus. We are in the first inning of what can be an extra-inning ball game. This is the beginning and not the end. We believe this hearing will give us good information about the prevalence of steroids in professional sports, shine light on the sometimes tragic results of steroid use by high school and college athletes and provide leads as to where our investigation will go next; leads from Senator Bunning about how to restore the integrity of the game; leads from medical experts about how to better educate all Americans about the real dangers of steroid use; leads from parents whose stories today will poignantly illustrate, like it or not, professional athletes are role models and their actions can lead to tragic imitation.

We are grateful to the players who have joined us today to share their perspective on the role and prevalence of performance enhancing drugs in baseball. Some have been vocal about the need for baseball to address its steroid problems, and we applaud them for accepting this calling. Others have an opportunity today to either clear their name, take public responsibility for their actions or perhaps offer cautionary tales to our youth. In total, we think the six current and former players offer a broad perspective on the issue of steroids in baseball, and we are looking forward to hearing from all of them.

Finally, we are fortunate to have with us a final panel representing Major League Baseball, the Players Association and front office management. This panel is quite frankly where the rubber hits the road. If the players are cogs, this is the machine. If the players have been silent, these are the enforcers and promoters of the code. Ultimately, it's Major League Baseball, the union and team executives that will determine the strength of the game's testing policies.

Ultimately, it's Major League Baseball and the union that will or will not determine the accountability or punishment. Ultimately, it's Major League Baseball and the union that can remove the cloud over baseball and maybe save some lives in the process. A famous poem starts, oh, somewhere in this favored land the sun is shining bright the band is playing somewhere and somewhere hearts are light. And somewhere men are laughing and somewhere children shout, but there is no joy in Mudville until the truth comes out. I now recognize the distinguished ranking member, Mr. Waxman.

Source: H. Hrg. 109-8, Committee on Government Reform, United States House of Representatives, March 17, 2005.

For the complete transcript of the hearing online, perform an Internet search for "f:23038.wais", including the quotation marks.

For more information on the impact of congressional hearings on non-governmental activities, see § 10.74, Hearings May Affect Public or Private Practices, the *Congressional Deskbook*, by Michael L. Koempel and Judy Schneider.

§1.100 HITS: Humor in Testimony—Casey Stengel

As with any human institution or endeavor, humor is quite often injected, intentionally or accidentally, into congressional hearing situations. In the following exchanges from the actual testimony before a 1958 hearing of the U.S. Senate Subcommittee on Anti-Trust and Monopoly, the venerable and loveable baseball great, Casey Stengel, gives the subcommittee a piece of his mind. This is a portion of his testimony in which Casey deals with the Congress's interest in intervening in, and possibly legislating on, an industry about which it knows little or nothing. One senator is trying hard to get Casey to say that baseball needs legislation and government intervention, and another senator is trying to pin Casey down about baseball as a monopoly. And be sure to check out Mickey Mantle's response to the question of whether he has any observations of his own at the conclusion of Casey's testimony.

To access the entire testimony and further commentary, go to: *<www.baseball almanac.com/quotes/casey_stengel_senate_testimony.shtml>*.

EXCERPTS OF CASEY STENGEL'S TESTIMONY:
July 9, 1958 Senate Anti-Trust and Monopoly Subcommittee Hearing

****

Senator Carroll: Do you feel, you have had experience through the years—

Mr. Stengel: That is true.

Senator Carroll: With the draft system, and the reserve clause in the contracts. Do you think you could still exist under existing law without changing the law?

Mr. Stengel: I think it is run better than it has ever been run in baseball, for every department.

Senator Carroll: Then, I come back to the principal question. This is the real question before this body.

Mr. Stengel: All right.

Senator Carroll: Then what is the need for legislation, if they are getting along all right?

Mr. Stengel: I didn't ask for the legislation. (Laughter).

Senator Carroll: Your answer is a very good one, and that is the question Senator Kefauver put to you.

Mr. Stengel: That is right.

Senator Carroll: That is the question Senator O'Mahoney put.

Mr. Stengel: Right.

Senator Carroll: Are you ready to say there is no need for legislation in this field, then, insofar as baseball is concerned?

Mr. Stengel: As far as I'm concerned, from drawing a salary and from my ups and downs and being discharged, I always found out that there was somebody ready to employ you, if you were on the ball.

Senator Carroll: Thank you very much, Mr. Stengel.

****

Senator Langer: Mr. Chairman, my final question. This is the Antimonopoly Committee that is sitting here.

Mr. Stengel: Yes, sir.

Senator Langer: I want to know whether you intend to keep on monopolizing the world's championship in New York City.

Mr. Stengel: Well, I will tell you, I got a little concerned yesterday in the first three innings when I saw the three players I had gotten rid of and I said when I lost nine what am I going to do and when I had a couple of my players I thought so great of that did not do so good up to the sixth inning I was more confused but I finally had to go and call on a young man in Baltimore that we don't own and the Yankees don't own him, and he is going pretty good, and I would actually have to tell you that I think we are more the Greta Garbo type now from success. We are being hated I mean, from the ownership and all, we are being hated. Every sport that gets too great or one individual, but if we made 27¢ and it pays to have a winner at home why would you not have a good winner in your own park if you were an owner. That is the result of baseball. An owner gets most of the money at home and it is up to him and his staff to do better or they ought to be discharged.

Senator Langer: That is all, Mr. Chairman. Thank you.

****

Senator Kefauver: Do you think the present commissioner ought to have the same power?

Mr. Stengel: There are sixteen men in baseball who own ball clubs. We will say that an individual can hardly make it any more unless he is wealthy. That is how it has grown. I would say the biggest thing in baseball at the present time now, and with the money that is coming in, and so forth, and with the annuity fund for the players, you can't allow the commissioner to just take everything sitting there, and take everything insofar as money is concerned, but I think he should have full jurisdiction over the player and player's habits, and the way the umpires and ball clubs should conduct their business in the daytime and right on up tight up here.

Senator Kefauver: Thank you very much, Mr. Stengel. We appreciate your presence here.

Senator Kefauver: Mr. Mantle, do you have any observations with reference to the applicability of the antitrust laws to baseball?

Mr. Mantle: My views are about the same as Casey's (laughter).

Source: S. Hrg. 85-(no number), Committee on the Judiciary, Anti-Trust and Monopoly Subcommittee, United States Senate, July 9, 1958.

§ 1.999 Chapter Summary

- Congressional testimony is a vital component of the legislative processes of government. Information gleaned through congressional committee hearings underpins and provides rationale for legislative decision-making and federal funding priorities, and informs Congress in its roles of overseeing, evaluating and investigating federal programs and policy issues important to all Americans. (§ 1.0)
- The authority and foundation for congressional hearings derive from the official rules of the United States Senate and House of Representatives and the guidelines established by their numerous committees. Committees organize and conduct hearings in concert with their relevant policy jurisdiction and mission, and they typically publish the hearing records of testimony, documents, and formal questions and answers that emanate from a hearing. Congressional committees operate under a formal set of rules and procedures that govern hearings and dictate how witnesses and testimony will be handled, how the hearings will be conducted, and how the committee will organize a hearing. (§ 1.0; § 1.2; § 1.3; § 1.4)
- For the benefit of researchers and those preparing hearing testimony, excellent sources are available to review hearings transcripts. (§ 1.5 and § 1.6)
- In a nutshell, the congressional hearings process is a formal method within the legislative branch of government for gathering, analyzing and critiquing information that underpins important congressional decisions and priorities. (§ 1.10)
- Congressional hearings and testimony are very useful and important to Congress because of the valuable information that is provided on a wide range of issues. Testimony provided through the numerous types of congressional hearings helps Congress determine priorities regarding legislation and other matters vital to the public interest. By adding to the public record on issues under review by committees, testimony educates, informs, and motivates lawmakers, and helps form consensus and political support for public policy issues. The delivery of testimony by those called as witnesses allows for valuable and important input by interested parties and policy stakeholders, as well as for the opportunity for Congress to hear divergent viewpoints. (§ 1.20)
- Two contrasting perspectives on the value of congressional hearings provide good context for understanding hearings. (§ 1.21 and § 1.22)
- Congressional hearings and witness testimony are everyday occurrences in the operations of congressional committees. Committees conduct hearings routinely in Washington in designated hearing rooms in the Capitol complex, as well as around the country in the form of field hearings that may be conducted in courthouses and city halls, at universities or virtually anywhere deemed appropriate by a committee. (§ 1.30)

- Making the record—a formal transcript of the proceedings of a hearing—is an important element of the hearings process. (§ 1.31)
- Policy and politics converge in congressional committee hearings, and, consequently, the hearings process is replete with political partisanship, discussion and analysis. (§ 1.32)
- A thorough understanding of the congressional committee system is a key to understanding the hearings process and the importance of witness testimony as vital components of the legislative process. (§ 1.40)
- There are several different types and purposes of congressional hearings in which witness testimony may be provided. A review of the descriptions and transcripts of actual hearings involving the testimony of witnesses provides an excellent method of understanding the purpose, value, and use of congressional hearings. (§ 1.50)
    1) Legislative Hearings (§ 1.51 and § 1.52)
    2) Budget and Appropriations Hearings (§ 1.53; § 1.54; § 1.55)
    3) Oversight and Investigative Hearings (§ 1.56 and § 1.57)
    4) Senate Advice and Consent Hearings: Nominations, Confirmations, and Treaties (§ 1.58 and § 1.59)
    5) Field Hearings (§ 1.60; § 1.61; § 1.62)
    6) Showcasing, Publicity, Celebrity, and Grandstanding Hearings (§ 1.63 and § 1.64)
    7) Public or Open Hearings and Closed Hearings (§ 1.65 and § 1.66)
- Each congressional hearing reflects its own unique committee culture, mission, and purpose. (§ 1.70)
- Congressional committee hearings can lead to many results and provide Congress with numerous benefits ranging from establishing the foundation for legislative measures to creating a public record of important public policy issues. (§ 1.80)
    1) Hearings Published for Public Record (§ 1.81 and § 1.82)
    2) Vital Education and Information for Congress (§ 1.83)
    3) Effective Public Policy Advocacy and Debate (§ 1.84 and § 1.85)
    4) Influence on Legislation and Other Committee Actions (§ 1.86 and § 1.87)
    5) Influence and Political Pressure on Executive Branch and Federal Regulatory Processes (§ 1.88 and § 1.89)
    6) Influence on Public Knowledge and Actions of Public and Non-Governmental Entities (§ 1.90; § 1.91; § 1.92)
- HITS: Humor in Testimony—As in so many areas of human endeavor, humor has its place in congressional hearings, particularly when Major League Baseball's immortal Casey Stengel is at the witness table. (§ 1.100)

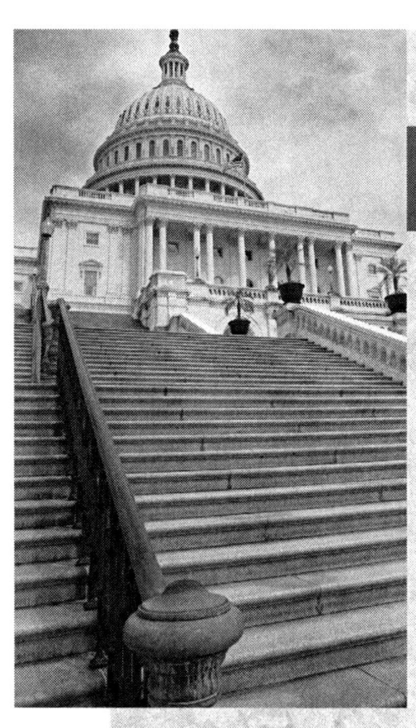

Chapter Two

Congressional Hearing Organization, Planning, and Preparation

Chapter Two

Section

Summary Table of Contents

§2.0 Introduction: The Committee Agenda

The "drivers" of a congressional hearing are the committee conducting it and that committee's agenda for the hearing. Committee leadership and professional staff engage in extensive planning and preparation for a congressional hearing. Through its chair, the committee calls the hearing, outlines its purpose and mission, invites witnesses, and executes the necessary logistics to organize and conduct the hearing.

Each committee of Congress operates with rules and guidelines that govern hearings and the role and expectations of witnesses. Any witness called to testify or organization invited to submit written testimony should first and foremost communicate and work cooperatively with the appropriate committee staff to understand the context and purpose of the hearing and the witness's role, as well as to be advised about the guidelines regarding preparation of a written statement and oral testimony to be delivered. In short, the committee's agenda and rules control and govern the hearing and the witness.

This chapter explains what is entailed in organizing and conducting a hearing by the committee, and what is involved in preparing for a hearing on the part of a witness. It describes committee rules and logistics; the hearing "players"; the types of witnesses and their selection; legal and procedural aspects of a hearing (such as subpoenas, depositions, and the rights of a witness); and the conduct of a hearing, including the typical order and format of proceedings. It also outlines the important formulas for effective congressional testimony and a successful hearing, from the perspectives of both a committee and a witness.

§2.1 Organization, Planning, and Preparation by the Committee

A congressional committee's decision to conduct a hearing triggers an array of administrative and substantive activities required to organize, plan, and prepare for the hearing on the part of both the committee and any witnesses. For the committee's part, most of this work is undertaken by committee staff, professional staff members whose job and loyalty are with the committee and its leadership. Many committees have a hearing clerk whose primary job is to assist with the organization, scheduling, and planning of hearings. While majority rule applies in the leadership and governance of a committee, and the chair of a committee typically wields the most control over decisions about hearings, many committees facilitate a cooperative working and planning relationship between the majority and minority committee members and staff. The minority party is usually guaranteed or provided the right to call witnesses of its own choosing. Nevertheless, the majority staff is usually in charge of planning committee hearings, and, consequently, the majority side of the aisle should be the first point of contact in most cases.

Committee staff attend to all administrative, logistical, and substantive aspects of hearing preparation. They are responsible for seeing that proper notification of the hearing is given through various formal and informal channels. They schedule a date, a hearing room, and the appropriate technical and administrative assistance to support the hearing, including scheduling an official hearing reporter and any media coverage. A committee hearing may be a one-day or part-day occurrence, or it may be extended over the course of two or more days, depending on the issues to be considered and the number of witnesses to be called. With the chair's and committee's direction, the staff issues invitations and subpoenas to witnesses. Committee staff also provide oral pre-hearing briefings for committee members, as well as occasionally for other members of the House or Senate and their staff, and for the media.

Committee staff also prepare written materials for the committee members, including background information, operational memoranda, issue outlines, statements, and other documents and materials required or requested by the chair and committee members. Quite often these written materials are contained in a folder or binder known as a briefing book for the committee chair's and members' review prior to a hearing, as well as for use during the hearing. (For more information on the committee's preparation of hearing documents and briefing materials, see § 2.8, Committee Preparation of Hearing Documents—Briefing Materials.)

Committee staff frequently use a number of outside sources to gather information in preparation for hearing. Included among these sources are federal executive branch departments and agencies; non-governmental public interest and private research organizations, such as universities, research institutes, trade associations, issue coalitions, and law and government relations consulting firms; and legislative service organizations (LSOs), such as the Congressional Budget Office (CBO), the Congressional Research Service (CRS) at the Library of Congress (LOC), and the Government Accountability Office (GAO). (For a list and explanation of congressional legislative service organizations, see § 5.130, Legislative-Branch Support Agencies, the *Congressional Deskbook*, by Michael L. Koempel and Judy Schneider.)

Among the duties of committee staff are contact and communication with witnesses. Staff often help identify and interview potential witnesses in preparation for a hearing. Committee staff communicate and work with witnesses to ensure an understanding of the hearing's purpose and the committee's agenda, the witness's role, and how the hearing will be conducted. Staff provide information to witnesses, including committee rules and guidelines, stylistic and formatting requirements for the prepared statement, and scheduling and logistical information such as time, place, room, layout, order of witness appearance, and hearing schedule.

Other administrative duties performed by committee staff include:

- setting up the hearing room;
- laying out briefing materials and other documents;

- reserving seating areas for the media, congressional staff, and witnesses;
- arranging for security and technology requirements;
- and providing committee liaison with all hearing participants.

§ 2.2 Organization, Planning, and Preparation by the Witness or Organization

The organizational, planning, and preparatory activities of a witness or organization planning to testify before a committee are both reactive and responsive to the committee's direction and guidelines, and driven by the witness's or organization's own agenda.

In response to a committee in preparation for a hearing, a witness should communicate with the committee staff person in charge of the hearing, follow all guidelines and rules for preparation, and generally work with committee staff to ensure the witness's understanding of the hearing's purpose and the committee's agenda. Being responsive to committee instructions and requests is an important step in establishing a rapport with the committee that sets the stage and tone for a successful appearance by a witness. Careful attention should be given to preparation details, such as providing the required numbers of copies of the witness statement, biographical information, and other requests of the committee. Promptness and efficiency are important in providing information and responses, and in participating in any pre-hearing briefings, the hearing itself, and any post-hearing follow-up.

For purposes of its own agenda, mission, and issues, the witness's organization should focus on preparing itself and its witness for the hearing. These activities constitute the bulk of the planning, preparatory work, and execution on the part of the witness and the organization. The key elements of this planning and preparation include a thorough review, understanding, and application of the following topics covered in the balance of this deskbook:

- "Preparation of Written Testimony" (Chapter 3)
- "Preparation of the Witness" (Chapter 4)
- "Presentation and Delivery of Oral Testimony" (Chapter 5)
- "Responding to Committee Questions" (Chapter 6)
- "Post-Hearing Activities and Follow-Up" (Chapter 7)

§ 2.3 Committee Rules, Policies, and Guidelines

Each congressional committee maintains its own set of rules and requirements for the conduct of and preparation for a hearing. Beyond the House and Senate rules (see House Rule XI at <*rules.House.gov*> and Senate Rule XXVI at <*rules.Senate.gov*>) that generally authorize hearings and set out some guidelines applicable to all committee panels, committees usually establish guidelines that conform both with the rules of their respective chamber and with that particular committee's mode of doing business.

Each committee publishes, usually on its web site and sometimes in print, its own rules, policies, and guidelines, which should be consulted and followed by those preparing to provide testimony at a committee hearing. (To access individual committee web sites to see committee rules and guidelines, go to <*www.House.gov*> and <*www.Senate.gov*>, and select the relevant committee link.) Many of the guidelines and policies are similar and common among most committees. However, each committee can establish unique rules of its own, so those preparing testimony for a hearing should be sure to work with committee staff, obtain that committee's rules, and become familiar with each committee's specific guidelines.

Among the guidelines and directives included in typical committee rules are specific provisions concerning procedures for hearings, including requirements for a committee quorum, public notice, timely distribution of documents to committee members, submission of witness statements, rights of the minority party to call witnesses, closed hearings, subpoenas, and sworn testimony.

Committee rules and hearing guidelines typically set out the committee's expectations of witnesses, including preparation and delivery of a certain number of copies of the statement; the required format of a written statement; biographical information about the witness; pre-hearing issue briefings and meetings in some cases; details regarding the format and conduct of the hearing proceedings; and post-hearing follow-up requests and requirements. These guidelines may be general in nature regarding logistics and preparation, or they may be specific, such as restrictions on statement length, document formatting, and length of a witness's presentation of testimony.

§2.4 Selected Excerpts Pertaining to Committee Hearings from Rule XI of the Rules of the House of Representatives—Procedures of Committees and Unfinished Business

Listed below are several excerpted portions of Rule XI of The Rules of the House of Representatives that pertain to committee hearings and related matters. The complete rules should be consulted for more information and detail. (To access the complete House rules, go to <*rules.House.gov*>.)

In general

1. (a)(1)(A) The Rules of the House are the rules of its committees and subcommittees so far as applicable.

****

Adoption of written rules

2. (a)(1) Each standing committee shall adopt written rules governing its procedure. Such rules—

(A) shall be adopted in a meeting that is open to the public unless the committee, in open session and with a quorum present, determines by record vote that all or part of the meeting on that day shall be closed to the public;

(B) may not be inconsistent with the Rules of the House or with those provisions of law having the force and effect of Rules of the House; and

(C) shall in any event incorporate all of the succeeding provisions of this clause to the extent applicable.

****

Regular meeting days

2. (b) Each standing committee shall establish regular meeting days for the conduct of its business, which shall be not less frequent than monthly. Each such committee shall meet for the consideration of a bill or resolution pending before the committee or the transaction of other committee business on all regular meeting days fixed by the committee unless otherwise provided by written rule adopted by the committee.

Additional and special meetings

2. *(c)(1)* The chair of each standing committee may call and convene, as the chair considers necessary, additional and special meetings of the committee for the consideration of a bill or resolution pending before the committee or for the conduct of other committee business, subject to such rules as the committee may adopt. The committee shall meet for such purpose under that call of the chair.

****

Committee records

2. *(e)(1)(A)* Each committee shall keep a complete record of all committee action which shall include—

in the case of a meeting or hearing transcript, a substantially verbatim account of remarks actually made during the proceedings, subject only to technical, grammatical, and typographical corrections authorized by the person making the remarks involved; and

a record of the votes on any question on which a record vote is demanded.

****

Open meetings and hearings

2. *(g)(1)* Each meeting for the transaction of business, including the mark-up of legislation, by a standing committee or subcommittee thereof (other than the Committee on Standards of Official Conduct or its subcommittees) shall be open to the public, including to radio, television, and still photography coverage, except when the committee or subcommittee, in open session and with a majority present, determines by record vote that all or part of the remainder of the meeting on that day shall be in executive session because disclosure of matters to be considered would endanger national security, would compromise sensitive law enforcement information, would tend to defame, degrade, or incriminate any person, or otherwise would violate a law or rule of the House. Persons, other than members of the committee and such non-committee Members, Delegates, Resident Commissioner, congressional staff, or departmental representatives as the committee may authorize, may not be present at a business or markup session that is held in

executive session. This subparagraph does not apply to open committee hearings, which are governed by clause 4(a)(1) of rule X or by subparagraph (2).

(2)(A) Each hearing conducted by a committee or subcommittee (other than the Committee on Standards of Official Conduct or its subcommittees) shall be open to the public, including to radio, television, and still photography coverage, except when the committee or subcommittee, in open session and with a majority present, determines by record vote that all or part of the remainder of that hearing on that day shall be closed to the public because disclosure of testimony, evidence, or other matters to be considered would endanger national security, would compromise sensitive law enforcement information, or would violate a law or rule of the House.

(B) Notwithstanding the requirements of subdivision (A), in the presence of the number of members required under the rules of the committee for the purpose of taking testimony, a majority of those present may—

> agree to close the hearing for the sole purpose of discussing whether testimony or evidence to be received would endanger national security, would compromise sensitive law enforcement information, or would violate clause 2(k)(5); or
>
> agree to close the hearing as provided in clause 2(k)(5).

****

2. (g)(3) The chair of each committee (other than the Committee on Rules) shall make public announcement of the date, place, and subject matter of a committee hearing at least one week before the commencement of the hearing. If the chair of the committee, with the concurrence of the ranking minority member, determines that there is good cause to begin a hearing sooner, or if the committee so determines by majority vote in the presence of the number of members required under the rules of the committee for the transaction of business, the chair shall make the announcement at the earliest possible date. An announcement made under this subparagraph shall be published promptly in the Daily Digest and made available in electronic form.

(4) Each committee shall, to the greatest extent practicable, require witnesses who appear before it to submit in advance written statements of proposed testimony and to limit their initial presentations to the committee to brief summaries thereof. In the case of a witness appearing in a nongovernmental capacity, a written statement of proposed testimony shall include a curriculum vitae and a disclosure of the amount and source (by agency and program) of each Federal grant (or sub-grant thereof) or contract (or sub-contract thereof) received during the current fiscal year or either of the two previous fiscal years by the witness or by an entity represented by the witness.

****

Quorum requirements

2. (*h*)(*1*) A measure or recommendation may not be reported by a committee unless a majority of the committee is actually present.

(2) Each committee may fix the number of its members to constitute a quorum for taking testimony and receiving evidence, which may not be less than two.

(3) Each committee (other than the Committee on Appropriations, the Committee on the Budget, and the Committee on Ways and Means) may fix the number of its members to constitute a quorum for taking any action other than one for which the presence of a majority of the committee is otherwise required, which may not be less than one-third of the members.

****

Calling and questioning of witnesses

2. (*j*)(*1*) Whenever a hearing is conducted by a committee on a measure or matter, the minority members of the committee shall be entitled, upon request to the chair by a majority of them before the completion of the hearing, to call witnesses selected by the minority to testify with respect to that measure or matter during at least one day of hearing thereon.

(2)(A) Subject to subdivisions (B) and (C), each committee shall apply the five-minute rule during the questioning of witnesses in a hearing until such time as each member of the committee who so desires has had an opportunity to question each witness.

(B) A committee may adopt a rule or motion permitting a specified number of its members to question a witness for longer than five minutes. The time for extended questioning of a witness under this subdivision shall be equal for the majority party and the minority party and may not exceed one hour in the aggregate.

(C) A committee may adopt a rule or motion permitting committee staff for its majority and minority party members to question a witness for equal specified periods. The time for extended questioning of a witness under this subdivision shall be equal for the majority party and the minority party and may not exceed one hour in the aggregate.

Hearing procedures

2.(*k*)(*1*) The chair at a hearing shall announce in an opening statement the subject of the hearing.

(*2*) A copy of the committee rules and of this clause shall be made available to each witness on request.

(*3*) Witnesses at hearings may be accompanied by their own counsel for the purpose of advising them concerning their constitutional rights.

(*4*) The chair may punish breaches of order and decorum, and of professional ethics on the part of counsel, by censure and exclusion from the hearings; and the committee may cite the offender to the House for contempt.

(*5*) Whenever it is asserted by a member of the committee that the evidence or testimony at a hearing may tend to defame, degrade, or incriminate any person, or it is asserted by a witness that the evidence or testimony that the witness would give at a hearing may tend to defame, degrade, or incriminate the witness—

(A) notwithstanding paragraph (g)(2), such testimony or evidence shall be presented in executive session if, in the presence of the number of members required under the rules of the committee for the purpose of taking testimony, the committee determines by vote of a majority of those present that such evidence or testimony may tend to defame, degrade, or incriminate any person; and

(B) the committee shall proceed to receive such testimony in open session only if the committee, a majority being present, determines that such evidence or testimony will not tend to defame, degrade, or incriminate any person.

In either case the committee shall afford such person an opportunity voluntarily to appear as a witness, and receive and dispose of requests from such person to subpoena additional witnesses.

Except as provided in subparagraph (5), the chair shall receive and the committee shall dispose of requests to subpoena additional witnesses.

Evidence or testimony taken in executive session, and proceedings conducted in executive session, may be released or used in public sessions only when authorized by the committee, a majority being present.

In the discretion of the committee, witnesses may submit brief and pertinent sworn statements in writing for inclusion in the record. The committee is the sole judge of the pertinence of testimony and evidence adduced at its hearing.

A witness may obtain a transcript copy of the testimony of such witness given at a public session or, if given at an executive session, when authorized by the committee.

****

Power to sit and act; subpoena power

2. *(m)(1)* For the purpose of carrying out any of its functions and duties under this rule and rule X (including any matters referred to it under clause 2 of rule XII), a committee or subcommittee is authorized (subject to subparagraph (3)(A))—

tc sit and act at such times and places within the United States, whether the House is in session, has recessed, or has adjourned, and to hold such hearings as it considers necessary; and

to require, by subpoena or otherwise, the attendance and testimony of such witnesses and the production of such books, records, correspondence, memoranda, papers, and documents as it considers necessary.

(2) The chair of the committee, or a member designated by the chair, may administer oaths to witnesses.

(3)(A)(i) Except as provided in subdivision (A)(ii), a subpoena may be authorized and issued by a committee or subcommittee under subparagraph (1)(B) in the conduct of an investigation or series of investigations or activities only when authorized by the committee or subcommittee, a majority being present. The power to authorize and issue subpoenas under subparagraph (1)(B) may be delegated to the chair of the committee under such rules and under such limitations as the committee may prescribe. Authorized subpoenas shall be signed by the chair of the committee or by a member designated by the committee.

****

Pay of witnesses

5. Witnesses appearing before the House or any of its committees shall be paid the same per diem rate as established, authorized, and regulated by the Committee on House Administration for Members, Delegates, the Resident Commissioner, and employees of the House, plus actual expenses of travel to or from the place of examination. Such per diem may not be paid when a witness has been summoned at the place of examination.

Source: Rules of the U.S. House of Representatives, Rule XI, Procedures of Committees and Unfinished Business. (To review the complete set of rules, go to <*rules.House.gov*>.)

§2.5 Selected Excerpts Pertaining to Committee Hearings from Rule XXVI of the Standing Rules of the Senate—Committee Procedure

Listed below are several excerpted portions of Rule XXVI of the Standing Rules of the Senate that pertain to committee hearings and related matters. The complete rules should be consulted for more information and detail. (To access the complete Senate rules, go to <*rules.Senate.gov*>.)

1. Each standing committee, including any subcommittee of any such committee, is authorized to hold such hearings, to sit and act at such times and places during the sessions, recesses, and adjourned periods of the Senate, to require by subpoena or otherwise the attendance of such witnesses and the production of such correspondence, books, papers, and documents, to take such testimony and to make such expenditures out of the contingent fund of the Senate as may be authorized by resolutions of the Senate. Each such committee may make investigations into any matter within its jurisdiction, may report such hearings as may be had by it, and may employ stenographic assistance at a cost not exceeding the amount prescribed by the Committee on Rules and Administration. The expenses of the committee shall be paid from the contingent fund of the Senate upon vouchers approved by the chairman.

2. Each committee shall adopt rules (not inconsistent with the Rules of the Senate) governing the procedure of such committee. The rules of each committee shall be published in the Congressional Record not later than March 1 of the first year of each Congress, except that if any such committee is established on or after February 1 of a year, the rules of that committee during the year of establishment shall be published in the Congressional Record not later than sixty days after such establishment. Any amendment to the rules of a committee shall not take effect until the amendment is published in the Congressional Record.

****

4. (a) Each committee (except the Committee on Appropriations and the Committee on the Budget) shall make public announcement of the date, place, and sub-

ject matter of any hearing to be conducted by the committee on any measure or matter at least one week before the commencement of that hearing unless the committee determines that there is good cause to begin such hearing at an earlier date.

(b) Each committee (except the Committee on Appropriations) shall require each witness who is to appear before the committee in any hearing to file with the clerk of the committee, at least one day before the date of the appearance of that witness, a written statement of his proposed testimony unless the committee chairman and the ranking minority member determine that there is good cause for noncompliance. If so requested by any committee, the staff of the committee shall prepare for the use of the members of the committee before each day of hearing before the committee a digest of the statements which have been so filed by witnesses who are to appear before the committee on that day.

(c) After the conclusion of each day of hearing, if so requested by any committee, the staff shall prepare for the use of the members of the committee a summary of the testimony given before the committee on that day. After approval by the chairman and the ranking minority member of the committee, each such summary may be printed as a part of the committee hearings if such hearings are ordered by the committee to be printed.

(d) Whenever any hearing is conducted by a committee (except the Committee on Appropriations) upon any measure or matter, the minority on the committee shall be entitled, upon request made by a majority of the minority members to the chairman before the completion of such hearing, to call witnesses selected by the minority to testify with respect to the measure or matter during at least one day of hearing thereon.

****

5. (b) Each meeting of a committee, or any subcommittee thereof, including meetings to conduct hearings, shall be open to the public, except that a meeting or series of meetings by a committee or a subcommittee thereof on the same subject for a period of no more than fourteen calendar days may be closed to the public on a motion made and seconded to go into closed session to discuss only whether the matters enumerated in clauses (1) through (6) would require the meeting to be closed, followed immediately by a record vote in open session by a majority of the members of the committee or subcommittee when it is determined that the matters to be discussed or the testimony to be taken at such meeting or meetings

(1) will disclose matters necessary to be kept secret in the interests of national defense or the confidential conduct of the foreign relations of the United States;

(2) will relate solely to matters of committee staff personnel or internal staff management or procedure;

(3) will tend to charge an individual with crime or misconduct, to disgrace or injure the professional standing of an individual, or otherwise to expose an individual to public contempt or obloquy, or will represent a clearly unwarranted invasion of the privacy of an individual;

(4) will disclose the identity of any informer or law enforcement agent or

will disclose any information relating to the investigation or prosecution of a criminal offense that is required to be kept secret in the interests of effective law enforcement;

(5) will disclose information relating to the trade secrets of financial or commercial information pertaining specifically to a given person if

(A) an Act of Congress requires the information to be kept confidential by Government officers and employees; or

(B) the information has been obtained by the Government on a confidential basis, other than through an application by such person for a specific Government financial or other benefit, and is required to be kept secret in order to prevent undue injury to the competitive position of such person; or

(6) may divulge matters required to be kept confidential under other provisions of law or Government regulations.

(c) Whenever any hearing conducted by any such committee or subcommittee is open to the public, that hearing may be broadcast by radio or television, or both, under such rules as the committee or subcommittee may adopt.

(d) Whenever disorder arises during a committee meeting that is open to the public, or any demonstration of approval or disapproval is indulged in by any person in attendance at any such meeting, it shall be the duty of the Chair to enforce order on his own initiative and without any point of order being made by a Senator. When the Chair finds it necessary to maintain order, he shall have the power to clear the room, and the committee may act in closed session for so long as there is doubt of the assurance of order.

(e) Each committee shall prepare and keep a complete transcript or electronic recording adequate to fully record the proceeding of each meeting or conference whether or not such meeting or any part thereof is closed under this paragraph, unless a majority of its members vote to forgo such a record.

****

7. (a)(1) Except as provided in this paragraph, each committee, and each subcommittee thereof is authorized to fix the number of its members (but not less than one-third of its entire membership) who shall constitute a quorum thereof for the transaction of such business as may be considered by said committee, except that no measure or matter or recommendation shall be reported from any committee unless a majority of the committee were physically present.

(2) Each such committee, or subcommittee, is authorized to fix a lesser number than one-third of its entire membership who shall constitute a quorum thereof for the purpose of taking sworn testimony.

****

10. (a) All committee hearings, records, data, charts, and files shall be kept separate and distinct from the congressional office records of the Member serving as chairman of the committee; and such records shall be the property of the Senate and all members of the committee and the Senate shall have access to such records. Each committee is authorized to have printed and bound such testimony and other data presented at hearings held by the committee.

Source: Standing Rules of the Senate, Rule XXVI, Committee Procedure. (To review the complete set of Senate rules, go to <*rules.Senate.gov*>.)

§2.6 Sample of Committee Rules, Directives, and Guidelines

Many examples of committee rules may be found on individual committee web sites accessed through links found on the web sites at <*www.Senate.gov*> or <*www.House.gov*>. One example of a typical set of rules includes the following rules established by the U.S. Senate Committee on Energy and Natural Resources.

Committee Rules

GENERAL RULES

Rule 1. The Standing Rules of the Senate, as supplemented by these rules, are adopted as the rules of the Committee and its Subcommittees.

MEETINGS OF THE COMMITTEE

Rule 2. (a) The Committee shall meet on the third Wednesday of each month while the Congress is in session for the purpose of conducting business, unless, for the convenience of Members, the Chairman shall set some other day for a meeting. Additional meetings may be called by the Chairman as he may deem necessary.

(b) Hearings of any Subcommittee may be called by the Chairman of such Subcommittee, Provided, That no Subcommittee hearing other than a field hearing, shall be scheduled or held concurrently with a full Committee meeting or hearing, unless a majority of the Committee concurs in such concurrent hearing.

OPEN HEARINGS AND MEETINGS

Rule 3. (a) All hearings and business meetings of the Committee and all the hearings of any of its Subcommittees shall be open to the public unless the Committee or Subcommittee involved, by majority vote of all the Members of the Committee or such Subcommittee, orders the hearing or meeting to be closed in accordance with paragraph 5(b) of Rule XXVI of the Standing Rules of the Senate.

(b) A transcript shall be kept of each hearing of the Committee or any Subcommittee.

(c) A transcript shall be kept of each business meeting of the Committee unless a majority of all the Members of the Committee agrees that some other form of permanent record is preferable.

HEARING PROCEDURE

Rule 4. (a) Public notice shall be given of the date, place, and subject matter of any hearing to be held by the Committee or any Subcommittee at least one week in advance of such hearing unless the Chairman of the full Committee or the Subcommittee involved determines that the hearing is non-controversial or that special circumstances require expedited procedures and a majority of all the Members of the Committee or the Subcommittee involved concurs. In no case shall a hearing be conducted with less than twenty-four hours notice. Any document or report that is the subject of a hearing shall be provided to every Member of the Committee or Subcommittee involved at least 72 hours before the hearing unless the Chairman and Ranking Member determine otherwise.

(b) Each witness who is to appear before the Committee or any Subcommittee shall file with the Committee or Subcommittee, at least 24 hours in advance of the hearing, a written statement of his or her testimony in as many copies as the Chairman of the Committee or Subcommittee prescribes.

(c) Each Member shall be limited to five minutes in the questioning of any witness until such time as all Members who so desire have had an opportunity to question the witness.

(d) The Chairman and Ranking Minority Member of the Committee or Subcommittee or the Ranking Majority and Minority Members present at the hearing may each appoint one Committee staff member to question each witness. Such staff member may question the witness only after all Members present have completed their questioning of the witness or at such other time as the Chairman and the Ranking Majority and Minority Members present may agree. No staff member may question a witness in the absence of a quorum for the taking of testimony.

BUSINESS MEETING AGENDA

Rule 5. (a) A legislative measure, nomination, or other matter shall be included on the agenda of the next following business meeting of the full Committee if a written request for such inclusion has been filed with the Chairman of the Committee at least one week prior to such meeting. Nothing in this rule shall be construed to limit the authority of the Chairman of the Committee to include a legislative measure, nomination, or other matter on the Committee agenda in the absence of such request.

(b) The agenda for any business meeting of the Committee shall be provided to each Member and made available to the public at least three days prior to such meeting, and no new items may be added after the agenda is so published except by the approval of a majority of all the Members of the Committee on matters not included on the public agenda. The Staff Director shall promptly notify absent Members of any action taken by the Committee on matters not included on the published agenda.

QUORUMS

Rule 6. (a) Except as provided in subsections (b) and (c), eight Members shall constitute a quorum for the conduct of business of the Committee.

(b) No measure or matter shall be ordered reported from the Committee unless twelve Members of the Committee are actually present at the time such action is taken.

(c) One Member shall constitute a quorum for the purpose of conducting a hearing or taking testimony on any measure or matter before the Committee or any Subcommittee.

VOTING

Rule 7. (a) A roll call of the Members shall be taken upon the request of any Member. Any Member who does not vote on any roll call at the time the roll is called, may vote (in person or by proxy) on that roll call at any later time during the same business meeting.

(b) Proxy voting shall be permitted on all matters, except that proxies may not be counted for the purpose of determining the presence of a quorum. Unless further limited, a proxy shall be exercised only upon the date for which it is given and upon the items published in the agenda for that date.

(c) Each Committee report shall set forth the vote on the motion to report the measure or matter involved. Unless the Committee directs otherwise, the report will not set out any votes on amendments offered during Committee consideration. Any Member who did not vote on any roll call shall have the opportunity to have his position recorded in the appropriate Committee record or Committee report.

(d) The Committee vote to report a measure to the Senate shall also authorize the staff of the Committee to make necessary technical and clerical corrections in the measure.

SUBCOMMITTEES

Rule 8. (a) The number of Members assigned to each Subcommittee and the division between Majority and Minority Members shall be fixed by the Chairman in consultation with the Ranking Minority Member.

(b) Assignment of Members to Subcommittees shall, insofar as possible, reflect the preferences of the Members. No Member will receive assignment to a second Subcommittee until, in order of seniority, all Members of the Committee have chosen assignments to one Subcommittee, and no Member shall receive assignment to a third Subcommittee until, in order of seniority, all Members have chosen assignments to two Subcommittees.

(c) Any Member of the Committee may sit with any Subcommittee during its hearings but shall not have the authority to vote on any matters before the Subcommittee unless he is a Member of such Subcommittee.

NOMINATIONS

Rule 9. At any hearing to confirm a Presidential nomination, the testimony of the nominee and, at the request of any Member, any other witness shall be under oath. Every nominee shall submit a statement of his financial interests, including those of his spouse, his minor children, and other members of his immediate household, on a form approved by the Committee, which shall be sworn to by the nominee as to its completeness and accuracy. A statement of every nominee's financial interest shall be made available to the public on a form approved by the Committee unless the Committee in executive session determines that special circumstances require a full or partial exception to this rule.

INVESTIGATIONS

Rule 10. (a) Neither the Committee nor any of its Subcommittees may undertake an investigation or preliminary inquiry unless specifically authorized by a majority of all the Members of the Committee.

(b) A witness called to testify in an investigation or inquiry shall be informed of the matter or matters under investigation, given a copy of these rules, given the opportunity to make a brief and relevant oral statement before or after questioning, and be permitted to have counsel of his or her choosing present during his or her testimony at any public or closed hearing, or at any unsworn interview, to advise the witness of his or her legal rights.

(c) For purposes of this rule, the terms "investigation" and "preliminary inquiry" shall not include a review or study undertaken pursuant to paragraph 8 of Rule XXVI of the Standing Rules of the Senate or an initial review of any allegation of wrongdoing intended to determine whether there is substantial credible evidence that would warrant a preliminary inquiry or an investigation.

SWORN TESTIMONY
Rule 11. Witnesses in Committee or Subcommittee hearings may be required to give testimony under oath whenever the Chairman or Ranking Minority Member of the Committee or Subcommittee deems such to be necessary. If one or more witnesses at a hearing are required to testify under oath, all witnesses at such hearing shall be required to testify under oath.

SUBPOENAS
Rule 12. No subpoena for the attendance of a witness or for the production of any document, memorandum, record, or other material may be issued unless authorized by a majority of all the Members of the Committee, except that a resolution adopted pursuant to Rule 10(a) may authorize the Chairman, with the concurrence of the Ranking Minority Member, to issue subpoenas within the scope of the authorized investigation.

CONFIDENTIAL TESTIMONY
Rule 13. No confidential testimony taken by or any report of the proceedings of a closed Committee or Subcommittee meeting shall be made public, in whole or in part or by way of summary, unless authorized by a majority of all the Members of the Committee at a business meeting called for the purpose of making such a determination.

DEFAMATORY STATEMENTS
Rule 14. Any person whose name is mentioned or who is specifically identified in, or who believes that testimony or other evidence presented at, an open Committee or Subcommittee hearing tends to defame him or otherwise adversely affect his reputation may file with the Committee for its consideration and action a sworn statement of facts relevant to such testimony or evidence.

BROADCASTING OF HEARINGS OR MEETINGS
Rule 15. Any meeting or hearing by the Committee or any Subcommittee which is open to the public may be covered in whole or in part by television broadcast, radio broadcast, or still photography. Photographers and reporters using mechanical recording, filming, or broadcasting devices shall position their equipment so as not to interfere with the seating, vision, and hearing of Members and staff on the dais or with the orderly process of the meeting or hearing.

AMENDING THE RULES

Rule 16. These rules may be amended only by vote of a majority of all the Members of the Committee in a business meeting of the Committee: Provided, That no vote may be taken on any proposed amendment unless such amendment is reproduced in full in the Committee agenda for such meeting at least three days in advance of such meeting.

Source: U.S. Senate Committee on Energy and Natural Resources.

§2.7 Advanced Copies of Witness Statement or Written Testimony, Biographical, and Other Information—Special Rules Regarding Truth in Testimony

Committee rules and guidelines usually require that a witness submit, by a certain deadline, a designated number of advanced copies of the witness's written hearing statement, biographical information about the witness, and, occasionally, other written materials about the hearing topic or the witness's organization. The deadline for submitting advanced copies of written testimony ranges from one to three days, but may vary depending on the committee and the nature of the hearing. Committees typically have guidelines about the number of copies to submit and, occasionally, require an executive or brief summary, particularly if the statement is lengthy. Consequently, it is important to determine each committee's individual deadline and other requirements.

A committee will usually outline these requests and related details in the letter of invitation to a witness to testify. These written materials provided by a witness are then included in the briefing books or folders prepared by committee staff for the use of members of the committee prior to and during the hearing. The materials are often summarized or excerpted by the committee staff for use by the committee during the hearing, especially in the question-and-answer portion. Copies of the materials are typically provided at the hearing, not only in the committee members' briefing packets, but also for the media, congressional staff, and the public.

It is important to consult with committee staff well in advance of the hearing to ensure complete compliance with committee rules, policies, practices, and requirements regarding preparation and submission of written materials. In particular, "Truth-In-Testimony" rules apply that require specific information from witnesses, such as advanced copies of testimony, biographical information, and financial information regarding grants and contracts, as described in the rules themselves. For the Senate rule, see Senate Rule XXVI, paragraph 4(b) at § 2.5, Selected Excerpts Pertaining to Committee Hearings from Rule XXVI of the Standing Rules of the Senate—Committee Procedure. For the House rule, see House Rule XI, clause 2(g)(4) at § 2.4, Selected Excerpts Pertaining to Committee Hearings from Rule XI of The Rules of the House of Representatives—Procedures of Committees and Unfinished Business, and the following explanation by the U.S. House of Representatives Committee on Rules.

TRUTH-IN-TESTIMONY RULES

Text of Rule:

SEC. 10. INFORMATION REQUIRED OF PUBLIC WITNESSES.—In clause 2(g) of rule XI, amend subparagraph (4) to read as follows:

"(4) Each committee shall, to the greatest extent practicable, require witnesses who appear before it to submit in advance written statements of proposed testimony and to limit their initial oral presentations to the committee to brief summaries thereof. In the case of a witness appearing in a nongovernmental capacity, a written statement of proposed testimony shall include a curriculum vitae and a disclosure of the amount and source (by agency and program) of any Federal grant (or subgrant thereof) or contract (or subcontract thereof) received during the current fiscal year or either of the two previous fiscal years by the witness or by an entity represented by the witness."

Summary of Rule:

Sec. 10. Information Required of Public Witnesses—Each committee shall require, to the greatest extent practicable, witnesses appearing in a non-governmental capacity to include with their advance written testimony a curriculum vitae and disclosure by source and amount of Federal government grants and contracts received by them and any entity they represent for the current and preceding two fiscal years. (Rule XI, clause 2(g))

Analysis of Rule (from Congressional Record, Jan. 7, 1997, p. H-13):

Section 10. Information Required of Public Witnesses: Committees shall require, to the greatest extent practicable, that non-governmental witnesses include as part of their written testimony that is already required by House Rules to be submitted in advance, both a curriculum vitae and a disclosure by source and amount of federal grants and contracts received by them and any organizations they represent at that hearing in the current and preceding two fiscal years, to the extent that such information is relevant to the subject matter of, and the witness' representational capacity at, that hearing . The purpose of these new requirements is to give committee members, the public, and the press a more detailed context in which to consider a witness' testimony in terms of their education, experience, and the extent to which they or the organizations being represented have benefited from Federal grants and contracts related to their appearance. It is not the intention of this section, for instance, to require individuals to disclose the amounts of Federal entitlements they have received, such as from Medicare or Social Security or other income support payments or individual benefits, or to require farmers to disclose amounts received in crop or commodity price support payments. Instead, the disclosure requirement is designed to elicit information from those who have received Federal grants or contracts for the purpose of providing the government or other individuals or entities with specified goods, services, or information. While failure to comply fully with this requirement would not give rise to a point of order against the witness' testifying, it could result in an objection to including the witness' written testimony the hearing record in the absence of such disclosure.

Source: Committee on Rules, U.S. House of Representatives <*rules.House.gov/Archives/truth_in_testimony.htm*>.

§2.8 Committee Preparation of Hearing Documents—Briefing Materials

Hearing preparation conducted by committee staff includes the writing and production of a number of written materials used by the committee prior to and during the hearing. Pre-hearing documents, such as backgrounders and hearing outlines, are helpful to the committee during the preparation stage. For the committee's use prior to and during the hearing, committee staff often prepare a briefing book, binder, or folder containing numerous written materials, including:

- background information on the hearing topics;
- a committee memorandum outlining the scope, purpose, goals and expected outcomes or goals of the hearing;
- an outline and description of topics and issues to be covered in a hearing;
- copies of prepared statements provided by witnesses;
- a roster or listing of witnesses;
- biographical information on witnesses;
- in-depth research on key issues;
- copies of bills;
- documents relevant to pending legislation or oversight matters;
- agency reports and information;
- formal research reports and results;
- relevant court decisions;
- media coverage and information;
- opening and other statements for the chair and members of the committee;
- suggested questions to be posed to witnesses by committee members; and
- any other information or background material requested by the chair and members of the committee.

Committee staff provide the chair and ranking member of the committee with opening statements that are typically read into the record or used as outlines for the committee leaders' initial oral statements at the hearing. Opening statements for rank-and-file committee members are usually prepared by their office or personal staff or by associate staff who have the responsibility for liaison with the committee on behalf of that member. Staff also provide committee members with prepared questions for use in engaging a witness following the testimony phase of the hearing. These scripted questions are usually organized thematically and are intended to expand the hearing record on a certain aspect of the hearing topic by soliciting additional information or explanation from a witness. Staff may also prepare follow-up written questions for a witness's response after the hearing.

For information on the preparation of hearing questions for committee members, see § 2.111, Prepared Questions for Committee Chair and Members. For information on a committee's preparation of post-hearing documents and follow-up questions, see § 7.3, Preparation of Post-Hearing Documents; and § 7.4, Preparation of Follow-Up Written Questions for Witnesses.

§2.9 Notice of Committee Hearing

Congressional committees are generally required to provide at least one week's public notice of a hearing and its date, time, location, and subject matter. Committee rules vary, so be sure to consult the rules of individual committees for more information. Notice requirements for the House of Representatives generally are found in House Rule XI, clause 2(g)(3). The Senate's general requirements are found in Rule XXVI, clause 4, of the Standing Rules of the Senate—Committee Procedure. (To access congressional committee rules, go to <*rules.House.gov*> or <*rules.Senate.gov*>.) Notices of hearings can be found in the Congressional Record's daily digest section, the Senate and House web sites (<*www.Senate.gov*> and <*www.House.gov*>), centralized committee scheduling services in each house, individual committee web sites (for access to links for each committee, go to <*www.Senate.gov*> and <*www.House.gov*>), and in a wide array of public policy journals and publications, including their web sites (see, for example, <*www.CQ.com*>).

§2.10 Congressional Hearing Room Layout and Logistics—The "Playing Field," Forum, and Venue

While there are many different sizes, shapes, and styles of congressional committee hearing rooms on Capitol Hill, the typical hearing room is an auditorium-styled room with a dais or raised bench at one end of the room, and with the bench or dais often semi-circular in style from one end to the other. This platform serves as the staging and seating area for members of the committee who face outward toward the witness table, audience, and committee room. The size and layout of committee hearing rooms vary widely in both the House and the Senate. Some large hearing rooms can accommodate 100–250 individuals in the room for general seating purposes, in addition to the seats for committee members and staff on the dais, and for witnesses, staff, and the media at special tables. Other smaller venues may hold only 20–50 people in the general seating areas.

The committee chair presides from the center seat position on the dais, with the ranking minority member in an adjacent chair and their committee colleagues flanking the center, usually with majority party members on one side and minority party members on the other, seated in order of their seniority on the committee. The committee staff director or chief counsel for both the majority and minority may sit next to their respective committee leaders, but most committee staff sit in chairs against the wall behind the members of the committee, yet within earshot and access of the committee members they serve who may need to consult with staff from time to time during a hearing.

On the main floor of the committee room, near and usually just beneath the chair or slightly off to one side, is a desk for a reporter or recorder of the proceedings who transcribes or tapes the hearing as it occurs. To one side of the room along the wall is usually a press table with chairs for print and broadcast journalists. There is also often a table for the personal staff of both members and non-members of the committee.

Squarely and directly in front of the chair, with only a "well," or small open area, as a buffer, is the witness table where witnesses appearing before the committee sit and deliver their testimony. Typically the first row or two of seating just behind the witness table is reserved for assistants, colleagues, support staff, and the briefing team of the witness, and for those who will be testifying later in the hearing.

Some hearing rooms, such as a large hearing room in the Senate Hart Building (Room 216), are equipped with considerable high-technology capability and amenities. These facilities can include special and expanded hearing room level space for the media complete with web access, upper-level viewing booths for senators, staff, and guests, and upper-level press booths for the broadcast media. To find out what technologies and facilities are available in a particular hearing room, contact the professional staff of that committee by telephone through the U.S. Capitol switchboard at 202-224-3121.

Most hearing rooms are typical auditorium-style with several rows of chairs for those in attendance, including interested parties and the general public. The entrance to the committee room is usually attended by a committee staff person and occasionally by a Capitol Hill security officer to control the flow and number of people in the room, and to assist with the admission and seating of those individuals who are waiting in line outside the hearing room or who arrive late.

To review a diagram of a typical hearing room, see § 2.12, Diagram of a Typical Committee Hearing Room Floor Plan.

§2.11 Congressional Committee Hearing Room Locations

Within the Capitol complex, various committee hearing rooms are located in areas in the Capitol building itself and in several buildings adjacent to the Capitol. In the Capitol building, several committee hearing rooms are located in either end of the Capitol, with House committee rooms located in the H-designated, or south end, of the building, and Senate committee rooms located in the S-designated, or north end, of the building.

On the House side of Capitol Hill, three major buildings—Rayburn, Cannon, and Longworth—serve as office space for representatives, their personal staffs, and all

§2.12 Diagram of a Typical Committee Hearing Room Floor Plan

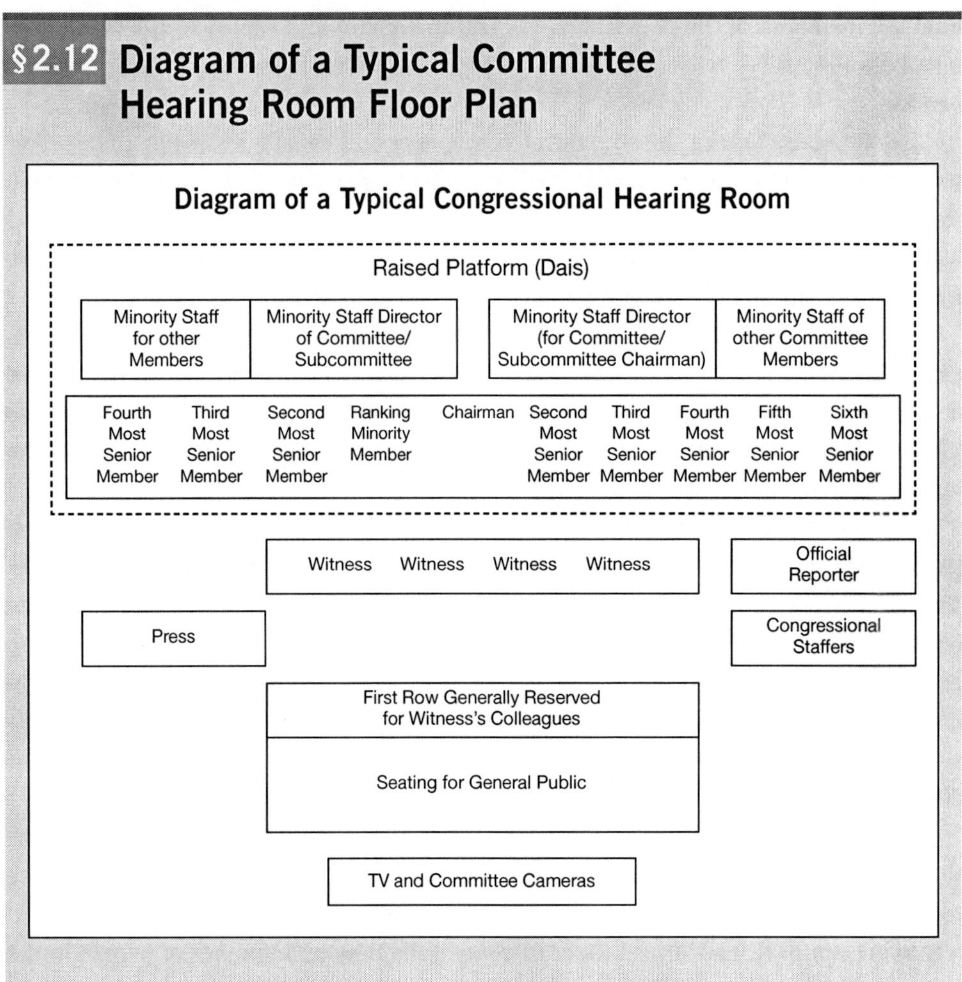

committees of the House of Representatives. The committee locations frequently include hearing rooms. There are no committee hearing rooms in the Ford Building.

Similarly, on the Senate side of Capitol Hill, the Russell, Dirksen, and Hart buildings house office space for senators, their personal staffs, and all committees. These committee locations also frequently include hearing rooms.

Congressional committees may be contacted telephonically through the U.S. Capitol switchboard at 202-224-3121, or via their respective web sites found as links on their respective chamber's web sites at <*www.Senate.gov*> and <*www.House.gov*>. For appointments and meeting locations, committee offices are located throughout the Capitol complex on Capitol Hill, and their room numbers are indicated on directories inside the entrance of each House and Senate building and the U.S. Capitol, as well as on directories located adjacent to each bank of elevators on all floors.

§2.13 Testimonial of a Congressional Expert on the Importance of Proper Hearing Organization, Preparation, and Planning

"For a federal government witness, the two primary goals of a hearing should be: 1) to effectively communicate your top points; and 2) to have no surprises. Thorough preparation for the witness is key to both. A witness should be prepared and able to deftly steer questioning back to the points he/she is trying to make without avoiding the question posed. And, while many Members of Congress and their staffs may believe that hearings with 'fireworks' are the successful ones, from the perspective of the government witness, the most successful hearings are usually the uneventful ones.

"A witness should also remember that clear, concise answers tend to be more effective. If a Member wants a more detailed response, he/she will ask a follow-up question. A witness with a long response may get fewer questions, but he/she risks losing control of the points to be made.

"Witnesses should not only be prepared on their key points, they should also have some idea what the interests of the individual Members of the Committee they are appearing before might be. Having this information, if possible, helps the witness to anticipate questions and be prepared with thoughtful answers."

Source: Cordia A. Strom, Assistant Director, Office of Legislative Affairs, Administrative Office of the U.S. Courts; Ms. Strom has held senior positions in all three branches of the federal government. On Capitol Hill, she was a professional staff member, House Committee on Appropriations; Chief Counsel, Subcommittee on Immigration and Claims, House Committee on the Judiciary; and Counsel, Subcommittee on Immigration and Refugee Affairs, Senate Committee on the Judiciary. In the executive branch, she was Counsel to the Director and Coordinator for Congressional Affairs, Office of the Director, Executive Office for Immigration Review; and Director, Legislative Affairs, Office of Legislative Affairs, Department of Homeland Security.

§2.14 The Essential Elements of an Effective and Successful Hearing

Common features of an effective and successful congressional hearing, from the perspectives of both a congressional committee and a witness, include:

- adherence to committee rules and guidelines, including promptness and limitation of time for speaking;
- execution of the proper roles of committee members, staff, and witnesses;
- timely submission of written statements and other requested materials;
- attention to hearing logistics and conduct;
- substantive "give-and-take" between the committee members and witnesses, especially during the question-and-answer portion of a hearing;
- effective education of the committee by those witnesses testifying; and

- a genuine "making of the record" and contribution to the policymaking process by witnesses whose testimony represents their particular stake in the issue under review.

The preferred and best elements of an effective and successful hearing, as well as the best practices involved in their conduct, are generally best understood from the perspectives of the presenter and recipient of testimony respectively—the witness and the committee. For more detail from each perspective, see the following two sections, § 2.15 and § 2.16.

§2.15 The Essential Elements of an Effective and Successful Hearing—The Committee's Perspective on What Constitutes an Effective and Successful Hearing

From a committee point of view, many factors contribute to an effective and successful hearing. The chair and committee members usually have a mission or purpose in mind when staging a hearing, and the success of most hearings is measured by the extent to which that mission or purpose is fulfilled. A committee wants to be educated and informed about the topic of the hearing. Its members want the hearing to establish a record on the issue at hand, complete with a transcription of that record for use in later deliberations. A committee seeks to engage experts who know the issue and can provide elucidating information about the hearing topic and its connection to proposed legislation, oversight objectives, or other goals of the committee. In a typical legislative hearing, for example, a committee seeks facts, advice, input, and perspectives, often from witnesses who represent disparate sources that can assist the committee in formulating legislative measures and making important policy decisions.

A committee typically expects factual and candid testimony from a witness, the full engagement and cooperation of those appearing before the committee, and an attitude and approach by the witness that reflect professionalism, respect, and dignity. Whatever a hearing's purpose, committee members want to be able to learn from the process, see their policymaking role more clearly regarding the hearing topic, form their own opinions in support of or opposition to an issue and related legislation or other action, and develop political consensus around the subject matter.

Finally, a committee typically wants to ensure that it provides an open forum for an "airing" and discussion of important policy issues in which stakeholders appear before the committee, present their respective policy positions, and genuinely feel that they have participated in an important aspect of the policymaking process. Procedurally, a committee appreciates a smoothly run and well-organized hearing involving careful preparation by committee staff and well-prepared witnesses.

§2.17 Threshold Questions for a Witness to Consider in Preparation for a Hearing

Hearing and testimony preparation should be approached with an understanding of committee needs and the political environment. Obtaining answers to questions such as the following will help the preparation team gain an understanding of the hearing context:

- What is the committee's purpose in holding the hearing?
- What is the occasion and type of hearing?
- Who are the other witnesses, and what is the proposed order of their testimony?
- What is the political environment? For example, what is the relationship between the chair and ranking minority member, and between majority and minority members of the committee and their staffs?
- Is there any relevant legislation or administration proposal pending?
- What will be the witness's role at the hearing?
- What type of questions will most likely be asked of the witness?
- Through what previous work or activity has the witness been involved with the topic of the hearing, and what special knowledge or expertise does the witness bring to the hearing and the committee?

Source: Adapted from Preparing for Congressional Testimony, Governmental Accountability Office (GAO), Nov. 2005, p. 3–7.

§2.16 The Essential Elements of an Effective and Successful Hearing—The Witness's Perspective on What Constitutes an Effective and Successful Hearing

From a witness's point of view, an effective and successful hearing essentially means adroitly communicating input on a policy matter to a committee through clear and concise testimony, being responsive in answering the committee's questions, and providing requested or volunteered materials for the committee's consideration. As a stakeholder in the subject matter of a hearing, a witness strives to make a compelling record and to convey to the committee his or her organization's perspectives and positions on the issues in a factual, straightforward, and convincing manner. The witness's role is to educate and advocate, and to provide commentary on the issue for the committee's consideration in the development of legislation or other measures.

A witness appreciates a well-organized, smoothly run hearing in which the expectations of the witness are made known in advance, and in which the witness is treated with respect and professionalism by the committee. A typical witness places a high value on the opportunity to weigh in for his or her organization in a hearing setting, and to participate in an important step in the enterprise of public policy development.

§2.18 The Essential Elements of Effective Congressional Testimony

As with elements of an effective and successful hearing, there are essential common features of effective and successful congressional testimony as well. Among them are a well-written statement for the record; a well-prepared witness; and oral testimony that is delivered in an articulate, clear, and concise manner. In similar fashion to understanding the elements of an effective and successful hearing, the preferred and best elements of effective and successful testimony, as well as the best operational practices, are best seen through the respective eyes of the witness and the committee, outlined in the following two sections.

For additional perspectives on effective congressional testimony, see Chapter 10, *Lobbying and Advocacy*, Deanna Gelak, TheCapitol.Net.

§2.19 The Essential Elements of Effective Congressional Testimony—The Committee's Perspective on Effective Congressional Testimony

For effective congressional testimony, a committee expects that a witness will:

- provide a thorough and well-written statement for the record;
- be prepared personally and professionally to provide oral testimony before the committee in an articulate, clear, concise, and helpful manner;
- be forthright and candid in his or her testimony;
- educate the committee by providing information otherwise not known or fully comprehended by the committee;
- explain all issues clearly;
- be professional and courteous in communicating with the committee;
- be responsive to questions posed by the committee both during and after the hearing; and
- provide other materials and information requested by the committee as a follow-up to the hearing.

A committee expects a witness to adhere to the committee's rules and guidelines relating to deadlines for the submission of statements and documents, as well as to the time limits for testifying and to requirements for statement formatting; to help make the record of the committee by providing a comprehensive statement; and generally to assist the committee in understanding the witness's perspective on the hearing topic and its potential relationship to legislation or other committee action.

§2.20 The Essential Elements of Effective Congressional Testimony—The Witness's Perspective on Effective Congressional Testimony

A witness's list of ideal components for effective testimony would include:

- providing a thorough and well-written statement for the record;
- being prepared both as an expert on the subject matter of the hearing and as an formidable orator presenting testimony before a committee;
- connecting with the committee through effective communications skills and relating the testimony to the interests of the committee;
- educating the committee on the subject of the hearing while also advocating the witness's or organization's position in a compelling manner;
- being professional, helpful, responsive, and courteous in all aspects of presenting testimony;
- adhering to committee rules and guidelines, including staying within the time restrictions for testifying and providing documents in the prescribed manner;
- making the record in such a way that is helpful to the committee as well as the witness;
- being responsive to questions posed by the committee both during and after the hearing; and
- providing other materials and information requested by the committee as a follow-up to the hearing.

For a more thorough discussion of the preparation of written and oral testimony and of the witness, see Chapter 3, "Preparation of Written Testimony," and Chapter 4, "Preparation of the Witness."

§2.21 Selection of Witnesses: How to Get Invited to Testify

Witnesses must be invited by a congressional committee in order to able to appear and testify at a hearing. A congressional committee basically has wide latitude and authority to invite whomever it wishes to testify before a hearing of the committee, and, in some instances, can even compel a witness to appear by using the power of a subpoena.

While many congressional committee hearings feature famous personalities, well-known authorities on a subject, government officials, or representatives of certain industries, nonprofit organizations and experts in government policy, individual citizens, and people from all walks of life have testified before committees as witnesses. The diverse range of witnesses includes farmers, small-business owners, small-town mayors, corporate executives, doctors, veterans, citizen activists, scholars, students, welfare recipients, and immigrants.

Witness selection is one of a committee's most important roles in preparing for a hearing, and thoughtful consideration goes into determining the witnesses to be invited, the order and format of their appearance, and the perspectives and viewpoints they will bring to the committee. Invited witnesses are usually experts or knowledgeable authorities such as members of Congress not on the committee holding the hearing, federal and state officials, representatives of private or public interest groups, spokespersons for business, industry and professional organizations, and private citizens.

In considering witness invitations, committees may weigh the need for fair representation of all viewpoints on an issue on the one hand, versus a strong, one-sided compelling presentation on the other hand. Because of the nature of some hearings, such as those held by appropriations and authorization committees respectively, certain witnesses from departments and agencies within the executive branch of government are invited and expected to appear and testify to justify and defend a budget request or a legislative proposal. In other instances, any number of non-governmental organizations or individuals may wish to testify before a committee on an issue for which they are a stakeholder, and, consequently, they make seek an invitation or offer to testify. Essentially, anyone potentially can be called or offer to appear as a hearing witness, but it is ultimately up to the committee to decide who will be invited. See § 2.22 through § 2.27 for various methods of being invited to testify.

§2.22 Selection of Witnesses: How to Get Invited to Testify—Committee Invitation to Testify

To appear before a committee as a hearing witness, one needs to be extended an invitation by the committee, usually in the form of a formal letter of invitation under the authority and signature of the chair, and occasionally the ranking member as well. The letter of invitation will set out the purpose, location, and time of the hearing, and describe the role of the witness. Usually included with the invitation will be a copy of the committee's rules or referral to the committee's web site that includes the rules of the committee.

A witness may be invited to appear in person to provide oral testimony, or merely to submit written testimony to be included in the record of the committee hearing. Other materials such as biographical, industry, and organizational information may also be requested of the witness. Committees generally extend invitations to key stakeholders of the issue that is the subject of the hearing. Typically, invitations are made to experts in the field; corporate and industry leaders; representatives of nonprofit organizations; federal, state, and local government officials; and those with special knowledge, experience or unique stories to tell. In preparation for a hearing, committee staff will usually help the committee identify and select witnesses, a process that occasionally involves interviews or informal communications with prospective witnesses. (For more information, see § 2.30–§ 2.39, Who Should Testify?)

§2.23 Sample of Committee Letter of Invitation to Testify

BARNEY FRANK, MA, CHAIRMAN

PAUL E. KANJORSKI, PA
MAXINE WATERS, CA
CAROLYN B. MALONEY, NY
LUIS V. GUTIERREZ, IL
NYDIA M. VELÁZQUEZ, NY
MELVIN L. WATT, NC
GARY L. ACKERMAN, NY
JULIA CARSON, IN
BRAD SHERMAN, CA
GREGORY W. MEEKS, NY
DENNIS MOORE, KS
MICHAEL E. CAPUANO, MA
RUBÉN HINOJOSA, TX
WM. LACY CLAY, MO
CAROLYN McCARTHY, NY
JOE BACA, CA
STEPHEN F. LYNCH, MA
BRAD MILLER, NC
DAVID SCOTT, GA
AL GREEN, TX
EMANUEL CLEAVER, MO
MELISSA L. BEAN, IL
GWEN MOORE, WI
LINCOLN DAVIS, TN
ALBIO SIRES, NJ
PAUL W. HODES, NH
KEITH ELLISON, MN
RON KLEIN, FL
TIM MAHONEY, FL
CHARLES WILSON, OH
ED PERLMUTTER, CO
CHRISTOPHER S. MURPHY, CT
JOE DONNELLY, IN
ROBERT WEXLER, FL
JIM MARSHALL, GA
DAN BOREN, OK

JEANNE M. ROSLANOWICK
STAFF DIRECTOR AND
CHIEF COUNSEL

U.S. House of Representatives
Committee on Financial Services
2129 Rayburn House Office Building
Washington, DC 20515

February 4, 2008

SPENCER BACHUS, AL, RANKING MEMBER

RICHARD H. BAKER, LA
DEBORAH PRYCE, OH
MICHAEL N. CASTLE, DE
PETER T. KING, NY
EDWARD R. ROYCE, CA
FRANK D. LUCAS, OK
RON PAUL, TX
STEVEN C. LATOURETTE, OH
DONALD A. MANZULLO, IL
WALTER B. JONES, JR., NC
JUDY BIGGERT, IL
CHRISTOPHER SHAYS, CT
GARY G. MILLER, CA
SHELLEY MOORE CAPITO, WV
TOM FEENEY, FL
JEB HENSARLING, TX
SCOTT GARRETT, NJ
GINNY BROWN-WAITE, FL
J. GRESHAM BARRETT, SC
JIM GERLACH, PA
STEVAN PEARCE, NM
RANDY NEUGEBAUER, TX
TOM PRICE, GA
GEOFF DAVIS, KY
PATRICK T. McHENRY, NC
JOHN CAMPBELL, CA
ADAM PUTNAM, FL
MICHELE BACHMANN, MN
PETER J. ROSKAM, IL
KENNY MARCHANT, TX
THADDEUS G. McCOTTER, MI
KEVIN McCARTHY, CA

The Honorable Thomas M. Wenham
Mayor
Village of Wellington
Executive Office
14000 Greenbriar Boulevard
Wellington, FL 33414

Dear Mayor Wenham:

The Financial Services Committee Subcommittee on Oversight and Investigations will hold a field hearing entitled "The Homeowners' Insurance Crisis and its Impact on Communities, Homeowners and the Economy" on Monday, February 11, 2008, at 1:00 p.m. at the Palm Beach County Commission Chambers, 301 North Olive Avenue, West Palm Beach, Florida, 33401. I am writing to confirm our invitation for you, or your designee, to testify at this hearing.

The field hearing will examine the costs to states and the insurance industry associated with providing relief from natural catastrophes in Florida as well as the current crisis related to the availability and affordability of homeowners' insurance in Florida and other disaster-prone areas. The field hearing will also explore the withdrawal of major insurance companies from offering policies in coastal areas, rising homeowners' insurance premiums and the resulting economic impact on state and local governments as well as a range of possible solutions to the homeowners' insurance crisis. The Subcommittee is especially interested in your views as a Mayor required to deal with this crisis and the effect on your city's tax base, local economy and overall fiscal health.

Please read the following carefully. It is intended as a guide to your rights and obligations as a witness under the Rules of the Committee on Financial Services and will be adhered to by the Subcommittee.

The Form of your Testimony. Under rule 3(d)(2) of the Rules of the Committee on Financial Services, each witness who is to testify before the Committee or its subcommittees must file with the Clerk of the Committee a written statement of proposed testimony of any reasonable length. Please also include with the testimony a current resume summarizing education, experience and affiliations pertinent to the subject matter of the hearing. This must be filed at least two business days before your appearance. Please note that changes to the written statement will not be permitted after the hearing begins. Failure to comply with this requirement may result in the exclusion of your written testimony from the hearing record. Your oral testimony should not exceed five minutes and should summarize your written remarks. The Chair reserves the right to exclude from the printed hearing record any

Source: Personal and professional files of William N. LaForge. *(Continued on page 96)*

§2.24 Selection of Witnesses: How to Get Invited to Testify—Invitation to Testify by Virtue of Institutional Role

Quite often, witnesses are invited by a committee to testify at a hearing because of a special institutional role the witness plays. Examples include:

- executive and judicial branch officials testifying on behalf of their department or agency with respect to proposed legislation, their budget submission, or

§2.23 Sample of Committee Letter of Invitation to Testify (continued)

The Honorable Thomas M. Wenham
Page 2

supplemental materials submitted with a written statement due to space limitations or printing expense.

Submission of your Testimony. Please deliver at least 50 copies of your proposed written statement to Felicia Goldstein, District Director, Office of Congressman Ron Klein, Palm Beach County District Office, 625 N. Flagler Drive, Suite 402, West Palm Beach, Florida.

The Rules of the Committee require, to the extent practicable, that you also submit your written testimony in electronic form. The preferred method of submission of testimony in electronic form is to send it via electronic mail to fsctestimony@mail.house.gov. The electronic copy of your testimony may be in any major file format, including WordPerfect, Microsoft Word, or ASCII text for either Windows or Macintosh. Your electronic mail message should specify in the subject line the date and the Committee or subcommittee before which you are scheduled to testify. You may also submit testimony in electronic form on a disk or CD-ROM at the time of delivery of the copies of your written testimony. Submission of testimony in electronic form facilitates the production of the printed hearing record and posting of your testimony on the Committee's Internet site.

Your Rights as a Witness. Under clause 2(k) of rule XI of the Rules of the House, witnesses at hearings may be accompanied by their own counsel to advise them concerning their constitutional rights. I reserve the right to place any witness under oath. Finally, a witness may obtain a transcript copy of his testimony given in open, public session, or in a closed session only when authorized by the Committee or subcommittee. However, by appearing before the Committee or its subcommittees, you authorize the Committee to make technical, grammatical, and typographical corrections to the transcript in accordance with the rules of the Committee and the House.

The Rules of the Committee on Financial Services, and the applicable rules of the House, are available on the Committee's website at . Copies can also be sent to you upon request.

The Committee on Financial Services endeavors to make its facilities accessible to persons with disabilities. If you are in need of special accommodations, or have any questions regarding special accommodations generally, please contact the Committee in advance of the scheduled event (4 business days notice is requested) at (202) 225-4247; TTY: 202-226-1591; or write to the Committee at the address above.

Should you or your staff have any questions or need additional information, please contact Sanders Adu at (202) 226-2888.

Sincerely,

Melvin L. Watt
Chairman
Subcommittee on Oversight and Investigations

MLW/sa

an issue being reviewed through the committee's oversight responsibilities;

- industry, company, or organizational leaders who represent the voice of the private sector;
- nonprofit or public-interest group leaders whose area of expertise is relevant to the hearing topic;
- public officials from state and local governments who are spokespersons for their constituents, communities, and respective political entities; and

- other individuals who represent and can speak for an entity that has a stake in the committee's deliberations.

§2.25 Selection of Witnesses: How to Get Invited to Testify—Invitation to Testify by Request

A person or organization wishing to testify before a committee, but not already invited to do so by the committee, may initiate contact with the committee staff to express interest in being invited to the hearing as a witness. This offer to testify should be made as early as possible to allow the committee time to evaluate potential witnesses during the preparation stages. It is also very helpful to have a representative or senator initiate the offer on behalf of an individual or organization, particularly if that person happens to be a member of the committee sponsoring the hearing.

The offer to testify by an individual, organization, and friendly member of Congress should lay out a compelling case why the requester's appearance as a witness would add substantially to the purpose and goal of the committee hearing. However, there is no guarantee that an offer to testify will result in a committee invitation. In lieu of appearing as a witness personally, or if an offer to testify in person is rejected, an outside interested party might also want to consider submitting a written statement for the record. (For more information on outside witness statements, see § 2.116, Outside Witness Statements—Written Statements for the Record.)

§2.26 Selection of Witnesses: How to Get Invited to Testify—Invitation to Testify by Recommendation

Committees will occasionally request or consider recommendations from organizations and individuals, in the public and private sectors, for the names of potential witnesses who would provide special or unique knowledge, expertise, background, or perspectives that would make those recommended witnesses valuable to the committee by virtue of testimony and input they would bring to a committee hearing and the making of its record. Before inviting witnesses to testify at a hearing, committees will sometimes use this method to cast a wide net to ensure that they are obtaining the best, most effective and most representative witnesses to testify on various or targeted positions on the subject matter of the hearing.

§2.27 Selection of Witnesses: How to Get Invited to Testify—Requirement to Testify under Subpoena

Most witnesses appear before a committee to testify willingly when invited by the chair or ranking minority member. Many witnesses, in fact, request to testify, and they consider an appearance before a congressional committee a privilege and opportunity to impart to Congress their respective viewpoints on the topic of the hearing.

When committees find themselves in situations in which a prospective witness will not agree to appear before the committee to testify voluntarily, or when committees choose on their own volition to require the appearance of a witness without issuing an invitation, the committees may compel the appearance of a witness by issuing a subpoena to that individual or organization under provisions that are in compliance with due process standards. Authority for the subpoena power in the House of Representatives is Rule XI, clause 2(m), and, in the Senate, Rule XXVI, paragraph 1. (To access House and Senate rules, go to *<rules.House.gov>* and *<rules.Senate.gov>*, respectively.) Committees are also empowered to subpoena documents and records associated with the compelled testimony of a subpoenaed witness.

Depending on the individual committee and its rules, issuance of a subpoena either requires majority approval by the committee members or a decision of the chair to whom that power is delegated in some instances. Subpoenas are not issued very frequently, and, when they are, it is usually in connection with investigative hearings that can involve individuals both inside and outside the realm of government. (For more information on testifying under subpoena, see § 2.39, Who Should Testify?—Testifying as a Result of a Committee Subpoena.)

§2.30 Who Should Testify?

There are several categories of witnesses that congressional committees tend to invite to testify frequently or routinely, largely premised on their positions in government, the private sector, public-interest organizations, stakeholder groups, or other special institutions. See § 2.31 through § 2.39 for information on these categories of likely potential witnesses.

§2.31 Who Should Testify?—Federal Executive, Legislative, and Judicial Branch Officials

Officials of the three branches of the federal government—executive, legislative, and judicial—often find themselves in the position of serving as a witness before a congressional committee hearing with regard to proposed legislation or recommendations for changes in federal law; advocating and justifying budgets; responding to congressional initiatives to make changes affecting the organization of government and the conduct of the various branches of government; and responding to regulatory and investigative oversight.

Federal executive branch officials, especially cabinet, subcabinet, and other high-ranking officials, both political and career, are frequently called to testify before a committee for a wide range of reasons. The type of hearing and the specific committee jurisdiction determine the nature of the government witness's appearance, which can occur in any number of scenarios before legislative, budget, appropriations, confirmation, oversight, or investigative hearings conducted by a wide array of committees in the Congress. Department and agency heads and their top management teams often appear as witnesses to request, advocate, explain, and justify programmatic legislative proposals and departmental and agency budget requests, as well as to provide information to committees that are conducting oversight or investigative hearings.

Within the separation of powers concept of the federal government, an appearance as a witness at a congressional committee hearing by an executive branch official is a recognized and approved manner of cross-branch communication that formally conveys information and engages both branches in the shared responsibility of policy-making. Presidential nominees for diplomatic, cabinet, judicial and other politically appointed positions requiring Senate confirmation appear as witnesses before the appropriate Senate committee for hearings on their qualifications for service. Whenever the president proposes a new policy or wishes to change existing law, officials from the White House, the Office of Management and Budget (OMB), and the department or agency with jurisdiction over that particular subject matter typically engage with Congress to discuss and debate the merits, and the hearing format is one of the most important forums for this dialogue. Within the annual budget and appropriations processes in Congress, officials throughout the executive branch are called upon and expected to appear as witnesses before the House and Senate budget and appropriations committees to defend and justify the president's annual budget request, and to provide detailed explanations for every aspect of the administration's requests and basic economic assumptions involving virtually every program of government, from the most costly defense and health-care programs to the most basic activity of a small agency.

Hearings that affect the operations of Congress itself also require appearances as witnesses before congressional committees by officials of the legislative branch of government, congressional committee leaders, rank-and-file members, and officers of the Senate and House serve as witnesses before committees that deal with the institution of Congress itself, including its organization, operations, budget, buildings, and facilities. Quite often, hearings of this type are "housekeeping" in nature and conducted only in one chamber because they deal exclusively with the operations of either the House or the Senate, which constitutionally are permitted to make and enforce their own internal and organizational rules. Legislative service organizations (LSOs), such as the Government Accountability Office (GAO), the Library of Congress (LOC), the Congressional Budget Office (CBO), and the Government Printing Office (GPO), are also frequent participants as witnesses before congressional committee hearings due to their roles in providing research, investigative, accounting and financial planning, and technical services and assistance to the Congress. (For a list and explanation of congressional legislative service organizations, see § 5.130, Legislative-Branch Support Agencies, the *Congressional Deskbook*, by Michael L. Koempel and Judy Schneider.)

Members of Congress also appear frequently as committee witnesses to support a bill they have introduced or a particular legislative proposal pending before a committee, to provide commentary on an existing federal program or policy, or to support the candidacy of an individual nominated for federal office. Members of Congress may testify before committees in their own or the other chamber. When appearing before a committee to testify, members of the House or Senate are typically accorded exceptional courtesy by their colleagues and allowed great latitude in making their statements.

Members of the federal judiciary, including Supreme Court justices and other Article III federal judges, appear as witnesses before the Senate Judiciary Committee for their respective confirmation hearings when they are nominated for service by the president. Supreme Court justices, federal judges, and officials of the Administrative Office of the United States Courts (AO) may also testify from time to time regarding the organization, operations, jurisdiction, and budget of the federal judiciary, as well as to provide perspectives and commentary on proposed legislation, current laws, and federal programs.

For more information regarding special considerations concerning executive, judicial, and legislative participation in congressional committee hearings, see § 2.68, Congressional Hearing Participants: The "Players"—Federal Departments and Agencies; § 3.23, Special Considerations Regarding Executive and Judicial Branch Testimony; § 3.24, Special Considerations Regarding Federal Legislative Branch Testimony; § 4.26, Witness Rehearsal of Oral Testimony and Answers to Questions: Preparation and Rehearsal by Federal Government Departments and Agencies; and § 4.40, Special Considerations Regarding Executive, Judicial, and Legislative Branch Witnesses.

For examples of hearing preparation and rehearsal methods used by federal agencies, see § 4.27 through § 4.31, Examples of Federal Agency Congressional Committee Hearing Preparation and Rehearsal Approaches and Methods.

§2.32 Who Should Testify?—Corporate, Business, and Association Representatives

Officials of corporations, trade associations and coalitions, and other business organizations are routinely called to testify before committees of Congress regarding proposed legislation or existing federal law, programs and policies, especially concerning how congressional actions might affect the market, business operations, the economy, and the end-users of goods, services and government programs. These witnesses represent the voice of business in the legislative policymaking process.

Private-sector spokespersons appear before committee hearings to support or oppose legislation affecting federal programs or policies that have or will have an impact on their particular industry. As direct stakeholders involved with the federal regulation of business, commercial interest representatives provide valuable commentary on the development, implementation, enforcement, impact, and substance of federal laws and regulations governing their industry and its products or services.

As legislation is considered by a committee, business and commercial organizations are in a unique position and have a special opportunity to provide private-sector perspectives, input and expectations with respect to laws and regulations affecting their respective industry and the U.S. economy. Examples would be a corporate CEO testifying on the impact proposed environmental laws would have on the company, its products or services, and its customers, and a trade association executive testifying on how a proposed change in the federal tax code would affect the association's membership.

For information on hearing preparation and rehearsal methods used by corporations and businesses, see § 4.33, Witness Rehearsal of Oral Testimony and Answers to Questions—Preparation and Rehearsal by Business and Corporate Offices.

For information on hearing preparation and rehearsal methods used by associations, see § 4.32, Witness Rehearsal of Oral Testimony and Answers to Questions—Preparation and Rehearsal by Trade Associations.

§2.33 Who Should Testify?—Nonprofit, Non-Governmental (NGO), Private and Voluntary (PVO), Public Interest and Advocacy Organizations, and Coalitions

Officials of nonprofit, non-governmental (NGO), private and voluntary (PVO), public interest and advocacy groups and coalitions, representing myriad issues affected by public policy decisions, appear as hearing witnesses to provide input from their vantage points on proposed legislation, federal funding or programs and policies under review through oversight. These interested parties provide a direct voice to Congress on issues of importance to their organizations and those members of the general public affected by both the organizations' activities and federal laws.

Typical examples of public interest and advocacy groups include associations seeking funds for research on a specific disease, groups whose mission is to represent consumers or taxpayers, and organizations that champion a certain side of a contentious policy issue such as reproductive rights, immigration reform, or financial accountability of lending institutions. Testimony from these organizations usually focuses narrowly on specific federal programs and policies with which the organization is specifically involved. Perspectives from these groups quite often tend to be different from the views of government and business. Their approach to hearings is usually very cause-oriented and advocacy-related.

For information on hearing preparation and rehearsal methods used by public interest and nonprofit organizations, see § 4.34, Witness Rehearsal of Oral Testimony and Answers to Questions—Preparation and Rehearsal by Nonprofit and Non-Governmental (NGOs), Private and Voluntary (PVOs), and Public Interest Organizations.

§2.34 Who Should Testify?—State and Local Government Officials

Governors, county supervisors, mayors, state legislators, and state regulatory agency officials often appear as witnesses to promote legislation that supports federal policies and programs that are beneficial to their state and local governments and their respective political constituencies. Governors are especially in a good position to champion states' rights issues when Congress is considering legislation that will lead to federal preemption of those rights. Quite often, state and local officials are in the best positions to inform the Congress on important federal funding programs such as food stamps, highway and transit programs, welfare and Medicaid, and to advocate for the support of these policies.

§2.35 Who Should Testify?—Citizens, Federal Program Participants, and End-Users

Individuals who are involved with specific federal programs are often called as hearing witnesses to provide commentary and evaluation on the effectiveness and benefits of those programs, particularly when programs are being reviewed for reauthorization or are the subject of oversight hearings. Committees are able to glean unique perspectives from certain categories of individuals who come into contact daily with federal programs. Examples include federal contractors, grant recipients, state and local governments, health and medical program providers and benefit recipients, and end-users of programs such as Social Security, federal housing, nutrition, and agricultural programs. The hearings process is also open to individual citizen requests to testify on any number of matters of public policy interest.

§2.36 Who Should Testify?—Government and Private Sector Experts and Research Organizations

Committees will often call as witnesses individuals from government, private-sector research organizations and others who are in a position to bring expert witness testimony to a committee hearing a particular topic. Typically, in addition to seeking expert input on the subject of a hearing, the committee is also looking for objective and nonpartisan perspectives, as well as timely commentaries from knowledgeable sources, that will be helpful to the committee in its decision-making on legislative and oversight matters.

Numerous private research groups, often called "think tanks," conduct studies and research on topics of significant public policy interest, and, consequently, scholars from those institutions are frequent witnesses at congressional committee hearings. The American Enterprise Institute, the Brookings Institution, and the Heritage Foundation are examples of private research institutions. Similarly, officials from government's in-house research components and other sources of authoritative information are frequently invited to testify to provide committees with the results of basic and applied research, studies, evaluations and analyses on a wide array of policy topics.

Examples of these groups include legislative service organizations (LSOs) such as the Government Accountability Office (GAO), the Congressional Research Service (CRS), and the Congressional Budget Office (CBO). The Government Accountability Office (GAO) is particularly adept at providing testimony because its mission includes preparing evaluations of federal programs and reporting to Congress either through the committee hearings process or through formal written reports. (For a list and explanation of congressional legislative service organizations, see § 5.130, Legislative-Branch Support Agencies, the *Congressional Deskbook*, by Michael L. Koempel and Judy Schneider.)

§ 2.37 Who Should Testify?—Witnesses Representing Special Geographic, State, and Congressional District Concerns and Perspectives

Witnesses who represent, or who are associated with, a special geographical, regional, or local issue, or occurrence are sometimes called to testify by committees who are interested in hearing a local or insider's perspective on a particular issue. Examples include victims of a flood or hurricane, firefighters who battle forest fires, commodities traders on one of the U.S. exchanges, or someone who was an eyewitness to a major event such as a grain bin explosion or a railroad accident.

On some occasions, witnesses from the committee chair's or a congressional member's home district or state might be called to testify to demonstrate the local impact of a law or policy, to underscore a problem that needs a solution, or to highlight the geographic depth and breadth of an organization and its activities. Examples would include a major city chief financial officer testifying on the impact of a new federal transit regulation on the city, a rancher testifying on the need for more available foreign agricultural guest workers to provide farm and ranch labor, and a local avionics manufacturer testifying on the economic impact of foreign imports on the manufacturer's community.

§ 2.38 Who Should Testify?—Use of Celebrity Witnesses

Celebrities from the entertainment world and other related industries are often invited to testify at congressional hearings to draw special attention to a particular issue or cause, especially in cases where the celebrity is personally involved with the topic of the hearing. Celebrity witnesses, quite often the official spokespersons for their chosen cause, appear before congressional committees to comment on a wide range of public policy issues, and to support or oppose numerous legislative proposals affecting those issues.

Examples include Elton John's testimony regarding HIV/AIDS research, Kim

Basinger's testimony regarding animal testing, and Michael J. Fox's appearance as a witness in support of Parkinson's disease research. Appearances by celebrities elevate the notoriety of the issue that is the topic of a hearing, and attract public and media attention to an issue, resulting often in the formation of political consensus and legislative traction.

For a sample of celebrity testimony, see § 1.64, Sample Celebrity Testimony: Michael J. Fox's Testimony before the Senate Appropriations Subcommittee on Labor, Health and Human Services, Education and Related Agencies.

For more examples of celebrity hearings, see § 8.44, Celebrity Witnesses, the *Congressional Deskbook*, by Michael L. Koempel and Judy Schneider.

For information on hearings that focus on publicity, celebrity and showcasing, see § 1.63, Showcasing, Publicity, Celebrity, and Grandstanding Hearings.

§2.39 Who Should Testify?—Testifying as a Result of a Committee Subpoena

Under the authority for subpoena power found in Rule XI of the Rules of the U.S. House of Representatives and in Rule XXVI of the Rules of the U.S. Senate, congressional committees are empowered to subpoena hearing witnesses in special situations in which invited witnesses refuse to appear before the committee voluntarily, or when a committee chooses to require an appearance in lieu of issuing an invitation. While each committee of Congress has the legal right to compel testimony by witnesses through the use of the subpoena power, committees use this power only as necessary and in rare instances, most often in the case of an investigative hearing.

Subpoenas are usually served on or delivered to potential witnesses by a United States marshal or by a designated committee staff member such as a committee investigator. How a subpoenaed witness responds to the committee is within the discretion of that individual. Subpoenaed witnesses may wish to seek legal counsel for clarification of the rules, an understanding of options, and protection of his or her constitutional rights. (See § 2.52, Rights of a Witness; and § 2.53, A Witness's Right to Legal Counsel.)

However, it is important to note that there are potential criminal and civil sanctions for failing to respond to a committee subpoena to appear before a committee. It is up to each congressional chamber to enforce subpoenas issued by its committees, usually in the form of a civil contempt resolution leading to a court decision regarding compliance, or a resolution referring the matter to the office of the U.S. attorney for possible criminal prosecution.

For more information on congressional subpoenas, see Rule XI of the Rules of the U.S. House of Representatives at <*rules.House.gov*>, and Rule XXVI of the Rules of the U.S. Senate at <*rules.Senate.gov*>.

For more information on testifying under a subpoena and on a witness's rights, see

§2.40 Sample of Use of Subpoena to Ensure Appearance of a Witness

"Facing a hostile congressional committee is never easy, but certain steps help. To paraphrase Woody Allen, the first rule is showing up. Steve Mendell, president of Westland/Hallmark Meat Co., ignored that one when he blew off an invitation to a Feb. 26 (2008) House Energy and Commerce Subcommittee hearing on his company's role in biggest beef recall in U.S. history. Mendell also ignored more than 15 phone calls from subcommittee staff, members said. That tack may work on relatives and salesmen, but it backfires on subpoena-wielding subcommittee chairmen like Energy and Commerce Oversight and Investigations Subcommittee Chairman Bart Stupak, D-Mich., who was eager to ask about millions of pounds of potentially tainted Westland beef consumed in schools. The subcommittee promptly subpoenaed Mendell, and Wednesday's hearing was no kinder for the delay."

Source: Dan Friedman writing in CongressDaily PM, Friday "Buzz" Section, March 14, 2008. Reprinted with permission of CongressDailyPM.

§ 2.27, Selection of Witnesses: How to Get Invited to Testify—Requirement to Testify Under Subpoena; § 2.52, Rights of a Witness; and § 2.53, A Witness's Right to Legal Counsel.

§2.50 Depositions Conducted by Committee Staff

In certain circumstances, committee staff members may be permitted to depose potential or scheduled witnesses to gather information in preparation for a hearing, particularly in investigative hearing situations. This formal manner of questioning a witness prior to a hearing is essentially taking testimony in private. The deposition may be administered under oath, may include both advanced written questions and a full transcript, and may involve witnesses whether or not they actually appear eventually in person before the committee. Quite often, deposed witnesses are accompanied by legal counsel.

Any witness called for a deposition should, directly or through legal counsel, have a clear understanding of the purpose and authority for the deposition, and may want to consult legal counsel who can provide advice on the substance and procedure of participating in a deposition, as well as ensure the constitutionally protected rights of the deposed witness. Committee practices regarding depositions vary greatly, and, because committee rules are often silent on the subject, resolutions by the respective chamber or committee are often the basis for authority to depose witnesses. Consult with a respective committee and the legal offices of the House or Senate for more information.

§2.51 Testifying Under Oath— Sworn and Unsworn Testimony

While congressional committees usually allow witnesses to proceed with their testimony under regular order and as unsworn witnesses, they do have the authority to place witnesses under oath, and occasionally committees exercise that option. Witnesses appearing before most congressional committee hearings proceed with presenting their testimony in an informal manner, under the direction and guidance of the committee chair, and without being administered an oath. This type of testimony is considered unsworn.

House, Senate, and committee rules provide for sworn testimony in which an oath is administered to a witness in the discretion of the chair or ranking minority member. While most hearings do not function with witnesses under oath, some committees, especially those dealing with intelligence and ethics issues, have special requirements for swearing in witnesses. Because of their nature or mission, some hearings are more prone to an oath being administered to witnesses, especially those involving investigations or confirmations. Most committees rarely use oaths or sworn testimony unless the nature of a hearing is investigative or the topic of the hearing is sensitive. Under 2 U.S.C. 191 of the United States Code, any member of Congress has the statutory authority to administer an oath to a witness.

For information on hearing procedure regarding administration of an oath, see § 2.93, Regular Order and Format of Proceedings: The Normal Procedural Conduct of a Hearing—Introduction and Order of Witnesses: Format for Witness Testimony. For more information about oaths and sworn testimony, see individual committee rules accessed through committee links available at <*www.Senate.gov*> and <*www.House.gov*>.

§2.52 Rights of a Witness

Witnesses who are called to testify before a congressional committee enjoy the basic rights and protections provided under the U.S. Constitution, as well as under any rules adopted by the Senate, the House, and their respective committees. Basic constitutional protections include First Amendment rights to free speech, assembly, and petition; Fourth Amendment rights against unreasonable search and seizure to obtain documents or information; and, Fifth Amendment rights against self-incrimination, including protection against being compelled to provide testimony or evidence against oneself that might be incriminating, unless immunity is granted. House and Senate rules, as well as some committee rules, provide added protections such as the right to legal counsel, the right to have counsel present to provide legal advice, the right to request that television cameras be turned off, the right in some cases to refuse to be photographed and to request that other witnesses be subpoenaed, the right of access to chamber and committee rules, and the right in certain instances to request that a hearing be closed.

The issues of a witness's rights and concerns about counsel, self-incrimination, and television coverage typically emerge in the context of investigative hearings of a controversial nature. While standards of due process and protection of individual rights are important in the congressional hearing forum, committee hearings are not judicial in nature, and rules of courts and judicial procedure generally do not apply. To be in the best position to protect a witness's rights both at law and before the Congress, it is important to consult individual committee rules and to work with the relevant committee staff to glean a complete understanding of witness rights. When in doubt, competent legal counsel should be consulted. For more information, see § 2.53, A Witness's Right to Legal Counsel, as well as the rules for each individual committee, accessed through committee links available at <*www.Senate.gov*> and <*www.House.gov*>.

Witnesses may also be entitled to reimbursement for per diem expenses and transportation, although these payments are generally used only in hardship cases. It is generally considered an honor and a privilege, and even a duty and obligation in some cases, for a witness to testify before a congressional committee. Testifying is part and parcel of a congressional function that includes many witnesses from outside government who are, more or less, expected to participate at their own expense. Consequently, there are no provisions for payment of witnesses other than for per diem and transportation expenses.

§2.53 A Witness's Right to Legal Counsel

Witnesses are generally entitled to legal counsel and representation any time they wish and at any stage of a hearing—prior, during, or after. However, the protocols involving use of, and consultation with, legal counsel during a hearing are within the purview of each individual committee, and are governed generally by House and Senate rules. Consequently, witnesses who intend or would like to bring legal counsel to a hearing should first consult with the relevant committee staff. In most cases, legal counsel is probably unnecessary, but it is certainly the prerogative of an individual witness.

Instances where legal counsel are frequently consulted include investigative hearings generally, and particularly when a witness has been subpoenaed, requested to submit to a deposition, wishes to protect and invoke his or her constitutional rights under the First, Fourth, and Fifth Amendments, or in any case where the witness may feel a potential encroachment on due process or equal protection standards. However, frequent consultation with counsel during the delivery of testimony or during the question-and-answer phase of a hearing is not favorably looked upon by committees in general.

For information on the use of legal counsel during the question-and-answer phase of a hearing, see § 6.40, Witness's Use of Legal Counsel during Questions and Answers.

§2.60 Congressional Hearing Participants: The "Players"

There are a number of important individuals and participants in a congressional hearing who play key roles in the process, production, and staging of a hearing. These individuals include the chair, ranking minority member, committee members and staff, non-committee members of Congress and their staff, witnesses and their support teams, federal agency representatives, the media, stakeholder and interest groups, the general public, and hearing room administrative staff. The following sections, § 2.61 through § 2.72, list and describe the major "players" in most hearing-room scenarios.

§2.61 Congressional Hearing Participants: The "Players"—Committee Chair

The committee chair, the highest-ranking member of the majority party on the committee, is the leader of the committee generally, as well as of the majority party members of the committee. The chair calls hearings, presides over the proceedings, and makes major decisions about the planning, organization, and conduct of hearings. The position of chair has great power over the hearings process, including leadership in decisions to hold hearings, selection of witnesses, and the setting of the committee's and a hearing's agendas. Subcommittee chairs have the same responsibilities for their respective subcommittees. The chair presides over the hearing from a seat in the center of the dais, maintains order during a hearing, makes statements that set the agenda and outline the hearing format, recognizes committee colleagues for statements and questions, welcomes and introduces witnesses who appear before the committee to testify, and engages witnesses in questioning to complete the record. All committee proceedings flow through the chair of the committee. On occasions when the chair cannot be present to preside over a hearing, he or she may delegate the role to a committee colleague.

§2.62 Congressional Hearing Participants: The "Players"—Ranking Minority Member

The ranking minority member, the highest-ranking member of the minority party on the committee, assists the chair when called upon and leads the minority side of the committee's membership. The ranking member speaks for the minority party members of the committee, helps ensure the minority's rights and participation in the hearings process, and provides leadership in making decisions for the minority involving the agenda, the selection of witnesses, committee member statements, and the questioning of witnesses. The ranking member typically sits next to the committee chair on the side of the dais designated for members of the minority party.

§2.63 Congressional Hearing Participants: The "Players"—Congressional Committee Members

The members of a congressional committee attend and participate in a hearing as the primary interested parties of the legislative panel that receives the testimony of witnesses and considers its content in the context of committee decisions on legislative and other matters. Depending on their own personal, professional, and congressional interests in a hearing topic, committee members may attend an entire hearing or just portions thereof. Consequently, committee members' attendance at any given hearing is subject to a number of variables, including the interest of the members in the hearing or topic, competing priorities in the members' schedules, and a duty or expectation to attend because of constituent interests or an obligation to the leadership or other committee members.

During a hearing, committee members typically make opening statements, listen to the testimony of witnesses, and engage the witnesses in questions after testimony has been presented. They sit in seats on the dais on their respective side of the political divide, usually in order of their seniority on the committee. Committee members constitute the primary target audience for witnesses who are testifying.

§2.64 Congressional Hearing Participants: The "Players"—Congressional Committee Professional Staff

Committee staff members are the worker bees who organize and prepare for the hearing. It is critical that witnesses establish a working relationship with the committee staff assigned to a particular hearing. They are a witness's primary source and contact. Staff make all the arrangements for the hearing, organize logistics that support the production and conduct of the hearing, and do the necessary handiwork of the chair and the committee. Committee staff work for the committee itself, not an individual member of the House or Senate. Usually majority party staff are hired by and report to the committee chair, and minority party staff are hired by and report to the ranking minority member. Occasionally committee members are allowed to appoint staff or have associate staff who also work in their personal offices.

During a hearing, committee staff support the leadership and members of the committee by ensuring that the room is well-organized, that the witnesses are present and prepared, and that the committee has all the necessary documents and materials, including their opening statements, background information, and questions for witnesses. Committee staff directors for the majority and minority typically sit beside or just behind their respective bosses. Other committee staff usually sit in chairs along the wall behind the dais where the committee members are seated, facing the witness and audience. Staff members are present and available to assist and consult with committee members throughout the hearing, and attend to any requests.

§2.65 Congressional Hearing Participants: The "Players"—Non-Committee Members and Personal Staff

On many occasions, members of the House or Senate who are not members of the committee staging a hearing will attend a hearing to testify, sometimes ask questions if permitted, or just listen and observe. While a committee gives preference to its own membership regarding time for statements and questions, the chair has the discretion to, and normally does, accord considerable courtesy to non-committee members in attendance, particularly when they appear to testify before the committee. In rare situations, non-committee members may even be invited to sit at the dais with the committee members, especially if the non-committee member is a leader or chair of another committee. Members of the House and Senate also testify before committees of the opposite chamber. The personal staff of committee members and non-committee members alike often attend hearings on behalf of their bosses, and they are typically seated at a special table for staff in the hearing room or in the general audience section. For the most part, their roles are to observe, listen, and take notes.

§2.66 Congressional Hearing Participants: The "Players"—Witnesses

Witnesses appearing before a committee to deliver testimony play a key role in the hearing process. Witnesses are called to provide information, education, and advocacy to assist the committee in making decisions on legislative and other measures under the committee's jurisdiction. They represent various perspectives on the topic of the hearing and play the role of an expert bringing vital information to the attention of the committee.

During a hearing, witnesses deliver statements in the form of oral testimony, and respond to questions posed by the committee members. While testifying, witnesses sit at a table facing the committee dais, either alone or in panels, as determined by the committee. (See § 2.10, Congressional Hearing Room Layout and Logistics: The "Playing Field," Forum, and Venue.)

For additional brief information on oral testimony, see § 2.95, Regular Order and Format of Proceedings: The Normal Procedural Conduct of a Hearing—Oral Testimony by Witnesses. For more complete information on preparation of a witness for a hearing, see Chapter 4, "Preparation of the Witness." For information on witness invitations, see § 2.21, Selection of Witnesses: How to Get Invited to Testify. For information regarding suggestions about who should testify, see § 2.30, Who Should Testify?

§2.67 Congressional Hearing Participants: The "Players"—Witness Support Teams

Witnesses occasionally are accompanied at a committee hearing by colleagues or staff who are available for consultation and assistance before and during the hearing. These individuals usually work with or for the witness and the organization represented by the witness. They provide technical assistance, information when called upon, and moral support for the witness. In many cases, they have assisted the witness in preparation for the hearing, and, thus, are in a position to help quickly locate information in the briefing materials that a witness may need to access.

In some cases, especially during the period of committee questioning, members of the support team may be called upon by the witness to provide details, explanations, or additional information that may not be known by the witness personally or be in the testimony or briefing materials used by the witness. Support team members typically sit just behind the witness table in the first row of seating. They can be particularly helpful to a witness during the questioning stage of oversight and investigative hearings when a committee is looking for detailed and specific information that may often include numbers and analyses.

For additional information on the use of briefing teams during rehearsal, delivery of testimony, and the question-and-answer phase of a hearing, respectively, see § 4.36, Witness Support: Use of Briefing Staff or Team; § 5.35, Utilizing a Briefing or Support Team; and § 6.36, Witness Use of Briefing or Support Team.

§2.68 Congressional Hearing Participants: The "Players"—Federal Departments and Agencies

Many congressional committee hearings feature representatives from federal departments and agencies as witnesses. Officials from executive branch organizations and the federal judiciary appear before numerous committees to deliver testimony on programs, policies, budgets, and appropriations requests. These officials provide committees of Congress with input and expert advice on legislative proposals, explanations and defense of the president's annual budget and appropriations requests, and responses to oversight and investigative inquiries.

When appearing as witnesses, government officials sit at the witness table to deliver their testimony. They are quite often accompanied by agency colleagues and support staff who assist them in ensuring a full and complete delivery of information to the committee. (See § 2.67, Congressional Hearing Participants: The "Players"—Witness Support Teams.) In many cases, government offices will also send staff to monitor committee hearings, especially when the hearing topic is a subject within an agency's purview and jurisdiction. Staff attending hearings to monitor the proceedings sit in the general seating section of the hearing room, or, on occasion, special seating may be provided at a table, much like the seating provided for the media and personal staff.

For examples and detailed outlines of how five federal agencies prepare for a congressional hearing, see § 4.27, Example of Federal Agency Congressional Committee Hearing Preparation and Rehearsal Approaches and Methods—National Aeronautics and Space Administration (NASA) Approach to Preparation; § 4.28, Example of Federal Agency Congressional Committee Hearing Preparation and Rehearsal Approaches and Methods—United States Agency for International Development (USAID) Preparation of Testimony and Witnesses; § 4.29, Example of Federal Agency Congressional Committee Hearing Preparation and Rehearsal Approaches and Methods—Internal Revenue Service (IRS) Preparation of Testimony and Witnesses; § 4.30, Example of Federal

Agency Congressional Committee Hearing Preparation and Rehearsal Approaches and Methods—Bonneville Power Administration (BPA) Preparation for Congressional Hearings; and § 4.31, Example of Federal Agency Congressional Committee Hearing Preparation and Rehearsal Approaches and Methods—National Science Foundation (NSF) Witness Preparation.

For more information regarding special considerations concerning executive, judicial and legislative participation in congressional committee hearings, especially with respect to written testimony preparation and oral testimony rehearsal, see § 2.31, Who Should Testify?—Federal Executive, Legislative, and Judicial Branch Officials; § 3.23, Special Considerations Regarding Executive and Judicial Branch Testimony; § 3.24, Special Considerations Regarding Federal Legislative Branch Testimony; § 4.26, Witness Rehearsal of Oral Testimony and Answers to Questions—Preparation and Rehearsal by Federal Government Departments and Agencies; and § 4.40, Special Considerations Regarding Executive, Judicial, and Legislative Branch Witnesses.

§2.69 Congressional Hearing Participants: The "Players"—The Media

Because committees frequently seek to publicize an issue or the committee's work on a legislative measure, the media are often a major target audience of a congressional hearing. The public exposure that a hearing may receive through media coverage can go a long way in focusing public attention on, and building public support for, an issue that has been the subject of public airing before a committee. In many instances, congressional hearings actually become a type of media strategy due to the coverage provided and the resulting increase in attention to a hearing topic or issue in the sphere of public opinion, as well as among government decision-makers.

C-SPAN actually covers and broadcasts a large number of hearings in both houses of Congress. To determine if a particular hearing will be covered live or taped, as well as when it will be broadcast, contact the committee conducting the hearing, or C-SPAN at <*www.c-span.org*>. C-SPAN also has a web site devoted to congressional hearing schedules that can be accessed at <*www.capitolhearings.org*>. For other television, radio, or cable coverage of congressional hearings, consult the hearing committee, the media source or your local broadcast listings.

Representatives of the print and broadcast media are usually invited and welcomed to cover open or public congressional hearings. House and Senate rules, as well as individual committee rules, govern media coverage of committee hearings. In most cases, committee hearings are open to the media when they are open to the public. The media are not allowed to attend and cover closed hearings.

Practically speaking, most hearings have little or no media coverage because of the sheer volume of hearings that are conducted and the rather ordinary nature of most hearings. Journalists are prone to attend and report hearings in which the subject matter is especially timely, controversial, or high-profile. They also tend to cover hearings involving celebrity witnesses and special angles of an issue. Committee chairs and staff often invite the media to attend a hearing and actually encourage media interest to help call attention to the subject of a hearing and to the work of the committee. Press conferences and interviews are often arranged before or after a hearing that attracts media coverage.

During a hearing, members of the media are usually provided seating space at a designated media or press table in a hearing room. Committee staff assist and direct the media in setting up cameras and audio devices, and they often provide the media with press releases, media information packets, copies of members' and witnesses' statements, and other information about the hearing, its purpose, and its topic. Committees may also announce and publicize their hearings on their committee web sites. To access committee web sites, see the links to congressional committees at <*www.House.gov*> and <*www.Senate.gov*>.

Members of the media may also approach a witness for an interview or information before or after a hearing. Consequently, a witness should be prepared for media encounters and interviews, and have an understanding of how the media work.

For more information about media coverage of congressional committee hearings, consult the House and Senate rules at <*rules.House.gov*> and <*rules.Senate.gov*>, as well as the rules of individual committees, accessed through <*www.House.gov*> and <*www.Senate.gov*>.

For information on the impact of congressional hearings on public policy debates, including media coverage, see § 1.84, Results and Outcomes of Hearings: Legislative and Regulatory Actions and Remedies—Public Policy Advocacy and Debate.

For information on preparing hearing-related documents for the media, see § 3.21, Important Documents: Drafting the Statement and Making the Record—Media Advisories, Press Kits, Backgrounders, and Releases.

For information on preparation of a witness to deal with the media, see § 4.41, Witness Contact with the Media.

For more information on media relations generally, see *Media Relations Handbook for Agencies, Associations, Nonprofits and Congress*, by Bradford Fitch.

§2.70 Congressional Hearing Participants: The "Players"—Interest Groups, Nonprofits, Non-Governmental Organizations (NGOs), Private and Voluntary Organizations (PVOs), and Other Stakeholders

Public and issue-oriented interest groups and organizations, including non-governmental (NGOs) and private and voluntary (PVOs) organizations, that are stakeholders in the issue or topic of a congressional hearing will often send representatives to the hearing to testify, observe, and lend either their support or opposition to a particular policy matter under review or discussion. Members of these organizations are often invited to testify, and, in those cases, the appointed witnesses have a seat at the witness table. Otherwise they are welcomed to attend a hearing to observe and listen just as any member of the public generally, in which cases they sit in the general seating area provided for the public.

These organizations typically include citizens' groups, public-interest entities, nonprofits, non-governmental, and private and voluntary organizations, and any number of associations or coalitions that concentrate their interests and efforts on a particular topic. They will often attend hearings to underscore their position on a public policy issue and to lend moral support to those testifying as witnesses or speaking from the dais as a member of the committee on their behalf.

§2.71 Congressional Hearing Participants: The "Players"— The General Public and the Audience

One of the most visible exercises of congressional activity is a committee hearing, and one of the most open and available opportunities for individual citizens to see their government at work is to attend a committee hearing and personally observe the process. Unless closed by vote of a committee's membership, congressional hearings are open and public for anyone to attend. Hearings typically are open in most cases unless they are closed by policy or committee decision because of security, intelligence, or confidentiality reasons. It is a right and privilege for the general public to attend congressional hearings, and to observe and hear a hearing's deliberations in person, as long as attendees do not breach committee rules regarding decorum and behavior.

Members of the general public or audience sit in the seating area provided by the committee, usually an auditorium-style seating area in the middle of the room facing the dais. In situations where the committee room becomes filled with people in attendance, the committee may arrange for an "overflow" room nearby. Lines outside committee rooms are frequent scenes, especially for popular hearings. In these cases, those individuals in line are permitted entry when space becomes available inside as people leave the hearing and seating becomes available. In most cases, uniformed Capitol Hill police officers control the door and entry to the committee hearing room.

The makeup of a congressional committee hearing audience can vary significantly for a number of reasons. On occasion, members of the public may just stop into a hearing for a few minutes to see what it is like, a very typical example being tourists or school children visiting Washington. Sometimes people generally interested in the hearing topic or witnesses will attend for their own personal or professional reasons. Many times the subject of a hearing draws an audience of individuals or groups that have a stake in a particular issue, program or policy, especially when the hearing topic is controversial or sensational, such as war powers, veterans benefits, immigration policy, abortion, treatment and interrogation of prisoners, and funding for research on medical and health issues. When executive branch officials testify, quite often an array of professional staff from a particular department or agency may attend the hearing either to observe or serve as resources for the witness.

§2.72 Congressional Hearing Participants: The "Players"—Official Hearing Reporter and Other Official and Administrative Personnel

The official hearing reporter is a professional reporter or stenographer designated and hired by a committee to make a complete record of the proceedings of a hearing. The reporter sits at a designated table near the front of the hearing room near the dais so that the entire proceedings may be observed and heard for purposes of making a complete and accurate record. Committees typically engage a commercial professional reporting service to transcribe the proceedings of hearings.

Other official personnel at a hearing might include a committee staff member near the entrance who assists in controlling traffic in and out of the hearing room, a uniformed Capitol Hill police officer who is stationed at the door to control admissions to the hearing room, and committee staff who may assist with hearing preparation and execution, as well as ensuring that the hearing room logistics are in order during the hearing. In addition to the committee's professional staff who assist the committee leadership and who are in charge of the hearing's organization (see § 2.64, Congressional Hearing Participants: The "Players"—Congressional Committee Professional Staff), other committee staff are often assigned press, clerical, and administrative duties during a hearing.

§2.80 The Targeted Audiences of a Witness's Testimony

A witness's targeted audience during a committee hearing is first and foremost the committee holding the hearing. A witness should direct his or her testimony toward the committee chair primarily and to all the members of the committee generally. Answers to questions should be directed to the member of the committee posing the question. The essential purpose of a hearing is for the committee to receive information through the testimony of witnesses, so witnesses should keep in mind at all times that they are addressing the committee directly.

Secondary targeted audiences, to whom a witness may also be explicitly or subtly addressing remarks or positions, include federal departments and agencies that might have representatives present at the hearing, the media, business and industry, trade associations, special interest groups, nonprofit and public-interest organizations, issue and program stakeholders, and the general public. In addition to the oral testimony and the live questions and answers that occur at a hearing, the written record of a hearing is also available to these targeted audiences. Witnesses should always be mindful that they are making a public record with their testimony and answers.

For more information, see § 3.12, Analysis and Targeting of the Committee and Audiences; § 4.14, Focusing the Witness on Targeted Audiences; § 5.42, Focus on the Primary Targeted Audience—the Committee; and § 6.33, Focusing on the Questioner during Questions and Answers.

§2.90 Regular Order and Format of Proceedings: The Normal Procedural Conduct of a Hearing

Each committee hearing operates from an agenda prepared for the chair and members by staff, in accordance with the stated purpose and mission of the hearing. Each individual committee decides the order and format of witness appearance and testimony. Committee hearing procedure is rather formal, but depending on the individual style of the chair, a hearing may be conducted formally or informally. Witnesses may appear before a committee one at a time to deliver testimony, or in groupings of witnesses called panels. Certain specific characteristics of the procedural order and format of a congressional committee hearing are considered standard, as described in the following sections, § 2.91 through § 2.102.

§2.91 Regular Order and Format of Proceedings: The Normal Procedural Conduct of a Hearing—Role of the Chair

The chair calls the committee hearing to order, serves as the presiding officer, maintains order, delivers an opening statement, ensures that the committee follows the agenda and the committee's rules, recognizes committee colleagues to deliver statements and ask questions of witnesses, and introduces and welcomes witnesses who appear before the committee to testify. All proceedings, recognitions, and rulings or directives of the committee rest with the power of the chair. The chair typically welcomes everyone to the hearing, announces the purpose and subject matter of the hearing, and outlines the procedure and format that will be followed.

§2.92 Regular Order and Format of Proceedings: The Normal Procedural Conduct of a Hearing—Opening Statements by Committee Members

Opening statements provide committee members an opportunity to make general remarks about the subject of the hearing and to stake out any policy positions, concerns, or questions they might have. The chair typically delivers the first opening statement, which may be general in nature regarding the hearing itself, as well as specific in nature regarding the chair's own perspectives. That statement usually includes an overview of the hearing, its subject and purpose, any relevant background, the committee's approach to the issue, and how the committee will proceed with the conduct of the hearing.

The ranking minority member usually delivers the second opening statement, and then committee members are recognized by the chair, successively in order of seniority on the committee and timing of appearance at the hearing, to deliver their opening statements. As a matter of practice, and in the interest of time, chairs will sometimes request that committee members' opening statements be submitted in writing for the record rather than summarized or read orally. As a matter of courtesy, chairs of committees are usually careful to recognize House or Senate members who are not members of the committee, but who appear at a hearing to observe and listen, and chairs may on some occasions offer those congressional colleagues a chance to make statements as well.

§2.93 Regular Order and Format of Proceedings: The Normal Procedural Conduct of a Hearing—Introduction and Order of Witnesses: Format for Witness Testimony

Once all committee members present have had an opportunity to deliver their opening statements at a committee hearing, the chair begins introductions of witnesses. Typically, witnesses are scheduled to appear according to a committee agenda which is shared with witnesses prior to the hearing. The order of introduction and format for the appearance of witnesses follow the committee's predetermined schedule, and are completely within the discretion of the committee. Witnesses may appear before the committee in solo fashion or as part of a panel, as determined by the committee. With the solo format, a witness presents testimony and then entertains questions from the committee before the next witness is called. With the panel format, witnesses grouped according to their position on the hearing topic or on other criteria determined by the committee, all present their testimony individually, and then take questions from the committee as a group.

The chair will usually welcome each witness, invite him or her to the witness table if they are seated elsewhere in the hearing room, make an introductory statement about the witness and the witness's organization, place the witness's written testimony in the record at that point, and suggest to the witness how to proceed. At the beginning of witness introduction, the chair will announce whether witnesses will be administered an oath, making their statements sworn testimony. If an oath is administered, the chair may swear in witnesses individually, by groupings or panels, or all at once. Most committees rarely require witnesses to testify under oath, but House, Senate, and committee rules allow for committee chairs to administer an oath to witnesses when a committee decides to proceed in that manner. (See § 2.51, Testifying under Oath—Sworn and Unsworn Testimony.)

Members of Congress, ranking government officials, and others deemed to be VIPs are typically scheduled to testify early in a hearing. In some cases, especially in confirmation hearings, members of the Senate or the House, who are friends of a witness or who represent a witness's home state or district, may appear to introduce a witness to the committee. This type of introduction occurs most frequently with nominees for federal executive positions such as cabinet officers, ambassadors and agency heads, as well as for nominees for federal judgeships.

§2.94 Regular Order and Format of Proceedings: The Normal Procedural Conduct of a Hearing—Use of Witness Panels

Committees will frequently group or align witnesses appearing before the committee to testify in panels that sit together at the witness table. Panels are formed variously according to the professional position and status of witnesses, their positions or predispositions on issues that are the subject of a hearing, and convenience and efficiency in support of the committee's processes and procedure. Prior to a hearing, committee staff will typically advise witnesses how the hearing will be organized, including whether witnesses will appear solo, in pairings, in panels, or in some other format.

In many instances, the witnesses in a particular panel have a common connection such as being from the same industry or representing the same side of an issue. When panels are used in committee hearings, all the witnesses on the panel are usually allowed to present their testimony before the committee begins questioning of the witnesses. Paneling of witnesses allows for the natural grouping of witnesses whose testimony may be similar on the hearing topic and whose answers to questions may reflect the same or similar perspectives. When one panel completes its testimony and answers all the questions asked by the committee, it is excused, and another panel is seated at the witness table.

§2.95 Regular Order and Format of Proceedings: The Normal Procedural Conduct of a Hearing—Oral Testimony by Witnesses

The central action of any congressional committee hearing is the in-person, real-time delivery of oral testimony by witnesses to the members of the committee. The verbal presentation of a witness's statement is the essence of the hearing format. A witness's oral testimony provides the committee with information and perspectives that can be considered and used by the committee in its further deliberations on legislative and other measures, and the testimony may lead to questions later posed by the committee to a witness. Witnesses sit at a designated witness table facing the dais on which the committee members sit, and they present their oral statement directly to the committee.

Formal written statements are usually required and inserted in the record, but oral testimony is generally intended to be a summation and highlighting of the witness's statement, especially in the context of the limited time allowed to testify, typically five to ten minutes, depending on the hearing and the committee's rules. Witnesses should strive to stay within prescribed time limits, and should present to a committee a succinct summary presentation of their case or position in clear-cut, easy-to-understand oration. It is preferred, and, in fact, usually expected, that a witness will not read his or her prepared written statement, which is made part of the record as a matter of course in most cases. House Rule XI, clause 2(g)(4) requires witnesses before House committees to limit oral testimony to a brief summary of their statement as much as is practicable. Senate rules do not impose such a general restriction on testimony before Senate committees, but some Senate committees place limits on the length of witness testimony.

Many witnesses operate from notes, outlines, or talking points in presenting oral testimony, while others actually read their prepared written statement or an abbreviated version thereof. Witnesses are recognized and introduced by the chair, and instructed how to proceed with their testimony before the committee.

For more information on oral testimony preparation, see § 4.11, Preparation and Use of Oral Statement Script or Outline; § 4.13, Delivering the Statement: To Read or Not to Read; and § 4.21, Witness Rehearsal of Oral Testimony and Answers to Questions —Relying on Oral Statement Script to Deliver Testimony.

Typically, a committee poses questions to individual witnesses after their respective testimony, but usually combines questions for witnesses appearing in panels until all members of the witness panel have delivered their testimony. On occasion, committees will utilize remote hearing formats, including teleconferencing and videoconferencing witnesses from locations other than the site of the hearing.

For complete coverage of the topic of preparing a witness for oral testimony, see Chapter 4, "Preparation of the Witness." For complete coverage of the topic of delivering oral testimony, see Chapter 5, "Presentation and Delivery of Oral Testimony." For complete coverage of the topic of the question-and-answer phase of a hearing, see Chapter 6, "Responding to Committee Questions."

§2.96 Regular Order and Format of Proceedings: The Normal Procedural Conduct of a Hearing—Time Limits for Oral Testimony

Committee rules often provide time restrictions for witnesses' testimony and limit witnesses to a brief summary statement. Brevity and succinctness in oral testimony are special virtues in a witness that are universally encouraged by committee chairs. The typical rule is five minutes, but some committees allow additional time—up to ten minutes or more—depending on the witness, the issue and the nature of the hearing, and committee chairs do have some discretion in allowing more time in certain instances. Committee staff will advise witnesses prior to the hearing about time limits, but witnesses should consult the committee rules and consult with staff to gain a complete understanding of the rules. (See House Rule XI, clause 2(g)(4). There is no similar Senate rule.)

Many committees use an encased electric clock placed on the witness table to help a witness keep track of time, or a light system to signal time, with the green light indicating to proceed, the yellow light announcing that time is about to expire, and the red light conveying that the prescribed time is over. Whatever system is utilized by a committee, a committee staff professional operates the device from the dais. Witnesses should adhere to time limits strictly, and, if additional time is needed, they might want to request an additional minute or two. Committee chairs have the discretion of enforcing time limits strictly or being lenient, although most committees attempt to strike a reasonable balance and be fair to all witnesses.

For more information on time limits for testimony and the use of timing devices, see individual House and Senate committee rules, accessed through links found at <*www.House.gov*> and <*www.Senate.gov*>, and contact the relevant committee for details. (For telephone contact, the U.S. Capitol switchboard number is 202-224-3121.) Also see § 4.22, Witness Rehearsal of Oral Testimony and Answers to Questions—Operating within Time Limits and Effective Use of the Clock.

§2.97 Regular Order and Format of Proceedings: The Normal Procedural Conduct of a Hearing—Committee Members' Questions and Witnesses' Responses

At the conclusion of oral testimony by witnesses, a committee may enter a period of questioning witnesses about their testimony, position on issues, organization, or any topic related to the hearing's purpose. Individual witnesses are usually questioned immediately after their testimony. Witnesses in a panel format are typically questioned by a committee after all witnesses in the panel have completed their testimony. The chair typically leads the questioning and then defers to other committee members for questions, usually on the basis of seniority and timing of arrival at the hearing, and usually with a focus on alternating between the majority and minority side of the aisle. Committee members' questions may be proffered to an individual witness or to an entire panel. Witnesses remain at the witness table during questioning, and their role is to respond to the questions briefly and accurately.

The question-and-answer period provides an environment for exploring issues in depth and for eliciting from witnesses explanations or clarifications of points covered in their testimony, as well as virtually anything the committee members wish to discuss. In question-and-answer exchanges with witnesses, committee members are able to expand on the statements of witnesses, offer divergent viewpoints, contribute additional text for the public record of the hearing, and elicit important information that can be helpful to the committee in formulating legislation and taking other actions. The opportunity for questioning witnesses also gives committee members an opening to make sometimes lengthy additional statements and to opine on virtually any aspect of the hearing's subject—before actually posing a question to a witness. In their responses to questions, witnesses have the opportunity to expand on comments made during their testimony and to accentuate the central points being made to the committee, as well as to clarify issues and provide additional information that might be of interest to the committee.

Some committees have established rules to limit the length of time its members may question a witness and engage in discussion, often ranging from five to ten minutes. Committees also utilize rounds of questioning by members in order to give all committee members a chance to ask questions within the time allotted. In the interest of courtesy and comity, congressional committee chairs usually attempt to accommodate committee members by according them with ample time to speak and pose questions to witnesses. Questions and talking points for committee members to use in questioning witnesses are usually prepared by committee staff.

For complete coverage of the topic of the question-and-answer phase of a hearing, see Chapter 6, "Responding to Committee Questions." For information on the rehearsal aspects of the question-and-answer phase of a hearing, see § 4.15, Witness Rehearsal of Oral Testimony and Answers to Questions; § 4.18, Witness Rehearsal of Oral Testimony and Answers to Questions—Practice "Runs" and Live Peer Review; § 4.19, Witness Rehearsal of Oral Testimony and Answers to Questions—Murder Boards" and Question-and-Answer "Dry Runs"; and § 4.23, Witness Rehearsal of Oral Testimony and Answers to Questions—Operating with the Use of a Briefing Book.

§2.98 Regular Order and Format of Proceedings: The Normal Procedural Conduct of a Hearing—Order of Questioning of Witnesses

The order of questioning of witnesses in a committee hearing is dependent on the chair's prerogatives. Each congressional committee enjoys the discretion to establish the order in which committee members question witnesses. Most committees begin with the chair and the senior members of the committee, and alternate calling on members from the majority and minority ranks of the committee to question witnesses. In some instances, committees utilize a system of recognizing members in the order in which they arrive at a hearing. The chair also has the flexibility in most cases to recognize committee members out of order to accommodate their schedules or conflicts. Witnesses appearing before a committee should consult the rules of individual committees, as well as with committee staff, to obtain guidance regarding the order of questioning. (Committee rules are accessible through committee links found at <*www.Senate.gov*> and <*www.House.gov*>.)

With respect to the order in which witnesses are questioned by the committee, individual witnesses are usually questioned immediately after their testimony, while witnesses in a panel format are typically questioned by the committee after all witnesses in the panel have completed their testimony. Witnesses should be prepared to answer a wide array of questions from members of the committee, although most committees, by rule or practice, tend to limit the scope of questioning to the subject matter of the hearing.

§2.99 Regular Order and Format of Proceedings: The Normal Procedural Conduct of a Hearing— Open and Closed Hearings

Most congressional committee hearings are open to the public. Committee staff will advise witnesses, usually well in advance of a hearing, if a hearing is going to be closed. The nature of the committee, the hearing purpose, and the subject matter will dictate whether a hearing is closed or not, and the parties involved with the hearing, including witnesses, will know and understand the situation as a matter of course due to their work and role.

Under House and Senate rules, as well as in practice, most hearings are open to the public. The rules and format for witnesses testifying in a closed hearing are basically the same internally. However, as may be appropriate with respect to their position or the information they are bringing to the committee, witnesses may be expected to keep the hearing's proceedings and all testimony confidential.

Closed, classified, or executive hearings are accessible only to those deemed necessary to the proceedings by the committee, and typically may include committee members and select staff, House and Senate colleagues if invited, and other invited and screened witnesses and officials from government agencies or the private sector. Those participating in closed hearings are sometimes required to have a certain level of security clearance, and the hearing rooms may be "swept" to guard against the possibility of surveillance or listening devices. Witnesses called to testify before a committee in a closed hearing will be briefed in advance by committee staff regarding rules, format, and expectations.

For more information on open and closed hearings, see § 1.65, Public or Open Hearings and Closed or Classified Hearings. For a sample notice of a closed and open hearing, see § 1.66, Sample of Open and Closed Hearings: Notices from the Senate Armed Services Committee.

§2.100 Regular Order and Format of Proceedings: The Normal Procedural Conduct of a Hearing— Participation by Non-Committee Members of Congress and Committee Staff

On some occasions, members of the Senate or House who are not members of a particular committee may appear at that committee's hearings to testify, observe, and hear the testimony and questioning of witnesses. Committee chairs typically extend courtesies to these non-committee members of Congress by allowing them to testify early in the proceedings and occasionally sit on the dais with the committee. Rarely are non-committee members allowed to ask questions of witnesses, but it does occur. Depending on the committee, there are numerous rules concerning participation by members of a committee in a hearing of a subcommittee on which they do not serve. Consult individual committee rules for the specifics. (Committee rules are accessible through committee links found at <*www.Senate.gov*> and <*www.House.gov*>.) Some congressional committees allow committee staff to question witnesses, usually through the authorization and direction of the chair.

§2.101 Regular Order and Format of Proceedings: The Normal Procedural Conduct of a Hearing—Committee Hearing Conclusion and Wrap-Up

When all witnesses have testified and all questions have been asked and answered, the chair usually brings the hearing to a close, sometimes with a summary or concluding statement about the hearing's content and value, next steps in the committee process, and potential action available to the committee. The chair typically thanks all witnesses and other participants, and addresses any follow-up activities that might be required.

§2.102 Regular Order and Format of Proceedings: The Normal Procedural Conduct of a Hearing—Committee Post-Hearing Follow-up and Expectations

At the conclusion of a committee hearing, there are occasionally follow-up actions to be considered. During a hearing, members of a committee will often ask questions to which witnesses do not have answers, totally or partially. In such instances, witnesses will offer to provide, and committees will expect, more complete answers or information in writing at a later date that will respond to unanswered or partially answered questions, that will allow the witness to expand on oral answers or testimony already provided, and that will allow a witness to provide written comments on issues raised at the hearing that were not included in his or her testimony or answers to oral questions.

Similarly, in addition to questions asked orally in real time at a hearing, committees will often provide witnesses with a list of written questions to be answered after the hearing and returned to the committee by a date certain. Committees will also sometimes offer or request that a witness work with the committee's staff on follow-up matters such as drafting of legislation, ensuring a complete hearing record, providing industry and other pertinent contact information, and delivering research, technical and other data for the committee's use and consideration. Committees have authority to keep a hearing record open for a period of time in order that additional information may be included in the formal hearing record.

In all circumstances involving a commitment of a witness to provide additional written material or information to a committee after a hearing, the witness should take great care to be responsive in a thorough and timely manner. Witnesses should attempt to work cooperatively with committee staff during post-hearing discussions and deliberations, especially as a committee is crafting legislation or preparing for markup of a bill. Witnesses should expect the opportunity to review the hearing record, to provide additional or corrected information for the record, and to receive a copy of the hearing transcript in most cases, although printed copies are often not available for lengthy periods of time.

For multi-day hearings, committee staff may be asked by the chair to prepare a summary of each day's testimony and significant questions and answers. When hearings are complete, committee staff may be authorized to have the transcript of the hearing's proceedings printed according to the official printing practices of the respective chamber and of the committee itself. Hearing transcripts are usually available for inspection in the offices of a committee at some point after a hearing.

Hearing transcripts are often printed for permanent record and committee use, and in some cases for public distribution, although there is no requirement under chamber or committee rules to print hearing transcripts. Committees are encouraged to post their proceedings, including hearing information and transcripts, on the web sites. Some committees allow witnesses to review their testimony, before it is included in the final hearing transcript, for the purpose of editing grammatical, transcription, and obvious factual errors or omissions. However, permission to make basic or substantive changes to witness testimony, statements, and answers in a transcript requires committee approval.

Post-hearing committee activities take many forms, depending on the nature of a hearing. At the conclusion of investigative hearings, committee staff are usually charged with the preparation of a report for the committee's review, approval, and release. The results of oversight hearings might include correspondence and other follow-up with the relevant executive branch department or agency, as well as the possibility of corrective legislation. Legislative hearings can lead to a markup of a bill and the writing of a report to accompany the committee print of the bill. Confirmation hearings set the stage for a committee vote on a nomination and an eventual report to the full Senate.

Committee staff also take care of administrative and logistical duties at the conclusion of a hearing, including restoring the committee hearing room to proper order, organizing all documents such as witness statements and answers to questions, dealing with the media, and handling all follow-up correspondence such as thank-you letters and requests for additional information.

For more information on post-hearing activities, see Chapter 7, "Post-Hearing Activities and Follow-Up."

§2.110 Sample Hearing Agenda

<http://edlabor.house.gov/hearings>

Hearings: House Committee on Education & Labor

Green Jobs and their Role in our Economic Recovery
Workforce Protections Subcommittee Hearing
10:00 AM, March 31, 2009
2175 Rayburn H.O.B.
Washington, DC

On Tuesday, March 31, the Subcommittee on Workforce Protections of the House Education and Labor Committee will hold a hearing to examine green jobs and their role in our nation's economic recovery. The American Recovery and Reinvestment Act set aside $50 billion in grants and tax incentives to promote energy efficiency and the renewable energy sector. Congress also approved the Green Jobs Act in 2007, a program to help train American workers for jobs in the renewable energy and energy-efficiency industries.

Archived Webcast »

Rep. Lynn Woolsey (CA) Opening Statement »

Witnesses:

William T. Bogart »
Dean of Academic Affairs and Professor of Economics,
York College York, Pa.

Kathy Krepcio »
Executive Director, John J. Heldrich Center for Workforce Development
at Rutgers University

Jerome Ringo »
President, The Apollo Alliance San Francisco

Robin Roy »
Vice President for Projects and Policy Serious Materials,
Sunnyvale, Calif.

Jill Sherman »
Gerding Edlen Development, Portland, Ore.

Clinton R. Wolfe »
Executive Director Citizens for Nuclear Technology Awareness,
Aiken, South Carolina

For shorter video excerpts of testimony, please visit our YouTube channel.

Source: Committee on Education and Labor, U.S. House of Representatives.

§2.111 Prepared Questions for Committee Chair and Members

Committee staff typically formulate, prepare, and script questions for the chair, and occasionally for other members of the committee, to ask of witnesses who appear before the committee. The committee professional staff prepare questions in advance of the hearing based on their reading of a witness's written statement and other information known to the staff person. The personal staff of committee members will most often prepare questions for their respective bosses. During the question-and-answer portion of a hearing, the committee chair and other committee members may ask these or other questions that they may develop during the hearing proceedings while listening to testimony.

Questions that are not asked and answered orally during the hearing are often submitted to a witness for written responses after the hearing. In some situations, committee staff will accept and consider written suggested questions from outside organizations to elucidate a particular issue or advance a certain viewpoint. These prepared questions may be friendly or hostile in nature to a witness, and it is completely within the discretion of the committee staff, and ultimately the committee chair and members, whether to ask or use such questions.

For more information on the question-and-answer phase of a congressional committee hearing, see Chapter 6, especially § 6.20, The Sources of Committee Hearing Questions, and § 6.11, Anticipating Questions: Being Prepared. For information on the types and origin of questions, see § 6.12, Friendly and "Softball" Questions; § 6.13, Unfriendly and Hostile Questions; and § 6.14, Pre-Scripted and "Planted" Questions. For more information on the preparation of committee documents, including questions for witnesses, see § 2.8, Committee Preparation of Hearing Documents—Briefing Materials.

§2.112 Scheduling and Timing of Hearings

Congressional committees schedule hearings as necessary according to the general schedules of their respective chamber. Committee chairs, with advice from committee members and staff, ultimately make decisions regarding the scheduling of hearings. Hearings on Capitol Hill are held when the House and Senate are in session, and at other times by permission or resolution of the respective chamber. Field hearings are scheduled with the approval of the committee chair. In most cases, committees determine the need for hearings and the timing involved, and then schedule hearings in an orderly fashion to meet room accommodations and other logistical needs.

Each congressional committee has committee hearing room space assigned to it under the rules of that particular chamber. Hearings are usually held during the regular workday of the House or Senate, and typically begin no earlier than 8:00 a.m. or 9:00 a.m. and conclude no later than 5:00 p.m. or 6:00 p.m. Depending on the hearing topic and interest of a committee, the duration of a hearing may be one or two hours,

§2.113 Sample Hearing Schedule

<www.capitolhearings.org/schedule.asp>

Senate Hearings Schedule

Wednesday, Apr. 22, 2009

10:00 am
Armed Services: Subcommittee on Readiness and Management Support
Hearings to examine the current readiness of United States ground forces.
SR-222

2:30 pm
Veterans' Affairs
Hearings to examine pending health related legislation.
SR-418

Thursday, Apr. 23, 2009

9:30 am
Energy and Natural Resources
Hearings to examine the nomination of Kristina M. Johnson, of Maryland, to be Under Secretary of Energy.
SD-366

Wednesday, May. 06, 2009

9:30 am
Veterans' Affairs
Hearings to examine pending benefits related legislation.
SR-418

Thursday, May. 21, 2009

9:30 am
Veterans' Affairs
Business meeting to markup pending legislation.
SR-418

Source: *<www.capitolhearings.org/schedule.asp>*.

several hours, most of a day, or even several days in length. It is within the discretion of the committee and its chair to determine how long a hearing will continue. The scheduling of hearings is closely connected to the timing of an issue, proposal, or directive of the committee or chamber leadership. Hearings may be conducted by resolution and permission of each house when that chamber is not in session.

§2.114 Alternatives to Traditional Hearing Formats

In addition to the traditional hearing format and venue entailing a single committee conducting a formal hearing, there are other non-traditional formats occasionally used by congressional committees, including some modern techniques.

One somewhat different format that has historically been used fairly often by congressional committees is the joint hearing, in which two or more committees or subcommittees pool their resources, interests, and legislative prowess to collaborate in the conduct of a hearing on the same subject. Quite often a joint hearing occurs when two or more committees have joint or sequential jurisdiction over a particular bill that has been introduced, or when the subject matter of the hearing is otherwise under the purview and consideration of more than one committee. The committee members sit together in combined fashion on the dais at the hearing, committee staff cooperate in organizing the hearing, and witnesses essentially are appearing before two or more committees at once to present testimony.

Some committees have begun to utilize forms of high-tech hearings, in which witnesses located elsewhere in the United States or virtually anywhere around the world are connected to the committee room to provide for communications by audio or video and audio together. This remote form of hearing access for witnesses helps address and alleviate cost and distance problems, as well as matters associated with unavailability or limitations on witness or committee time and travel. One such hearing included testimony by an astronaut who happened to be in space at the time of the hearing.

In lieu of formal hearings, some congressional committees have also experimented with more informal types and formats of official communication with witnesses such as "round tables." For example, the Senate Foreign Relations Committee has begun using a format of round-table discussions with a variety of witnesses referred to as visitors. The discussions occur around a hollow square table, with committee members and visitors interspersed to facilitate a more casual environment and more informal discussion. Meeting notices are sent to committee members just as with committee hearings, and a court reporter is present to transcribe the discussion.

In similar fashion, the Senate Finance Committee utilized round tables in preparation for the 2009 debate on health-care reform. The series of informal discussions sponsored by the committee afforded more witnesses an opportunity to participate, without the usual structure and formalities of a committee hearing. The absence of both required formal statements and adherence to time limits facilitated more opportunity for dialogue and discussion between witnesses and committee members. While the round table format has seen limited use thus far, it may be a harbinger of the future as congressional committees search for new and better ways to gather information.

§2.115 Committee Quorum Requirements

Congressional committees are required to have a quorum of their members present at a hearing to receive testimony. Under the general rules of each chamber, individual committees in both chambers are permitted to determine their own quorum rule determining the number of committee members required to be present for the committee to receive testimony from a witness. In the House of Representatives, under Rule XI, section (h) (2), each committee may set a quorum number not less than two. In the Senate, under Rule XXVI, paragraph 7(a)(2), each committee is authorized to set a quorum number that is less than the one-third requirement for almost all other committee business, essentially ensuring that one senator may take sworn and unsworn testimony.

In practice, committee member attendance at hearings will often consist of the bare minimum number to achieve a quorum, sometimes just the chair, or maybe the chair and one or two other members, depending on the committee, the nature of the hearing and its subject, and the witnesses involved. Many committees informally operate with only one member present at a hearing, but this practice may sometimes be subject to a challenge through a point of order by another committee member.

On the other hand, some hearings draw the entire committee membership or a large contingency on both sides of the political aisle. Staff of each congressional committee can provide specific quorum rules for their respective panel, as well as expectations for member attendance at a specific hearing. For more information and details on quorum requirements, see the rules of each chamber (<*rules.Senate.gov*> and <*rules.House.gov*>) and the rules for each committee, accessed through committee links available at <*www.Senate.gov*> and <*www.House.gov*>).

§2.116 Outside Witness Statements— Written Statements for the Record

In connection with hearings, congressional committees will usually invite or allow written statements for the record, typically called outside witness statements, to be submitted by individuals or organizations who do not have the opportunity to appear in person to testify orally at a hearing, but who wish to add to the record of the committee's hearing concerning a particular issue. These documents are essentially written statements that will be included in the written transcript of a hearing just as oral testimony will be included. This procedure allows a committee to invite, solicit, and benefit from statements that provide input to the committee from a wide array of organizations from whom the committee would or might not otherwise be able to hear.

Conversely, outside witness statements also give outside organizations a chance to weigh in on the topic of the hearing by providing a written statement without having to appear in person to testify before a committee. Prior to a hearing or series of hearings, committees will invite outside witness statements if they choose, and establish deadlines for submission and format guidelines for the written statements. The rules and policies of a committee generally govern this opportunity to provide input to the committee, so anyone interested in submitting an outside witness statement should contact the staff of the committee sponsoring the hearing to determine whether a statement is an option, and, if so, what are the specific rules for submission of the statement, such as length, format, and due date.

§2.117 Sample of Committee Guidelines Regarding Outside Witness Statements

Senate Appropriations Subcommittee on Transportation, Housing and Urban Development, and Related Agencies

Outside Witness Testimony Instructions

FY 2010 Appropriations

GUIDELINES

Format:

Testimony (and supporting material) should be a maximum of four (4) pages, on 8½ x 11 paper, single sided, single spaced, and have a 1" margin. Do not include a cover page. At the top of the first page list the name of the organization submitting testimony, the subcommittee for which the testimony has been prepared, and the Department and/or Agency the testimony is addressing.

Delivery:

Please e-mail testimony to Tranhud@appro.senate.gov with the subject line "OWT." We will only accept testimony formatted in Word Perfect and Microsoft word. Please DO NOT SEND PDF files. Electronic submission only, testimony sent via the US mail or by Fax will not be accepted. Include contact information (phone, fax, e-mail, and address).

Deadline:

All material must be received no later than Monday, May 25, 2009. This deadline will be strictly enforced.

Thank you.

Subcommittee on Transportation, Housing
and Urban Development, and Related Agencies
Committee on Appropriations
United States Senate, SD-131
Washington, DC 20510
202-224-7281

Source: U.S. Senate Appropriations Subcommittee on Transportation, Housing and Urban Development, and Related Agencies.

For more information on written statements and testimony, see Chapter 3, "Preparation of Written Testimony," especially § 3.35, Written vs. Oral Testimony: When Written Witness Statements Suffice; and § 3.36, Purpose of Written-Only Witness Statements.

§2.118 Forms of Address—Use of Titles for Committee Members and Staff

In a congressional committee hearing context, committee leadership, members and staff should be recognized and addressed according to their official titles. A male chair should be referred to as Mr. Chairman. A female chair should be addressed as Madam Chair, Madam Chairman, or Madam Chairwoman, as she prefers. The ranking minority member may be referred to as the Ranking Minority Member or as Senator, Representative, or Congressman/woman, depending on the committee's chamber. Members of a Senate committee should be addressed as Senator, and members of a House committee should be recognized as Representative, Congressman, or Congresswoman. References to committee professional staff and other officials in the hearing room might include Committee Chief Counsel (for the majority and minority), Professional Staff Member, Clerk, Hearing Reporter, and Guard. References to the committee as a body should be to the committee by its official name.

§2.119 Behavior and Decorum in a Committee Hearing

Congressional committees have an expectation of professional, polite, and courteous behavior by all participants and attendees at a hearing. With a constant eye on hearing room decorum, the chair presides over a hearing, and is responsible for keeping the proceedings of a hearing orderly and dignified. If there is an incident of bad behavior by a witness or anyone else in a hearing room, the chair may address those persons to stop or correct the behavior, and, when deemed necessary, may further enlist the assistance of Capitol Hill police officers to escort the offending individuals from the hearing room.

House, Senate, and committee rules set out standards for behavior and decorum, as well as remedies available to the chair and committee on those occasions when an individual is unruly, disruptive, or uncooperative. House Rules give a committee chair the authority to ". . . punish breaches of order and decorum, and of the professional ethics on the part of counsel, by censure and exclusion from the hearings; and the committee may cite the offender to the House for contempt." (House Rule XI, Hearing Procedures, clause 2 (k)(4).)

Senate Rules provide that, "Whenever disorder arises during a committee meeting that is open to the public, or any demonstration of approval or disapproval is indulged in by any person in attendance at any such meeting, it shall be the duty of the Chair to enforce order on his own initiative and without any point of order being made by a Senator. When the Chair finds it necessary to maintain order, he shall have the power to clear the room, and the committee may act in closed session for so long as there is doubt of the assurance of order." (Senate Rule XXVI, clause 5 (d).) In extreme cases where criminal behavior is apparent or suspected, Capitol Hill police officers are empowered to arrest the suspected individuals.

To access the complete rules of the House and Senate, go to <*rules.House.gov*> and <*rules.Senate.gov*>.

§2.120 HITS: Humor in Testimony—H. Ross Perot

Humor is part of human nature, and like any human institution, congressional committee hearings have their fair share of humorous and comedic moments. Consider excerpts from the testimony and exchanges in a 1993 hearing of the Joint Committee on the Organization of Congress that featured as a witness H. Ross Perot. (*<www.archive.org/stream/operationsofcongrp1993unit/>*.)

Operations Of The Congress: Testimony Of H. Ross Perot

****

Mr. Perot. I cannot overemphasize how critical our financial situation is. We are $4 trillion in debt. Just to put it in perspective, we have gone $130 billion more into debt since election day. Time is critical. Our current annual increase in the national debt exceeds the cost to fight and win World War II. That should help the ordinary citizen to understand the size of the growth of the debt. All ordinary income taxes paid by people west of the Mississippi are used just to pay the interest on the debt.

The magnitude of the debt was not discussed in prior political campaigns. It was in this last campaign. I used to refer to it as a crazy aunt we kept in the basement. All the neighbors knew she was there, but nobody ever talked about her.

She was out of the basement all during the campaign. I think she went to the Inaugural Ball this time.

[Laughter.]

****

Mr. Perot. They want the President to have a line item veto. I know that is controversial with Congress, but there are a few reasons. Number one, there is a lot of pork. Number two, it gives him a chance to get rid of it. Number three, it gives us a chance to see if he does get rid of it.

The one thing I will promise you all is a program called Pork of the Month where we will get into this stuff as long as it lives so that it will not be dead and buried because our people across the country—and there are millions of them who have come together—feel very strongly that every single penny—and this is an important point. The people keep track of their pennies. They get really nervous when we round off to the nearest $50 billion here in Washington, DC.

[Laughter.]

****

Mr. Perot. Again, I am not a lawyer, so we get a good lawyer to figure out how to do this and do it constitutionally. But my suggestion as a layman—we would obviously have to talk to lawyers—would be to prohibit any foreign individual or company from hiring Americans to lobby or directly or indirectly influence our Government.

We are back to money. If a foreign company has a problem in our country and they need to talk to Commerce or they need to talk to trade negotiators, there should be all sorts of avenues for them, but it shouldn't be by buying influence. One country spent $400 million lobbying in 1988, more than the next 12 countries combined. And they had a good year.

[Laughter.]

****

Mr. Dreier. I will look forward to getting into it further.

I wanted to raise the issue of this budget which has been submitted to us just briefly. I saw in your testimony that you said in referring to the American people, "They absolutely do not want tax and spending programs first with only the possibility of cuts and savings at a later time."

In 1981 and 1982, as we looked at the budget that came before us, there were $3 in spending cuts for every $1 in taxes increased. We all know what happened. We got the $98.5 billion tax increase and we're still waiting for those spending cuts. We have heard this was two for one. You wisely point out a $1.83 disparity from the 1990 budget summit is actually $2.37 in spending increases for every $1.

Mr. Perot. When you're from Texas, you always understate everything.

Mr. Dreier. And we in California have a tendency to exaggerate.

[Laughter.]

****

Chairman Boren. It is not coincidental that the Political Action Committees give nine to one to sitting incumbents versus challengers because they are the people whose doors they need to open to come in to see to talk about legislation. No wonder, then, the people have the perception that we don't listen to all the American people equally.

As they say in some media programs, I am going to give Senator Cohen the final word, after which point we will stand in recess.

Senator Cohen. Thank you very much, Mr. Chairman.

As one of the new Founding Fathers—

[Laughter.]

Senator Cohen. Let me assure Mr. Dreier that while the House may have a Rules Committee which is much more efficient, the Senate does have a far greater sense of equity to allow the kind of bipartisanship displayed on this committee than does the House. Perhaps that is one of the reasons why so many House Members are eager to move to the Senate so that they can then operate under the aegis of Senator Boren.

[Laughter.]

Source: S. Hrg. 103-15, Joint Committee on the Organization of Congress, Operations of the Congress: Testimony of H. Ross Perot, March 2, 1993. (Full transcript of hearing available through the U.S. Government Printing Office Superintendent of Documents, Mail Stop: SSOP, Washington, DC 20402-9328; ISBN 0-16-040618-8.)

§2.999 Chapter Summary

- A congressional committee and its agenda drive the organization, planning and preparation for a committee hearing. (§ 2.0)
- The organization, planning, and preparation of a hearing by a congressional committee include a number of administrative and substantive activities that are usually carried out by a committee's professional staff. (§ 2.1)
- Congressional hearing organization, planning, and preparation by a witness entail working with the committee staff, following committee rules and guidelines, providing the committee with a number of key written documents, and rehearsing for the delivery of oral testimony before the committee. (§ 2.2)
- Rules of the House of Representatives, the Senate, and individual committees in both chambers set out guidelines and requirements for the conduct and preparation of congressional committee hearings. (§ 2.3; § 2.4; § 2.5; § 2.6)
- Witnesses are required by House, Senate, and committee rules and policies—including "Truth-in-Testimony" rules—to provide committees with advanced copies of witness statements and other related written information. (§ 2.7)
- Congressional committee staff prepare briefing materials for the committee chair and members. Included in a briefing book or folder are copies of witness statements, introductory remarks, prepared questions, and other information about the hearing topic and the witnesses. (§ 2.8)
- Congressional committees are required to provide public notice of committee hearings, including time, date, location, and subject matter. (§ 2.9)
- Within the Capitol complex, there are numerous Senate and House committee hearing rooms that vary in shape, size, and style. (§ 2.10; § 2.11; § 2.12)
- The perspectives of a congressional expert underscore the importance of proper hearing organization, preparation and planning. (§ 2.13)
- From both a committee's and a witness's perspective, there are many essential elements of an effective and successful hearing, including the edification of the committee members, helpful testimony from witnesses, and the making of a thorough hearing record. (§ 2.14; § 2.15; § 2.16)
- In preparation for a congressional hearing, key threshold questions for a witness to consider include the purpose, occasion, and type of hearing; the witnesses' roles; and the questions that may be asked by the committee. (§ 2.17)
- From both a committee's and a witness's perspective, there are several essential elements of effective congressional testimony, including a well-written statement, professionally delivered oral testimony, and responsive answers by a witness to questions posed by a committee. (§ 2.18; § 2.19; § 2.20)
- To be selected as a witness to testify at a congressional hearing, an individual or organization must be invited by the committee sponsoring the hearing under one of the several methods to assist in this process. (§ 2.21)

1) Committees have the authority to invite anyone they wish to testify at a hearing. A formal invitation from a committee, usually in the form of a letter, is almost always a requirement. (§ 2.22 and § 2.23)
2) Some witnesses are invited to testify by virtue of a role or position they hold in government or the private sector. (§ 2.24)
3) Anyone wishing to testify before a congressional hearing may offer to do so by contacting the committee conducting the hearing, although there is no guarantee that an invitation will be extended. (§ 2.25)
4) Committees will sometimes request or consider recommendations from organizations or individuals for names of potential witnesses to testify at a hearing. (§ 2.26)
5) When an invited witness refuses to appear to testify before a congressional committee hearing, or when a committee chooses to require an appearance in lieu of issuing an invitation, committees are empowered to issue a subpoena compelling an appearance before the committee. (§ 2.27)

- There are several categories of witnesses who tend to be called to testify, including government officials, business leaders, public-interest organization representatives, and issue stakeholders. (§ 2.30)
  1) Federal Executive, Legislative and Judicial Branch Officials (§ 2.31)
  2) Corporate, Business, and Association Representatives (§ 2.32)
  3) Non-Profit, Non-Governmental (NGO), Private and Voluntary (PVO), Public Interest and Advocacy Groups and Coalitions (§ 2.33)
  4) State and Local Government Officials (§ 2.34)
  5) Citizens, Federal Program Participants, and End Users (§ 2.35)
  6) Government and Private Sector Experts and Research Organizations (§ 2.36)
  7) Witnesses Representing Special Geographic, State, and Congressional District Concerns and Perspectives (§ 2.37)
  8) Use of Celebrity Witnesses (§ 2.38)
  9) Testifying as a Result of a Committee Subpoena (§ 2.39 and § 2.40)
- In some cases, congressional committees authorize committee staff members to depose potential or scheduled witnesses prior to a committee hearing. (§ 2.50)
- Congressional committees have the authority to place witnesses under oath to make their oral statements sworn testimony. (§ 2.51)
- Witnesses who appear before a congressional committee to testify are afforded basic rights and protections under the U.S. Constitution, as well as under Senate, House, and committee rules. (§ 2.52)
- Subject to House and Senate rules, witnesses generally are entitled to legal counsel and representation prior to, during, and after a congressional hearing. (§ 2.53)

- A wide array of individuals and participants constitute the key "players" in any congressional committee hearing. (§ 2.60)
  1) Committee Chair (§ 2.61)
  2) Ranking Minority Member (§ 2.62)
  3) Congressional Committee Members (§ 2.63)
  4) Congressional Committee Professional Staff (§ 2.64)
  5) Non-Committee Members of Congress and Staff (§ 2.65)
  6) Witnesses (§ 2.66)
  7) Witness Support Teams (§ 2.67)
  8) Federal Departments and Agencies (§ 2.68)
  9) The Media (§ 2.69)
  10) Interest Groups, Nonprofits, Non-Governmental Organizations (NGOs), Private and Voluntary Organizations (PVOs), and Other Stakeholders (§ 2.70)
  11) The General Public (§ 2.71)
  12) Official Hearing Reporter and Other Official Administrative Personnel (§ 2.72)
- A witness's targeted audiences in a congressional committee hearing are primarily the committee itself, followed by secondary targets such as federal agencies, the media, private organizations, and the general public. (§ 2.80)
- The regular order, format, and procedural conduct of a congressional committee hearing are determined by the committee holding the hearing, and generally include a number of standard practices and operations. (§ 2.90)
  1) Role of the Chair (§ 2.91)
  2) Opening Statements by Committee Members (§ 2.92)
  3) Format for Witness Testimony (§ 2.93)
  4) Use of Witness Panels (§ 2.94)
  5) Oral Testimony by Witnesses (§ 2.95)
  6) Time Limits for Testimony (§ 2.96)
  7) Committee Members' Questions and Witnesses' Responses (§ 2.97)
  8) Order of Questioning Witnesses (§ 2.98)
  9) Open and Closed Hearings (§ 2.99)
  10) Participation by Non-Committee Members of Congress and Committee Staff (§ 2.100)
  11) Committee Hearing Conclusion and Wrap-up (§ 2.101)
  12) Committee Post-Hearing Follow-up and Expectations (§ 2.102)
- Questions for the chair and members of a congressional committee are prepared by staff for the purpose of engaging witnesses in a question-and-answer period following the delivery of testimony. (§ 2.111)

- Congressional hearings are scheduled by committees as needed and in concert with the general schedules of the House and Senate. (§ 2.112 and § 2.113)
- In addition to the traditional hearing format and venue, congressional committees occasionally conduct joint hearings and use modern techniques such as high-tech communications and informal discussions with witnesses. (§ 2.114)
- Congressional committees are subject to rules requiring a certain number of committee members to be present at a hearing to constitute a quorum. (§ 2.115)
- Committees often invite outside organizations to submit written statements for the hearing record in lieu of appearing personally to testify. (§ 2.116 and § 2.117)
- Certain forms of address or titles are preferred when addressing congressional committee members and staff. (§ 2.118)
- Congressional committees conduct hearings, and expect witnesses to comport themselves, according to standard norms of behavior and decorum, and they are empowered to deal with unruly and disruptive situations. (§ 2.119)
- HITS: Humor in Testimony—Like any human institution, congressional committee hearings have moments of comic relief and humorous testimony, especially when Ross Perot makes an appearance to testify. (§ 2.120)

Chapter Three

Preparation of Written Testimony

Chapter Three

Section

Summary Table of Contents

§3.0 Introduction and Overview

Written congressional testimony, known also as a written statement, is the official written document representing a witness's prepared testimony for a congressional committee in conjunction with a formal hearing on a certain topic or issue. The preparation of well-drafted, informative, and compelling written testimony in advance of a congressional committee hearing is a critical ingredient in the success formula for any hearing, both from the perspective of a committee and a witness. Well-written testimony lays out the case and message a witness brings to the committee, and provides a sound foundation for a witness's oral testimony. Typically, a written witness statement serves as the basis for a witness's oral presentation, which is usually a shortened summary of the written statement.

Excellence in the preparation of a written statement is paramount because high-quality written testimony serves as the basic witness document for a hearing, makes the public record of the witness's position before the committee, and generally serves as a lynchpin for everything that follows—oral testimony by the witness, questions from the committee, and post-hearing follow-up matters. Written statements of witnesses are routinely distributed to a wide array of audiences beyond the committee holding the hearing, including other members of Congress, congressional staff, the media, private sector interests, public interest organizations, and the general public.

Those involved in the drafting of written testimony or a written statement should carefully attend to the highest standards of excellent writing, including the elements of thoughtful preparation and research, a substantive case and content that provide both education and advocacy, and proper style, layout, format, syntax, and grammar.

This chapter covers the vital aspects of preparing effective written testimony, and explains the nature, differences, and importance of both written and oral testimony. It discusses methodologies, approaches, and preparatory tools and perspectives, and it describes several important documents for consideration and use in developing the written statement. The chapter outlines the basic manuscript components, format, and layout of a written statement, and provides several samples of actual statements submitted to congressional committees. It also provides suggestions on building a strong substantive case and developing compelling arguments in both written and oral testimony.

§3.2 Written Goal Statement and Thesis: Getting Started with the Basic Theme

To crystallize and focus on the basic theme and subject matter of written testimony, statement preparers are wise to develop a written goal statement and thesis, much as is often done in preparing for a research paper or project. A goal statement can be as simple as one or two sentences that state the essence of the message to be conveyed in the testimony. Similarly, a thesis can be a few sentences or bullet points that capture the basic direction of the testimony.

§3.1 Congressional Committee Staff Perspective on the Importance of Drafting an Effective, Informative, and Compelling Witness Statement

"Written testimony is an opportunity for advocates (public or private) to gain a foothold in the official record and to explain the position they wish to advance clearly and wholly from their perspective. Unlike a live hearing setting, where interruptions from members are possible and trains of thought can be derailed, a cogent and properly articulated written statement is the one vehicle in which the totality of a position can be laid out in the order best designed to promote a logical explanation to and persuasion of the intended audience, usually Committee staff or other individuals who will play a role in the final crafting of legislation. Therefore, it is of extreme importance that any written statements be crafted in an effective and highly efficient form that will capture the interest of the reader, be brief enough to not overly consume staff's limited time, and contain a logical and persuasive argument sufficient to achieve the desired outcome."

Source: Galen Fountain, Esq., Staff Director and Professional Staff Member, United States Senate Appropriations Subcommittee on Agriculture, Rural Development, Food and Drug Administration, and Related Agencies.

Using one or both devices helps a writer identify and describe the basic theme of the testimony. In most cases, preparers and writers have a goal statement and thesis in mind, but it is helpful to reduce them to writing to induce creative thought and to stay on script. They do not need to be formal by any means, and they are basically a personal tool to help guide and keep the writer on course. Once a well-thought-out goal statement and thesis are in place, they can be used as a measure or standard for content in the actual statement, with an eye on ensuring that anything written in the statement supports the basic theme, goal statement, and thesis of the testimony.

In the preparation of witness testimony, developing a written goal statement and thesis is essentially answering a key, two-part, threshold question: "What is the basic goal of the witness statement, and what should be the thesis and theme of its content?" (For examples, see § 3.3, Sample Goal Statement, Thesis, and Theme.)

§3.3 Sample Goal Statement, Thesis, and Theme

Below are samples of a goal statement, a thesis, and a theme. To review the text of the written statement which these samples support, see § 3.31, Sample of Written Statements—Statement Prepared for House Appropriations Subcommittee on Transportation in Support of Federal Funding for Clean Air Research.

- **Sample goal statement:** The Central California Ozone Study (CCOS) Coalition needs and requests $500,000 from the Department of Transportation (DOT) to conduct vital research on the sources of ozone air pollution so the state can comply with federal clean air standards.
- **Sample thesis:** With adequate support from the federal government, CCOS is in a position to help better understand the nature of the ozone problem across the central California region, thus providing a strong scientific foundation for preparing the next round of state and federal attainment plans.
- **Resulting basic theme:** The Central California Ozone Study (CCOS) is designed to enable central California to meet Clean Air Act requirements for ozone State Implementation Plans (SIPs), as well as to advance fundamental science for use nationwide. For fiscal year 2004, our coalition is seeking funding of $500,000 from DOT through highway research funds. DOT is a key stakeholder because federal law requires that transportation plans be in conformity with SIPS. Determining the emission and air quality impacts of motor vehicles is a major part of the CCOS effort.

§3.4 Methodology and Approach: Managing the Preparation Stage

At an early stage in the preparation of witness testimony, the writer should determine the methodology and approach to be used in managing the statement preparation process and in proceeding to the actual drafting. All good writers develop and have their own methodology and approach to producing a quality written product. Those preparing witness testimony and statements should do likewise. Whether the task at hand is a solo project for a writer or will entail a team of colleagues, managing the preparation stage of witness statement production is an important enterprise that deserves thought and attention.

Those preparing witness testimony will find the task much easier and streamlined, with a much higher quality end-product, if there is a sense of organization and methodology to the process, rather than approaching the project like a last-minute term paper or proceeding helter-skelter. While individual styles and approaches vary widely, it is prudent to have a sense of direction and leadership that should ideally be provided by a principal writer or a team leader.

Methodology and approach, in their simplest forms, are really just figuring out how to get one's hands around the project or task at hand, in this case the writing of a witness statement. Many federal agencies and private organizations have protocols, practices, and policies in place to deal with the preparation of written testimony. Some organizations approach the preparation of testimony on a case-by-case basis. For purposes of developing or sharpening a witness's statement, the succeeding sections suggest a variety of checklist steps, tools, and processes that should be helpful in any approach to drafting a superb written statement.

§3.5 Liaison with Committee Staff: Building a Good Working Relationship

One of the key first steps in approaching the preparation of a witness statement is working closely with the professional staff of the committee holding the hearing. Preparers of testimony ideally should have direct communication with the staff person responsible for organizing the hearing or for providing liaison with witnesses. It is preferable to meet with that staff person, if possible, to establish a good working relationship, to gain a full understanding of the hearing's purpose and what is expected of the witness, and to learn about the committee's rules and guidelines for witness statements. Committee staff are usually very willing to be helpful to witnesses and preparers of witness statements to help ensure the best possible written product for the committee's use. A witness, the statement preparer, or the witness's organization should have an established relationship with committee staff, or should develop one.

§3.6 Adherence to Committee Instructions, Rules, Format, Expectations, and Culture

Preparation of witness testimony demands adherence on the part of both the witness and the preparer of written testimony to a committee's rules, guidelines, and instructions with respect to the production and advanced transmittal of a written statement. Chamber and committee rules should be consulted to ensure compliance with basic instructions. Committees usually have guidelines for witness and statement preparation posted on the committee web site or available in print copy by request or accompanying the letter of invitation to testify. Witnesses and preparers are also well-served by gaining an understanding of a committee's culture, agenda, and expectations through meetings and discussions with committee staff and others who know the committee well. To access chamber rules, go to *<rules.House.gov>* and *<rules.Senate.gov>*. To see individual committee rules, go to *<www.House.gov>* and *<www.Senate.gov>* to access links that will take you to individual committee sites and rules.

§3.7 Research and Sources of Information

The research phase of preparation for the writing of a witness statement is intended to answer very basic questions: What information does the writer need to craft the statement, and what sources will be necessary to provide that information?

As with most writing projects, preparation of a quality witness statement requires good, solid research on the issue that is the topic of the hearing, and on the position and approach to be advocated or discussed in the testimony. This research can be basic or applied, formal or informal, as need dictates. However, it is important that the witness and the preparer of the statement operate from a strong position of knowledge and understanding of the issue to ensure the excellence of the content and quality of the witness statement.

To develop the body of information needed to provide a foundation for writing the statement, the preparer should consult whatever internal and external sources are available and necessary. In many cases, the organization itself will have a research office or function that can provide the requisite information. Sometimes original research is required, whether basic and long-term in nature or more applied and short-term. Anecdotal evidence and information quite often will provide an adequate base of information, while other situations require the collection and analysis of data, the use of questionnaires or interviews, or a review of available targeted literature and web sites.

Most witnesses who testify are making an appearance on behalf of an organization or institution that typically has an existing base of information available for use in preparing a witness statement. However, when there is limited or a shortage of available research, information or data, preparers may have to utilize traditional approaches to research, as well as contemporary search engine methods on the Internet.

For a complete discussion of research and reference advice, techniques, information and resources, see *Real World Research Skills: An Introduction to Factual, International, Judicial, Legislative, and Regulatory Research*, Peggy Garvin, The Capitol.Net.

§3.8 Issue Analysis and Topic Outline

Once a goal statement and thesis have been developed, and appropriate research has been conducted, the key issues to be covered in written testimony should be analyzed and outlined. The writer should review the research materials and other information available about the issues, analyze that information for the basic salient points, and draft an issue or topic outline that lays out the essential points to be covered in the witness statement. This process and the written outline itself do not have to be formal in nature. They are essentially preparatory tools intended to be helpful to the person drafting the statement. The outline may be in a topic outline, brief narrative/full-sentence notations, bullet-point format, or any style or outline format that is comfortable and workable for the writer. The point is to reduce to writing the basic elements that will comprise the substantive content of the witness statement.

§3.9 Political Analysis and Landscape

Because witness testimony is presented to a congressional committee in the context of the consideration of public policy issues, a witness and a preparer of a witness statement should conduct a political analysis of the issues at hand and have a firm understanding of the political landscape in which the hearing and the testimony are taking place. This type of analysis does not require consultation with political consultants or government experts, but, rather, it entails gaining an understanding of the various political perspectives on the topic of the hearing and the subject matter of the witness statement.

Witnesses and statement writers should determine what, if any, positions or opinions have been expressed on the subject matter by both political parties in each house of Congress, as well as by the White House, the Office of Management and Budget (OMB), and the federal department or agency with jurisdiction over the subject matter. It is important to know if various congressional committees have staked out positions on the issue or have begun their own hearings or review. Answers need to be determined to questions such as whether the topic has been the subject of recent media coverage, political commentary, and debate in any quarter of government, especially if the topic is controversial or has the possibility of becoming controversial.

Conducting a thorough and candid assessment of any political impact on, or political implications involving, the key issue of a hearing and the subject matter of a witness statement will afford the statement writer the opportunity to factor in that vital intelligence in the development of the witness statement and the framing of the witness's approach and position.

For more information on partisanship and political analysis, see § 1.32, Partisanship and Political Analysis: Where Policy and Politics Converge; § 5.11, Recognizing and Understanding Partisanship; and § 6.25, Dealing with Partisanship and Political or Policy Agendas.

§3.10 Issue Context and Stakeholders

Before writing the first word of a witness statement, the writer should gain a full understanding of both the issue context and the stakeholders involved. Determining upfront the context in which an issue is being considered or discussed by a committee is vital to a complete understanding of how a witness's statement will fit into the hearing scenario. Is the issue at hand a "hot-button" topic in the media? Or is the subject matter rather routine?

Similarly, it is important for a witness and author of a witness statement to understand the various stakeholders involved in the issue or topic of the hearing. Stakeholders are basically those individuals and organizations that care about an issue, one way or another. They may "drive" the issue, as decision-makers in Congress do, or they may derive benefit or detriment from the outcome or results of the issue and its application, as federal program participants, regulated industry, or end-users of federal laws and regulations. Identifying and analyzing the key players who have a stake in an issue are important steps in understanding the complete picture surrounding an issue. Information gleaned from a stakeholder analysis can be very helpful to a witness and statement writer in formulating an incisive witness statement.

§3.11 Opposition Research

Knowing the thinking and position of opponents on an issue in the public policy arena can be very helpful to a witness and statement writer in understanding the entire picture surrounding the topic, and can also help define and sharpen the witness's position and approach. Researching the writings, web sites, hearing statements, media reports, industry information and any other available sources in print or online can provide helpful intelligence for use in producing a witness statement.

These are the operative questions regarding opposition research: "What is the other side's position on the issue, and how is it being communicated?" With the answers to these questions, a statement writer can incorporate perspectives and responses that would otherwise go unknown and unmentioned.

§3.12 Analysis and Targeting of the Committee and Audiences

Before commencing a draft of a witness statement, the writer should identify the appropriate targeted audiences of the witness testimony, including first and foremost the committee itself, and then analyze those audiences to ensure that the statement is properly focused and directed toward the intended audiences.

The operative questions for the witness and statement author should be, "What and who are the rightful targeted audiences of the witness's testimony?" and "How should the witness statement be crafted to ensure the most compelling message is delivered to those audiences?"

Since the committee is usually the prime target and audience of witness testimony, a formal statement should be drafted with a thorough understanding of the committee's focus and needs; the current political environment surrounding the issue; and the need to provide the committee with accurate and helpful information representing the perspectives of the witness. Witnesses and statement drafters should carefully consider the purpose and type of hearing being conducted; other stakeholders including fellow witnesses; the politics of the hearing subject matter; the existence of any current law or proposed legislation on the topic of the hearing; and any current or timely circumstances that might have a bearing on the issue of the hearing.

A witness and the statement drafter should study the composition of the committee holding the hearing, and gain an understanding of the backgrounds, experiences, and interests of each member in order to know whether there are any special connections to the subject matter of the hearing and the witness's testimony. A witness and statement author should also review other potential audiences intended by the witness as recipients of the message in the witness's testimony. These audiences can include other members of Congress, executive branch departments and agencies, the private business sector, public-interest organizations, the media, and the general public.

For more information, see § 2.80, The Targeted Audiences of a Witness's Testimony; § 4.14, Focusing the Witness on Targeted Audiences; § 5.42, Focus on the Primary Targeted Audience—the Committee; and § 6.33, Focusing on the Questioner during Questions and Answers.

§3.13 Important Documents: Drafting the Statement and Making the Record—A "Road Map"

In the enterprise of writing a substantive and powerful witness statement, there are several documents that can be drafted to:

1) support the ultimate statement and final product;

2) help define and build the case for the issue that is the subject of the statement; and

3) use the basic statement information for related purposes in creating other documents.

These documents, and the approach and activities necessary to produce them, can constitute for the statement author an outline or a "road map" for the enterprise of crafting written testimony and related materials:

- Goal statement, thesis and general theme for the statement (see § 3.2 and § 3.3);
- Methodology and approach (see § 3.4);
- Liaison with committee staff and rules (see § 3.5 and § 3.6);
- Research needs (see § 3.7);
- Analyses of the issue (see § 3.8), political landscape (see § 3.9), stakeholders (see § 3.10), opposition positions (see § 3.11), and targeted audiences (see § 3.12);
- Topic outline draft (see § 3.8);
- Basic script draft (see § 3.14);
- Final statement for the record (see § 3.17); and
- Other documents as may be deemed helpful and necessary (see § 3.14 through § 3.22 for information and guidance on the writing of basic documents).

§3.14 Important Documents: Drafting the Statement and Making the Record—Basic Script: The Essence of the Witness Statement's Case and Content

The basic script is intended to reflect the complete essence of the content of the statement and the case or message to be conveyed to a committee by a witness. Preferably using a topic outline as a guide, the statement writer's first serious drafting exercise is to develop the basic script for the witness statement—an original cut of a draft statement that includes all the elements and information developed and gathered during the earlier preparation, research, and analysis phases.

This first draft of a statement is typically rough in nature, in that while it basically incorporates all the ingredients to make the statement whole, informative, and compelling, the actual writing may still be raw, and much of the content may need reordering and considerable editing. It is important at this stage to develop a comprehensive statement that captures all the aspects of the purpose, theme, and message of the witness's testimony and reason to be appearing before a committee. While certainly relying on research and other information for basic text, the writing exercise can often be almost "free think" and "stream of consciousness" in nature, allowing the writer to cover all the important angles without regard at that moment to what a final product will look like. Refining and editing the statement will follow in time.

§3.15 Important Documents: Drafting the Statement and Making the Record—The "White Paper": The Complete Case Supporting the Witness Statement and Its Message

While not an absolute requirement of a witness statement drafting enterprise, the development of a longer "white paper" has a number of benefits that can assist the witness statement author in the production of the actual testimony and a number of other related documents. In fact, some witness statement writers utilize a "white paper" approach in lieu of preparing a topic outline, and simply draw information from the expanded work to draft the actual final product witness statement.

This more comprehensive document provides an opportunity to collect all the research, analysis, education, and advocacy related to the testimony statement preparation in one major writing. The "white paper" can be a valuable stand-alone tool to provide to congressional committees and others who are interested in reading more detail than is included in the actual witness statement. In most cases, the "white paper" not only includes all the information and content that will be included in the final formal witness statement, it also often serves as a reserve or library for the totality of vital issue material and information that can be tapped in the development of other documents such as executive summaries, media and staff backgrounders, presentation talking points, correspondence, briefing books and materials, question-and-answer modules, and press releases.

§3.16 Important Documents: Drafting the Statement and Making the Record—Executive Summary and the Famous One-Pager

There is a long-standing saying on Capitol Hill that if you really want to get a congressional staffer's attention, provide her or him with a one-page summary of your issue, not a long dissertation. The famous one-pager concept stems from the need for congressional staff to be able to read and digest a lot of material about a lot of different issues in a short period of time. The one-pager provides a digest or abstract that serves the purposes of brevity and succinctness, and also conveys a basic theme or message. The business world knows the one-pager as an executive summary.

Whether it is called a one-pager or executive summary, this document is valuable in providing congressional staff and others with a quick-hit amount of information about an important topic. In the congressional hearings world, and particularly related to witness testimony, committees often request or expect such a document to be provided by a witness in order for the staff to include the document in committee members' briefing books or materials, as well as to be able to use it as a guide and reference regarding a witness's anticipated statement before the committee.

Some statement authors develop a one-pager or executive summary directly from a written topic outline produced early in the statement preparation process. Others draw a one-pager from the content of a basic statement script or a "white paper." Unless requested or required by a committee, the one-pager is an optional document, but it can be helpful both in the development of a final formal statement and in serving as a stand-alone document that has multiple educational and advocacy applications. Some witnesses like to use a one-pager or topic outline as notes for the actual oral delivery of a witness statement before a committee.

To review a sample of an executive summary, see § 3.30, Sample of Written Statements—Statement Prepared for House Judiciary Subcommittee on Courts and Intellectual Property in Opposition to the Split of the 9th Circuit Court of Appeals.

§3.17 Important Documents: Drafting the Statement and Making the Record—Formal Statement for the Record: The Final Product

The formal witness statement is the one that counts—the writing that makes the record. It is the finished product. Because it will become part of the official record of a hearing, great care should be taken in its preparation to ensure a superb product with meaningful content, correct format and layout, proper grammar, and adherence to the rules and guidelines of the committee sponsoring the hearing.

Utilizing some combination of preliminary steps and documents undertaken and produced in preparation for the drafting of the formal statement, including the goal statement, thesis, theme, research, topic outline, basic script, and white paper, the statement writer should strive to craft a compelling document that includes the features of education and advocacy, and that targets both the topic of the hearing and the message and goal of the witness.

From the standpoint of content and substance, the statement should be replete with information that makes the witness's basic case before a committee on the particular topic of the hearing. Stylistically, the statement should comport with committee requirements regarding pagination, type, font, format and layout, margins, cover page, and length.

To review samples of actual formal statements, see § 3.29 through § 3.33.

§3.18 Important Documents: Drafting the Statement and Making the Record—Narrative, Outline, or Notes Used as Script for Oral Presentation

While subject to personal style, approach, and preferences, a written script for use by a witness in delivering the actual testimony is a very important and helpful document. This is the written document on the witness table in front of the witness from which the witness makes his or her oral statement to the committee. Some witnesses choose to use the actual formal written statement, and either read it outright or use it as an outline, perhaps with annotations or side notes, from which to deliver their oral testimony. Others prefer a reduced narrative, a topic outline, notes or bullet points to use as a script for their oral remarks to the committee. A topic outline can be in the form of numbered or bulleted items, or it can be an actual narrative that is the actual language the witness intends to read or, preferably, state to the committee in a conversational style.

Depending on individual style, a witness should decide which method is preferable, and then produce the appropriate written document to support that approach. In any case, the basic information to be included is readily available in the formal statement and other documents already prepared, so it is usually just a matter of organizing the material, making it flow thematically, and ensuring that it is both as complete as necessary while also being succinct, compelling, and to the point of the hearing.

With respect to best or preferred practices, it is highly recommended that a witness not read the official written statement or any other document, but, rather that a witness summarize the testimony orally with the help and use of a written script for reference, and within the prescribed time allowed by the committee.

The content of the document used to deliver oral testimony can differ substantially from the actual written statement presented to the committee in several ways, although the basic theme, goal, thesis, and content should remain the same in both. The script used at the hearing to present oral testimony should be only as long as the prescribed time for testifying allows. It should focus on a central theme, with supporting points, data and explanations, but not dwell on too many major points or too much detail. It should allow for a crisp, punchy, and informative presentation that is clearly and easily understood and grasped by the committee. Remember that the full written statement for the committee will be made part of the hearing record, in addition to the oral testimony of the witness, so the oral portion of testimony should concentrate on the big points and major elements of the case being made.

To ensure that the hearing script helps guide the witness to a stellar performance, there are several stylistic pointers that should be considered for inclusion in the actual script that are intended to help make the witness's testimony more effective, compelling and well-received.

- Ensure that the basic thematic message of the testimony is stated upfront through use of a headline statement encapsulating the basic message that is being conveyed to the committee. Highlight that theme in bold for quick and easy reference. So the witness can verbally underscore, bracket, label, or otherwise emphasize the theme by highlighting the importance and significance of the message, use key words and phrases, often known as "oral cues," such as "first," "primary," "main," "basic," "threshold," or "key" message or theme.
- So that the witness can lay down a marker of urgency, time sensitivity, or event relationships related to the theme and message of the testimony, use phrases or oral cues such as ". . . critical change is needed at this time . . . ," ". . . in response to a current crisis or recent event . . . ," ". . . the need for action stems directly from Congress's or an agency's deadline for follow-up . . . ," and ". . . to avert a major problem or avoid a negative result . . ."
- Relate the basic message or theme of the testimony to the timeliness of, and connection to, the committee's consideration of the issue or relevant legislation. Help the committee understand why the witness's message is important and applies directly to them and the committee's actions.
- Use the tactic of enumeration where possible throughout the testimony. This method of communication entails the use of numbers, counting off various points, and demonstrating numerical priority of issues in the testimony as they are being delivered, by using key phrases such as, "first and foremost . . . ," ". . . the next largest priority is . . . ," and ". . . the final key ingredient is . . ." Enumeration is a form of oral cue that is also a verbal marker or attention-getter. It helps convey information in manageable portions and "sound bites" through the use of the verbal punctuation of preceding a comment with a number or a term of priority reference, and thus aids in helping the committee members to hear, focus on, understand, and retain the basic message of a witness. It also conveys to the committee that a sound case is being made with a strong sense of organization and purpose. Be sure to write enumerated phrases into the script so that the witness can rely on them as oral cues and verbal markers during presentation of oral testimony.
- To support enumerated points that are made during oral testimony, a witness should employ the use of specifics such as examples, vignettes, data, anecdotes, best- and worst-case scenarios, and research results. These additional supporting facts amplify and bolster a key point being made in the testimony. Provide this valuable supporting information in the written script that the witness will use in delivering testimony, and be sure to highlight

or set them apart on the page for emphasis, ease in reference and reading, and impact on the committee.

- Sometimes it is also helpful to provide explanations of context, connections, and rationale for a point that is being made in the testimony. This additional supportive information makes the point more understandable to the committee, and allows the members to see the big picture on the one hand, or to drill down to an underpinning or foundation on the other hand. Be sure that this type of information is included in the script in a manner that is succinct and to the point for ease both in use by the witness and understanding by the committee.

To review an actual operational document utilized as the narrative script for delivery of oral testimony, see § 3.34, Sample of Oral Statement—Written Document Used as Reference to Deliver Oral Testimony.

For more information regarding witness preparation and use of an oral witness statement, see § 4.11, Preparation and Use of Oral Statement Script or Outline.

For information on the preferred manner of delivering testimony with use of a prepared document, see § 4.13, Delivering the Statement: To Read or Not to Read.

For information on rehearsing oral testimony by using a prepared script, see § 4.21, Witness Rehearsal of Oral Testimony and Answers to Questions—Relying on the Oral Statement Script to Deliver Testimony.

For information on using written text or script to delivery oral testimony at the actual hearing, see § 5.30, Organization and Use of Written Text to Deliver the Oral Testimony.

For a complete discussion of the presentation of oral testimony, see Chapter 5, "Presentation and Delivery of Oral Testimony."

§3.19 Important Documents: Drafting the Statement and Making the Record—The Briefing Book

While not directly related to the enterprise of writing the witness statement per se, production of a briefing book can be an important exercise in preparing for the hearing. A briefing book typically consists of any documents, research materials, and other information that may be helpful to a witness during a hearing. It is especially useful as a quick-reference tool during questioning by a committee.

If utilized, a briefing book usually is placed on the witness table in front, and perhaps a little to one side, of the witness for quick access and referral during the hearing. In addition to containing the basic documents, it can also include prepared answers to potential questions, lists and numbers, and other resources that need to be quickly accessible to a witness during a hearing, especially during the question-and-answer phase, but also on occasion during the testimony phase.

Having all the documents at hand at the witness table can be helpful on occasions when a committee member might inquire about a passage in the formal statement, a research or "white paper," or other materials provided earlier to the committee. Consequently, a witness should have ready access to any such materials during the hearing in order to be able to address questions or to provide clarifications. A tabbed briefing book provides a good system for cataloguing those items, and serves as a quick and easy reference system for a witness. Briefing books may include any number of documents that are easy-to-use references for the benefit of a witness, including FAQs and question modules. For more information on FAQs and question modules, see § 3.22, Important Documents: Drafting the Statement and Making the Record—FAQs and Question Modules.

For more information on the briefing book and its use, see § 4.23, Witness Rehearsal of Oral Testimony and Answers to Questions—Operating with the Use of a Briefing Book; § 5.33, Organization and Use of Prepared Written Support Materials; § 6.21, Preparing Answers in Advance to Expected or Anticipated Questions; and § 6.34, Witness Use of a Briefing Book to Answer Committee Questions.

§3.20 Important Documents: Drafting the Statement and Making the Record—Background Information for Congressional Committees and Staff

Utilizing the various written materials already prepared for a witness to use at a congressional hearing, a witness or those in charge of writing documents may also wish to produce issue papers, information sheets, and other background materials for the congressional committee and staff, whether requested or unsolicited. These materials should be easy to produce because the basic content is already prepared and available in other documents. These background materials on specific aspects of the testimony or other issues can be helpful to a committee, and their preparation and presentation to a committee before or after a hearing connote a sense of professionalism and thorough preparation on the part of a witness.

§3.21 Important Documents: Drafting the Statement and Making the Record—Media Advisories, Press Kits, Backgrounders, and Releases

Similar to the documents discussed in § 3.20 above, a witness or those in charge of writing documents for a hearing may wish to prepare various written materials for the media, including media advisories, press kits, issue backgrounders, and press releases. These informative materials should be easy to produce because the basic substance and content are available in other documents that have already been produced. The author need only reformat the materials to suit the particular need and purpose of the materials that will be directed toward print and broadcast journalists. These materials can be very helpful to the media as they attempt to understand and report a hearing and its topic, and the preparation of these informative documents for the media provides a witness and his or her organization with opportunities to publicize the organization and its position on issues discussed at a hearing.

Media and press materials, especially in briefing format, can also be very helpful to a witness who may face media inquiries before or after a hearing. It is always possible that a witness may experience an "ambush interview" when it is least expected.

For more information on media participation in hearings, see § 2.69, Congressional Hearing Participants: The "Players"—The Media.

For information on preparation of a witness to deal with the media, see § 4.41, Witness Contact with the Media.

For thorough coverage and discussion of media relations and media-related aspects of public appearances, consult *Media Relations Handbook for Agencies, Associations, Nonprofits and Congress*, Bradford Fitch, The Capitol.Net.

§3.22 Important Documents: Drafting the Statement and Making the Record—FAQs and Question Modules

It is sometimes helpful for a witness or those preparing written materials for a hearing to produce scripted or "canned" questions and answers that anticipate questions and issue details that might be of interest to a committee, the media or the general public. Some organizations prepare FAQs—frequently asked questions—or question modules that provide answers to questions that often arise concerning a certain subject matter.

FAQ documents are typically a series of several enumerated written questions followed immediately by scripted answers to each. Question modules tend to be formatted on stand-alone pages that pose one question and provide one answer per page, and may be a bit longer with more detail than FAQs. These documents are valuable in "pre-answering" likely questions that may be asked by a committee, or in clarifying certain aspects of an issue. Because of their generic and versatile utility, these informative documents can be used with any number of audiences.

FAQs and question modules are often included in a witness's briefing book or folder for use at the witness table during a hearing. For more information on briefing books, see § 3.19, Important Documents: Drafting the Statement and Making the Record—The Briefing Book. For more information on FAQs and question modules, see § 6.21, Preparing Answers in Advance to Expected or Anticipated Questions; and § 6.35, Witness Use of Answer Modules and FAQs in Responding to Committee Questions.

§3.23 Special Considerations Regarding Executive and Judicial Branch Testimony

Officials of the federal executive and judicial branches who testify before a congressional committee face different and additional challenges and requirements in the preparation of written testimony. First, the testimony that is presented is a form of official cross-branch communication that must be carefully and thoughtfully prepared because of the dynamics and interaction among the three branches of government. Secondly, the department, agency, or office preparing the testimony must adhere to internal protocols regarding the preparation, review, vetting, and clearance of official statements by the appropriate officials.

Each department and agency in the executive branch, in coordination with the Office of Management and Budget (OMB), as well as the Administrative Office of the U.S. Courts on behalf of the federal judiciary, has protocols and guidelines in place for its respective office's preparation and review of congressional testimony. Testimony and official statements emanating from either branch and provided to the Congress are closely scrutinized and tightly controlled so that there is an assurance of coordination, correct message, accuracy, responsiveness, and general appropriateness reflected in the documents. Executive branch departments and agencies will be guided to a large extent in many cases by the Office of Management and Budget (OMB), as well as by the White House policy office, to ensure adherence to, and consistency with, administration policies and priorities. The Administrative Office of the U.S. Courts plays a similar role for the judiciary to ensure consistency of policy as determined by the Judicial Conference of the United States.

Federal executive branch entities and the Administrative Office of the U.S. Courts also have their own methodologies and approaches regarding the preparation of written testimony, as well as their own formats and styles for writing and producing statements. Witnesses and preparation teams within the executive or judicial branch should consult their respective organization's guidelines and protocols for preparing congressional testimony.

For examples of detailed guidance provided by executive branch agencies regarding congressional testimony preparation and clearance procedures, go to:

1) United States Army source: <*www.hqda.army.mil/ocll/DOC/Info%20Paper%20-%20Clearing%20Hearing%20Statements.doc*>; and

2) National Aeronautics and Space Administration (NASA) source: <*http://nodis3.gsfc.nasa.gov/iso_docs/pdf/H_OWI_1311_L_001_B_.pdf*>.

For more information regarding special considerations concerning executive, judicial, and legislative participation in congressional committee hearings, see § 2.31, Who Should Testify?—Federal Executive, Legislative and Judicial Branch Officials; § 2.68, Congressional Hearing Participants: The "Players"—Federal Departments and Agencies; § 3.24, Special Considerations Regarding Federal Legislative Branch Testimony; § 4.26, Witness Rehearsal of Oral Testimony and Answers to Questions—Preparation and Rehearsal by Federal Government Departments and Agencies; and § 4.40, Special Considerations Regarding Executive, Judicial, and Legislative Branch Witnesses.

§3.24 Special Considerations Regarding Federal Legislative Branch Testimony

Quite often members of Congress, representatives of congressional committees and offices, and legislative service organizations (LSOs) find themselves in a position to testify before congressional committees. Individual members of the U.S. Senate and the U.S. House of Representatives enjoy the opportunity to appear before committees in both houses of Congress, and frequently testify before committees in support of legislation they have introduced, or to comment on their views about a particular issue pending before a committee. The preparation of testimony in these cases is the responsibility and prerogative of the individual member of Congress, and members' staff should work with the appropriate committee staff to ensure compliance with committee rules and guidelines.

Officials from administrative offices of the Congress, such as the Clerk of the House, the Secretary of the Senate, the respective chambers' Sergeant at Arms, and the U.S. Capitol Police, for example, are also called to testify before congressional committees on occasion. Those offices' staff typically work closely with committee staff to ensure the production of appropriate testimony and materials for a hearing.

Professional staff from legislative service organizations (LSOs), such as the Congressional Budget Office (CBO), the Congressional Research Service (CRS) at the Library of Congress (LOC), and the Government Accountability Office (GAO) testify frequently and regularly before a wide array of congressional committees. CBO's mission and message in testifying are usually focused on the budget implications and impact of a proposed measure or program. CRS provides congressional committees with a very valuable service in helping to supply nonpartisan research results and issue analyses. Through both committee testimony and special reports, GAO provides congressional committees and members with expert and detailed analyses of federal programs, executive branch operations, and the use of federal funds to support and enforce the laws and regulations of the land.

Each of these unique entities has its own special protocols and guidelines for preparing congressional testimony. Furthermore, CRS has a significant in-house expertise on the congressional committee and hearing processes, and, consequently, it is a very credible and reliable resource on those subjects. Similarly, GAO has considerable internal experience and expertise, not only in the production of testimony, but also in providing training on the precise subjects of this treatise—preparing and delivering congressional testimony. (For a list and explanation of congressional legislative service organizations, see § 5.130, Legislative-Branch Support Agencies, the *Congressional Deskbook*, by Michael L. Koempel and Judy Schneider.)

For more information on special considerations regarding legislative witnesses, see § 2.31, Who Should Testify?—Federal Executive, Legislative, and Judicial Branch

Officials; and § 4.40, Special Considerations Regarding Executive, Judicial, and Legislative Branch Witnesses.

§3.25 Visual and Stylistic Layout for Statements

A formal written witness statement that is provided to a committee should comport with the best writing practices and styles, and it should utilize a user-friendly visual layout. It is important for the optics of the statement to be attractive and inviting so that the statement appears to be an "easy read." The use of short or medium-sized paragraphs, enumeration and bullet points, succinct opening and closing paragraphs, and a wide array of other stylistic elements (see § 3.26, Key Stylistic Elements) will contribute to an effective, well-written statement that is appealing to the eye of the reader.

To review samples of several statements, see § 3.29 through § 3.33, Samples of Written Statements.

§3.26 Key Stylistic Elements

As with any effective written statement, the writing of congressional witness testimony should incorporate key stylistic elements to make the statement effective and compelling. Because of committee-imposed limitations on the length of a statement, and the need to convey the witness's position in just a few pages of text, it is usually preferable to utilize a direct and hard-hitting writing style. Statement authors would be well-advised to approach the writing project by stating the theme, providing factual justification and examples in support of the case, drawing logical conclusions, and making recommendations to the committee.

An effective witness statement often incorporates a deductive layout including:

- a thesis;
- the enumeration of facts;
- the notation of key details about the issue;
- a few paragraphs laying out the basic case or position of the witness; and
- conclusions, requests for action, and suggested remedies.

The writing style should be clear, with the use of concise sentences. The writer should utilize:

- good syntax;
- proper English;
- action verbs;
- sufficient concrete examples to illustrate points;
- consistent terminology and definitions; and
- a simple, straightforward approach throughout the document.

To review samples of several statements, see § 3.29 through § 3.33, Samples of Written Statements.

§3.27 Written Testimony Components: Manuscript Format, Layout, and Content

Effective written congressional testimony consists of a number of components that provide a simple and logical format and layout for a statement, and that incorporate purposeful content that adds value, information, and advocacy, as well as a professional and well-communicated message. The following items are key components to consider for inclusion in a formal statement document.

1) **Title Page**—Committee rules generally dictate whether a title page is required or permitted. (See congressional committee rules by accessing committee links at <*www.House.gov*> and <*www.Senate.gov*>.)

A title page should include:

- the name, title and organizational affiliation of a witness;
- the name of the congressional committee and the respective chamber;
- the topic of the statement; and
- the date.

To see a sample title page, go to § 3.30.

2) **Introductory Information in Lieu of a Title Page**—If a title page is not permitted or utilized, an introductory set of phrases and information, included just prior to the beginning of the statement text, can be used to accomplish the same goal of providing important information about a witness, an organization, and the hearing topic. For an illustration, see the opening phrases of the sample statement at § 3.32.

3) **Opening Greeting**—The typical opening greeting for witness testimony and for use by a witness testifying is "Mr. Chairman," "Madam Chairman," or "Madam Chairwoman" followed by "and Members of the Committee." These should be the opening words at the beginning of the text of any witness statement. For an illustration, see the introductory sentence of the Formal Statement at § 3.30.

4) **Thematic Introduction**—The opening paragraphs should include:

- information about the purpose of the appearance by a witness and his/her organization;
- the thesis of the witness's message and the theme of the testimony;
- a statement about the importance of the issue and its connection to public policy;
- any necessary background, such as history with the issue, expertise, and the definition or scope of terms and issues; and
- a brief topic outline of messages and case points that the witness statement will convey.

For examples of opening, introductory paragraphs, see the sample statements at § 3.30 through § 3.33.

5) **Main Body of Statement Text or Narrative**—The middle paragraphs of a witness statement should include:

- the development of the essence of the witness's case, message, and theme;
- notation of important supporting information; and
- enumeration of recommendations and requested remedies.

This portion of the statement, typically the longest part of the statement, is the heart of witness testimony in terms of education, information, and advocacy, and should include all the necessary elements and arguments to support the position of the witness on the topic of the hearing.

For examples of main thematic paragraphs, see the sample statements at § 3.30 through § 3.33.

6) **Conclusion and Closing**—The final paragraphs should:

- indicate the conclusion of the testimony;
- summarize the case and messages of the witness;
- briefly repeat the major or key points of the case;
- include a call to action, if appropriate;
- invite questions from the committee;
- offer follow-up assistance; and
- thank the committee for the opportunity to testify.

For an example, see the "Conclusion" section of the sample statement at § 3.30.

§ 3.28 Use of Graphics and Visuals

The effective use of graphics and visuals in written testimony is an important method of supporting themes and case points being made in the message development of a statement. When properly used, graphics can support, enhance, and add great value to a written statement and to the testimony of a witness. Utilizing a chart, graph, matrix, or listing of bulleted items in congressional testimony, for example, can help elucidate an important fact or assertion, demonstrate a trend, or illustrate the magnitude of an issue or situation.

Graphics should be used strategically and not as a crutch. Their purpose should be clear and well-defined, and should support the narrative text and message of the statement and the testimony of the witness. Graphics should be simple, to the point, and easily understood. Actual graphics should be professionally produced, incorporated strategically in a written statement, and enlarged adequately for use and reference by the witness during oral testimony at a hearing. It is important for a graphic to be introduced and explained in the narrative of a written statement.

Witnesses should consult with committee staff and rules prior to a hearing to ensure a complete understanding of the use of graphics, if permitted.

For more information on a witness's use of graphics, see § 4.24, Witness Rehearsal of Oral Testimony and Answers to Questions—Use of Graphics and Visuals; § 5.70, Effective Use of Visual Aids, Charts, and Graphics; and § 5.71, Sample of Design and Use Guidelines to Ensure Visual Aids Have Their Desired Impact.

§ 3.29 Samples of Written Statements

There is no ideal or perfect witness statement. Style, purpose, subject matter, content, and hearing type all dictate the substance, flow, and focus of a witness statement to a very large extent. However, it can be valuable for a witness and author of a statement to review samples of well-written statements to see the application and use of key ingredients and elements of style, layout, format, and content, as discussed in § 3.25, § 3.26, and § 3.27, as well to see the application and use of various methods for building a case and developing the argument, as discussed in § 3.40 through § 3.48.

The hearings' transcripts and records of most congressional committees also provide a wealth of sources for testimony and witness statements, and can be accessed either through individual committee links found at *<www.House.gov>* and *<www.Senate.gov>*; a visit to the offices of congressional committees to review printed editions of hearings; or through the Library of Congress's excellent legislative reference site at *<Thomas.gov>*.

In § 3.30 through § 3.33 below are four sample congressional witness statements in the forms in which they were prepared and presented to various congressional committees. These samples offer a variety of styles and approaches for consideration and use, and include good examples of key stylistic features that make a statement more compelling, and case-building methods that make a statement more powerful and substantive. See the head note before each sample for an explanation of the key content and stylistic elements of the statement being highlighted.

Source for all statements: Personal and professional files of William N. LaForge.

§ 3.30 Sample of Written Statements— Statement Prepared for House Judiciary Subcommittee on Courts and Intellectual Property in Opposition to the Split of the 9th Circuit Court of Appeals

This document is an example of a formal written statement submitted to a subcommittee prior to a hearing. It utilizes a cover page. Note how the statement is laid out by topic with the use of Roman numerals and capital letters. Notice also how recommendations for action are included in the final paragraphs of items I and II. Preceding the official statement is an executive summary that provides a "quick look" at the statement's basic content for those who do not have or take the time to read the entire formal statement. (See § 3.16, Important Documents: Drafting the Statement and Making the Record—Executive Summary and the Famous One-Pager.) Finally, this document is the basic text from which was crafted the actual witness statement presented at the hearing—the literal words actually uttered by the witness to the committee. To see that document, go to § 3.34, Sample of Oral Statement—Written Document Used as Reference to Deliver Oral Statement.

STATEMENT OF

WILLIAM N. LAFORGE

CHAIRMAN
COMMITTEE ON GOVERNMENT RELATIONS
FEDERAL BAR ASSOCIATION

BEFORE THE
SUBCOMMITTEE ON COURTS AND INTELLECTUAL PROPERTY
COMMITTEE ON THE JUDICIARY
U.S. HOUSE OF REPRESENTATIVES

CONCERNING
THE FINAL REPORT OF THE
COMMISSION ON STRUCTURAL ALTERNATIVES
FOR THE FEDERAL COURTS OF APPEALS

JULY 22, 1999

EXECUTIVE SUMMARY

The Federal Bar Association is vitally interested in the proposed reorganization of the Court of Appeals for the Ninth Circuit because it is the only national bar association that has as its primary focus the practice of federal law. Of the 15,000 attorneys in private and government practice across the nation who belong to the FBA, over 2,700 practice in the Ninth Circuit. With such a regional and national constituency, the FBA has its feet in both camps—as the beneficiary of direct experience with the structure and operation of the Ninth Circuit, and as a stakeholder in the well-being of the entire federal court structure and the uniform administration of justice.

The FBA applauds the recommendation of the Commission on Structural Alternatives for the Federal Courts of Appeals (White Commission) against splitting the Ninth Circuit into two or more circuits. In our prior comments and testimony before the White Commission, the FBA strongly argued against such a split. Instead the FBA favors increased innovation and experimentation by the Ninth Circuit to arrive at solutions that advance the court's efficiency and effectiveness. As the White Commission Report acknowledges, the Ninth Circuit long has been a crucible for experimentation in management and disposition of a growing federal court caseload. Many of the innovations employed by the Ninth Circuit in the past have proven successful, and thus, are proven mechanisms for other circuits to implement as they encounter problems associated with growth of caseload and court size.

The FBA believes that the White Commission's proposed division of the Circuit into three semi-autonomous adjudicative units, and corresponding *en banc* revision, is not in the best interests of the Circuit, its adjudicatory processes, litigants appearing before it, and the interests of justice. It is not likely to increase the uniform application of federal law, and certainly not within the state of California. It is not likely to make the law more predictable. It is not likely to speed the court's decision-making or create cost-savings for litigants. It is not likely to lead to fewer conflicts in decisional law. It is not likely to enhance the integrity of or the respect for the federal courts. Furthermore, it is not likely to ease the weight of the Ninth Circuit's caseload, nor enhance or simplify litigation. Indeed, the proposal would in many respects accomplish the contrary. The structure and processes of a court are not its ends. They are the means to the end of serving the administration of justice. Rather than passing structure-oriented legislation that may or may not prove desirable with experience, the FBA recommends that Congress encourage and charge the Ninth Circuit to proceed with continued innovation and flexibility.

The FBA believes that the well-being of the Ninth Circuit and the federal court system are best served by increased Congressional attention to two other concerns: the assurance of timely filling of judicial vacancies; and the reversal of the trend to federalize crimes in areas traditionally reserved to the states. Both of these concerns relate directly to the capacity of courts to render justice fairly and swiftly. Indeed, we recommend that Congress, prior to the passage of any further federal criminal legislation, procedurally require of itself the generation of a "judicial impact statement" that projects the additional caseload and costs that such legislation may create.

FORMAL STATEMENT

Good afternoon, Mr. Chairman and Members of the Subcommittee. The Federal Bar Association (FBA) thanks the House Judiciary Committee, Subcommittee on Courts and Intellectual Property, for the opportunity to offer comments concerning the Final Report of the Commission on Structural Alternatives for the Federal Courts of Appeals (White Commission). We testified before the White Commission at its San Francisco hearings in May, 1998, and we offered written comments to the Commission concerning its draft report last fall.

The FBA remains vitally interested in this matter because we are the only nation-wide bar association that has, as its primary focus, the practice of federal law. Of our 15,000 members across the United States, over 2,700 of them practice in the Ninth Circuit. With those demographics, the FBA has its feet in both camps. We are the beneficiary of direct experience with the structure, caseload, adjudication and operation of the Ninth Circuit and of that Circuit's own continuing efforts to address its circumstances. At the same time, we occupy a perspective that necessarily embraces the well-being of the entire Federal Court system. In that capacity, we appreciate the opportunity to continue to help shape solutions to problems associated with growth of caseload management and adjudication as they affect the due administration of justice in the federal appellate judiciary.

At the outset, we will address the report's proposals concerning division of the

Ninth Circuit and, in the future, other circuits as they continue to grow. We also propose that Congress take certain broad actions, apart from structural initiatives, that we believe will reduce the stress on the circuit courts, regardless of their structure.

I. Division of the Ninth Circuit

The FBA applauds the Commission's recommendation against splitting the Ninth Circuit into two or more circuits. Both in our written statement and in our testimony before the Commission at its San Francisco hearing in May 1998, the Federal Bar Association—like the state officials, the U.S. Department of Justice, the American Bar Association, and most of the state and local bar associations that have addressed the issue—strongly argued against such a split.

Although eschewing splitting the Ninth Circuit, the Commission report proposes adjudicative division of the circuit, with specific and detailed suggestions for implementing that division, including a "circuit division" for resolving inter-division conflicts and a revised *en banc* procedure. As well, the report recommends certain experimental efforts, such as two judge panels and district court appellate panels, to relieve decisional pressure.

As the report acknowledges, the Ninth Circuit long has been a crucible for experimentation in management and disposition of the growing federal court caseload. Many of the innovations of the Ninth Circuit have proven successful, and thus, are proven mechanisms for other circuits to implement as they encounter problems associated with growth of caseload and court size.

Indeed, even as these hearings are held, the Ninth Circuit is reexamining many of its procedures in order to experiment with innovations that might lead to greater efficiency and effectiveness. In order to do so, the Circuit has constituted a 10-member Evaluation Committee that is chaired by Senior Circuit Judge David R. Thompson and includes representatives from that court, its district courts, the bar, and academia. The committee will examine the Circuit's limited *en banc* process, the monitoring of panel opinions, regional considerations, and disposition times, among other issues.

The White Commission's report proposes several creative structural approaches and additional mechanisms for grappling with many of these same issues. They seem to serve three overarching principles that the Commission has concluded are desirable in conceiving a circuit structure and operation.

- First, an appeal should be decided largely by circuit judges who reside in the region from which the appeal emanates.
- Second, the judges who reside in a particular region of the circuit, where there are relatively homogenous interests and culture, are best able to work together to develop the body of law particularly applicable to that region.
- Finally, a smaller body of judges, all from a particular region of the circuit, would be better able to monitor the panel decisions from within that region and to adopt procedures for doing so.

In our view, however, the proposals that are designed to implement these principles create issues that suggest caution and flexibility. For instance, it well might be that legal issues of unique regional concern within a circuit can be resolved more satisfactorily by judges from within that region, though that would not seem to be a given. The much larger portion of appellate issues and caseload, however, are not regionally unique. Experience with the specific division structure proposed in the report might well reflect some achievement of greater sensitivity in resolution of essentially regional issues. At the same time, experience also might demonstrate that the price of achieving this—occasioned by lack of inter-division *stare decisis* and of meaningful *en banc* review—is a significant compromise of jurisprudential integrity of the circuit as an institutional structure.

In an effort, at least in part, to accommodate regionalism, the White Commission's report, and now the implementing bill in the Senate, S.253, propose a system that is convoluted and unwieldy. A circuit structure of multiple, semi-autonomous adjudicative units with their separate *en banc* processes and an appellate division to resolve potential "square conflicts" actually seems to go in the wrong direction.

A sound proposal for reform should countenance swifter administration of justice, uniform decisions and application of federal law, fewer conflicts, less cost to the litigants, and increased predictability. Splitting the decisional function within the circuit—with little intra-circuit accountability for uniformity and precedent and with a concomitant layering of additional intra-circuit review in an effort, though likely futile, to correct these flaws—does none of this.

We will not burden these comments with exhaustive discussion of these and other concerns. Neither will we reiterate the numerous significant criticisms of the division approach that others—including the large majority of chief judges of the other circuits —have addressed. Suffice to say at this point that, at a minimum, they raise yellow flags that signal caution.

The White Commission report offers Congress a vision that looks beyond the present and well into the future. Such a vision, however, must recognize and reflect on the risk of significant adverse harm, not just the possibility of improvement in certain areas. Congress must take care to acknowledge that, as creative and positive as any particular scheme or structure might seem to be, only experience will prove the point.

Based on this realization, we urge that Congress build upon the Ninth Circuit's tradition as a crucible for change and experimentation and transform it into a laboratory that will illuminate for itself and other circuits the rocky roads, as well as the smooth and promising ones. Congressional focus on the Ninth Circuit over the last five years seems to have provided appropriate stimulus for that circuit to be ever bolder in its rulemaking to respond to the need for sound reform. These continuing efforts and the work of the Evaluation Committee should be given a fair opportunity to succeed before a potentially wrenching structural approach is embraced.

To the extent that Congress may feel compelled to legislatively ensure continuing focus on reform within the circuit, we suggest that Congress enact legislation that will authorize the Ninth Circuit to implement sensible initiatives, including reform of the *en banc* process, in an effort to determine, in practice, what does and does not work.

The structure and processes of a court are not the ends. They are the means to the end of serving the principles identified by the White Commission that are implicit in its recommendations. Rather than pass legislation that would pour concrete around a new structure that may or may not prove desirable with experience, the FBA recommends that Congress permit—even charge—the Ninth Circuit to blaze the trail through experiment and flexibility. In this manner, the judges and practitioners of the Ninth Circuit can discover the most efficient and effective appellate structure and procedure, for the sake not just of the Ninth Circuit but of those that follow. Make no mistake—it is the future of the entire federal judiciary and the citizens that it serves that is at stake.

II. Other Relief on Circuit Stress

A. Judicial Vacancies

In our written and oral presentations to the White Commission, the Federal Bar Association urged the Commission to note for the attention of the Congress and the President the vital importance to the health of the federal judiciary and the well-being of all our citizens in promptly filling judicial vacancies. No structural innovation will work if judges are not appointed to already-existing, Congressionally approved judicial seats (to say nothing of reasonable expansion of those seats on certain courts).

Although the House of Representatives institutionally does not play a role in that process, we recognize that Members of this chamber provide important input into both the nomination and confirmation of individual judges. In that context, we respectfully urge that Members of the House exert all available influence to ensure timely filling of judicial vacancies. Empty seats on the bench ill serve our Nation just as surely as vacant seats in the Congress.

B. Federalization of State Crimes

Additionally, in our testimony before the White Commission, the Federal Bar Association discussed with the Commission the importance of focusing attention on the impact on the judiciary of the proliferation of new federal criminal statutes. Surely, there are appropriate occasions for federalization of a crime—occasions in which a federal statute would not merely duplicate a state statute, but where some additional aspect makes federal treatment appropriate. But crimes that adequately are addressed in state courts do not belong in federal courts.

In the course of considering the issues involved in the White Commission's report, we urge Congress to acknowledge the substantial impact that its actions in this regard have on federal court caseloads. Before Congress passes another single new criminal statute, we urge Congress to require of itself a "judicial impact statement" that projects the additional caseload and costs that such legislation will create.

CONCLUSION

The Federal Bar Association offers these comments and suggestions in the spirit of assisting Congress in grappling with these important questions. We remain available to be of service to the Subcommittee on this and other matters concerning the courts and the administration of justice. Thank you for the opportunity to appear before you today.

Source: Personal and professional files of William N. LaForge.

§3.31 Sample of Written Statements— Statement Prepared for House Appropriations Subcommittee on Transportation in Support of Federal Funding for Clean Air Research

This document is an example of a statement submitted to a subcommittee for the hearing record as an "outside witness statement." No oral testimony by the witness of record was presented at the hearing. The coalition submitting the statement desired to make a written request for funding and to make a public record of its position, but it did not need to testify in person in this instance. Note how the opening paragraph lays out the basic request, the middle paragraphs make the case for the funding, and the final paragraph summarizes and restates the request. Also notice the listing of key coalition participants on the cover page, a practice that boosts the credibility of the coalition, its message, and its statement for the record.

STATEMENT OF THE CALIFORNIA INDUSTRY AND GOVERNMENT CENTRAL CALIFORNIA OZONE STUDY (CCOS) COALITION

SUBMITTED TO THE
APPROPRIATIONS SUBCOMMITTEE ON TRANSPORTATION
UNITED STATES HOUSE OF REPRESENTATIVES

BY

ALAN C. LLOYD, Ph.D.
CHAIRMAN, CALIFORNIA AIR RESOURCES BOARD

BARBARA PATRICK
CHAIR, CCOS POLICY COMMITTEE
MEMBER, CALIFORNIA AIR RESOURCES BOARD
MEMBER, SAN JOAQUIN VALLEY APCD AND KERN COUNTY SUPERVISOR

LYNN TERRY
DEPUTY EXECUTIVE OFFICER, CALIFORNIA AIR RESOURCES BOARD

JOHN DAMASSA
CCOS PROGRAM MANAGER, CALIFORNIA AIR RESOURCES BOARD

MARK BOESE
DEPUTY AIR POLLUTION CONTROL OFFICER, SAN JOAQUIN VALLEY APCD

MANUEL CUNHA, JR.
PRESIDENT, NISEI FARMERS LEAGUE

CATHERINE H. REHEIS-BOYD
VICE PRESIDENT, WESTERN STATES PETROLEUM ASSOCIATION

LES CLARK
VICE PRESIDENT, INDEPENDENT OIL PRODUCERS AGENCY

APRIL 11, 2003

Mr. Chairman and Members of the Subcommittee:

On behalf of the California Industry and Government Central California Ozone Study (CCOS) Coalition, we are pleased to submit this statement for the record in support of our fiscal year 2004 funding request of $500,000 from the Department of Transportation (DOT) for CCOS as part of a Federal match for the $9.1 million already contributed by California State and local agencies and the private sector.

Most of central California does not attain federal health-based standards for ozone and particulate matter. The San Joaquin Valley is developing new State Implementation Plans (SIPs) for the federal ozone and particulate matter standards in the 2002 to 2004 timeframe. The San Francisco Bay Area has committed to update their ozone SIP in 2004 based on new technical data. In addition, none of these areas attain the new federal 8-hour ozone standard. SIPs for the 8-hour standard will be due in the 2007 timeframe—and must include an evaluation of the impact of transported air pollution on downwind areas such as the Mountain Counties. Photochemical air quality modeling will be necessary to prepare SIPs that are approvable by the U.S. Environmental Protection Agency.

The Central California Ozone Study (CCOS) is designed to enable central California to meet Clean Air Act requirements for ozone State Implementation Plans (SIPs) as well as advance fundamental science for use nationwide. The CCOS field measurement program was conducted during the summer of 2000 in conjunction with the California Regional PM_{10}/PM_{25} Air Quality Study (CRPAQS), a major study of the origin, nature, and extent of excessive levels of fine particles in central California. CCOS includes an ozone field study, a deposition study, data analysis, modeling performance evaluations, and a retrospective look at previous SIP modeling. The CCOS study area extends over central and most of northern California. The goal of the CCOS is to better understand the nature of the ozone problem across the region, providing a strong scientific foundation for preparing the next round of State and Federal attainment plans. The study includes six main components:

- Developed the design of the field study
- Conducted an intensive field monitoring study from June 1 to September 30, 2000
- Developing an emission inventory to support modeling
- Developing and evaluating a photochemical model for the region
- Designing and conducting a deposition field study
- Evaluating emission control strategies for upcoming ozone attainment plans

The CCOS is directed by Policy and Technical Committees consisting of representatives from Federal, State and local governments, as well as private industry. These committees, which managed the San Joaquin Valley Ozone Study and are currently managing the California Regional Particulate Air Quality Study, are landmark examples of collaborative environmental management. The proven methods and established teamwork provide a solid foundation for CCOS. The sponsors of CCOS, representing state, local government and industry, have contributed approximately $9.1 million for the field study. The federal government has contributed $3,730,000 to support some data analysis and modeling. In addition, CCOS sponsors are providing $2 million of in-kind support. The Policy Committee is seeking federal co-funding of an additional $6.25 million to complete the remaining data analysis and modeling and for a future deposition study. California is an ideal natural laboratory for studies that address these issues, given the scale and diversity of the various ground surfaces in the region (crops, woodlands, forests, urban and suburban areas).

There is a national need to address national data gaps and California should not bear the entire cost of addressing these gaps. National data gaps include issues relating to the integration of particulate matter and ozone control strategies. The CCOS field study took place concurrently with the California Regional Particulate Matter Study - previously jointly funded through Federal, State, local and private sector funds. Thus, the CCOS was timed to enable leveraging the efforts of the particulate matter study. Some equipment and personnel served dual functions to reduce the net cost. From a technical standpoint, carrying out both studies concurrently was a unique opportunity to address the integration of particulate matter and ozone control efforts. CCOS was also cost-effective since it builds on other successful efforts including the 1990 San Joaquin Valley Ozone Study. Federal assistance is needed to effectively address these issues.

For fiscal year 2004, our Coalition is seeking funding of $500,000 from DOT through highway research funds. DOT is a key stakeholder because federal law requires that transportation plans be in conformity with SIPS. The motor vehicle emission budgets established in SIPs must be met and be consistent with the emissions in transportation plans. Billions of dollars in federal transportation funds are at risk if conformity is not demonstrated for new transportation plans. As a result, transportation and air agencies must be collaborative partners on SIPs and transportation plans. SIPs and transportation plans are linked because motor vehicle emissions are a dominant element of SIPs in California as well as nationwide. Determining the emission and air quality impacts of motor vehicles is a major part of the CCOS effort. In addition, the deposition of motor vehicle emissions and the resulting ozone is a nationwide issue.

Thank you very much for your consideration of our request.

Source: Personal and professional files of William N. LaForge.

§3.32 Sample of Written Statements— Statement Prepared for Senate Appropriations Subcommittee on Agriculture, Rural Development, and Related Agencies in Support of Federal Funding for Turfgrass Research

This document is an example of a statement, submitted for a subcommittee hearing record as an "outside witness statement," that includes the use of a powerful first paragraph laying out the requests succinctly, followed by enumerated sections that explain and justify each request, and a compelling conclusive summary. Note how the statement also includes a sidebar listing the components of a national strategy on the subject matter, an excellent way to demonstrate the correlation of the funding request with an existing public policy program. Notice also that there is no title page. In this instance, the committee disallowed cover pages for outside statements. To get around that directive, yet still include important information about the organization and witness of record, the document includes the relevant introductory verbiage at the very beginning just prior to the statement itself. For emphasis, certain parts of the statement are also in bold type.

STATEMENT OF KEVIN N. MORRIS
Executive Director, National Turfgrass Evaluation Program,
Presented to the Appropriations Subcommittee on Agriculture, Rural Development, and Related Agencies, United States Senate, March, 2002

Mr. Chairman and Members of the Subcommittee:

On behalf of the National Turfgrass Evaluation Program (NTEP), I appreciate this opportunity to provide the Subcommittee with the turfgrass industry's perspective in support of continuation of the $55,000 appropriation for the National Turfgrass Evaluation Program (NTEP) included in the President's fiscal year 2003 budget request for the Agricultural Research Service (ARS). Also, I appreciate the opportunity to present to you the turfgrass industry's need and justification for continuation of the $490,000 appropriated in the Presidents's fiscal year 2002 budget for the full-time turfgrass scientist position within ARS. In addition, I appreciate the consideration of an additional appropriation of $3,500,000 for the establishment of a national turfgrass research laboratory, as a part of the national turfgrass research initiative proposed by ARS, with ten new research scientist positions.

1) Justification of $55,000 Appropriation Request for Program Support. Once again, NTEP and the turfgrass industry come to the appropriations process to request continuation of the $55,000 basic program support in the ARS budget for NTEP's activities at Beltsville. We appreciate the Subcommittee's continuation of this amount as in previous fiscal years, and hope that you will agree with us that this request is justified for the ensuing fiscal year.

The National Turfgrass Evaluation Program (NTEP) is unique in that it provides a working partnership that links the federal government, turfgrass industry and land grant universities together in their common interest of turfgrass cultivar development, improvement and evaluation. The National Turfgrass Evaluation Program is the primary means by which cultivated varieties of turfgrass are evaluated in this country. It provides unbiased information on turfgrass cultivar adaptations, disease and insect resistance and environmental stress tolerance. The public and private sectors of the turfgrass industry use this information to develop cultivar recommendations for home owners, sod producers, sports turf and parks managers, golf course superintendents and highway vegetation managers.

Our nation's awareness of safety is at an all-time high. Turfgrass provides multiple benefits to society including child safety on athletic fields, environmental protection of groundwater, reduction of silt and other contaminants in runoff, green space in home lawns, parks, golf courses, etc. With the advancements being made to turfgrasses that require less pesticides, water and other inputs as well as other efforts to improve integrated pest management programs, recycling, etc., the USDA has a unique opportunity to take positive action in support of the turfgrass industry. With a minuscule investment of Department funds, in relative terms within USDA's budget, a tremendous return can be gained for society and the turfgrass industry.

While the vast majority of the USDA's funds have been and will continue to be directed toward traditional "food and fiber" segments of U.S. agriculture, it is important to note that turfgrasses (e.g., sod production) are defined as agriculture in the Farm Bill and by many other departments and agencies. Further, it is estimated by the Economic Research Service that the turfgrass industry, in all its forms, is a $35-40 billion industry. It should also be noted that the turfgrass industry is the fastest growing segment of U.S. agriculture, while it receives essentially no federal support. There are no subsidy programs for turfgrass, nor are any desired.

For the past seventy years, the USDA's support for the turfgrass industry has been modest at best. The turfgrass industry's rapid growth, importance to our urban environments, and impact on our daily lives warrant more commitment and support from USDA. Failing to support the National Turfgrass Evaluation Program, would be a tremendous oversight of a major opportunity. USDA's basic support of NTEP at the $55,000 level does not cover all costs. In fact, NTEP represents an ideal partnership of the public and private sectors in terms of program cost sharing. The NTEP relies most heavily on turfgrass industry (i.e., public sectors, end-users) support. However, it is essential that the USDA maintain its modest financial support and work closely with NTEP. The turfgrass industry relies heavily on NTEP for unbiased information. Discounting this support will also eliminate a highly reliable and credible level of objectivity that is associated with the NTEP program.

2) Justification of $490,000 Appropriation Request for the ARS Scientist Position as well as $3,500,000 Appropriation Request for the Establishment of a National Turfgrass Research Laboratory

NTEP and the turfgrass industry are requesting the Subcommittee's

support for $490,000 continuing funding for the full-time scientist staff position at ARS, focusing on turfgrass research, that was appropriated in the fiscal year 2002 budget. We also request that the Subcommittee appropriate an additional $3,500,000 for establishment of the initial stage of a national turfgrass research laboratory within USDA, ARS, which ARS estimates will be a $20 million venture over several years of development. This laboratory would address the specific need of collecting, evaluating and enhancing turfgrass germplasm. For this undertaking, we ask that five new scientist positions be created and located at the Beltsville Agricultural Research Center in Beltsville, MD. In addition, we ask that five new scientist positions be created to conduct watershed-level modeling research on turfgrass and development of management systems to minimize surface runoff and groundwater impacts from turf inputs. These five positions may be located at existing ARS centers of watershed quality/modeling expertise.

Our society is becoming increasingly more urbanized. Currently, turfgrasses impact more than 90% of all people in the U.S. through exposure to home lawns, business landscapes, roadsides, parks, or recreational turf on a daily basis. As more and more cropland is converted to houses, office parks, shopping centers, etc., the acreage of turfgrass is increasing exponentially. However, with the increasing urbanization comes a greater demand on resources, such as potable water. Also, with the general public experiencing heightened awareness of the environment and its protection, use of inputs such as fertilizer, pesticides and water on turfgrass areas is coming under greater scrutiny. In some jurisdictions, use of these inputs will either be banned or severely restricted for turfgrass use. In addition, the urbanization of America is leading to an overuse of current recreational facilities such as parks, athletic fields and golf courses. New facilities are being considered or constructed, many on abandoned sites such as landfills, industrial wastelands, gravel pits or mine spoils. Turfgrasses in these areas will play an important role in reclamation vegetation, recreational turf or both.

The USDA needs to initiate and maintain ongoing research on turfgrass development and improvement for the following reasons:

The value of the turfgrass industry in the U.S. is $35–$40 billion annually. Turfgrass is the number one or two agricultural crop in value and acreage in many states (i.e. MD, PA, FL, NJ, NC).

1. As our society becomes and more urbanized, the acreage of turfgrass will increase significantly. Consequently, state and local municipalities will require the utilization of other water sources (i.e. effluent, reclaimed, etc.), reduction of pesticide use and elimination of nutrient runoff from turfgrass. However, demand on recreational facilities will increase while these facilities, for safety reasons, will still be required to provide safe, attractive athletic fields, parks and grounds.
2. Private and university research programs are working to develop improved turfgrasses, but they do not have the time nor resources to

identify completely new sources of beneficial genes in commonly used species or the usefulness of potential new species. In addition, new plant materials collected by these institutions most often are not placed in the National Plant Germplasm System for use by all interested parties. Additionally, long-term research to identify and transfer desirable genes from other species (turfgrass or other crop species) is not being undertaken by public and private interests. ARS scientists working with turfgrass will enhance the ongoing research and development currently underway within the public and private sectors of the turfgrass industry.

3. Water management is a key component of healthy turf and has direct impact on nutrient and pesticide losses into the environment. New and improved technologies are needed to monitor turf stresses and to schedule irrigation to achieve the desired turf quality. Increasing demands and competition for potable water make it necessary to use water more efficiently for turf irrigation. Technologies are needed to more efficiently and uniformly apply irrigations to achieve desired turf quality for the intended use. Also, there is greater competition for potable water. Therefore, to increase water availability for turf irrigation, waste water (treated and untreated) from both animal and municipal sources as well as from food processing plants must be utilized. Some of these waste waters contain contaminants such as pathogens, heavy metals, and organic compounds. consequently, movement and accumulation of these contaminants in the atmosphere, soil profile, and ground water must be determined.
4. USDA conducted significant turfgrass research from 1920-1988. However, since 1988, no full-time scientist has been employed by USDA, Agricultural Research Service (ARS) to conduct turfgrass research specifically.
5. Research on florist, nursery and ornamental crops is significant within USDA, industries with far less public and commercial value than turfgrass.

A new turfgrass research scientist position within USDA, ARS was created by Congress in the FY2001 budget. Accordingly, in January 2001, the turfgrass industry met with USDA, ARS officials to discuss the position description, hiring process, facilities needed, etc. for the new position. ARS welcomed the new position but felt strongly that just one person working in turfgrass research would be ineffective in addressing the needs and concerns of the industry. Therefore, in January 2002, ARS held a customer workshop to gain valuable input from turfgrass researchers, golf course superintendents, sod producers, lawn care operators, athletic field managers and others on the research needs of the turfgrass industry. As a result of the workshop, ARS is developing and proposing a national strategy to address the specific needs and concerns within the turfgrass industry. The highlights of this strategy are below:

A NATIONAL STRATEGY FOR ARS TURFGRASS RESEARCH

Research. Objectives: Conduct long-term basic and applied research to provide knowledge, decision-support tools and plant materials to aid in designing, implementing, monitoring and managing economically and environmentally sustainable turfgrass systems including providing sound scientifically based information for use in the regulatoryprocess.

Research Focus: To make a significant contribution in developing and evaluating sustainable turfgrass systems, ARS proposes developing research programs in six major areas:

Component I. Turf Germplasm, Genetics, and Genomics

Rationale: Grasses that better resist diseases, insects, drought, traffic, etc. are deparately needed. Also, a better understanding of the basic biology of turfgrass species is essential.

Component II. Soil Management for Turf

Rationale: Research is needed to characterize limitations to, turf growth and development in less than optimum soils and to develop cost-effective management practices to overcome these limitations.

Component III. Turf Water Supply and Use

Rationale: New and improved technologies are needed to monitor turf stresses and to schedule irrigation to achieve desired turf quality but with greater efficiency or using other water sources.

Component IV. Turf Pest Control and Management

Rationale: New tools and management practices are needed to adequately control weeds, diseases, insects and vertebrate pests while reducing input costs and pesticide use.

Component V. Environmental Aspects of Turf

Rationale: The need is great to quantify the contribution of turf systems to water quality and quantify of vital importance in addressing the potential role of turf systems in environmental issues.

Component VI. Integrated Turf Management

Rationale: To develop needed tools for turf managers to select the best management practices for economic sustainability as well as environmental protection.

The turfgrass industry is very excited about this new proposal and wholeheartedly supports the efforts of ARS. Since the customers at the workshop identified turfgrass genetics/genomics and water quality/use as their top priority areas for ARS research, for fiscal year 2003, the turfgrass industry requests that the following units be established within USDA, ARS:

A turfgrass genomics unit (five new positions) to conduct the following research:

1. **Plant Germplasm Collection and Evaluation:** *The new position created in the FY2001 budget will fulfill these duties.*

2. **Genomics/Genetics Studies:** a molecular geneticist or cytogeneticist to betterunderstand the genomics of various turfgrass species, collected wild germplasm and their evolution.
3. **Transfer of Desirable Genes:** a molecular geneticist to identify desirable genes and how they may be transferred to current turfgrass species.
4. **Evaluation and Enhancement of Genetically Altered Grasses:** a turfgrass breeder to evaluate and enhance the genetically altered plants from the program.
5. **Turfgrass Entomology:** an entomologist to identify insect resistant germplasm and evaluate promising new species and potential releases.
6. **Turfgrass Pathology:** a pathologist to identify disease resistant germplasm and evaluate promising new species and potential releases.

A turfgrass water quality/systems unit (five new positions) to conduct the following research:

1. **Watershed Modeling:** to first conduct watershed modeling of existing turf systems on a regional basis. This research is essential to document the contribution of turf to the overall quality of surface and groundwater in the U.S.
2. **Management Systems:** this unit also needs to conduct research on management systems designed to reduce/eliminating any runoff and groundwater contamination from turf inputs.

In conclusion, on behalf of the National Turfgrass Evaluation Program and the turfgrass industry across America, I respectfully request that the Subcommittee continue the vital $55,000 appropriation for the National Turfgrass Evaluation Program (NTEP) as well as the $490,000 appropriated in fiscal year 2002 for the new turfgrass scientist position within the Agricultural Research Service. I also request that the Subcommittee appropriate an additional $3,500,000 for the establishment of a turfgrass genetics/genomics unit and a turfgrass water quality/systems unit within USDA, ARS.

Thank you very much for your assistance and support.

Source: Personal and professional files of William N. LaForge.

§3.33 Sample of Written Statements— Statement Prepared for Senate Appropriations Subcommittee on Labor, Health and Human Services, Education, and Related Agencies in Support of Hospital Funding

This document is an example of an "outside witness statement" for a subcommittee hearing record. It is brief and succinct. It makes excellent use of enumerated examples to support the case and request, as well as bulleted statistics to support the premise of need.

TESTIMONY FOR U.S. SENATE
Labor/Health and Human Services/Education Subcommittee

Dr. J. Philip Hinton
Chief Executive Officer
Community Medical Centers
Fresno, California
April 1, 2003

Mr. Chairman and Members of the Subcommittee:

My name is Dr. Philip Hinton and I am the Chief Executive Officer of Community Medical Centers in Fresno, California. Community Medical Centers is a not-for-profit, locally owned healthcare corporation that is committed to improving the health of the community. I am pleased to provide the subcommittee with a request for assistance in securing federal monies for a critical project in the Central San Joaquin Valley that would improve access to healthcare to the residents of Fresno County.

These are challenging times for those providing healthcare across the country. Recent events have highlighted the crisis that the healthcare system in this country is facing:

Recently, the week of March 10, 2003 was designated as national "Cover the Uninsured" week, publicizing the plight of over 41 million people across America lacking health insurance and resulting in the introduction of several initiatives in Congress to address the situation.

The recent introduction of S. 412, the Local Emergency Health Services Reimbursement Act of 2003, recognizing the need for the federal government to reimburse counties in southern and central California for emergency health care to undocumented residents.

Recent news articles reporting that emergency departments in hospitals across the country are overcrowded by uninsured and Medicaid populations. In the last 10 years, there has been an average increase in hospital emergency department visits by 33% while over 500 hospital emergency departments have closed. Due to a lack of health insurance, many are forced to resort to treatment at hospital emergency rooms rather than access primary care physicians.

It is clear that this crisis requires bold initiatives and leadership.

Community Medical Centers, located in Fresno, took over the County of Fresno's obligation for indigent healthcare in a 1996 landmark agreement. Since that time, Community has been providing inpatient and outpatient services to the residents of this community - regardless of their ability to pay. The availability of healthcare to all in Fresno County is a challenge at best. With a county boasting a population of 800,000, Fresno has some sobering statistics:

- An unemployment rate at 15% (almost three times the national average)
- Over 25% of the residents in the county living below the poverty line
- Over 30% of the residents in the county without health insurance (almost double the national average)

- The third highest asthma mortality rate in the nation
- The highest rates of teen pregnancy in the state
- The highest incidence of diabetes among the Hispanic population
- Late or no prenatal care for pregnant women
- Some of the lowest immunization rates in the nation (62% at age 2 versus 79% nationally)

These statistics point to the need to aggressively address the healthcare needs for the county in a comprehensive manner and offer an opportunity for Fresno County to serve as the perfect laboratory for such an experiment. Community has developed the concept of a primary healthcare network comprised of a local healthcare providers, Federally Qualified Health Centers, county health and human services agencies, schools and churches. A critical link to this network is the Community Caremobile, a doctor's office on wheels that travels to communities with no access to healthcare. The network will work to deliver both preventive and primary healthcare to the residents of Fresno County.

Key to this network is a hub known as the Ambulatory Care Center to be located on the campus of the Regional Medical Center in downtown Fresno. We are requesting $17.5 million in funding for the Ambulatory Care Center and have identified the following program for this $17.5 million request: the HHS Health, Resources and Services Administration (HRSA) Buildings and Facilities earmark in the fiscal year 2004 appropriations bill for Labor/HHS/Education. Because this program is specifically designated for buildings and facilities, we request your assistance in securing as much of the $17.5 million as possible through this program for the Ambulatory Care Center.

Although the challenges facing the healthcare community at the national level are significant, these challenges are magnified in the Central Valley beginning with the 30% of the residents of Fresno County lacking any form of health insurance. The result is the need to become creative and innovative in one's approach to providing health care. The concept of creating a hub, the Ambulatory Care Center in downtown Fresno, to be linked to a vast network of clinics and healthcare providers throughout the county is the only possible way to address the great need for accessible primary healthcare. By your providing significant funding for the Ambulatory Care Center, we can begin to address a severe crisis and improve the lives of many in Fresno County.

Source: Personal and professional files of William N. LaForge.

§3.34 Sample of Oral Statement—Written Document Used as Reference to Deliver Oral Testimony

As explained above in § 3.18, Important Documents: Drafting the Statement and Making the Record—Narrative, Outline or Notes Used for Oral Presentation, it is helpful for a witness to utilize a written document from which to deliver oral testimony before a committee. This written document, quite often different from the official written statement provided a committee, but nevertheless containing all the pertinent points to be covered, can be in the form of a narrative statement, topic outline, or notes.

For more information on the importance, development and use of an oral statement script, see § 4.11, Preparation and Use of Oral Statement Script or Outline; § 4.13, Delivering the Statement: To Read or Not to Read; § 3.18, Important Documents: Drafting the Statement and Making the Record—Narrative, Outline, or Notes Used for Oral Presentation; § 4.21, Witness Rehearsal of Oral Testimony and Answers to Questions—Relying on the Oral Statement Script to Deliver Testimony; and § 5.30, Organization and Use of Written Text to Deliver the Oral Testimony.

The following statement is a sample of a narrative outline actually used in the delivery of oral testimony before a House Judiciary Subcommittee. Above, at § 3.30, Sample of Written Statements—Statement Prepared for House Judiciary Subcommittee on Courts and Intellectual Property in Opposition to the Split of the 9th Circuit Court of Appeals, see the accompanying formal written statement prepared for submission to the committee in advance of the hearing. Review, compare, and contrast it with the narrative below, which was taken from that original written statement and actually used to present the testimony.

ORAL STATEMENT OF

WILLIAM N. LAFORGE
CHAIRMAN
COMMITTEE ON GOVERNMENT RELATIONS
FEDERAL BAR ASSOCIATION

BEFORE THE
SUBCOMMITTEE ON COURTS AND INTELLECTUAL PROPERTY
COMMITTEE ON THE JUDICIARY
U.S. HOUSE OF REPRESENTATIVES

CONCERNING
THE FINAL REPORT OF THE
COMMISSION ON STRUCTURAL ALTERNATIVES
FOR THE FEDERAL COURTS OF APPEALS

JULY 22, 1999

Mr. Chairman and Members of the Subcommittee:

My name is William LaForge, and I appear today on behalf of the Federal Bar Association—the FBA.

The Federal Bar Association has a major stake in the issues articulated in the White Commission Report and before this subcommittee today because we are the only nationwide bar association with its primary focus on the practice of federal law.

The FBA's 15,000 members nationwide have a direct stake in the well-being, independence and integrity of the Federal judiciary.

At the same time, our 2700 members practicing in the 9th Circuit have direct experience with the structure, caseload, adjudication, and operation of the 9th Circuit - as well as with that Circuit's own continuing efforts to address its problems.

The Federal Bar's position on the 9th Circuit per se and on the White Commission Report was developed over a period of thorough consideration, including testimony before the commission itself.

Today, I am pleased to represent FBA's national president, Adrienne Berry of Kentucky, and our membership across the country, in highlighting 3 basic areas of concern:

- Reorganization of the 9th Circuit;
- the filling of judicial vacancies; and,
- the federalization of state crimes.

The FBA supports the recommendation of the White Commission against splitting the 9th Circuit into 2 or more circuits. Instead, the FBA favors increased innovation and experimentation by the 9th Circuit to arrive at solutions that advance the court's efficiency and effectiveness.

As the commission's report acknowledges, the 9th Circuit long has been a crucible for experimentation in management and disposition of a growing federal court caseload. Many of the innovations employed by the 9th Circuit in the past have proven successful, and, thus, are proven mechanisms for other circuits to implement as they encounter problems associated with growth of caseload and court size.

However, the FBA believes that the Commission's proposed division of the Circuit into 3 semi-autonomous adjudicative units, and corresponding en banc revisions, are NOT in the best interest of the Circuit, its adjudicatory processes, litigants appearing before it, and the interests of justice.

That remedy is not likely to increase the uniform application of federal law - certainly within California. It is not likely to make the law more predictable, nor speed the court's decision-making. It will not create cost-savings for litigants. It is not likely to lead to fewer conflicts in decisional law, nor ease the weight of the 9th Circuit's caseload. It will not enhance or simplify litigation. Indeed, the proposal would in many respects accomplish the opposite effects by haplessly layering, dividing and isolating.

A special comment on the politics of this issue:

Splitting the 9th Circuit—legislatively or adjudicatively—to remedy the problem of political or ideological differences or disapproval with the opinions emanating from the 9th Circuit, is inappropriate in the view of the Federal Bar Association.

Altering basic judicial structure on political grounds is shortsighted and misguided, and would, in the opinion of the Federal Bar, violate the basic tenets of judicial independence and integrity.

To those in the Congress who may advance or hide behind a political motivation on this issue, beware of that for which you ask, because the political winds are bound to change.

To the extent that Congress may feel compelled legislatively to ensure continuing focus on reform within the circuit, the FBA recommends that Congress enact legislation that will authorize the 9th Circuit to implement sensible initiatives, including reform of the en banc process, in an effort to determine, in practice, what does and does not work.

Rather than pass legislation that would pour concrete around a new structure that may or may not prove desirable with experience, Congress should permit—even charge—the 9th Circuit to blaze the trail through experiment and flexibility—and create a model to be used by other circuits in the future.

For my final 2 points, I would note that the FBA believes the best interests of the 9th Circuit and the entire federal court system would be served by increased Congressional attention to 2 major concerns:

- the assurance of timely filling of judicial vacancies, and,
- the reversal of the trend to federalize crimes in areas traditionally left to the states.

As we commented before the White Commission, the prompt filling of judicial vacancies is critical to a healthy federal judiciary. NO structural innovation will work if excessive vacancies continue.

While you as House members do not play an institutional role in advice and consent, your state and regional delegation influence—and especially your political party input—are sure ways you can help the process.

Regarding the problem with federalization of state crimes, the FBA recommends that Congress require of itself the generation of a "judicial impact statement" before the passage of any further federal criminal legislation.

Viewing your legislative actions through a prism such as this would enable you to forecast and guard against unnecessary additional caseloads and costs that new legislation might create.

We ask that this committee implement a judicial impact review and analysis procedure before reporting out your next piece of criminal legislation.

Mr. Chairman, thank you for affording the Federal Bar Association this opportunity to appear today and contribute to this oversight and discussion.

Source: Personal and professional files of William N. LaForge.

§3.35 Written vs. Oral Testimony: When Written Witness Statements Suffice

On many occasions, a written witness statement provided to a committee for a hearing record will suffice in lieu of an actual personal appearance by a witness before a committee to present oral testimony. These documents are frequently referred to as "outside witness statements." These written statements may be requested by a committee, or voluntarily offered by a witness or organization, subject to the committee's rules and guidelines regarding outside witness statements.

Written statements prepared for a hearing are usually included in the hearing record verbatim. When a witness makes an appearance before a committee to testify, the witness's actual spoken words during oral testimony are also included in the record. On occasions when a witness or organization is not given an opportunity to testify, chooses not to do so, or deems a personal appearance to testify unnecessary, it is, nevertheless, often beneficial that a written statement be provided for the hearing record. For more information on outside witness statements, see § 2.116, Outside Witness Statements—Written Statements for the Record.

§3.36 Purpose of Written-Only Witness Statements

As explained in § 3.35 above, outside witness statements are often submitted to a committee for inclusion in the hearing record in lieu of oral, in-person testimony before the committee. These written-only statements serve the purposes of making the official record, providing helpful information to a committee, and transmitting to a committee the position and recommendations of an outside organization.

As part of the official hearing record of a committee, these written statements may be used for reference and citation purposes, may be consulted and relied upon by a committee in its decision-making regarding legislative action, and demonstrate that an outside organization cares enough about an issue and a hearing to submit an official statement for the record. For more information on outside witness statements, see § 2.116, Outside Witness Statements—Written Statements for the Record.

§3.37 Compliance Deadlines

Congressional committees establish compliance deadlines for the submission of written statements. For witnesses planning to testify in person before a committee, a formal written statement is typically required by committee rule or guideline to be submitted to the committee a specific number of days before the hearing. For other written statements for the committee hearing record, but not in preparation for an appearance to testify before a committee in person, committees usually have rules or guidelines outlining due dates and other specifications for "outside witness statements" and for statements requested or invited by a committee. Quite often, these due dates are after the actual hearing date, but before the hearing record is finally closed at the committee's discretion.

For more information about submitting advanced copies of witness statements, see § 2.7, Advanced Copies of Witness Statement or Written Testimony, Biographical and Other Information—Special Rules Regarding Truth in Testimony. For more information on outside witness statements generally, see § 2.116, Outside Witness Statements—Written Statements for the Record. For specific information about committee deadlines, consult individual committee rules accessible via committee links available at <*www.House.gov*> and <*www.Senate.gov*>.

§3.38 Sample of Congressional Committee Instructions for Providing Written Testimony

House Committee on Appropriations
Subcommittee on the Departments of Commerce, Justice, and State, the Judiciary and Related Agencies

INSTRUCTIONS FOR PROVIDING WRITTEN TESTIMONY FOR FISCAL YEAR 2005

The Subcommittee on Commerce, Justice, State and the Judiciary will not be scheduling any outside witness hearings on the fiscal year 2005 budget. As in past years, interested parties may submit written testimony to be included in the official record. Testimony must be received **no later than 5:00 pm on April 9, 2004** for it to be included in the printed hearing volume. Current mail handling measures have complicated Congressional mail procedures. The Subcommittee strongly recommends submitting testimony via electronic mail.

To send via standard mail your written statements must:

- Not exceed four pages;
- Be singled-spaced on 8.5 by 11 inch letter size paper;
- Be at least 12 point font and one inch margins;
- Clearly state in the first paragraph the agency, program, and amount of money involved in the request;
- Clearly indicate your name, title, and institutional affiliation at the top of the first page; and
- Not include color and detailed photos since the hearing volume will be photographically reproduced. However, use of charts and tables and the use of appropriate bold type and bullets are acceptable, as long as they are within the four page maximum length.

You should send four individually stapled, unfolded copies, and one original, unstapled copy to:

Subcommittee on Commerce, Justice, State, the Judiciary
and Related Agencies H309, The Capitol
U.S. House of Representatives
Washington, DC 20515-6017
Attention: CJS Detailee

* Note: If sending testimony by any means other than electronically, allow an additional 3 to 4 days for delivery (the deadline is still 5:00 pm on April 9, 2004).

As an alternative, you may submit your testimony as an electronic mail attachment to (<*Approp.Commercejustice@mail.house.gov*>). Your written statement must meet all of the above standard mail requirements except for the multiple copy requirement. Submit your testimony EITHER electronically or through the postal mail service.

The Rules of the House require additional information from nongovernmental witnesses. According to clause 2(g)(4) of Rule XI,

> In the case of a witness appearing in a nongovernmental capacity, a written statement of proposed testimony shall include a curriculum vitae and a disclosure of the amount and source (by agency and program) of each Federal grant (or sub-grant thereof) or contract (or subcontract thereof) received during the current fiscal year or either of the two previous fiscal years by the witness or by an entity represented by the witness.

Consistent with this rule, the Subcommittee requests that all public written testimony be accompanied by the curriculum vitae and disclosure described above. This supplementary information is not subject to the page limitation for written testimony.

Thank you again for your interest in the activities of the Subcommittee on Commerce, Justice, State, the Judiciary and Related Agencies. If you have any questions or require further information, please contact the Subcommittee staff at 202-225-3351.

Source: Committee on Appropriations, U.S. House of Representatives.

§3.39 Purposes of Oral Statements and Witness Testimony

In contrast to the purposes of written statements, as outlined in § 3.35 and § 3.36, the purposes of oral statements delivered in the form of testimony by a witness at a congressional hearing include accommodating a face-to-face presentation to the committee by the witness in person; the opportunity for a committee to hear directly and personally from a witness and not just rely on information available in a written text; and the interpersonal dynamics of two-way communication that is triggered by oral testimony and continued in a subsequent question-and-answer period.

Oral testimony should be brief enough to fit within the prescribed time limit, educational and informative for the committee members, and succinct and punchy enough to gain the attention of the committee panel. Oral testimony is a witness's one shot at addressing a committee in person to make the record, state, and advocate a policy position, represent the views of an organization, capture the attention and interest of a committee, educate a committee as it formulates legislation on a particular subject matter, and make requests and recommendations concerning the topic of a hearing. Witnesses should be thoroughly prepared to testify and make their appearance before a committee count.

For an example of a narrative outline used to deliver oral testimony, see § 3.34, Sample of Oral Statement—Written Document Used as Reference to Deliver Oral Statement.

For more information on oral statements and witness testimony in general, see Chapter 5, "Presentation and Delivery of Oral Testimony."

§ 3.40 Building the Case and Developing the Argument

In developing the content and text of a written witness statement, the author should focus on building an effective and compelling case for the position or issue being presented to a committee, as well as on the development of sound and persuasive arguments and rationale that support the position or issue. Building a good case and developing sound arguments include utilizing several writing conventions or features such as:

- using education, persuasion, and argumentation (§ 3.41);
- explaining issues, facts, and remedies (§ 3.42);
- describing witness credibility (§ 3.43);
- using a succinct position outline (§ 3.44);
- explaining public policy rationale, support, and reasoning (§ 3.45);
- framing the issue properly (§ 3.46);
- distinguishing from the opposition's position (§ 3.47); and
- connecting with the committee and its membership (§ 3.48).

These writing approaches and methods are explored more fully below in § 3.41 through § 3.48.

§ 3.41 Building the Case and Developing the Argument—Committee Advocacy: Education, Persuasion, and Argumentation

Advocacy is an important ingredient of congressional testimony. In one form or another, every written witness statement involves the need for educating the committee; attempting to persuade it to take, or refrain from taking, certain action; and presenting a line of arguments for or against a particular issue or position. An effective written statement should include sufficient information about the issue or policy that is the subject of the hearing, its impact and results on stakeholders, and the position of the witness or statement provider, to constitute a thorough education of the committee.

Based on a foundation of information intended to educate the committee, the statement should also focus on advocating the position or interests of the witness or organization submitting the statement by setting out a compelling and persuasive case. A witness statement should both educate and advocate. To enhance the educational and advocacy aspects of a statement, the writer should include a series of arguments for or against the issue or position by enumerating supportive data such as:

- examples;
- anticipated results;
- success stories;
- positive vignettes;
- horror stories and worst-case scenarios;

- policy rationale;
- factual details;
- recommendations;
- potential remedies; and
- illustrative points that distinguish the witness's position from that of others or the status quo.

For more information generally on effective written advocacy, see Chapter 11, "Written Advocacy," in *Common Sense Rules of Advocacy for Lawyers*, Keith Evans, TheCapitol.Net.

§3.42 Building the Case and Developing the Argument—Explanation of Issues, Facts, and Remedies Sought

An effective, compelling written witness statement should include a carefully crafted explanation of the issues under consideration by the committee and included in the witness's position, the facts from the perspective of the witness as they apply to the issue at hand, and any remedies, solutions, or recommendations that the witness is suggesting for the committee's consideration.

As the statement is developed to achieve its educational and advocacy goals, attention should be given to including just the right amount of information about the issues and facts so that the reader will grasp them quickly and easily. A statement author should stick to the basics, and avoid either overloading the statement with unnecessary details, or under-explaining the issues and facts by clinging to sweeping generalities and unsupported assumptions.

The reader should be able to glean from the description of issues and facts just enough information to comprehend the case the witness is making. The statement should also include a clear description of any remedies, solutions, or recommendations being proffered by the witness, with the focus on helping the committee to understand and see a way to agree with the position of the witness.

§3.43 Building the Case and Developing the Argument—Witness Standing and Credibility

Beginning with the statement's title page or witness information that immediately precedes the opening paragraph of the statement, a witness should clearly advance his or her standing and credibility or that of the represented organization. It is important for a committee to understand who is offering the statement, and in what capacity the witness is bringing information to the committee. The witness and his or her organization, as well as all those being represented in the statement or at a hearing, should be clearly identified.

A witness wants the committee to know and understand that he or she is an expert on the subject of the hearing, a key stakeholder of the committee's policy decisions, an effective representative of a particular organization and point of view, and a unique communicator of important information that can be of help to the committee in its decision-making. The importance of the standing and credibility of a witness rests in the gravitas provided by either the witness personally or the organization being represented by the witness.

A committee needs to know it is hearing from someone who has special knowledge, interests, ideas, and recommendations. Periodically throughout the statement, references should be made to the witness's or organization's place and role in the issue area, its expertise and knowledge, its unique position on the issue or policy under consideration, and the impact of the committee's decision and action on the witness or organization. When a committee understands that a witness is stating a position or providing information on behalf of a sizeable or important stakeholder or constituent group, the impact of the witness statement and its message is much greater.

§3.44 Building the Case and Developing the Argument—Importance of Succinct Position Outline

Effective written witness testimony should include a statement, placed early in the document, that succinctly lays out the position of the witness on the issue or subject of the hearing. The statement should outline the general thesis or position, followed by an enumeration of its key components. This early statement announces to the committee the direction of the testimony, and outlines what will be discussed throughout the text. For example, if a witness is requesting research funding for a special project, the position outline should crisply include the basics of the request for the funding, the nature of the project, and how the funds will be utilized. Details should then follow in the main body of the testimony.

§3.45 Building the Case and Developing the Argument—Public Policy Rationale, Support, and Reasoning

Witnesses before congressional committees should always remember that they are engaged in education and advocacy in the public policy arena. While commercial, nonprofit, public interest and other non-governmental enterprises are vital and important, virtually every issue that is the subject of public policy decision-making—legislating, regulating and lawmaking—has to have a sound foundation in public policy. In the congressional hearings process, this rule of thumb applies to the oral and written testimony presented to committees by witnesses. Whatever the issue of a hearing, and whatever topic is the focus of a witness statement, it should be grounded in a legitimately sound public policy rationale.

Consequently, witness statements should be written in such a way that the public policy underpinning of an issue is clearly understood and advocated, and so that the case being made by a witness is understandable and saleable from a public policy perspective. Witness statements should be written with an eye toward answering the questions, "Why and how should the federal government be involved with this issue?" and "Why should this committee consider, and Congress legislate on, this particular matter?"

§3.46 Building the Case and Developing the Argument— Framing the Issue

In building a case in support of, or opposition to, an issue in the congressional committee hearings context, a witness statement should accurately and convincingly frame the issue in a manner that is understandable for purposes of both education and advocacy. This does not mean use of a clever headline or one-liner that is sensational in nature. Rather, it means characterizing the issue in an intellectually honest and straightforward manner for educational purposes, while also providing an accurate description that will advance the advocacy goals of the statement. The two are not mutually exclusive.

In the early 1990s, there was a famous ballot initiative case in a Midwestern state in which the proponents were attempting to place on the fall election ballot the opportunity for voters to consider the notion that residents of that state had "the right to know" all the ingredients in packaged food products (as opposed to just the highest concentration of ingredients). The proponents of this measure captured a lot of attention and support with their framing of the issue as "the right to know." The proposal and its characterization were accurate and honest, but certainly did not consider all angles. The opponents, business and manufacturing interests throughout the state, developed a counter-characterization they entitled "the billion dollar tax," because that would be the cost to producers and manufacturers—and eventually consumers—if the additional package labeling requirements became law.

Both sides presented their best cases to the public and cleverly campaigned on their respective framing of the issue: "the right to know" versus "the billion dollar tax." In the end, business interests and "the billion dollar tax" argument prevailed.

While all issues do not lend themselves to clear black-and-white framing distinctions, written testimony should likewise include a concise, accurate, and straightforward framing of the issue so that the facts involved and the position of the witness are communicated in a clear and understandable way, as well as in a compelling and persuasive manner.

§3.47 Building the Case and Developing the Argument— Distinguishing from Opposition Position: Comparing, Contrasting, and Categorizing

In the context of congressional testimony, an effective way to build the case and develop arguments for or against a particular issue or position is to distinguish the position of the witness from that of the opposition or other parties. A straightforward statement distinguishing one's position from others helps build the case you are attempting to make, while giving the reader a very different perspective on the matter. It can be helpful to your case and to the committee for the written statement to point out that "... our perspective on this issue is very different from another witness's position ...," or "... we are recommending a remedy to this policy concern that is unlike any other the committee has heard." These comments strengthen your case and attract the committee's attention because they offer something different.

The use of comparisons, contrasts, and categorizations are also helpful in setting one's issue or position apart from others. For example, comparing your position to a similar one recently approved by a committee, or to current law or policy, gives your position and statement credibility. Setting up contrasts between and among various perspectives can help support your case, while providing a committee with effective education, choices, and advocacy. Likewise, the use of categorizations—identifying a position or issue by categories, fields, or areas in which they typically fall or by which they are typically known—helps to build a case by clearly describing issues in terms (categories) understood by a committee. Distinguishing comments or data in a statement can be expressed affirmatively or negatively, depending on the issue, the style of the writer, and the focus of the distinction being made.

§3.48 Building the Case and Developing the Argument—"Playing" to the Committee Audience and Connecting to Members' Interests

In the drafting of a congressional witness statement, a witness or statement author should keep in mind not only the committee's interest in the subject matter per se, but its focus on various connections to the subject matter as well. To gain that level of understanding typically requires knowledge of the committee's history, as well as the track record of individual committee members, in dealing with the subject matter. Quite often that information can be obtained by a search and reading of committee and public documents and other publications, as well as through inquiries of committee staff. While written statements should not include information or perspectives that merely pander to the committee or its members, it is sometimes helpful and perfectly acceptable to make reference to an issue or situation that connects the committee or a committee member to the issue at hand.

For example, a comment referencing the results of an earlier hearing on the same subject would not only reinforce to the committee that the witness is aware of the committee's work on an issue, it would also bolster the witness's case and credibility by demonstrating a valuable or familiar connection or reference for the committee's consideration. Likewise, referencing a committee member's special interest or involvement in an issue, such as a member's previous professional activities regarding the issue in the private sector, can draw extra attention to the issue, while also helping the committee and its members relate to the position of the witness and the case being made in the written statement.

§3.49 Dissecting Written Witness Testimony or Statements in a Nutshell— The Essential Written Components and Documents in Developing a Statement

In a nutshell, the essential written components or documents in developing effective written congressional committee testimony or statements include:

1) Written Goal, Thesis, and Basic Theme (§ 3.2 and § 3.3);

2) Topic Outline (§ 3.8);

3) Draft Statement—Basic Script (§ 3.14);

4) Other Optional Helpful Written Documents: White paper (§ 3.15); Executive Summary/One-Pager (§ 3.16); Outline for Oral Presentation (§ 3.18); Briefing Book (§ 3.19); Committee Background Information (§ 3.20); Media Information (§ 3.21); FAQs and Question Modules (§ 3.22); and

5) Formal Statement for the Record—the Finished Product (§ 3.17).

§3.50 Dissecting Written Witness Testimony or Statements in a Nutshell— The Essential Formatting and Layout Components in Developing a Statement

(For a complete discussion, see § 3.27, Written Testimony Components: Manuscript Format, Layout, and Content.)

In a nutshell, the essential components of the format and layout of effective written text for congressional testimony or statements include:

1) Title Page (§ 3.27, #1);

2) Introductory Information in Lieu of a Title Page (§ 3.27, #2);

3) Opening (§ 3.27, #3);

4) Thematic Introduction (§ 3.27, #4);

5) Main Body of Statement Text or Narrative (§ 3.27, #5); and

6) Conclusion and Closing (§ 3.27, #6).

§3.51 Dissecting Written Witness Testimony or Statements in a Nutshell— The Essential Methods for Building the Case and Developing the Argument

(For more complete information, see § 3.40, Building the Case and Developing the Argument.)

In a nutshell, the essential components of building the case and developing the arguments for congressional testimony or statements include:

1) Committee Advocacy: Education, Persuasion, and Argumentation (§ 3.41);

2) Explanation of Issues, Facts, and Remedies Sought (§ 3.42);

3) Witness Standing and Credibility (§ 3.43);

4) Importance of Succinct Position Outline (§ 3.44);

5) Public Policy Rationale, Support, and Reasoning (§ 3.45);

6) Framing the Issue (§ 3.46);

7) Distinguishing from Opposition Position: Comparing, Contrasting, and Categorizing (§ 3.47); and

8) "Playing" to the Committee Audience and Connecting to Members' Interests (§ 3.48).

§3.52 HITS: Humor in Testimony— Mark Twain

There are moments in the history of congressional committee hearings in which someone larger than life has had the opportunity to testify and, moreover, to deliver a message to a committee that is both serious and humorous at once.

One such occasion involved Samuel Langhorne Clemens, better known as Mark Twain and widely considered to be the greatest humorist of 19th-century American literature, who contributed a major piece of humor in the context of his testimony before a congressional hearing in 1906.

Assuming his public persona by notably wearing a white suit that became his signature uniform, the 71-year-old author appeared before the Congressional Joint Committee on Patents to share his thoughts on a pending copyright bill.

Twain was the main and final witness of the hearing, which was held in the Congressional Reading Room of the Library of Congress. Before an unusually large crowd for a congressional hearing, Twain expressed his strong support for copyright protection for authors, artists, and musicians. His testimony, part-serious, part-humorous, was considered to be very influential in the eventual development of copyright law.

Remarks of Samuel Langhorne Clemens before the Congressional Joint Committee on Patents, December, 1906

COPYRIGHT HEARINGS, DECEMBER 7 TO 11, 1906.

ARGUMENTS

BEFORE THE

COMMITTEES ON PATENTS

OF THE

SENATE AND HOUSE OF REPRESENTATIVES, CONJOINTLY,

ON THE BILLS

S. 6330 AND H. R. 19853.

TO AMEND AND CONSOLIDATE THE ACTS RESPECTING COPYRIGHT.

DECEMBER 7, 8, 10, AND 11, 1906.

WASHINGTON:
GOVERNMENT PRINTING OFFICE.
1906.

(Continued on page 193)

Source: Arguments before the Committees on Patents of the Senate and House of Representatives, Conjointly, on the Bills S. 6330 and H.R. 19853 To Amend and Consolidate the Acts Respecting Copyright, 59th Cong. 116-121 (1906) (statement of Samuel L. Clemens). Statement accessible online at: <*www.TCNTwain.com*>.

Remarks of Samuel Langhorne Clemens before the Congressional Joint Committee on Patents, December, 1906

(continued)

FIFTY-NINTH CONGRESS.

COMMITTEE ON PATENTS OF THE SENATE.

ALFRED B. KITTREDGE, OF SOUTH DAKOTA, *Chairman*.

MOSES E. CLAPP, OF MINNESOTA.
REED SMOOT, OF UTAH.
PHILANDER C. KNOX, OF PENNSYLVANIA.
STEPHEN R. MALLORY, OF FLORIDA.
MURPHY J. FOSTER, OF LOUISIANA.
ASBURY C. LATIMER, OF SOUTH CAROLINA.

THOMAS B. ROBERTS, *Clerk*.

COMMITTEE ON PATENTS OF THE HOUSE OF REPRESENTATIVES.

FRANK D. CURRIER, NEW HAMPSHIRE, *Chairman*.

SOLOMON R. DRESSER, PENNSYLVANIA.
JOSEPH M. DIXON, MONTANA.
EDWARD H. HINSHAW, NEBRASKA.
ROBERT W. BONYNGE, COLORADO.
WILLIAM W. CAMPBELL, OHIO.
ANDREW J. BARCHFELD, PENNSYLVANIA.
JOHN C. CHANEY, INDIANA.
CHARLES McGAVIN, ILLINOIS.
WILLIAM SULZER, NEW YORK.
GEORGE S. LEGARE, SOUTH CAROLINA.
EDWIN Y. WEBB, NORTH CAROLINA.
ROBERT G. SOUTHALL, VIRGINIA.
JOHN GILL, JR., MARYLAND.

EDWARD A. BARNEY, *Clerk*.

2

(Continued on page 194)

Remarks of Samuel Langhorne Clemens before the Congressional Joint Committee on Patents, December, 1906
(continued)

TABLE OF CONTENTS.

3

(Continued on page 195)

Remarks of Samuel Langhorne Clemens before the Congressional Joint Committee on Patents, December, 1906
(continued)

4 TABLE OF CONTENTS.

(Continued on page 196)

Remarks of Samuel Langhorne Clemens before the Congressional Joint Committee on Patents, December, 1906

(continued)

STATEMENT OF MR. SAMUEL L. CLEMENS.

Mr. CLEMENS. I have read the bill. At least I have read such portions of it as I could understand; and indeed I think no one but a practiced legislator can read the bill and thoroughly understand it, and I am not a practiced legislator. I have had no practice at all in unraveling confused propositions or bills. Not that this is more confused than any other bill. I suppose they are all confused. It is natural that they should be, in a legal paper of that kind, as I understand it. Nobody can understand a legal paper, merely on account of the language that is in it. It is on account of the language that is in it that no one can understand it except an expert.

Necessarily I am interested particularly and especially in the part of the bill which concerns my trade. I like that bill, and I like that extension from the present limit of copyright life of forty-two years to the author's life and fifty years after. I think that will satisfy any reasonable author, because it will take care of his children. Let the grandchildren take care of themselves. "Sufficient unto the day." That would satisfy me very well. That would take care of my daughters, and after that I am not particular. I shall then long have been out of this struggle and independent of it. Indeed, I like the whole bill. It is not objectionable to me. Like all the trades and occupations of the United States, ours is represented and protected in that bill. I like it. I want them to be represented and protected and encouraged. They are all worthy, all important, and if we can take them under our wing by copyright, I would like to see it done. I should like to have you encourage oyster culture and anything else. I have no illiberal feeling toward the bill. I like it. I think it is just. I think it is righteous, and I hope it will pass without reduction or amendment of any kind.

I understand, I am aware, that copyright must have a term, must have a limit, because that is required by the Constitution of the United States, which sets aside the earlier constitution, which we call the Decalogue. The Decalogue says that you shall not take away from any man his property. I do not like to use the harsher term, "Thou shalt not steal." But the laws of England and America do take away property from the owner. They select out the people who create the literature of the land. Always talk handsomely about the literature of the land. Always say what a fine, a great monumental thing a great literature is. In the midst of their enthusiasm they turn around and do what they can to crush it, discourage it, and put it out of existence. I know that we must have that limit. But forty-two years is too much of a limit. I do not know why there should be a limit at all. I am quite unable to guess why there should be a limit to the possession of the product of a man's labor. There is no limit to real estate. As Doctor Hale has just suggested, you might just as well, after you had discovered a coal mine and worked it twenty-eight years, have the Government step in and take it away—under what pretext?

The excuse for a limited copyright in the United States is that an author who has produced a book and has had the benefit of it for that term has had the profit of it long enough, and therefore the Government takes the property, which does not belong to it, and

(Continued on page 197)

Remarks of Samuel Langhorne Clemens before the Congressional Joint Committee on Patents, December, 1906
(continued)

COPYRIGHT HEARINGS. 117

generously gives it to the eighty-eight millions. That is the idea. If it did that, that would be one thing. But it does not do anything of the kind. It merely takes the author's property, merely takes from his children the bread and profit of that book, and gives the publisher double profit. The publisher and some of his confederates who are in the conspiracy rear families in affluence, and they continue the enjoyment of these ill-gotten gains generation after generation They live forever, the publishers do.

As I say, this limit is quite satisfactory to me—for the author's life, and fifty years after. In a few weeks, or months, or years I shall be out of it. I hope to get a monument. I hope I shall not be entirely forgotten. I shall subscribe to the monument myself. But I shall not be caring what happens if there is fifty years' life of my copyright. My copyrights produce to me annually a good deal more money than I have any use for. But those children of mine have use for that. I can take care of myself as long as I live. I know half a dozen trades, and I can invent a half a dozen more. I can get along. But I like the fifty years' extension, because that benefits my two daughters, who are not as competent to earn a living as I am, because I have carefully raised them as young ladies, who don't know anything and can't do anything. So I hope Congress will extend to them that charity which they have failed to get from me.

Why, if a man who is mad—not mad, but merely strenuous—about race suicide should come to me and try to get me to use my large political or ecclesiastical influence for the passage of a bill by this Congress limiting families to 22 children by one mother, I should try to calm him down. I should reason with him. I should say to him, "That is the very parallel to the copyright limitation by statute. Leave it alone. Leave it alone and it will take care of itself." There is only one couple in the United States that can reach that limit. Now, if they reach that limit let them go on. Make the limit a thousand years. Let them have all the liberty they want. You are not going to hurt anybody in that way. Don't cripple that family and restrict it to 22 children. In doing so you are merely offering this opportunity for activity to one family per year in a nation of eighty millions. It is not worth the while at all.

The very same with copyright. One author per year produces a book which can outlive the forty-two year limit, and that is all. This nation can not produce two authors per year who can create a book that will outlast forty-two years. The thing is demonstrably impossible. It can not be done. To limit copyright is to take the bread out of the mouths of the children of that one author per year, decade, century in and century out. That is all you get out of limiting copyright.

I made an estimate once when I was to be called before the copyright committee of the House of Lords, as to the output of books, and by my estimate we had issued and published in this country since the Declaration of Independence 220,000 books. What was the use of protecting those books by coypright? They are all gone. They had all perished before they were 10 years old. There is only about one book in a thousand that can outlive forty-two years of copyright. Therefore why put a limit at all? You might just as well limit a family to 22. It will take care of itself. If you try to recall to your

(Continued on page 198)

Remarks of Samuel Langhorne Clemens before the Congressional Joint Committee on Patents, December, 1906

(continued)

118 COPYRIGHT HEARINGS.

minds the number of men in the nineteenth century who wrote books in America which books lived forty-two years you will begin with Fennimore Cooper, follow that with Washington Irving, Harriet Beecher Stowe, and Edgar A. Poe, and you will not go far until you begin to find that the list is limited. You come to Whittier and Holmes and Emerson, and you find Howells and Thomas Bailey Aldrich, and then the list gets pretty thin and you question if you can find 20 persons in the United States in a whole century who have produced books that could outlive or did outlive the forty-two year limit. You can take all the authors in the United States whose books have outlived the forty-two year limit and you can seat them on one bench there. Allow three children to each of them, and you certainly can put the result down at 100 persons. Add two or three more benches. You have plenty of room left. That is the limit of the insignificant number whose bread and butter are to be taken away. For what purpose? For what profit to anybody?

Nobody can tell what that profit is. It is only those books that will outlast the forty-two-year limit that have any value after ten or fifteen years. The rest are all dead. Then you turn those few books into the hands of the pirate—into the hands of the legitimate publisher—and they go on, and they get the profit that properly should have gone to wife and children. I do not think that is quite right. I told you what the idea was in this country for a limited copyright.

The English idea of copyright, as I found, was different, when I was before the committee of the House of Lords, composed of seven members I should say. The spokesman was a very able man, Lord Thring, a man of great reputation, but he didn't know anything about copyright and publishing. Naturally he didn't, because he hadn't been brought up to this trade. It is only people who have had intimate personal experience with the triumphs and griefs of an occupation who know how to treat it and get what is justly due.

Now that gentleman had no purpose or desire in the world to rob anybody or anything, but this was the proposition—fifty years extension—and he asked me what I thought the limit of copyright ought to be.

"Well," I said, "perpetuity." I thought it ought to last forever.

Well, he didn't like that idea very much. I could see some resentment in his manner, and he went on to say that the idea of a perpetual copyright was illogical, and so forth, and so on. And here was his reason—for the reason that it has long ago been decided that ideas are not property, that there can be no such thing as property in ideas.

I said there was property in ideas before Queen Anne's time, that it was recognized that books had perpetual copyright then. Doctor Hale has explained why they reduced it to forty-two years in Queen Anne's time. That is a very charitable explanation of that event. I never heard it before. I thought a lot of publishers had got together and got it reduced. But I accept Doctor Hale's more charitable view, for his information is more than mine and he is older than I am, but not much older. He is older, but not much older.

That there could be no such thing as property in an intagible idea. He said, "What is a book? A book is just built from base to roof with ideas, and there can be no property in them."

(Continued on page 199)

Remarks of Samuel Langhorne Clemens before the Congressional Joint Committee on Patents, December, 1906

(continued)

COPYRIGHT HEARINGS. 119

I said I wished he could mention any kind of property existing on this planet, property that had a pecuniary value, which was not derived from an idea or ideas.

"Well," he said, "landed estate—real estate."

"Why," I said, "Take an assumed case, of a dozen Englishmen traveling through the South—Africa—they camp out; eleven of them see nothing at all; they are mentally blind. But there is one in the party who knows what that harbor means, what this lay of the land means; to him it means that some day—you can not tell when—a railway will come through here, and there on that harbor a great city will spring up. That is his idea. And he has another idea, which is to get a trade, and so, perhaps, he sacrifices his last bottle of Scotch whisky and gives a horse blanket to the principal chief of that region and buys a piece of land the size of Pennsylvania. There is the value of an idea applied to real estate. That day will come, as it was to come when the Cape-to-Cairo Railway should pierce Africa and cities should be built, though there was some smart person who bought the land from the chief and received his everlasting gratitude, just as was the case with William Penn, who bought for $40 worth of stuff the area of Pennsylvania. He did a righteous thing. We have to be enthusiastic over it, because that was a thing that never happened before probably. There was the application of an idea to real estate. Every improvement that is put upon real estate is the result of an idea in somebody's head. A skyscraper is another idea. The railway was another idea. The telephone and all those things are merely symbols which represent ideas. The washtub was the result of an idea. The thing hadn't existed before. There is no property on this earth that does not derive pecuniary value from ideas and association of ideas applied and applied and applied again and again and again, as in the case of the steam engine. You have several hundred people contributing their ideas to the improvement and the final perfection of that great thing, whatever it is—telephone, telegraph, and all."

So if I could have convinced that gentleman that a book which does consist solely of ideas, from the base to the summit, then that would have been the best argument in the world that it is property, like any other property, and should not be put under the ban of any restriction, but that it should be the property of that man and his heirs forever and ever, just as a butcher shop would be, or—I don't care—anything, I don't care what it is. It all has the same basis. The law should recognize the right of perpetuity in this and every other kind of property. But for this property I do not ask that at all. Fifty years from now I shall not be here. I am sorry, but I shall not be here. Still, I should like to see it.

Of course we have to move by slow stages. When a great event happens in this world, like that of 1714, under Queen Anne, it stops everything, but still, all the world imagines there was an element of justice in that act. They do not know why they imagine it, but it is because somebody else has said so. And that process must continue until our day, and keep constantly progressing on and on: First twenty-eight years was added, and then a renewal for fourteen years; and then you encountered Lord Macaulay, who made a speech on copyright when it was going to achieve a life of sixty years,

(Continued on page 200)

Remarks of Samuel Langhorne Clemens before the Congressional Joint Committee on Patents, December, 1906

(continued)

120 COPYRIGHT HEARINGS.

which reduced it to forty years—a speech that was read all over the world by everybody who does not know that Lord Macaulay did not know what he was talking about. So he inflicted this disaster upon his successors in the authorship of books. It has to undergo regular and slow development—evolution.

Here is this bill, one instance of it. Make the limit the author's life and fifty years after, and, as I say, fifty years from now they will see that that has not convulsed the world at all. It has not destroyed any San Francisco. No earthquakes concealed in it anywhere. It has changed nobody. It has merely fed some starving author's children. Mrs. Stowe's two daughters were close neighbors of mine, and—well, they had their living very much limited.

That is, to my mind, about what I was to talk about. I have some notes—I don't know in which pocket I put them—and probably I can't read them when I find them.

There was another thing that came up in that committee meeting. I would rather get the advantage of a lord than most anyone. He asked me on what ground I could bring forth such a sort of monstrosity as that—the idea of a perpetual copyright on literature.

He said, "England does not do that." That was good argument. If England doesn't do a thing, that is all right. Why should anybody else? England doesn't do it. England stands for limited copyright, and will stand for limited copyright, and not give unlimited copyright to anybody's books.

I said, "You are excepting one book."

He said, "No; there is no book in England that has perpetual copyright."

I said, "Yes; there is one book in England that has perpetual copyright, and that is the Bible."

He said, "There is no such copyright on the Bible in England."

But I had the documents with me, and I was able to convince him that not only does England confer perpetual copyright upon the Old and New Testaments, but also on the Revised Scriptures, and also on four or five other theological books, and confers those perpetual copyrights and the profits that may accrue not upon some poor author and his children, but upon the rich and competent, who can take care of themselves without perpetual copyright. There was that one instance of injustice, the discrimination between the author of the present day and the author of thousands of years ago, whose copyright had really expired by the statute of limitations.

I say again, as I said in the beginning, I have no enmities, no animosities toward this bill. This bill is plenty righteous enough for me. I like to see all these industries and arts propagated and encouraged by this bill. This bill will do that, and I do hope that it will pass and have no deleterious effect. I do seem to have an extraordinary interest in a whole lot of arts and things. The bill is full of those that I have nothing to do with. But that is in line with my generous, liberal nature. I can't help it. I feel toward those same people the same sort of charity of the man who arrived at home at 2 o'clock in the morning from the club. He was feeling perfect satisfaction with life—was happy, was comfortable. There was his house weaving and weaving and weaving around. So he watched his chance, and by and by when the steps got in his

(Continued on page 201)

Remarks of Samuel Langhorne Clemens before the Congressional Joint Committee on Patents, December, 1906
(continued)

neighborhood he made a jump and he climbed up on the portico. The house went on weaving. He watched his door, and when it came around his way he climbed through it. He got to the stairs, went up on all fours. The house was so unsteady he could hardly make his way, but at last he got up and put his foot down on the top step, but his toe hitched on that step, and of course he crumpled all down and rolled all the way down the stairs and fetched up at the bottom with his arm around the newel post, and he said, "God pity a poor sailor out at sea on a night like this."

The committee adjourned until 10 o'clock a. m. to-morrow.

SATURDAY, *December 8, 1906—10 o'clock a. m.*

The committee met at the Senate reading room, Congressional Library, jointly with the House Committee on Patents.

Present: Senators Kittredge (chairman), Clapp, Smoot, Mallory, and Latimer; Representatives Currier, Hinshaw, Bonynge, Campbell, Barchfeld, Chaney, McGavin, Legare, and Webb.

The CHAIRMAN. The committee would like to hear from Mr. Montgomery first.

The LIBRARIAN. Mr. Montgomery, Mr. Chairman, would like to note, for the information of the committee, some difficulties that might be experienced by the Treasury Department in actually applying the provisions of section 30—is that it, Mr. Montgomery?—as to importations.

Mr. MONTGOMERY. Section 30 and section 16. I did intend to say something about the cataloguing of the title entries, the inability of customs officers to detect these illegal importations; but if I am to confine my statement to section 30, I will do so.

The LIBRARIAN. Mr. Montgomery, are you the official in the Treasury Department who has particularly to do with importations?

Mr. MONTGOMERY. Yes, sir.

The LIBRARIAN. From this end—that is, in the main Department?

Mr. MONTGOMERY. Yes, sir; I expect I had better make a litttle broader statement.

The CHAIRMAN. How much time do you wish, Mr. Montgomery?

Mr. MONTGOMERY. Five minutes, I should say, will be enough.

STATEMENT OF C. P. MONTGOMERY, ESQ., LAW CLERK, CUSTOMS DIVISION, TREASURY DEPARTMENT.

Mr. MONTGOMERY. The Treasury Department is required by existing law to render protection to the copyright proprietor by preventing importations which infringe his rights, and it is also required to protect certain of our industries—typesetting, for instance—against importations of books, etc., copyrighted in the United States, but manufactured abroad. To aid the Treasury and Post-Office Departments in executing the law, the act of 1891 provides for the publication and distribution weekly of catalogues of title entries. These title entries, which show the various titles of copyrighted books and other articles, now number over a million and a half. In order that

§3.999 Chapter Summary

- The preparation of well-drafted, informative, and compelling written testimony in advance of a congressional committee hearing is a critical ingredient in the success formula for any hearing. (§ 3.0)
- In a convincing testimonial, a congressional committee professional staff member provides important perspectives on the importance of drafting an effective, informative, and compelling witness statement. (§ 3.1)
- A written goal statement and thesis can help crystallize and focus on the basic theme and subject matter of written testimony. (§ 3.2 and § 3.3)
- In the preparation of witness testimony, the author should determine the methodology and approach to be used in managing the statement preparation stage and in drafting the statement. (§ 3.4)
- To ensure an understanding of the committee's expectations regarding the preparation of witness statements, preparers of congressional witness testimony and statements should work closely with the professional staff of the committee holding the hearing, as well as consult committee rules and instructions. (§ 3.5 and § 3.6)
- Preparation of a quality witness statement requires effective research and adequate sources of information. (§ 3.7)
- Building on a goal statement, a thesis and appropriate research, the author of a witness statement should analyze and outline the key issues. (§ 3.8)
- A witness and a preparer of a witness statement should conduct a political analysis of the issues before the committee and have a firm understanding of the political landscape and the public policy context. (§ 3.9)
- Before drafting a statement, the author of witness testimony should have a keen understanding of the issue context and related stakeholders. (§ 3.10)
- An understanding of the thinking and position of opponents to the witness on a public policy issue can be helpful in the formation of an issue position and the drafting of a written statement. (§ 3.11)
- Before commencing a draft of a witness statement, the writer should identify the appropriate targeted audiences of the witness testimony, including primarily the committee itself. (§ 3.12)
- Several important documents can be utilized in the construction of a substantive witness statement that makes a powerful record. (§ 3.13)
  1) Basic Script: the Essence of the Witness Statement's Case and Content (§ 3.14)
  2) The "White Paper": The Complete Case Supporting the Witness Statement and its Message (§ 3.15)
  3) Executive Summary and the Famous One-Pager (§ 3.16)
  4) Formal Statement for the Record (§ 3.17)

5) Narrative, Outline, or Notes Used for Oral Presentation (§ 3.18)
6) The Briefing Book (§ 3.19)
7) Background Information for Congressional Committees and Staff (§ 3.20)
8) Media Advisories, Press Kits, Backgrounders, and Releases (§ 3.21)
9) FAQs and Question Modules (§ 3.22)

- Federal executive and judicial branch officials who testify face unique and additional requirements and challenges in the preparation of written testimony. (§ 3.23)
- Members of Congress and representatives of special legislative branch offices frequently testify before congressional committees. (§ 3.24)
- A formal written congressional committee statement should reflect best writing practices and styles, and utilize a user-friendly visual and stylistic layout. (§ 3.25)
- The writing of congressional witness testimony should incorporate key stylistic elements to make the statement effective and compelling. (§ 3.26)
- Effective witness testimony consists of a number of components that provide a simple and logical format and layout, and incorporates purposeful content that adds value, helpful information, and advocacy to the statement. (§ 3.27)
- The effective use of graphics in written testimony can enhance a formal statement and add value to the witness's message to a committee. (§ 3.28)
- Selected samples of written congressional witness statements provide examples of various styles, approaches, content, case and message development, formatting and layout, and other best practices. (§ 3.29)
  1) Statement Prepared for House Judiciary Subcommittee on Courts and Intellectual Property in Opposition to the Split of the 9th Circuit Court of Appeals (§ 3.30)
  2) Statement Prepared for House Appropriations Subcommittee on Transportation in Support of Federal Funding for Clean Air Research (§ 3.31)
  3) Statement Prepared for Senate Appropriations Subcommittee on Agriculture, Rural Development, and Related Agencies in Support of Federal Funding for Turfgrass Research (§ 3.32)
  4) Statement Prepared for Senate Appropriations Subcommittee on Labor, Health and Human Services, Education, and Related Agencies in Support of Hospital Funding (§ 3.33)
- It is helpful for a witness appearing before a congressional committee to testify to utilize a written document as a guide and reference. (§ 3.34)
- In certain situations, only a written witness statement is necessary for inclusion in the hearing record of a committee. (§ 3.35)
- In lieu of oral testimony, written "outside witness statements" can provide valuable information to a committee, convey the position of an outside

witness or organization on the topic of the hearing, and make an adequate hearing record on the issue. (§ 3.36)

- Witnesses and authors of written testimony should consult with and adhere to committee compliance deadlines for the submission of written statements. (§ 3.37 and § 3.38)
- While similar in content and purpose to written congressional testimony and statements, the oral testimony and statements of witnesses have their own unique purposes. (§ 3.39)
- In developing the content and text of a written witness statement, the author should focus on building an effective and compelling case, as well as sound and persuasive arguments, in support of the witness's position. Several writing approaches and methods apply. (§ 3.40)
  1) Committee Advocacy: Education, Persuasion, and Argumentation (§ 3.41)
  2) Explanation of Issues, Facts, and Remedies Sought (§ 3.42)
  3) Witness Standing and Credibility (§ 3.43)
  4) Importance of Succinct Position Outline (§ 3.44)
  5) Public Policy Rationale, Support, and Reasoning (§ 3.45)
  6) Framing the Issue (§ 3.46)
  7) Distinguishing from Opposition Position: Comparing, Contrasting, and Categorizing (§ 3.47)
  8) "Playing" to the Committee Audience and Connecting to Members' Interests (§ 3.48)
- In a nutshell, in the process of developing and drafting a witness statement, the writer should consider and utilize certain essential written components and documents. (§ 3.49)
- In a nutshell, in the process of developing and drafting a witness statement, the writer should consider and utilize certain essential formatting and layout components. (§ 3.50)
- In a nutshell, in the process of developing and drafting a witness statement, the writer should consider and utilize some essential methods for building the case and developing the argument. (§ 3.51)
- HITS: Humor in Testimony is demonstrated in the person and words of the famous American author and humorist, Mark Twain, himself. (§ 3.52)

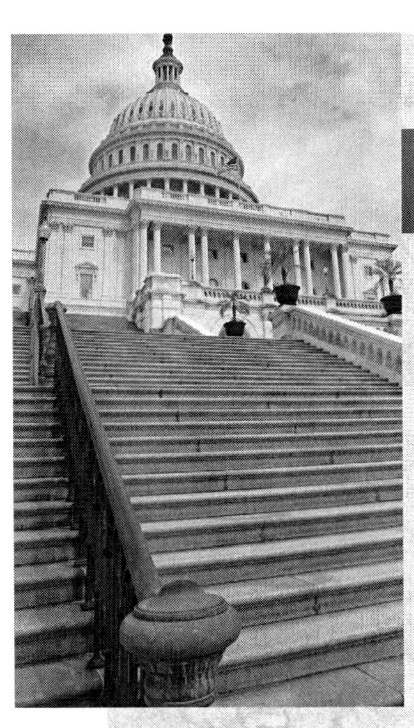

Chapter Four

Preparation of the Witness

Chapter Four

Section

Summary Table of Contents

§4.0 Introduction and Overview

A critical ingredient of any successful hearing and high-quality oral testimony from the perspective of both the committee and the witness is a well-prepared witness. To be an effective witness, one should understand the role of a witness and engage in studious preparation to testify before a congressional committee hearing.

The central role of a witness is essentially to present testimony and to answer committee questions. However, with that role comes a number of subparts and expectations that, if executed well, lay the foundation for a successful witness appearance. A committee expects a witness to be well-prepared personally and professionally to testify before the committee in an articulate, clear, concise, and helpful way. A committee looks to a witness for candor, helpful information, effective communication of a message, and responsiveness to questions.

In the hearing context, a successful and effective witness seeks to educate and inform a committee; to provide top-quality written and oral statements; to present oral testimony that conveys a compelling case and important information in a professional, convincing, and courteous manner; and to answer the committee's questions in a forthright and succinct way.

This chapter focuses on how to prepare to be an effective witness, describes the key methods and elements of witness preparation, provides explanations on how to fulfill the role of a witness, discusses the use of prepared materials and witness rehearsals, includes numerous samples of preparatory guidelines, outlines what a witness should expect, and serves as a workable preparatory checklist for witnesses and those engaged in helping a witness prepare for a hearing.

For more information on the essential elements of an effective and successful hearing from both a committee's and a witness's perspective, see § 2.14, The Essential Elements of an Effective and Successful Hearing; § 2.15, The Essential Elements of an Effective and Successful Hearing—The Committee's Perspective on What Constitutes an Effective and Successful Hearing; and § 2.16, The Essential Elements of an Effective and Successful Hearing—The Witness's Perspective on What Constitutes an Effective and Successful Hearing.

For more information on the essential elements of effective congressional testimony from both a committee's and a witness's perspective, see § 2.18, The Essential Elements of Effective Congressional Testimony; § 2.19, The Essential Elements of Effective Congressional Testimony—The Committee's Perspective on Effective Congressional Testimony; and § 2.20, The Essential Elements of Effective Congressional Testimony—The Witness's Perspective on Effective Congressional Testimony.

For information on congressional testimony as a lobbying strategy, and for additional perspectives on effective congressional testimony, see Chapter 10, *Lobbying and Advocacy*, Deanna Gelak, TheCapitol.Net. See especially § 10.61, Step-by-Step-Checklist for Testifying before Congress or Preparing a Witness.

§4.2 Testimonials of Two Congressional Experts on the Importance of Preparing a Witness to Testify before a Congressional Committee

"Careful and thorough preparation of a Congressional committee witness is extremely important to ensure that the witness is responsive to the committee and in a position to advocate persuasively for an organization's position on a particular issue or on legislation. Preparation and rehearsal should include familiarizing a witness with the necessary information to educate the committee and make a compelling case, as well as providing a witness with a good understanding of what to expect at the hearing, including the political climate, interests and predispositions of committee members, and other reality checks. Rehearsal sessions such as 'murder boards' are particularly effective in preparing a witness to handle committee questions deftly. Adequate preparation by a witness is essential to a successful committee appearance."

Source: Brenda Becker, Senior Vice President, Global Government Affairs, Boston Scientific Corporation; Formerly Assistant to the Vice President for Legislative Affairs, Office of Vice President Cheney; Assistant Secretary for Legislative Affairs, Department of Commerce for Secretary Donald L. Evans; Vice President, Congressional Communications, Blue Cross and Blue Shield Association.

"Testifying is just one of many potential turning points in the legislative process but it is a high-profile opportunity to either shine or set your issue back. The key is to be prepared for anything and then to relax and engage the committee members. Reading testimony scores no points so force yourself to work off a script using bulleted talking points and an extemporaneous style so you can be interactive with the committee members. Witnesses must spend ample time in advance summarizing the material, practicing the main points—out loud—and anticipating potential questions. The best testimony is not a show or stiff presentation, but a conversation that enables you to demonstrate your confidence in your position."

Source: Nancy Perry, Vice President, Government Affairs, The Humane Society of the United States.

§4.1 The Importance and Value of Witness Preparation

"Practice. Practice. Practice!" "It's better to over-prepare than to under-prepare." "Garbage in, garbage out." "Proper preparation prevents poor performance."

All these aphorisms, despite being overworked clichés, apply when approaching the preparation of a witness to testify before a congressional committee.

It is important to practice—to rehearse—but it is more important to rehearse properly, with a clear sense of mission, purpose, and expectation in mind. Unless a witness is a terrifically accomplished presenter who needs little to no warm-up, witness preparation is a critical stage in pre-hearing activities. Even if a witness has testified many times before, is considered the consummate expert, and has a reputation for, and history of, outstanding presentations, some preparation is wise—just to be sure and fully prepared.

The witness personally and those helping to prepare the witness should take great care to ensure that adequate preparation is planned and executed. Under-preparation should never be an option, and over-preparation, usually checked and adjusted in the process along the way, is a much better alternative. It is far better for a witness to leave a hearing feeling he or she had more to say or answer than to feel inadequate in the presentation or unable to field the committee's questions well.

The time and effort a witness devotes to preparation can, and usually does, pay huge dividends. If the background material studied and the written statement reviewed by a witness are poor-quality work products, it is difficult to expect anything but a less-than-stellar performance at a hearing. Good solid research, data, and preparation materials, plus a top-quality written statement, are vital to support excellent witness performance. Consequently, it behooves a witness and those assisting the witness to approach witness preparation in a methodical, organized, and thorough manner.

A witness's appearance to testify before a congressional committee is the "big show." Testifying before a committee presents the opportunity for a witness to educate and inform the committee, advocate a position, sell an idea, and engage in a question-and-answer dialogue that can serve the interests of both the committee and the witness. Leaving the preparation of a witness—and the witness's hearing performance—to happenstance and guesswork should be non-starters for any professional and responsible organization.

§4.3 How to Be an Effective Witness: A Start-Up Checklist

To be an effective witness, whether a first-timer or a veteran, an individual needs to exhibit several key qualities, understand the role of a witness, and manage expectations. Novice witnesses will want to rehearse a little more than a veteran to gain the necessary confidence and familiarity with the process and its flow. With experience will come greater comfort and skill in being an effective witness. Some common characteristics of an outstanding witness include:

- Follow the instructions and guidelines provided by the committee staff and rules. (See § 2.2 through § 2.7.)
- Prepare thoroughly, including ample rehearsals, but don't "over-prepare" or panic. (See § 4.5.)
- Be totally familiar with the subject matter of the hearing. As a witness, you are considered an expert. (See § 4.5 and § 4.9.)

- Be confident. Remember that you know more about the subject matter than anyone else in the room. (See § 4.5.)
- Participate in the preparation of the written testimony, review it carefully, and take "ownership" of the testimony. (See § 3.13.)
- Develop and follow a script for oral testimony, and stick to it. (See § 4.11 and § 4.21.)
- Anticipate and prepare for a line of questions from the committee, including potentially hostile questions. (See § 4.15 and § 4.18.)
- Engage the committee in a natural, friendly, and professional manner. Be yourself. (See § 4.25.)
- In communicating with the committee, proceed in as conversational, yet respectful, a manner as possible. Consider the committee members to be your peers. (See § 4.25.)
- Make your case and key points early and often to provide a lasting impression. (See § 5.30, § 5.32, § 5.52, and § 5.53.)
- Relax! Take your time and nail your presentation. (See § 4.5 and Chapter 5.)
- Be responsive to questions and give good answers. If you don't have an answer, just say so, and offer to provide it to the committee in writing later. (See Chapter 6.)
- Follow up diligently and in a timely manner with any responses to written questions, information or action promised. (See Chapter 7.)

§4.4 What to Expect as a Witness

There are a number of important considerations and perspectives that a witness should keep in mind when preparing for a hearing. Beyond those items noted below, for more information on the nature and culture of hearings, see § 1.70, The Psychology and Culture of Congressional Hearings: Mission, Education, Information, and Advocacy.

- A congressional committee holding a hearing is interested in gaining information from a witness that will educate the committee and be helpful to the committee in its work, and that will help make a public record of a timely issue.
- A committee's environment—the hearing room—may be large or small, but will typically be set up with a witness table facing a dais where committee members sit. (See § 2.10 through § 2.12 for more information about hearing room layout, logistics, and locations.)
- Committee procedures and the order of business typically include opening statements by the chair and committee members, introduction of witnesses, testimony by witnesses, and questions from the committee for witnesses to answer. (For more information on committee hearing processes, order of business, and procedures, see § 2.90 through § 2.101.)

§4.5 Tips for First-Time Witnesses

- Brace against too much advice. Decide on an approach to preparation, stick with it, and select your own team. Adequate preparation is important, but don't create or allow a frenzied atmosphere during the preparation stage.
- Be confident and relaxed in your preparation, and those traits will likely carry over to your performance at the hearing. Remember that you know (or should know) more about the subject of your testimony than anyone else. You are the expert.
- Call on your experience as a professional within your organization and area of expertise, and in your approach to being a presenter. Capitalize on your good speaking qualities and work on those that need a boost.
- Study the subject matter and the written materials prepared for the hearing. Become an expert if you are not already one. The committee expects helpful information and a strong performance from you. Prepare to deliver both.
- Don't over-prepare. Prepare as much as you and your preparation team feel you should, but don't overdo it under the mistaken impression that saturation leads to excellence. When you nail the preparation, call it a day and move on.
- Prepare in such a way that you will stay calm, professional, and in control throughout the testimony phase of the hearing, as well as during questions and answers. Stick to your script, message, and goal.
- Provide good, straightforward answers to questions, and be candid. If you don't know an answer, offer to provide it to the committee in writing as a post-hearing follow-up matter.

- Committee hearings are usually relatively formal under a prescribed order of business. Committees typically treat witnesses professionally and respectfully, and engage them in the enterprise of making an important public record on key issues.
- The witness's testimony will be delivered from a seat at the witness table directly in front of, and facing, the dais where the committee members sit. A witness may testify alone or be part of a panel of witnesses, as the committee chooses. Materials for use by a witness in testifying may be placed on the table for reference.
- Following the testimony of a witness, committee members have wide latitude in asking questions of a witness, and they appreciate engaged witnesses who provide complete and candid answers. (For information

§4.6 Threshold Questions for a Witness to Consider in Preparation for a Hearing

Hearing and testimony preparation should be approached with an understanding of committee needs and the political environment. Obtaining answers to questions such as the following will help the preparation team gain an understanding of the hearing context:

- What is the committee's purpose in holding the hearing?
- What is the occasion and type of hearing?
- Who are the other witnesses, and what is the proposed order of their testimony?
- What is the political environment? For example, what is the relationship between the chair and ranking minority member, and between majority and minority members of the committee and their staffs?
- Is there any relevant legislation or administration proposal pending?
- What will the witness's role at the hearing be?
- What type of questions will most likely be asked of the witness?
- With what previous work or activity has the witness been involved with the topic of the hearing, and what special knowledge or expertise does the witness bring to the hearing and the committee?

Source: Adapted from Preparing for Congressional Testimony, Governmental Accountability Office (GAO), Nov. 2005, p. 3–7.

on the question-and-answer portion of a hearing, see Chapter 6, "Responding to Committee Questions.")

- A committee's professional staff members who organize a hearing are available to provide advice and assistance to invited witnesses as they prepare for a hearing.

§4.7 Witness Preparation Team Meeting and Organization

In many cases involving the preparation of congressional testimony and the witness, it is helpful to utilize a team approach. Depending on an organization's and witness's circumstances, the preparation team may be a group of professionals or a single individual who is assigned the task of preparing the testimony and the witness, or, in some cases, the witness may do all the preparation personally.

If a team approach is employed, early in the process of witness preparation it is helpful to have a meeting of the preparation team or briefing staff, with or without the witness personally, as circumstances may dictate, to kick off the process and get organized. This meeting should focus on organizing the preparation timeline, materials, priorities, and scheduled events such as due dates for materials, briefings, and rehearsals. It also provides an opportunity to assess additional needs for information, materials, and overall preparation. The mission of the preparation meeting (and other similar meetings that may follow) is to organize, advance, and keep on track the process of getting the witness ready to testify at a hearing.

§4.8 Briefing the Witness

Once the preparation or briefing team has had an opportunity to meet and begin the process of preparation for a hearing, but early enough in the process for the witness personally to become actively engaged in the preparatory stage, the witness should be briefed on the process and timeline of preparation, the written testimony and materials to be used, and the methods of rehearsal that will be employed.

Depending on the witness's preferences and the protocols and practices of a particular organization, the witness may wish to be more or less involved with each phase of preparation. However, the purposes of the initial briefing, as well as subsequent briefings during the preparation stage, are to ensure that the witness is fully engaged and invested in the preparatory process, and that everything that needs to be done to prepare the witness is, in fact, underway.

§4.9 Witness Familiarization with the Hearing Issue and Subject Matter of the Testimony

As soon as practicable in the witness preparation stage, a witness should become familiar with the issue of the hearing and the subject matter of the testimony. This is a critical step in preparing to be an effective witness. Usually the witness is a principal or officer in the organization being asked to testify, so it is natural for that individual to be somewhat or very familiar with the hearing topic already. However, even in the best of circumstances in which the witness is the head of, or a top official for, an organization, he or she should be deliberative and diligent in preparing for a hearing.

To ensure adequate preparation as a knowledgeable or expert witness before a committee, a witness should spend time reading and reviewing pertinent organizational and outside information about the issues to be covered in the hearing. The witness should understand the committee and legislative process, and the type, purpose, and goal of the hearing. The witness should also have a firm grasp of the nature and context of the testimony he or she will present to the committee.

It is often a valuable exercise for a witness to conduct targeted reviews of materials and information from a variety of sources from both inside and outside the organization, including:

- **Previous hearings**—Consulting the hearing records or transcripts of previous hearings on the same or a related issue, especially before the same committee, can provide excellent sources of information about the issue at hand, the perspectives of the committee and its members, likely questions to be asked, and previously considered strategies and remedies. In its training materials, the United States Government Accountability Office (GAO) lists a number of key questions that can be answered through a review of previous congressional testimony and hearing records:

- What testimony has been given where presenters were in identical or somewhat similar situations?
- How did they deal with particular issues that might be causing you concern?
- What kinds of questions did committee members ask them?
- What kinds of responses did the witness make?
- How might those answers be improved?
- What were the major concerns of the chair, the ranking minority member, or other opinion leaders on the committee?
- What positions have members taken?
- What hints do those concerns and positions provide for your preparation, testimony, and answers?
- How do the chair and ranking minority member conduct hearings?

Source: Delivering Testimony, Participant Manual, United States Government Accountability Office (GAO), January 2007; for more information on GAO, go to *<www.gao.gov>*.

- **Media coverage and news clips**—Reviewing broadcast and print journalism coverage of an issue that is the subject of a hearing can provide valuable information and perspectives in preparing for a hearing on that same subject. It can be especially helpful to review media reports and news clips from the home states and congressional districts of the members of a committee to discern press coverage and perspectives on a local level.
- **Congressional inquiries, correspondence and questions**—A review of congressional contacts with the witness's organization can often provide a unique glimpse into the thinking, interests, and perspectives of Capitol Hill offices and committees. For government agencies, an analysis of congressional inquiries and correspondence may be helpful in preparation for a hearing. For organizations outside government, previous questions or inquiries made of the organization by Congress may provide helpful information during hearing preparation.
- **Issue analysis**—A thorough analysis of the issue that is the topic of the hearing is a highly recommended tool in the preparation of a witness for a hearing. This consideration especially applies if there have been recent public activities, incidents, or events that relate to the issue of the hearing and that have drawn public attention and scrutiny. For more information about the issue analysis, see § 3.8, Issue Analysis and Topic Outline.

- **Stakeholder analysis**—A thorough analysis of the various interests—players and people—involved in a particular issue that is the subject of a hearing can be helpful to a witness in preparing for hearing testimony. This approach is especially helpful in determining the "drivers" of an issue, those who benefit from or are harmed by it, and the universe of those who care about the issue for any reason. Conducting a stakeholder analysis can also help identify differing positions and perspectives on a given issue that can be helpful to a witness in formulating a more strategic approach to his or her role as a witness. For more information about the stakeholder analysis, see § 3.10, Issue Context and Stakeholders.
- **Opposition research**—Knowing the various and differing positions on a particular policy issue under consideration by a committee can be valuable and helpful information for a witness preparing to testify before a committee. For more information about opposition research, see § 3.11, Opposition Research.

§4.10 Witness Review and Study of Prepared Written Materials

As soon as practicable in the witness preparation phase, a witness should begin a review and study of the prepared written materials developed for the hearing. First and foremost, this review should include the official written statement prepared for the committee in advance of the hearing. That document encapsulates the witness's message, case, and arguments that are to be made in the testimony delivered at the committee hearing.

To the extent possible, it is preferable for a witness personally to be involved in the production and review of those documents early on, but that engagement is dependent on the nature, protocols, and practices of the organization, as well as on the individual preferences of the witness. The witness and the preparation team should also review the research and operational materials prepared for the hearing, including the briefing book or folder, background information, white papers or research data, FAQs, and question modules.

For more information on the key written materials used in preparation for a congressional committee hearing, see § 3.13 through § 3.22.

§4.11 Preparation and Use of Oral Statement Script or Outline

As soon as practicable in the witness preparation process, the witness (and the witness preparation team, as well, if one is employed) should determine what type of document will actually be used as a reference by the witness to deliver the testimony at the hearing. This document is the scripted narrative or outline placed in front of the wit-

§4.12 Tips for Visual Layout of Oral Statement Used in Testifying before a Congressional Committee

It is important that the document to be used by a witness in delivering testimony is laid out in an organized, simple, easy-to-read, and easy-to-use format. Whether a witness chooses to utilize a narrative script, a topic outline, or a bullet-item list (or the actual written statement prepared for the committee in advance), the written document on the table in front of the witness should be designed and formatted so that the witness is able to utilize and refer to it with ease and comfort.

Tips for Visual Layout of Oral Statement

- Use a large font (14 or 16 point)
- Highlight key portions of the script such as the beginning phrase of each sentence or bullet point
- Do NOT use all caps (capitalized letters do not have ascenders and descenders that provide visual cues for quick recognition when reading)
- Double space
- Leave wide margins
- Leave a very, very wide footer (about a third of the page) so that when you read the statement, your eyes/head will not bow down to look at the bottom of the page
- Use indents or "overhanging indents" for each paragraph start, or even each sentence
- Print only on one side of each page
- Never split a sentence on to 2 pages

ness at the witness table that is referenced and relied upon by the witness in the delivery of oral testimony.

In addition to becoming familiar with the complete contents of the official written statement, the witness should especially become thoroughly familiar with the oral statement script—in whatever format is chosen for use—and, during rehearsals, the witness should develop the ability and comfort to rely on that operational document to deliver the testimony. While it is important for a witness to have a keen familiarity with all the written documents prepared for a hearing, the witness should devote special attention to the presentation script, which should be utilized by the witness in rehearsals in preparation for the actual hearing appearance.

For more information on the importance and crafting of an oral statement script, see § 3.18, Important Documents: Drafting the Statement and Making the Record—Narrative, Outline or Notes Used for Oral Presentation.

To review an actual operational document utilized as the narrative script for delivery of oral testimony, see § 3.34, Sample of Oral Statement—Written Document Used as Reference to Deliver Oral Testimony.

For information on the preferred manner of delivering testimony with use of a prepared document, see § 4.13, Delivering the Statement: To Read or Not to Read.

For information on rehearsing oral testimony by using a prepared script, see § 4.21, Witness Rehearsal of Oral Testimony and Answers to Questions—Relying on the Oral Statement Script to Deliver Testimony.

For information on using written text or script to delivery oral testimony at the actual hearing, see § 5.30, Organization and Use of Written Text to Deliver the Oral Testimony.

§4.13 Delivering the Oral Statement: To Read or Not to Read

In presenting oral testimony to a committee, a witness preferably should operate from an outline, notes, or a narrative script rather than merely read a statement to the committee, and a witness should rehearse that presentation during the preparatory phase leading up to the hearing.

While House and Senate committee rules and practices dictate the format of oral presentations by witnesses at congressional hearings to some extent, common sense and traditional concepts of good delivery form should essentially prevail in the style a witness chooses to use in presenting testimony to a committee. It is true that many, perhaps even most, witnesses merely read a statement to a committee, quite often the actual written statement submitted earlier to the committee. However, that is not the best form and style. It is far better to speak to a committee during the delivery of testimony from a prepared summary of the official statement or other forms of outline notes or narrative scripts. With the investment of some time, effort, and practice, a witness can develop a better approach to the delivery of oral testimony that will more effectively convey a witness's message and case to a committee.

During preparation to testify at a committee hearing, a witness should become familiar with committee rules and guidelines regarding testimony presentation, including limits on the time allowed to testify and the resulting need to limit oral testimony to a brief summation of the witness's positions, arguments, and the basic content of the written testimony already provided to the committee for inclusion in the hearing record. Because a hearing can be lengthy, time limits are necessarily imposed on witnesses. Consequently, in the interest of time, and because the committee has the benefit of having the witness's written statement prior to the hearing, it is typically unnecessary for a witness to read the full written statement.

Moreover, it is the better practice not to read the official statement because doing so tends to tilt a witness's presentation and delivery to possible tedious repetition, dry recitation, and sometimes a mediocre or even boring presentation. It is much more preferable to present oral testimony with the use of notes, an outline, or a narrative script so that the witness can utilize a briefer and more succinct summary variation of the written statement that allows for a more conversational, effective, and interesting delivery. This preferred style and format of testimony delivery deserve careful planning and rehearsal by a witness.

Consequently, a witness should practice the delivery of oral testimony in a manner that utilizes notes or a narrative script, as the witness elects, and preferably not simply read a statement to the committee.

For more information on drafting preparatory notes for use during testimony, see § 3.18, Important Documents: Drafting the Statement and Making the Record—Narrative, Outline or Notes Used for Oral Presentation.

To review an actual operational document utilized as the narrative script for delivery of oral testimony, see § 3.34, Sample of Oral Statement—Written Document Used as Reference to Deliver Oral Testimony.

For information on witness involvement with the preparation and use of a document for utilization in testifying at a hearing, see § 4.11, Preparation and Use of Oral Statement Script or Outline.

For more information on rehearsing oral testimony by using a prepared script, see § 4.21, Witness Rehearsal of Oral Testimony and Answers to Questions—Relying on Oral Statement Script to Deliver Testimony.

For information on using written text or script to deliver oral testimony at the actual hearing, see § 5.30, Organization and Use of Written Text to Deliver the Oral Testimony; and § 5.41, Speak to the Committee Members—Don't Read to Them.

§4.14 Focusing the Witness on Targeted Audiences

During preparation for a hearing, a witness should focus extensively on the target audiences and "publics" that are the aim of the testimony. Keeping in mind that the committee itself is the primary focus helps to guide the direction and emphasis of the testimony toward that target. But it is also helpful to be mindful of other targeted audiences for which the testimony is intended and might have some significance, including federal agencies, the media, private organizations, business interests, and the general public. Sizing up the anticipated targets, and planning a delivery of testimony that is directed toward select audiences, help a witness sharpen and focus the message, information, and arguments to be conveyed in the oral testimony.

For more information on a witness's targeted audiences, see § 2.80, The Targeted Audiences of a Witness's Testimony; § 3.12, Analysis and Targeting of the Committee and Audiences; § 5.42, Focus on the Primary Targeted Audience—the Committee; and § 6.33, Focusing on the Questioner during Questions and Answers.

§4.15 Witness Rehearsal of Oral Testimony and Answers to Questions

The core activity of witness preparation is a witness's rehearsal of the oral testimony and answers to expected or possible committee questions. Rehearsals can take many forms and utilize many methods, and a witness and his or her organization should determine which ones are best suited for their need. As with any practiced or rehearsed endeavor, a witness should devote time and study to the effort of testimony rehearsal to ensure a quality performance at the hearing. The various methods of rehearsal and related issues discussed in § 4.16 through § 4.25 below can be altered to accommodate personal interests and preferences, and can generally be used in any combination and variation.

It is recommended that a witness preparing for a hearing not only review and consider the topics below and elsewhere in this chapter, but also the entirety of Chapter 5, "Presentation and Delivery of Oral Testimony," and Chapter 6, "Responding to Committee Questions." See especially § 5.73, The Top Twenty Tips of the Trade for the Delivery of Oral Testimony by a Witness.

Additionally, it may be helpful to a witness during preparation to watch a live hearing or to review recordings of actual hearings to "get a feel" for the flow and dynamics of committee hearings. Committees in both the House and Senate utilize video broadcasting and taping technologies for their hearings on committee cable channels administered by their respective chambers. Many committees post live and archived webcasts of their hearings on their respective committee web sites. To see the webcasts of numerous hearings available for viewing, go to the individual committee sites accessible through <*www.House.gov*> and <*www.Senate.gov*>, and proceed to the links for menus of webcasts. See the Back of the Book for more information on this source. C-SPAN also provides a full archive of hearings on the Web at <*www.c-spanvideo.org*>.

§4.16 Witness Rehearsal of Oral Testimony and Answers to Questions—Hearing Simulation or Mock Hearing

One method of rehearsal involves the creation of a mock hearing which is essentially a "pretend" version of the real thing or a hearing simulation, sometimes called a simulated hearing exercise.

The preparation team or staff assigns different colleagues to play various roles at the mock hearing, thus simulating the circumstances and environment of the actual hearing. The witness engages with these role players by practicing the delivery of his or her testimony before a made-up committee panel, and then answering questions—all intended to be a reasonable facsimile of what will likely occur on the hearing day.

Mock hearings tend to include all aspects of both the testimony delivery and the question-and-answer period, with the players attempting to replicate the experience the witness is likely to have before an actual congressional committee. Mock hearings are usually conducted with the use of a script start to finish without interruption or discussion, and with evaluation and critique afterward. While one or more mock hearings can be conducted in preparation for a hearing, sometimes a mock hearing is utilized as a dress rehearsal just prior to the actual hearing.

§4.17 Sample of Simulated Hearing Exercise Outline

Below is a simulated hearing exercise outline prepared by the Government Accountability Office (GAO) for use in its training program for GAO witnesses.

SIMULATED HEARING EXERCISE

Overview—This module provides a simulated experience of a real committee hearing. Participants will have an opportunity to present testimony and be questioned by mock committee members, as well as observe and ask questions themselves.

Objectives—At the end of this module, you will be better able to

- organize congressional testimony
- deliver congressional testimony
- answer questions about your congressional testimony

Opening Statement—Based on either of the following options, prepare a five minute opening statement. Your name and topic should be at the top of the first page, or on a cover page. Bring four copies of your testimony; one for yourself to read and three others for the members of the mock Congressional committee consisting of your trainer and several GAO class participants or other trainers. Draft, organize, and support your opening statement along the guidelines discussed during the first day of training. Also, prepare at least a half-dozen paragraph length answer modules incorporating the answering techniques discussed in training. The simulated hearing exercise will be videotaped and you will be provided feedback. The tapes will be given to you after the training.

Options—Prepare a five minute opening statement on a GAO report or other work-product that you have helped draft. Be sure you are sufficiently familiar and current on the GAO material to give testimony. Be sure your testimony states your main message and is organized into three enumerated points. Prepare to answer questions on your testimony by drafting a half-dozen answer modules.

Witnesses—Each participant will have an opportunity to deliver an opening statement. After the opening statement, the participant will be questioned for 10-15 minutes. Depending on the witness' option choice, the witness will testify on a panel or alone. The exercise will be reviewed and critiqued by the instructor. Participants will also provide feedback.

Members of Congress—Each participant will also have the opportunity to role-play a member of Congress. When questioning witnesses, participants should be as friendly, neutral or hostile as they like. Questions should be kept as short as possible, so as to keep the focus on the witness' answer and give the questioner time to ask several questions. Employ follow-up questions or questions on a different aspect of the issue, depending on the witness' response.

Observers' Guide—Most of the time, participants will either be delivering testimony or questioning witnesses. But during one hearing exercise, you will have the chance to observe the mock hearing. Several questions that might contribute to insightful observation as follows:

Note: Participants are requested to use the Observation Form to provide feedback to the witness after each question.

- Was the "bottom line" or main message well labeled and concise? What was the main message presented in the opening statement?
- Was the credibility of GAO in general and/or the witness in particular developed? Was the scope (or limitation) of the report, study, or analysis mentioned?
- Can you readily identify the two, three, or four main points the testifier made in support of GAO's message? What were they?
- What were the three best answers the witness gave? What made them good?
- What were the two weakest answers the witness gave? What made them weak? How might the answer have been improved?
- Comment on the witness' delivery. What were some of the speaker's strengths? Identify two or three aspects about the witness' delivery that were effective.
- Identify one or two aspects of the witness' delivery that could be improved. What improvements would you suggest?
- Are there any other comments you would like to make to the witness? If so, what?

Job Aid

Planning the Testimony

- Anticipate Partisan Nature
- Appreciate Role of Media
- Review Previous Hearings
- Survey Opposing Positions
- Format Transcript
- Plan Visual Aids
- Practice Microphone Adjustment
- Anticipate Questions
- Plan Answer Modules

Introduction of Testimony

- Greet Chair and committee members
- Identify the topic/request of GAO
- **Label** the main **message** of the testimony
- Employ a **stem** to invite enumeration

Body of Testimony

- **Enumerated** point (Reason)
- **Enumerated** point (Reason)
- **Enumerated** point (Reason)

Conclusion of Testimony

- Summary/Restated enumerated reasons
- Close-off (possible reference to significance)

Module Summary—The witnesses should review the feedback from the instructor and other participants. The witness should review the video tape of his/her testimony.

Source: United States Government Accountability Office, Participant Manual, Delivering Testimony, GAO Learning Center, Simulated Hearing Exercise, January 2007.

§4.18 Witness Rehearsal of Oral Testimony and Answers to Questions—Practice "Runs" and Live Peer Review

Another more informal method of rehearsal entails the use of practice "runs" or sessions in which a witness practices his or her testimony before a group of colleagues or the preparation team. Practice "runs" of the oral testimony may be conducted any number of times to satisfy the witness and the preparation team, often with intermittent critique and commentary by onlookers as the witness is presenting the statement. This type of rehearsal is sometimes referred to as live peer review because those observing the witness have the opportunity to review and critique the performance of the witness live and in real time.

§4.19 Witness Rehearsal of Oral Testimony and Answers to Questions—"Murder Boards" and Question-and-Answer "Dry Runs"

While it is obviously important to rehearse the actual oral testimony to be delivered by a witness, as described in the suggested exercises in § 4.16 and § 4.18 above, it is likewise very important to prepare a witness for the question-and-answer portion of a hearing. Many organizations prepare their witnesses to answer questions by using a "murder board" or "dry run" format.

"Murder boards" are mock panels or groups of individuals from the organization or witness preparation team who put a witness through a series of questions, including difficult questions. Sometimes called "grilling" the witness, this exercise forces a witness to respond to a number of questions, occasionally hostile, in preparation for the real hearing, and it helps a witness callous against and prepare for especially difficult and troublesome questions that might be asked by a committee. "Dry runs" are a more informal method of posing questions to a witness in practice sessions, allowing the witness to respond, and then critiquing the response.

For more information on preparing for and handling committee questions, see Chapter 6, "Responding to Committee Questions."

§4.20 Witness Rehearsal of Oral Testimony and Answers to Questions—Videotaped and Critiqued Drills

Another approach to preparing a witness for both oral testimony and the question-and-answer portion of a hearing is the use of videotaping. In this exercise, the witness is filmed while delivering his or her testimony in a rehearsal or "mock hearing," or is filmed while answering questions posed by a "murder board" or "dry-run" panel of colleagues. This method of rehearsal allows a witness to view himself or herself in performance mode, thus allowing for shared critique with colleagues or the preparation team as the witness attempts to make adjustments necessary for the best possible performance. It is a particularly valuable tool in helping a witness see and understand testimony delivery style, body language, gestures, eye contact, and general demeanor as a witness.

§4.21 Witness Rehearsal of Oral Testimony and Answers to Questions—Relying on the Oral Statement Script to Deliver Testimony

One of the most important aspects of preparation for a hearing is the witness's rehearsal of the actual oral testimony by using an oral statement script or outline format of his or her choosing. A witness should become completely familiar with the script, should develop a comfort level in using and referring to it, and should have an operational sense of reliance on the document as *the script* throughout oral testimony.

A witness should know the script well enough to have a professional ease in utilizing the document without actually reading it, and should more or less employ a combination of memorized lines and frequent referral to the script, while maintaining eye contact and a conversational tone with the committee. It is important to practice oral testimony delivery with the use of the document that has been prepared for use at the actual hearing. Be sure to include and rehearse key stylistic pointers noted in the section on crafting the oral script, § 3.18, Important Documents: Drafting the Statement and Making the Record—Narrative, Outline, or Notes Used for Oral Presentation.

For more information on the importance and crafting of an oral statement script, see § 3.18, Important Documents: Drafting the Statement and Making the Record—Narrative, Outline, or Notes Used for Oral Presentation.

To review an actual operational document utilized as the narrative script for delivery of oral testimony, see § 3.34, Sample of Oral Statement—Written Document Used as Reference to Deliver Oral Testimony.

For more information regarding witness preparation and use of an oral witness statement, see § 4.11, Preparation and Use of Oral Statement Script or Outline.

For information on the preferred manner of delivering testimony with use of a prepared document, see § 4.13, Delivering the Statement: To Read or Not to Read.

For information on using written text or script to delivery oral testimony at the actual hearing, see § 5.30, Organization and Use of Written Text to Deliver the Oral Testimony.

§4.22 Witness Rehearsal of Oral Testimony and Answers to Questions—Operating within Time Limits and Effective Use of the Clock

During rehearsals, a witness should specifically practice delivering oral testimony so that it fits within the time prescriptions laid out by the committee holding the hearing. It is important to operate within the time limit allowed a witness, and there is no guarantee that a committee chair will be charitable in granting additional time, even if requested to do so. Typically the time limit is five minutes, although the range may vary widely among committees. Be sure to consult with committee staff and rules to gain a complete understanding of time limitations for testimony.

Consequently, it is wise during practice sessions to become accustomed to the time pressure of the presentation so that the flow of testimony at the actual hearing will be smooth, concise, and time-perfect. Effective use of the clock will demonstrate to the committee that a witness is prepared and willing to be cooperative with the committee's processes and rules. If it is imperative to have an extra minute or two for presentation, a witness may certainly make that request of the chair. However, it is preferable not to have to rely on that tactic, and it is more likely than not that a chair might deny such a request out of an abundant caution to be fair to all witnesses.

To determine time limits for individual committees, contact the relevant committee and consult with committee rules that may be accessed through committee links found at <*www.Senate.gov*> and <*www.House.gov*>.

For more information on time limits for oral testimony, see § 2.96, Regular Order and Format of Proceedings: The Normal Procedural Conduct of a Hearing—Time Limits for Oral Testimony.

§4.23 Witness Rehearsal of Oral Testimony and Answers to Questions—Operating with the Use of a Briefing Book

If a witness is going to have and utilize a briefing book or some sort of folder or notebook of information at a hearing, witness rehearsals should include the familiarization with, use of, and reliance upon those materials for a variety of informational needs, including, for example, checking facts or statistics, referring to relevant correspondence, and seeking an answer to a question posed by the committee. While the contents and use of a briefing book are often left to the prerogative and style of the witness, such a resource can be very helpful during the testimony and the question-and-answer phases of a hearing.

The briefing book, often tabbed or indexed by subject or item, may include a copy of the testimony, an executive summary, background research and materials, potential questions and answers, and committee information. Some organizations also like to include a copy of the committee invitation, handout materials (if needed or used), graphs and charts, biographies of committee members, and the witness's scheduling information and travel itinerary.

During the rehearsal stage, a witness should practice locating and referring to the contents of the briefing book to develop the ability to use the references with ease and speed at the hearing. Rehearsals should include use of the briefing book by the witness in delivering oral testimony (for example, to refer to a document or quote from correspondence or a statute), and in answering questions posed by the committee (for example, locating facts or statistics to cite in answering a committee question).

Briefing books or folders are particularly helpful to a witness in cataloguing and referencing answers to possible questions that a committee might address.

For more information on the use and importance of a briefing book, see § 3.19, Important Documents: Drafting the Statement and Making the Record—The Briefing Book.

For information on the use of a briefing book and other materials at a hearing, see § 5.33, Organization and Use of Prepared Written Support Materials.

For information on the use of a briefing book during the question-and-answer phase of a hearing, see § 6.34, Witness Use of a Briefing Book to Answer Committee Questions.

§4.24 Witness Rehearsal of Oral Testimony and Answers to Questions—Use of Graphics and Visuals

If graphics or visuals in any form, especially charts, matrices, drawings or graphs, are to be used or referred to by a witness during a congressional hearing, the witness should practice using those graphics during hearing rehearsals. A witness should develop a smooth and easy style in handling, discussing and showing the graphics, in concert with the oral statement being used in the testimony. This choreography is important to ensure a professional and understandable flow to the testimony and the application of graphics used to support it.

A witness should ensure that the graphics are large enough to be seen clearly by the committee, and that they are simple, straightforward, and not overloaded with data and numbers. To ensure a smooth delivery on hearing day, a witness should use, present, and discuss the graphics during rehearsal just as he or she would do in the hearing itself, including movement of and pointing to graphics, and the use of props or aides such as stands, tables, easels, and electronic technology, which should be doubly checked for readiness to ensure it works.

For more information on utilizing graphics, see § 3.28, Use of Graphics and Visuals. For information on the use of graphics and visual aids at a hearing, see § 5.70,

Effective Use of Visual Aids, Charts, and Graphics; and § 5.71, Sample of Design and Use Guidelines to Ensure Visual Aids Have Their Desired Impact.

§4.25 Witness Rehearsal of Oral Testimony and Answers to Questions—Speaking Style, Demeanor, and Format

During witness rehearsals, whatever form they may take, a witness should work to perfect his or her speaking style, demeanor, and format. Essentially, this means speaking in a professional and direct, yet conversational style, addressing the committee panel respectfully as a knowledgeable professional and a peer, delivering the testimony in a speaking format that is clear, concise, logical, and understandable, and sticking to the script and staying on the message of the testimony.

For information on the personal appearance, attire, and demeanor of a witness, see § 4.42, The Witness's Personal Appearance, Attire, and Demeanor: Looking and Acting the Part.

For information on effective communications skills to ensure clear presentations, see § 5.9, Relying on Preparation, Best Instincts, and Good Communications Skills; and § 5.40, Sticking to the Script in Delivering Testimony.

For information on speaking techniques, see § 5.44, Importance of Voice Variation, Inflection, Projection, Clarity, Quality, Tone, and Tenor.

For information on eye contact, body language, and gestures, see § 5.45, Importance of Eye Contact, Body Language, and the Use of Gestures.

For more information on speaking style and testimony delivery format, see § 5.50, Presentation Format and Order; and subsequent sections through § 5.59.

For an outline of best-practice tips for a witness, see § 5.73, The Top Twenty Tips of the Trade for the Delivery of Oral Testimony by a Witness.

§4.26 Witness Rehearsal of Oral Testimony and Answers to Questions—Preparation and Rehearsal by Federal Government Departments and Agencies

Across the range of the federal government's executive departments and agencies, the offices responsible for congressional relations and legislative liaison utilize a wide array of methods, approaches, and protocols to prepare for congressional committee hearings, including the preparation of written testimony and the witness who will appear before the committee.

Typically governmental entities have their own internal policies, guidelines, methodologies, and exercises, including various forms of rehearsals and practice sessions for witnesses. These policies and protocols are often informal, handled in an ad hoc fashion, and, in many cases, not even reduced to writing. Since many executive branch entities have no written process outline or guidance on preparing witnesses, often the process of preparing witnesses is drawn from the institutional memory of a department or agency, usually relying on career professionals who have prepared numerous witnesses over the years, and who engage the department and officials in preparation and rehearsals for testifying at hearings as needed. Consequently, hearing preparation is often handled by experienced and knowledgeable congressional relations and legislative affairs professional staff who gather intelligence, coordinate written materials, brief witnesses, and conduct rehearsals and role-playing.

Many departments and agencies do have some form of general written guidelines and format for hearing preparation, with some even having preparation notebooks or manuals. Some departments and agencies keep these materials close for internal use, although there is really nothing particularly secretive about them. But essentially, most executive branch legislative operations proceed informally and rely on historical, tried-and-true practices and methods utilized within their own department or agency. Most departments and agencies employ some form of rehearsal such as a mock hearing or "murder board," many utilize briefing books and briefing sessions, and one department, as a matter of long-time practice, even negotiates the matter of the order of witnesses with congressional committees to ensure that its witnesses representing the administration are in the first panel of a hearing in most cases and separated from other witnesses.

In general, and for the most part, the examples of rehearsal methods and activities discussed in § 4.16 through § 4.25 are representative of the approaches and protocols utilized by most federal departments and agencies.

A generic look at a cross-section of departmental and agency practices and activities related to hearing preparation might include the following outline:

- Poll members of the relevant committee and gather intelligence to get a sense of the agenda, key issues, and potential members' questions;
- Arrange a conference call or face-to-face meeting for selected members of the committee with the witness on a need basis to discuss key issues prior to the hearing;
- Provide the witness with biographical information for all committee members, along with a listing of departmental or agency facilities, activities, and spending in the states and districts of all committee members;
- Provide the witness with any special information about committee members, legislation, or issues of interest;
- Review all congressional correspondence and inquiries for connections to members of the relevant committee holding the hearing; and
- Conduct rehearsal or practice sessions for the witness, such as simulated hearings and "murder boards," and involve internal departmental or agency personnel and resources as needed, depending on the issues, committee, and witness.

For more information regarding special considerations concerning executive, judicial and legislative participation in congressional committee hearings, see § 2.31, Who Should Testify?—Federal Executive, Legislative and Judicial Branch Officials; § 2.68, Congressional Hearing Participants: The "Players"—Federal Departments and Agencies; § 3.23, Special Considerations Regarding Executive and Judicial Branch Testimony; and § 3.24, Special Considerations Regarding Federal Legislative Branch Testimony; and § 4.40, Special Considerations Regarding Executive, Judicial, and Legislative Branch Witnesses.

§4.27 Example of Federal Agency Congressional Committee Hearing Preparation and Rehearsal Approaches and Methods—National Aeronautics and Space Administration (NASA) Approach to Preparation

(*Be sure to check out the unique NASA "countdown" approach in the template.*)

- Identify issues of concern to members of Congress based on knowledge of issues and previous congressional hearings/correspondence/direction.
- Determine if administrator or other NASA witness should attend the hearing.
- Consult with program offices regarding hearing issues.
- Prepare associate administrator/witness for hearing. Preparation may include items such as: scheduling meetings to review testimony and preparatory sessions to address sample questions that may be asked at the hearing.
- Task program offices to prepare issue papers by specific due date. Due date is determined by date of hearing and lead time required to prepare materials.
- Review issue papers and obtain appropriate clearances. Determination of who should clear is based on knowledge, judgment, and experience of legislative office. If the issue paper addresses a topic that has overlapping areas affecting multiple program offices, the issue paper is cleared through all affected offices.
- Develop briefing book for the administrator and include issue papers in the book. Development of the briefing book is an iterative process. To insure that the current version of the book is maintained each issue paper contains a date stamped on the paper which reflects the most current version of the document. The Office of Legislative Affairs maintains the master copy of the book to which everyone may go to obtain the current version of the material.
- Schedule and hold hearing preparatory meetings, including review of testimony, briefing book and possible questions that might be asked at the hearing. The deputy associate administrator of Legislative Affairs/LAS makes determination which program offices should attend preparatory meeting based on issues to be discussed, experience, and knowledge of programs.
- Determine if follow-up required after preparatory session.

- If yes, task program office to prepare additional white papers for briefing book and obtain them for inclusion. Incorporate new material/issue papers in administrator's briefing book and date stamp to reflect most current version of material.
- Determine if additional preparatory meetings are required. This determination is made based on: (1) whether the meetings are requested by the witness or (2) if program offices determine additional sessions are needed to cover new or emerging issues. If additional prep meetings are required, proceed to new schedule of rehearsals. If not, proceed to submission of testimony to Capitol Hill.

****

TEMPLATE—NASA Hearing Countdown Schedule

T-14 days NASA Receives Confirmed Invite from Committee/Subcommittee

T-13/14 days Strategy Meeting with Witness(es)

T-12 days OLIA Issues Call for Written Testimony, White Papers and Q&A

T-7 days Draft Written Testimony/White Papers/Q&A due to OLIA

OLIA Distributes Draft Written Testimony for Agency Clearance to Relevant Offices

OLIA Distributes White Papers/Q&A for Review to Relevant Offices

Hearing Backup Book Provided to Witness(es)

As needed Hearing Prep Meeting(s)/Murder Board(s) Scheduled with Witness

T-6 OLIA Notifies PAO of Hearing Date/Time

T-5 days Agency Clearance of Written Testimony

Draft Written Testimony Provided to OMB for Clearance

Draft Oral Statement due to OLA

T-3 days Written Testimony Cleared by OMB

T-2/3 days Electronic Copy of Written Testimony and Witness Bio Provided to Committee (within time limit specified by the Committee/Subcommittee)

T-3 days Written Testimony Sent to Printers

T-1/2 days Hard Copies of Written Testimony Hand Delivered to Committee/Subcommittee

T-1/2 days Witness Courtesy Visits with Committee/Subcommittee Leadership and/or other key Members, as appropriate

T-Hearing Depart for Hearing

T+24 hours Top-Level Summary of Hearing Highlights to OLIA

T+3 days Hearing Memo for the Record Distributed to HQ OICs, CDs and OLIA HQ and Center Contacts

Template assumes NASA received confirmation of hearing 2 weeks in advance of hearing. It is not uncommon for hearings to be called with less than 2 weeks notice. In those instances, the countdown will need to be revised to reflect a schedule that will be responsive to Committee/Subcommittee direction.

Source: Adapted from Congressional Hearing Preparation, Office of Legislative and Intergovernmental Affairs, National Aeronautics and Space Administration (NASA), and from other documents provided by that office. For a detailed outline of a governmental agency process for preparing testimony, back-up material, and witnesses for congressional hearings, and to see the complete NASA document, go to: <*http://nodis3.gsfc.nasa.gov/iso_docs/pdf/H_OWI_1311_L_001_B_.pdf*>.

§4.28 Example of Federal Agency Congressional Committee Hearing Preparation and Rehearsal Approaches and Methods—United States Agency for International Development (USAID) Preparation of Testimony and Witnesses

Major Functional Series 500: Management Services
ADS Chapter 554 – CONGRESSIONAL WITNESSES

554.1 Authority
Foreign Assistance Act of 1961, as amended
International Security Assistance Act of 1978

554.2 Objective
To provide clear, informative, and uniform testimony by USAID officials before congressional committees.

554.3 Responsibility
The Bureau for Legislative and Public Affairs (LPA) is responsible for coordinating and preparing the testimony of USAID officials before congressional committees.

USAID offices/bureaus or officers are responsible for notifying LPA immediately of any request for an appearance before a congressional committee and for maintaining the confidentiality of the proceedings of closed congressional committee hearings that they attend.

554.4 Definitions (See ADS GLOSSARY)

CLOSED HEARINGS
CONGRESSIONAL TESTIMONY

554.5 POLICY
The following are the official Agency policies and corresponding essential procedures:

554.5.1 CONGRESSIONAL TESTIMONY
The Bureau for Legislative and Public Affairs (LPA) shall coordinate, prepare, and follow-up on all appearances before House and Senate committees by USAID officials, including, but not limited to:

a) hearings on the foreign assistance and P.L. 480 authorization and appropriations bills;

b) hearings on other legislation of interest to USAID; and

c) hearings investigating specialized fields in which USAID may provide expert testimony.

E554.5.1 Congressional Testimony
When a USAID Office/Bureau or officer outside LPA receives a request for appearance before a congressional committee, the office/bureau or officer shall notify LPA of the request immediately.

E554.5.1a Preparation of Testimony
LPA shall coordinate the selection of witnesses, schedule all witness appearances, and as appropriate, provide briefing support before and during testimony. LPA shall advise on the form and content of all witness statements and inform the witness of submission deadlines and clearance requirements. In all instances, copies of the witness statement must be submitted to LPA in time to permit delivery to the appropriate committee no later than 48 hours before the scheduled hearing, as required by Committee rules.

E544.5.1b Statements for the Record
Following the hearing, LPA shall coordinate with USAID bureaus and offices the editing of the hearing transcript and the preparation of required inserts and responses to questions for the record of the hearing.

554.5.2 CONFIDENTIALITY OF CLOSED HEARINGS
USAID employees who appear before or attend closed hearing sessions of a congressional committee must maintain all information which is the subject of discussion or consideration on a confidential basis, whether or not national security is involved, until the record of the congressional hearing is published and enters the public domain. Under no circumstances shall any USAID employees discuss, or act in such a way as to disclose inadvertently, any matter that has been the subject of consideration before such congressional committee hearings.

E554.5.2 Confidentiality of Closed Hearings – N/A

554.6 Supplementary Reference – N/A

Source: United States Agency for International Development (USAID), Automated Directives System (ADS) policy chapter on Congressional Testimony; *<www.usaid.gov/policy/ads/500/554.pdf>*.

§4.29 Example of Federal Agency Congressional Committee Hearing Preparation and Rehearsal Approaches and Methods—Internal Revenue Service (IRS) Preparation of Testimony and Witnesses

Legislative Affairs prepares testimony and briefing materials for the Commissioner and other executives for hearings (other than appropriations), which have an average of nearly 30 annually. Major program policy issues are often identified and resolved during the hearing process.

Other hearing related tasks include:

- coordinating with other Service activities to prepare materials;
- responding to congressional inquiries on the hearing topic;
- arranging briefings with the Commissioner and other top Service officials and with congressional staff (as requested);
- monitoring the hearing; and
- performing follow-up duties such as responding to additional questions, editing the transcripts and developing inserts for the record.

Legislative Affairs Division's Role in The Legislative Process

- track selected bills and monitor their progress
- analyze bills for administrative implications for taxpayers and IRS
- handle congressional inquiries on these bills
- keep involved IRS functions aware of developments on these bills
- prepare responses for Commissioner to draft and final GAO reports (reports are frequently used at hearings)
- if no IRS testimony is requested on a bill/topic, activities are limited to attending hearings and markups, gathering relevant information, etc.
- If IRS testimony is requested on a bill/topic, activities include-
    - preparing opening statement for Commissioner or other witness
    - preparing briefing materials for Commissioner and other top officials—referencing relevant GAO reports
    - handling congressional inquiries on the hearing topic
    - arranging briefings with the Commissioner and other top Service officials—arranging briefings with congressional staff (as requested)
    - clearing opening statement with Treasury and OMB; providing copies to the Committee; sending copies to IRS executives
    - monitoring the hearing
    - performing follow-up activities (responding to additional questions, editing the transcript, developing inserts for the record, etc.)
    - publishing explanatory materials on the subject/event as needed (Legislative Fact Sheets for Congress, Legislative Affairs Updates for IRS executives)

- meet with involved functions on implementation issues (especially those requiring early action by IRS)
- prepare and coordinate Service-wide implementation plan
- monitor implementation plan for functional compliance
- publish explanatory materials on the bill/plan as needed (Legislative Fact sheets for Congress, Legislative Affairs Updates for IRS executives)

Source: Internal Revenue Service (IRS), Congressional Affairs Program Guide; *<www.irs.gov/irm/part11/irm_11-005-002.html>*.

§4.30 Example of Federal Agency Congressional Committee Hearing Preparation and Rehearsal Approaches and Methods—Bonneville Power Administration (BPA) Preparation for Congressional Hearings

157.1 PURPOSE The purpose of this chapter is to establish guidelines to:

A. Provide a general description of the roles of the offices involved in the Congressional hearings; and

B. Lay out the steps to be taken in preparing for Congressional hearings.

C. BPA is periodically called upon to provide testimony at Congressional hearings on topics involving activities in all BPA program areas. Being fully prepared for these hearings often requires a great deal of staff work, in a short period of time, from a variety of BPA organizations. Recognizing the short notice often provided, the objectives of these guidelines are to ensure that:

1. BPA has prepared testimony responsive to the concerns of those calling the hearing;
2. BPA witnesses are fully prepared on the issues and questions that may arise and are aware of the background of the committee members; and
3. Necessary follow-up activities occur in a timely manner.

D. Separate guidelines, describing the roles of the Regional Relations Manager and Business Services have been developed for BPA's budget hearings. These hearings differ from those described above in that they reoccur each year and are generally scheduled some time in advance.

157.2 RESPONSIBILITIES

A. The Washington, DC, office is the primary contact point for Members of Congress, their staffs, and the committee staffs. As a result, the Washington, DC, office is most often the first to learn about a pending Congressional hearing involving BPA. It is their responsibility to ensure that the Regional Relations Manager and affected program offices are notified of the hearing at the earliest possible time. The Washington, DC, office is also responsible for:

1. Analyzing Congressional concerns;
2. Recommending and implementing legislative strategy;
3. Providing input on the substance of BPA testimony;

4. Identifying potential issues and questions;
5. Providing input on, and implementing, the strategy for hearing presentations;
6. Obtaining clearance by OMB/DOE;
7. Developing and arranging witnesses' Washington, DC, itineraries;
8. Coordinating Washington, DC, press contacts;
9. Briefing US legislators, their staffs, and executive officials;
10. Attending hearings and noting all follow-up requests;
11. Obtaining hearing transcripts; and
12. Obtaining clearance on revised transcripts

B. **Regional Relations** is responsible for coordinating BPA's headquarters preparation efforts. That is, to ensure that the steps described are carried out as smoothly and efficiently as possible. Regional Relations is responsible for:
1. Establishing BPA's internal schedule for hearing preparations;
2. Editing and collating the briefing book and related materials;
3. Analyzing Congressional concerns;
4. Providing input on, and final review of, BPA testimony;
5. Identifying potential issues and questions;
6. Providing input on the strategy for hearing presentations;
7. Informing offices of hearing developments;
8. Producing the hearing book for the Administrator and DOE;
9. Coordinating BPA witness travel;
10. Participating in development of witnesses' Washington, DC, itineraries; and
11. Coordinating transcript review and other follow-up activities.

C. **In those instances when Congressional hearings are held in the Northwest**, Regional Relations assumes the logistical responsibilities performed by the Washington, DC, office for hearings held in Washington, DC. Those responsibilities may include arranging for hearing rooms and times, developing itineraries for witnesses, attending hearings, and noting follow-up requests. The Washington, DC, office will, in all cases, provide advice and review on hearing strategy and documents.

D. **Program Offices:** The specific program office involved in the preparation efforts for a Congressional hearing will vary depending on the topic of the hearing. The involved offices are responsible for developing the testimony and other materials necessary for BPA to be clear, accurate, and responsive to Congressional concerns. The program offices are responsible for:
1. Preparing testimony;
2. Identifying potential issues and questions;
3. Providing input on hearing strategy; and
4. In some cases, presenting testimony at the hearing.

E. **General Counsel** can have two roles in preparation efforts for Congressional hearings. They will review the testimony of BPA witnesses and contribute to planning the hearing strategy. In addition, they may, for Congressional hearings involving legal issues, serve as the program office and be involved in all of the activities listed above for program offices.

F. **Budget Support, Business Services,** has a special role in the Congressional appropriations hearings process which is described under separate guidelines. However, for all other Congressional hearings, this office will be in the clearance process, etc.

157.3 GUIDELINES

A. **Hearing Notice:** Being fully prepared for a Congressional hearing depends largely on how much time is available to plan, write, and review our testimony. For this reason, it is crucial that any informal notice of a hearing at which BPA will be asked to attend be used to initiate preparations for the hearing. The following guidelines will ensure that these preparations begin with the first formal or informal notice.

1. A formal Congressional hearing invitation from a committee chairperson to the Administrator will be time-dated and copies sent immediately to the Regional Relations Manager and the Vice President, Washington, DC, office.
2. When the Washington, DC, office receives notice of a hearing, they will contact the Administrator's office, Regional Relations and the pertinent program offices.
3. Program offices will notify Regional Relations when they are informed of a hearing at which BPA will be asked to provide testimony. Regional Relations will then report this information to the Washington, DC, office.

B. **Hearing Strategy:** Once notified of a pending Congressional hearing, Regional Relations will schedule a strategy meeting of all involved program offices, representatives from the Washington, DC, office, and General Counsel. This meeting will accomplish the following:

1. Identify issues/questions that may arise at the hearing;
2. Identify the approach for handling those issues/questions;
3. Develop a presentation order or structure;
4. Identify BPA witnesses;
5. Identify the lead program office;
6. Identify Regional Relations, Washington, DC, office, General Counsel and program office staff involvement;
7. Plan any needed graphics and production; and
8. Develop a schedule for preparation work.

C. **The results of the strategy session** will be confirmed by a memo prepared by Regional Relations. This memo will serve as the work plan, describing who does what and by when.

D. **Testimony Preparation and Review.** Following the strategy session, the involved staffs will gather the necessary information and prepare draft testimony and other related materials. Copies of these materials are to be delivered to Regional Relations for compiling and review.

1. Regional Relations staff will coordinate the internal review of all hearing materials, etc.
2. Regional Relations will transmit the proposed testimony to the Washington, DC, office for their review and to obtain necessary DOE and OMB approvals.

E. **Hearing Briefing Book.** Regional Relations will prepare for each Congressional hearing a briefing book containing the following materials:
   1. Committee invitation;
   2. Testimony and summary;
   3. Handouts (if needed);
   4. Potential questions and answers;
   5. Background materials;
   6. Biographies of committee members; and
   7. Itinerary for hearing trip.

F. **Regional Relations** will prepare copies of the briefing book for each witness. Reference copies will also be produced, to be kept in the Washington, DC, office, Regional Relations, and appropriate program offices.

G. **Briefing of Hearing Participants:** Depending on the issues and on the need for coordination between the various BPA witnesses, a briefing on the completed testimony and hearing strategy will be held prior to the witnesses leaving for Washington, DC. The Vice President, Washington, DC, office or his/her staff, will brief the witnesses generally the day before or the morning of, the hearing to communicate any recently identified concerns of the committee members.

H. **Hearing Follow-up.** Following each hearing, transcripts of the proceedings are obtained by the Washington, DC, office. The transcripts are then sent to Regional Relations, who will distribute a copy to the lead program office and each BPA witness for review. Transcripts are to be reviewed for accuracy and any supplemental materials or activities needed either for the record or as follow-up. After this review, the transcripts should be returned to Regional Relations for compiling of the comments and transmittal back to the Washington, DC, office.

I. **The Washington, DC, office** will be responsible for noting any additional actions or information requested by the committee or needed as a part of BPA's participation in the Congressional hearing. The Washington, DC, office will notify Regional Relations and the appropriate program offices of requested actions or information. Regional Relations will enter the request into the executive correspondence system and monitor program office compliance.

Source: Bonneville Power Administration Manual, Chapter 157, Guidelines for Congressional Hearings Preparation. Access at: *<www.bpa.gov/ebr/bpamanual/CHAPTERS/00000157.doc>*.

§4.31 Example of Federal Agency Congressional Committee Hearing Preparation and Rehearsal Approaches and Methods—National Science Foundation (NSF) Witness Preparation

Witness Preparation for National Science Foundation (NSF) Congressional Hearings

- Congressional Affairs Section determines NSF witness based on hearing type and issue, if not specifically requested by Committee

  - Director/Deputy Director
  - Assistant Director/Expert
- Congressional Affairs identifies issues of concern to Members of Congress and incorporates into testimony and Qs (Questions) and As (Answers)
- Written testimony
  - Congressional Affairs seeks advice from program officer for technical aspects of testimony
  - Congressional Affairs clears testimony through NSF and OMB
- Mock Hearing
  - Generally for Director/Deputy Director
  - Subject matter experts are usually done only upon request
- Congressional Affairs prepares briefing books for witness
  - OMB cleared testimony
  - Other witnesses testimony
  - Members' bios
  - Qs & As developed by Congressional Affairs
  - Other relevant material (press releases, award abstracts, etc.)
- Congressional Affairs staff attends hearing with witness

Source: National Science Foundation Congressional Affairs Section.

§4.32 Witness Rehearsal of Oral Testimony and Answers to Questions—Preparation and Rehearsal by Trade Associations

Most trade associations that are involved with public policy issues and that provide witnesses to testify on Capitol Hill prepare their witnesses with some combination and use of the methods, activities, and approaches outlined in § 4.16 through § 4.25.

Since associations represent a wide array of members from a particular industry, sector, or issue category, those preparing witnesses to testify do so with a careful eye on representing the best interests of all the members of the organization. Preparation of witnesses must include approaches that will allow a witness to represent those interests adequately when testifying, while also educating the committee and advocating on behalf of the association's positions.

Many associations, including some of the largest organizations in the country, conduct witness preparation in an informal manner, relying mostly on group discussions and briefings to prepare for hearing appearances. Many officials, members or representatives of associations are quite experienced as witnesses, so the need for preparation can often be minimal. It usually falls to the professional staff of an association to provide whatever preparation and rehearsal will be utilized to ensure that its witnesses are well-prepared to testify on Capitol Hill.

For more information on testifying by association representatives, see § 2.32, Who Should Testify?—Corporate, Business, and Association Representatives.

§4.33 Witness Rehearsal of Oral Testimony and Answers to Questions—Preparation and Rehearsal by Business and Corporate Offices

U.S. business, corporate, and commercial interests that engage in public policy debate very often send officials to Capitol Hill to testify before congressional committees. For hearing and witness preparation and rehearsals, these private sector interests typically utilize the approaches and methods described in § 4.16 through § 4.25.

Some companies have no formal preparatory guidelines or protocol in writing, but, rather, informally rely on internal government relations professional staff and officials, often located in their Washington offices, who typically prepare witnesses on a need basis from institutional memory and experience. Many corporate government relations offices prepare testimony for their respective witnesses. Others utilize their relationship with trade associations or outside counsel to prepare the basic witness statements. Preparation of a corporate or business witness may include briefings on what to expect at a hearing, issue familiarization, materials to review, potential committee questions and suggested answers to study, and rehearsals such as a "murder board" to provide the witness with a real-world "feel" for what can sometimes be a tough grilling by a committee.

For more information on testifying by business and corporative officials, see § 2.32, Who Should Testify?—Corporate, Business, and Association Representatives.

§4.34 Witness Rehearsal of Oral Testimony and Answers to Questions—Preparation and Rehearsal by Nonprofit, Non-Governmental (NGOs), Private and Voluntary (PVOs), and Public Interest Organizations

Numerous nonprofit, non-governmental (NGOs), private and voluntary (PVOs), and public interest organizations are engaged in various public policy debates and issues, and, consequently, they frequently send witnesses to Capitol Hill to testify. These organizations generally follow preparation and rehearsal methods and approaches similar to those discussed in § 4.16 through § 4.25.

Some organizations describe their approaches to preparation and rehearsals as informal, involving pre-meetings with witnesses to discuss the issues and the hearing topic, but without the use of any written guidelines or activity checklist. Nonprofit groups generally consider congressional committee hearings to be excellent opportunities for the advocacy of their own particular policy or issue positions. Their testimony tends to reinforce their organization's own mission and policies, and quite often nonprofit witnesses must address difficult or controversial issues and questions when appearing before a committee. Consequently, their preparation of witnesses reflects their own priorities and goals, as well as the need to be responsive to a committee.

For more information on testifying by nonprofit and non-governmental organizations, see § 2.33, Who Should Testify?—Nonprofit, Non-Governmental (NGO), Private and Voluntary (PVO), Public Interest, and Advocacy Organizations and Coalitions.

§4.35 Pre-Hearing Adjustments to Statements and Presentation

One of the purposes and outcomes of preparation generally, and witness rehearsals more specifically, is to enable the witness and preparation team to make any necessary changes or adjustments to the oral testimony prior to the actual hearing moment. Rehearsals have a way of exposing weaknesses, and the adjustments and corrections necessary to overcome these weaknesses should be made in subsequent rehearsals and highlighted in briefings with the witness.

Adjustments to consider might include a change in facts, correction of an erroneous statement, correction of an improper citation of a statement or publication, an updating of data or numbers to support the case, and the need to add new or additional elements to the testimony that have been requested by the committee or a party associated with the witness, such as the Office of Management and Budget (OMB) for government agencies, and the parent organization of the witness testifying. The witness and the preparation team should consider the testimony a "living and working" document or work product that is subject to change right up to the time of the hearing.

§4.36 Witness Support: Use of Briefing Staff or Team

To assist a witness with logistics and presentation at a hearing, many organizations and witnesses utilize a support or briefing team, or a group of professional staff members, who constitute an advisory and resource panel that often sits directly behind the witness on the first row of seating in the hearing room. These individuals may be the same professionals who serve on the witness preparation team, if there is one (see § 4.7, Witness Preparation Team Meeting and Organization), or they may be an entirely different group, at the prerogative of the witness.

The witness support team serves the functions of assisting the witness in locating information and resources during the hearing (quite often in the briefing book), clarifying points and providing details, occasionally providing answers when called upon by the witness or the committee, assisting with any immediate research needs during the question-and-answer period, and generally supporting the witness with data and background information. Any witness support team should prepare and rehearse for a hearing alongside the witness to ensure the proper execution of its duties and a coordinated effort when the hearing day arrives.

For more information, see § 2.67, Congressional Hearing Participants: The "Players"—Witness Support Teams. For information on the use of briefing or support teams at a hearing, see § 5.35, Utilizing a Briefing or Support Team; and § 6.36, Witness Use of Briefing or Support Team.

§4.37 Rehearsing the Use of a Microphone

During hearing rehearsals, a witness should practice using a microphone if at all possible. While there are many styles and designs of microphone, it is important for a witness to be able to deliver the witness statement and address the committee during questions and answers using a microphone with ease, comfort, and professionalism. Use of a live sound system during rehearsals will afford a witness the opportunity to get a feel for how a microphone works and how sensitive it is, to learn how to adjust the microphone as needed, and to hear her or his voice in an amplified fashion. To determine the type or style of microphone that will be used at a hearing, call the committee staff to inquire, or visit the hearing room in advance of the hearing to see for yourself. Committee staff can provide guidance on how to adjust and use a microphone. (Congressional committees may be reached by telephone through the U.S. Capitol switchboard at 202-224-3121.)

For more information on use of the microphone during a hearing, see § 5.22, Effective Use of a Microphone.

§4.38 The Day of the Hearing: Thinking and Planning Ahead

On the day of a congressional committee hearing, it is advisable for a witness to arrive early, preferably before the hearing activities for the day begin, to scope out the hearing room layout and become familiar and comfortable with the surroundings. It is helpful to get a feel for the positioning of the witness table in the hearing room, and to observe how the microphone, sound system, and time limitation device operate. It is wise to make a final contact with the committee professional staff before the hearing commences, especially to get an idea of any changes to the agenda, to understand the order of witness presentations, and to learn of any last-minute details or revisions.

It is also courteous and professional to make an informal introduction of the witness to the committee chair and members, if they are present and available with adequate time prior to the rap of the gavel, even if the witness is not scheduled to testify until later in the hearing's proceedings. All of these hearing day issues should be discussed with the witness during the preparation stage leading up to the hearing.

For more information on witness activities, thought processes, and other elements of the actual hearing day, see Chapter 5, especially § 5.6, Going Up in the Stands: The Thirty-Thousand Foot Perspective—Keeping It All in Context; § 5.7, Getting Down to Basics and Details; § 5.9, Relying on Preparation, Best Instincts, and Good Communications Skills; § 5.10, Getting a Handle on the Hearing Room Environment; § 5.20, Just Before the Hearing . . . ; § 5.21, At the Hearing Table . . . ; and § 5.22, Effective Use of a Microphone.

§4.39 What a Witness Should Expect and Assess at the Hearing

During the preparation and rehearsal stage, it is important for a witness to get a "feel" for what will actually occur in the hearing room. In terms of what is expected of the witness by the committee and how the process will generally flow, see § 4.4, What to Expect as a Witness. For a discussion on the nature and culture of congressional committee hearings generally, see § 1.70, The Psychology and Culture of Congressional Hearings: Mission, Education, Information, and Advocacy.

Additional elements and expectations of a committee hearing that are good for a witness to keep in mind during preparation, and that should be included in witness briefings and rehearsals, include:

- **Committee chair**—focus on the committee chair through whom all the hearing's proceedings flow;
- **Committee members**—know the members' names, political party, who is actually present and absent, and their seating position on the dais;
- **Hearing room logistics and layout**—notice the positioning of the "players" and have an understanding of the flow of the hearing's business;
- **Witness table**—note the position of the witness table in front of, and facing, the committee, with a microphone used by witnesses and a clock or timing device to relay the amount of time for testifying;
- **Attendance and audience**—notice the size and layout of the hearing room, observe the audience, and inquire of committee staff about the audience makeup and hearing attendance;
- **Media presence**—notice existence and credentials of media representatives;
- **Demeanor and style**—observe the demeanor and style of the committee chair and members to get a feel for the communications environment;
- **Questions and answers**—committee members often spend considerable time and effort asking questions of witnesses, and may also give lengthy speeches or monologues prior to asking actual questions;
- **Expect distractions and interruptions**—distractions such as chamber votes that arise and other matters such as lunch breaks might cause periodic recesses throughout a hearing, and the order of business may be interrupted by the committee's attempt to extend professional courtesies to colleagues by allowing them to speak early or out of order;
- **Postponements and continuances**—occasionally a hearing or a portion of a hearing must be rescheduled or continued (to a later time on the same day or to another day) due to a last-minute conflict for committee members, the unavailability of a witness or the need for more time than originally scheduled for the hearing;

- **Courtesies**—committee chairs and members usually bend over backward to extend courtesies to each other, to non-committee member colleagues from the House and Senate, and to witnesses;
- **Flexibility**—in general, be prepared for anything in the way of changes, flow, logistics, location, and timing.

§4.40 Special Considerations Regarding Executive, Judicial, and Legislative Branch Witnesses

Officials of the federal executive, judicial, and legislative branches who testify before a congressional committee appear and are treated basically the same as outside witnesses at a hearing, although perhaps with more deference and courtesy, or adversity, depending on the issue and parties.

For executive and judicial officials, their appearance as witnesses is a form of official cross-branch communication that must be carefully and thoughtfully prepared and delivered because of the dynamics and interaction among the three branches of government. Many executive branch agencies and judicial representatives are routinely expected to testify at certain hearings, such as budget, appropriations, and legislative hearings affecting their organization's respective area of jurisdiction.

Testimony that is provided to the Congress from either the executive or judicial branch is closely scrutinized and tightly controlled by the respective testifying branches so that there is an assurance of coordination, correct message, accuracy, responsiveness, and general appropriateness reflected in the documents. Witnesses representing executive branch departments and agencies will be guided to a large extent by their own internal protocols and guidelines, as well as, in many cases, by the Office of Management and Budget (OMB) and the White House policy office, to ensure adherence to and consistency with administration policies and priorities. To ensure consistency of policy as determined by the Judicial Conference of the United States, the Administrative Office of the U.S. Courts (AO) plays a similar role for the judiciary when judges or other court officials appear as witnesses before congressional committees.

With respect to legislative branch witnesses, members of Congress, representatives of congressional committees and offices, and legislative service organizations (LSOs) often find themselves in a position to testify before congressional committees. Individual members of the U.S. Senate and the U.S. House of Representatives frequently testify before committees in support of legislation they have introduced, or to comment on their views about a particular issue pending before a committee. Officials from administrative offices of the Congress, such as the Clerk of the House, the Secretary of the Senate, the respective chambers' Sergeant at Arms, and the U.S. Capitol Police, for example, are also called to testify before congressional committees on occasion.

Professional staff from legislative service organizations (LSOs), such as the Congressional Budget Office (CBO), the Congressional Research Service (CRS) at the

Library of Congress (LOC), and the Government Accountability Office (GAO) testify frequently and regularly before a wide array of congressional committees. CBO's mission and message in testifying are usually focused on the budget implications and impact of a proposed measure or program. CRS provides congressional committees with a very valuable service in helping to supply nonpartisan research results and issue analyses. Through both committee testimony and special reports, GAO provides congressional committees and members with expert and detailed analyses of federal programs, executive branch operations, and the use of federal funds to support and enforce the laws and regulations of the land.

Each of these unique entities has its own special protocols and guidelines for testifying before committee hearings. Furthermore, CRS has a significant in-house expertise on the congressional committee and hearing processes, and, consequently, it is a very credible and reliable resource on those subjects. Similarly, GAO has considerable internal experience and expertise in providing training on the precise subjects of this treatise—preparing and delivering congressional testimony. (For a list and explanation of congressional legislative service organizations, see § 5.130, Legislative-Branch Support Agencies, the *Congressional Deskbook*, by Michael L. Koempel and Judy Schneider.)

For more information regarding special considerations concerning executive, judicial and legislative participation in congressional committee hearings, see § 2.31, Who Should Testify?—Federal Executive, Legislative, and Judicial Branch Officials; § 2.68, Congressional Hearing Participants: The "Players"—Federal Departments and Agencies; § 3.23, Special Considerations Regarding Executive and Judicial Branch Testimony; and § 3.24, Special Considerations Regarding Federal Legislative Branch Testimony. For information on preparation and rehearsal of testimony by federal government entities, see § 4.26, Witness Rehearsal of Oral Testimony and Answers to Questions—Preparation and Rehearsal by Federal Government Departments and Agencies.

§4.41 Witness Contact with the Media

Depending on the nature of a hearing topic and the extent of associated public and media interest, a witness may be likely to encounter representatives of the media before or after a hearing. Print and broadcast journalists frequently attend hearings to cover a committee's action, report on the hearing subject matter, and look for other related stories. It is not unusual for a witness to walk out of a hearing room and be surrounded by reporters pushing microphones in the witness's face while cameras are rolling in the background. Witnesses also occasionally conduct press conferences before or after a congressional committee hearing.

A witness should be fully prepared to deal with the media in order to continue advancing his or her organization's message and best case. It is prudent during witness rehearsal to include a mock press interview to familiarize a witness with the tactics of the press and with the proper ways to respond to media questions. This preparation should include a press conference setting, a conventional interview format, and an "ambush" interview. It is also important to prepare and utilize press briefing materials and other information that will be helpful to a witness and to the media. To some extent, being able to answer press inquiries and provide the media with written and oral information is an extension and continuation of the communication process that a witness provides in testifying before a committee.

The Government Accountability Office (GAO), which sends hundreds of professional staff members to Capitol Hill each year to testify, recommends the following considerations and ground rules for those occasions when a witness is confronted with a press interview, especially one that is spontaneous.

1) Ask the reporter's name and affiliation.

2) Ask the purpose of the interview. What's the story?

3) Ask that cameras, lights, and microphones be kept at a reasonable distance.

4) Keep the interview confined to the original subject.

5) Remember that the reporter is looking for information—a good quote.

6) Never say "No comment."

7) Do not go "off the record."

8) Ask for a retake on a fumbled answer.

9) Break off the interview after a reasonable time. Let reporters know where they can reach you for follow-up.

10) Ask when the interview will be broadcast or appear.

Source: United States Government Accountability Office, Participant Manual, Delivering Testimony, GAO Learning Center, Simulated Hearing Exercise, January 2007.

For information on preparing hearing-related documents for the media, see § 3.21, Important Documents: Drafting the Statement and Making the Record—Media Advisories, Press Kits, Backgrounders, and Releases.

For more information on media participation in hearings, see § 2.69, Congressional Hearing Participants: The "Players"—The Media.

For more information on media relations generally, and on how to prepare for interviews and other encounters with representatives of the press, see *Media Relations Handbook for Agencies, Associations, Nonprofits and Congress*, by Bradford Fitch.

§4.42 The Witness's Personal Appearance, Attire, and Demeanor: Looking and Acting the Part

During the preparation phase prior to a congressional hearing, a witness should develop an understanding of the appropriate dress standard and personal demeanor for someone who is appearing before a congressional committee to testify at a hearing.

Consultation with professional committee staff can provide excellent guidelines, and the preparation team should ensure that a witness is fully briefed on the personal aspects of appearing before a committee.

Generally business attire is considered appropriate for an appearance as a witness before a congressional committee. Business suits or at least coat and tie for gentlemen, and business suits or dress ensembles for ladies, are preferable. "Business dress" is a common standard. Witnesses should be appropriately groomed. A professional appearance goes a long way in helping to convey a professional message. On occasion, different dress standards may apply, particularly when a witness is representing a special ethnic, religious, or cultural group or organization. To be sure in planning for appropriate dress and to avoid possible embarrassment, it is prudent to consult with committee staff prior to hearing.

A witness's demeanor and attitude throughout a hearing should be engaging, personable, and professional. He or she should be communicative and should attempt to be helpful to the committee. While seated at the witness table, a witness should face the committee at all times and maintain an upright posture, with both hands resting on the witness table or on the testimony document before the witness. An effective witness utilizes good eye contact with the members of the committee, conveys serious and professional body language, and uses hand gestures to underscore and accentuate points in the testimony.

A witness's speaking style and tone should be natural to the witness, and as conversational as possible, but with an emphasis on clearly and concisely communicating a message, a story, and a case to the committee. The delivery of testimony should be direct, simple and evenly paced—not too fast or too slow. Voice inflections are helpful in varying the presentation, making it interesting to the committee, and helping to communicate the importance of a message. Monotone deliveries can put a committee to sleep.

An effective hearing witness knows, looks, and plays her or his role and part. Appropriate witness attire and demeanor are important considerations that should not be overlooked, and that should be addressed during rehearsals to help ensure that a witness is fully prepared for hearing day.

For more information on various aspects of personal demeanor and performance on hearing day, see § 5.36, Establishing the Witness's Own Comfort Zone; § 5.37, Demonstrate a Commanding Presentation Style and Demeanor; and § 5.43, Make a Personal Connection with the Committee. Also see § 4.25, Witness Rehearsal of Oral Testimony and Answers to Questions—Speaking Style, Demeanor and Format; § 5.44, Importance of Voice Variation, Inflection, Projection, Clarity, Quality, Tone, and Tenor; and § 5.45, Importance of Eye Contact, Body Language, and the Use of Gestures.

§4.43 Helpful Tips for Preparation and Briefing Teams

The witness preparation or briefing team can help the witness to prepare for testimony by:

- talking early and often with the witness;
- letting the witness know where certain points in the testimony could lead a member;
- anticipating committee questions;
- providing examples for Q&A;
- practicing with the witness, especially Q&A in a murder board;
- providing backup material or a short briefing book in a format that the witness can use, and
- getting the witness to the Hill early on the day of the hearing.

Source: Helping the Witness to Prepare: Points to Keep in Mind; Preparing for Congressional Testimony, United States Government Accountability Office, November 2005.

§4.44 Witness Preparation Checklist: Keeping the Important Things in Mind

These are important touch points for a witness to consider during preparation for a hearing, whether or not a preparation or briefing team is utilized.

- Identify and review the major issues and topics of interest and concern to the committee.
- Communicate with the committee staff.
- Understand your role as a witness at this particular hearing.
- Study and master the issues to be covered at the hearing.
- Ensure the proper and timely preparation and production of written materials and important documents, including the official statement.
- Consult with appropriate individuals and offices internally within your organization, and obtain any necessary clearances.
- Conduct a document review far in advance of the hearing.
- Develop a briefing book or background information folder.
- Schedule and conduct preparatory meetings and briefings with the internal organization team to review testimony, briefing books, questions and answers, and other plans.
- Brief committee members and staff as requested or needed.
- Schedule and conduct rehearsal sessions as needed.
- Assess the need for additional documents, background, or other preparation.

§4.45 Recommended General Approaches to Preparation for the Question-and-Answer Phase

1) Understand your role.
2) Anticipate questions. What questions would you ask if you heard your testimony? What questions are the committee members likely to be interested in? What related recent events might you be questioned about?
3) Prepare modules. Answer modules are concise responses consisting of a one sentence, or at most two sentence, direct answer, followed by another two or three short sentences of elaboration.
4) Practice answer modules. Practice them out loud, so you can hear them in your "mind's ear." Realize that questions will not always be asked exactly as you had anticipated, and that you will have to adapt your module answers. Always be prepared to segue into your answer.
5) Simulate a question-and-answer session. If at all possible, try to actually simulate a question-and-answer session. Present your news release to several colleagues and/or people in your press office. Have them ask questions. Answer them as best as possible. What questions did you correctly anticipate? How might those answers be improved? What questions caught you unprepared, and how can they be better answered? Be sure to explicitly request feedback from the participants on how well you did and possible areas for improvement.

Source: United States Government Accountability Office, Participant Manual, Delivering Testimony, GAO Learning Center, Simulated Hearing Exercise, January 2007.

For more information on responding to committee questions during a hearing, see Chapter 6, "Responding to Committee Questions."

- Conduct a "dress rehearsal" or final simulation session just prior to the hearing.

§4.46 Follow the Rules and Be Prepared

The following article underscores the importance of a witness being prepared, following the rules and engaging fully with a committee in the context of a congressional hearing. A Washington lawyer and former chief counsel of the Ethics Committee of the U.S. House of Representatives outlines some valuable pointers and expectations for those called to testify before a congressional committee and for counsel who may be representing them.

IF CONGRESS CALLS, KNOW THE RULES

When an executive is asked to testify before a committee, don't treat it like a trial

William V. O'Reilly
Legal Times
February 9, 2009

Your chief executive officer has received a letter signed by the chairman of a congressional committee or subcommittee, inviting him to testify at a congressional hearing. You need to act quickly. Such letters often seek testimony very soon—sometimes within a week, but rarely beyond a few weeks. Documents may be requested even sooner. How do you respond?

Experienced in-house lawyers may think that they can easily handle this situation. After all, much of the work involved in responding to a congressional inquiry seems to call upon the same skills, techniques and judgment required in civil or criminal litigation. But the most common misstep made in responding to a congressional inquiry is to approach it like a trial.

Congressional hearings are different. You are on their turf, and you must play by their rules.

Some witnesses appear especially oblivious of this. During the February 2008 hearings of the House Committee on Oversight and Investigations into alleged steroid use in baseball, Roger Clemens (354 wins, 4,672 strikeouts, 95 mph fastball) apparently thought it wise to interrupt Chairman Henry Waxman's concluding remarks. Waxman gaveled the legendary pitcher into silence. "Now is not the time to argue with me," Waxman said.

But even more experienced witnesses can make mistakes. With the usual quadrennial prediction of an explosion of Capitol Hill investigations, now is a good time to review some of the things that make a congressional hearing unique.

AHEAD OF TIME

Most requests for congressional testimony are made in letters from the relevant committee or subcommittee chairs rather than through subpoenas. Don't be lulled. Congressional committees have expansive subpoena power, although they rarely need to exercise it. Treat a letter request as seriously as you would a subpoena.

In all but the truly exceptional case, do not waste time pondering legal challenges to the committee's jurisdiction, the scope of its inquiry, or the relevance of the witness's testimony. Those arguments will fall on deaf ears if you raise them with committee staff, and your ability to raise them in a court is both limited and risky. (The court is unlikely to hear your argument unless you are defending a contempt enforcement proceeding, which your company would probably prefer to avoid.)

Thorough preparation is of course key to managing testimony, and building a relationship with committee staff is fundamental to preparation. Begin by calling staff to learn what you can about the purpose of the hearing or overall investigation. Determining whether the hearing is part of general oversight or fact-finding, or whether the committee is looking for a likely piñata on a high-profile issue, will help to define your strategy. Read the committee rules. Visit the committee's Web site. Learn whether your witness will testify alone or on a panel. If he is on a panel, learn the identity of the other witnesses and their anticipated testimony.

Prepare a written statement if committee rules allow. The statement should be brief and should emphasize any helpful themes; it should not be argumentative. Rehearse the most likely questions and answers—and then think of unlikely questions and work on those answers, too.

Recognize from the outset that many of the rules counsel rely on to help clients in other venues do not necessarily apply. As part of the legislative branch, committees might not consider various common-law privileges, including the attorney-client privilege, to apply at all or at least not to the extent they do in judicial proceedings.

Identify promptly any privileges or other limitations on testimony that you believe may apply, and prepare your witness to recognize when those privileges should be invoked. If you conclude that he should refuse to testify at all on Fifth Amendment grounds, tell committee staff well before the hearing. Depending on the importance of the testimony, the committee may seek immunity for your witness from a federal court. Alternatively, the committee may force him to publicly invoke the Fifth Amendment. (While your CEO may not be comforted to know he would not be the first to decline to testify, you can point to the extreme example of an entire panel of witnesses invoking the Fifth, as occurred at a September 2006 hearing of a House Energy and Commerce subcommittee investigating the use of pretexting to gather personal information.)

Similarly, if it is clear that the committee plans to inquire into privileged matters, such as attorney-client communications, and your CEO intends to rely on the privilege to refuse to testify on those particular matters, tell committee staff. They may not agree to avoid the questions entirely, but sometimes there are ways to approach the issue that do not make the witness appear to be stonewalling.

Like much else in Congress, hearings often constitute a zero-sum game: The interest of some lawmakers in making a witness look bad gives rise to a competing interest among other lawmakers to claim unfair treatment. Talk to both minority and majority committee staff well before the hearing to learn whether they have such differing views on the issues and the roles of the witnesses, and work with staff favorable to your position to explore ways to provide helpful testimony.

IN THE HOT SEAT

Once on Capitol Hill, a witness should assume that none of the lawmakers now peering down at him have read his written testimony and so should plan to make an opening statement, if permitted. Keep it short, and emphasize themes.

It is possible that few committee members will be present at any given moment during the hearing. Most committees require at least two members to be there to hear testimony, but lawmakers often come and go throughout the hearing. As a result, the newly arrived may ask questions or make statements virtually identical to those made moments before, which can give hearings a "Groundhog Day" quality.

Thorough preparation will help ensure that your witness gives consistent responses.

Counsel has a very limited role once the hearing begins. The committee wants the witness to speak, not his lawyer, and you should therefore not count on being permitted to object to particular questions or to otherwise interact with lawmakers during the hearing. (Waxman had to frequently remind Clemens' counsel of this.) Lawyers are generally not allowed to sit at the witness table, but are relegated to seats behind the witness. Frequent requests by the witness to consult with his lawyer are not viewed favorably.

Maintain low expectations. As with most civil depositions, your goal will likely be to avoid harm to the CEO and the company rather than to achieve some positive result. If you assume that the hearing's primary purpose is make political points, rather than to develop a comprehensive factual record, you are less likely to be frustrated or disappointed.

One thing that doesn't differ from judicial proceedings: The witness should listen carefully to the question. Make sure your CEO understands that he can ask to hear the question again. He can ask for clarification—but recommend that he do so without insulting the questioner.

Then he should answer the question as succinctly and directly as possible. If he can return to one of your themes, he should do so, but he should do it in the context of a responsive answer.

And don't lie. A false statement under oath is perjury. Even if the witness is unsworn, false statements may be criminally prosecuted under 18 U.S.C. § 1001 or § 1505.

The time to identify any partisan issues regarding the testimony (and to benefit from them) was before the hearing. During the hearing, if partisan lines are being sharply drawn among the committee members, the witness is better served not to try to align himself with either side. Leave politics to the professionals.

AFTER THE SHOUTING

With limited exceptions all congressional hearings are public. Transcripts or videos may be available—although sometimes, committees will decline to provide you with a transcript, particularly if the testimony was taken in executive session (i.e., not publicly) or is otherwise considered confidential.

If a transcript is available, read it. Assume that others are reading it also and that any mistakes, misstatements, or even minimally controversial statements will be reported in the press.

If you believe the transcript contains material errors, contact committee staff immediately in writing and ask that the transcript be corrected. While they may not do so, you have created a record of the error.

If, on the other hand, the transcript is correct, but your CEO misspoke or would like to say something additional or different, you should also prepare something in writing. But weigh the value of getting that additional information into the congressional record. Before submitting anything, contact committee staff for a little chat. The risk is that your CEO will be invited back for another hearing.

William V. O'Reilly is a trial practice partner in the Washington, D.C., office of Jones Day. From January 2006 to August 2008, he served as chief counsel and staff director for the House Ethics Committee. The views expressed here are his own. He can be contacted at woreilly@jonesday.com.

§4.47 HITS: Humor in Testimony—Mock Hearing on UFOs

While humor occasionally finds its way into real-life congressional testimony and adds a unique dimension to what can otherwise be dull, boring, and dry subject matter at times, the following example of humor in testimony is actually included in a mock congressional hearing that was fabricated by its authors to replicate their view of what a hearing on the topic of UFOs might have been like in the 1950s. Reflecting the popular sensationalism of the possibility that UFOs exist, this exchange between the witness and the committee chairman, Senator Mo Lasses, provides a blend of research evidence and skepticism of both government and the existence of UFOs with good old-fashioned humor.

For this HITS sample, authors Francis Ridge and Jerry Washington, who research and write about UFO sightings and related phenomena, developed the mock hearing based on information in Edward Ruppelt's book, *The Report on Unidentified Flying Objects*. New York: Doubleday (1956), which is an account of his experiences, research and findings regarding UFOs. Ruppelt was head of the U.S. Air Force's investigation into unidentified flying objects from 1951 to 1953, and as the leader of Project Blue Book on the subject, he coined the term "unidentified flying object" in lieu of using "flying saucer." What follows are excerpts from the faux testimony. To see the text in its entirety, go to: <*www.nicap.org/mock.htm*>.

A MOCK CONGRESSIONAL HEARING
The Ruppelt Record
By Francis Ridge & Jerry Washington

It is now common knowledge that several official UFO projects came into being as a result of officialdom's concern over the presence of strange objects in our nation's skies—especially since the advent of the "Atomic Age." With the situation reaching critical mass in the late 1940s and '50s, Project Sign, then Grudge, and ultimately, Blue Book, was born.

Edward J. Ruppelt, a captain in the U.S. Air Force, was put in charge of the Project in 1951 and given the unenviable task of getting to the truth of the matter in the face of official obfuscation and stonewalling. A skeptic at heart, Ruppelt changed his tune eventually when confronted with the mounting evidence to the contrary. As a result, Blue Book's official conclusion was that there were a number of cases involving "Unknowns" that could not be explained away - a surprisingly candid admission under the circumstances.

It is in that spirit of truth and honesty that we've cooked-up the following exchanges from a mock hearing, circa 1956, during which Capt. Ruppelt (utilizing his actual quotes) testifies before a skeptical Congress. The Committee Chairman, Senator "Mo Lasses"—a man more interested in grandstanding than anything else—has the floor.

****

CC: Good morning, Captain Ruppelt.

CR: Good morning, sir.

CC: Captain Ruppelt, we understand that you were head of Project Blue Book for two years, from September 1951 to some time in 1954.

CR: Yes, Sir.

CC: So, tell me, Captain. Regarding your, uh, "flying saucers," has the Air Force ever taken the reports of these things seriously?

CR: Yes sir, it has. On September 23, 1947, the chief of the Air Technical Intelligence Center, one of the Air Force's most highly specialized intelligence units, sent a letter to the Commanding General of the then Army Air Forces. The letter was in answer to the Commanding General's verbal request to make a preliminary study of the reports of unidentified flying objects.

CC: And what, pray tell, did this letter say?

CR: The letter said that after a preliminary study of UFO reports, ATIC concluded that, to quote from the letter, the reported phenomena were real. The only problem that confronted the people at ATIC was, "Were the UFOs of Russian or interplanetary origin."

CC: Whoa! Slow down there. That's a lot for this ol' peapicker to digest. (Spoken in his best Southern drawl, Senator Mo then takes a deep breath, using the pregnant pause to shift his immense heft around in his over-stuffed leather chair).

CC: All right now. Let's carry on. Do you know of any higher placed Air Force officers or project scientists who actually bought into this?

CR: Into what sir?

CC: This outer-space idea? It's pretty far-fetched, to put it mildly.

CR: There was a group among intelligence circles that thought the UFO's were interplanetary spaceships. They ranged from generals and top-grade scientists on down. And "maybe they're interplanetary"—with the "maybe" bordering on "they are"—was the opinion of several high-ranking officers in the Pentagon, so high that their personal opinion was almost policy.

CC: Well how come we're just now hearing about it? Didn't any of these people attempt to tell the public their conclusions?

CR: Well, yes. There were two factions. One believed the spaceship answer but felt we should clamp down on information until we had all the answers. Another group favored giving more facts to the public, including the best cases, the unsolved movies of UFOs, and the Air Force conclusions. A press showing of the "Tremonton" UFO movie—which the Navy analysts said showed unknown objects under intelligent control—was planned early in 1953.

CC: Well, if that's so, what happened to this plan?

CR: A new policy went into effect: "Don't say anything!"

CC: A cover-up, in other words?

CR: Those would be your words, Sir.

CC: Okay. Then could you tell me what, if anything, transpired as a result of that letter?

CR: The (1947) letter strongly urged that a permanent project be established at ATIC to investigate and analyze future UFO reports. It requested a priority for the project, a registered code name, and an overall security classification.

CC: And whatever became of that?

CR: ATIC's request was granted and Project Sign, the forerunner of Project Grudge and Blue Book was launched.

CC: So that's when all of this started; this flying saucer business that got the Air Force's knickers in an uproar began in September of that year?

CR: Although a formal project for UFO investigation wasn't set up until September of 1947, the Air Force had been vitally interested in UFO reports since June 24, 1947, the day Kenneth Arnold made the original UFO report.

CC: The record, as I read it here says, that quite a few sightings occurred both before and after the Arnold sighting. Just how concerned was the Army Air Force about all this? How would you best describe the situation?

CR: By the end of July 1947 the UFO security lid was down tight. The few members of the press that did inquire about what the Air Force was doing got the same treatment you would get today if you inquired about the number of thermonuclear weapons stockpiled in the U.S.'s atomic arsenal.

CC: So this was considered a serious situation by the powers-that-be?

CR: These memos and pieces of correspondence showed that the UFO situation was considered to be serious, in fact, very serious.

CC: And confusion reigned until then, right? When would you say folks started to get a handle on the situation?

CR: This confused speculation lasted only a few weeks. Then the investigation narrowed down to the Soviets and took off on a much more methodical course of action.

CC: Well, naturally. So, by the end of the year things really must have calmed down.

CR: Yes sir. While they were still convinced that UFOs were real objects, the people at ATIC began to change their thinking. Those who were convinced that the UFOs were of Soviet origin now began to look towards outer space; not because of any evidence that UFOs came from there, but because of their conviction that UFOs existed and only some unknown race with a highly developed state of technology could build such vehicles.

CC: Yes, well that's a pretty fanciful notion, Captain. Was that ever put into writing?

CR: In intelligence, if you have something to say about some vital problem you write a report that is known as an "Estimate of the Situation." A few days after the DC-3 was buzzed [Chiles-Whitted case, July 24, 1948], the people at ATIC decided that the time had arrived to make an Estimate of the Situation.

CC: And what was that estimate?

CR: The "situation" was the UFOs; the "estimate" was that they were interplanetary!

CC: Whatever happened to this estimate?

CR: It got as far as General Hoyt S. Vandenburg, then Chief of Staff, before it was batted back down. The General wouldn't buy interplanetary vehicles. The report lacked proof. A group from ATIC went to the Pentagon to bolster their position but had no luck, the Chief of Staff couldn't be convinced.

CC: Sounds like my kind of soldier. What happened next?

CR: The top Air Force's command refusal to buy the interplanetary theory didn't have any immediate effect upon the moral of Project Sign because the reports kept pouring in.

CC: Would you continue to categorize those reports of being of serious nature, Captain?
(Whether it's due to his mush-mouthed delivery or the fawning, greased, obsequious leer that accompanies it, Senator Mo has a talent for making even an innocent question sound patronizing).

CR: Yes sir, I would. Then radar came into the picture. For months the anti-saucer faction had been pointing their fingers at the lack of radar reports, saying, "If they exist, why don't they show up on radarscopes?" When they showed up on radarscopes the UFO theory won some converts.

CC: So tell me, Captain Ruppelt. How many official reports had they gotten by this time?

CR: By the end of 1948, Project Sign had received several hundred good reports. Out of those, 167 had been saved as good reports. About three dozen were classified as "Unknowns." At the same time, more and more work was being pushed off to the other investigative organization that was helping ATIC. The kickback on the Top Secret Estimate of the Situation was beginning to dampen a lot of enthusiasm. It was definitely a bear market for UFOs. A bull market was on the way, however.

CC: And the "moonpies" who believed in the interplanetary explanation, whatever happened to them?

CR: These people weren't a bunch of nuts or crackpots, Sir. They ranged down through the ranks from generals and top-grade civilians. On the outside civilian scientists backed up their views.

****

CC: Once again, Captain Ruppelt, you have been most helpful. At this time we'll break for lunch and call on the testimony of some of the other men involved in the Air Force study concerning this fascinating, but puzzling subject.

****

Hearing author note: Though liberties were taken with Capt. Ruppelt's syntax on occasion, in order to match this format, none were taken with out the substance of his statements and/or the implications thereof intact. All of Ruppelt's quotes used in this article can be found in his book "The Report on Unidentified Flying Objects."

Source: Excerpts reprinted with permission of authors Francis Ridge and Jerry Washington, and the NICAP web site. To view the entire fascinating exchange, go to: <*www.nicap.org/mock.htm*>.

§4.999 Chapter Summary

- A well-prepared witness is a critical ingredient of a successful hearing and high quality oral testimony. (§ 4.0)
- It is important for a congressional hearing witness to rehearse the oral delivery of testimony and the answers to potential questions posed by a committee. (§ 4.1)
- Two experts on Congress and committee hearings underscore the importance of effective preparation and rehearsal by a witness planning to testify before Congress. (§ 4.2)
- Effective and outstanding witnesses, whether novices or veterans, exhibit several key common characteristics that can be considered a checklist for witnesses preparing to testify. (§ 4.3)

- There are several important practical considerations and perspectives that a witness should ponder when preparing to testify at a congressional hearing. (§ 4.4)
- First-time witnesses are wise to consider a checklist of helpful pointers and tips that can make their first hearing experience more effective and rewarding. (§ 4.5)
- An effective witness is wise to approach a hearing with a keen understanding of the committee's needs and the political environment. (§ 4.6)
- Utilizing a witness preparation team that organizes the preparation phase and prepares the witness prior to a hearing can be very helpful to a witness. (§ 4.7)
- When utilizing a witness preparation team, a witness should be briefed on the process and timeline of preparation, the written testimony and materials to be used, and the methods of rehearsal that will be employed. (§ 4.8)
- Early in the process of preparation, a witness should become familiar with the issue of the hearing and the subject matter of the testimony. There are numerous sources for consultation to become more fully prepared. (§ 4.9)
- Early in the process of preparation, a witness should begin a review and study of the prepared written materials developed for the hearing, especially the official written statement prepared for the committee. (§ 4.10)
- Early in the process of preparation, a witness and the preparation team should determine and develop the document that will be used as a reference or script by the witness to deliver testimony at the hearing. (§ 4.11)
- It is important that the document used by a witness to deliver testimony be laid out in an organized, simple, easy-to-read, and easy-to-use format as suggested by a checklist of commonly used formatting features. (§ 4.12)
- In presenting oral testimony to a committee, a witness preferably should operate from an outline, notes, or a narrative script rather than merely read a statement to the committee, and a witness should rehearse that presentation during the preparatory phase leading up to the hearing. (§ 4.13)
- During preparation for a hearing, a witness should focus on the target audiences and "publics" that are the aim of the testimony. (§ 4.14)
- A witness's rehearsal of both oral testimony and answers to prospective questions posed by a committee is the core activity of witness preparation for a hearing, and there are several methods of rehearsal and related activities that can be utilized by a witness and a preparation team, regardless of the nature of the organization. (§ 4.15)
  1) Hearing Simulation or Mock Hearing (§ 4.16)
  2) Sample of Simulated Hearing Exercise Outline (§ 4.17)
  3) Practice "Runs" and Live Peer Review (§ 4.18)
  4) "Murder Boards" and Question-and-Answer "Dry Runs" (§ 4.19)

5) Videotaped and Critiqued Drills (§ 4.20)
6) Relying on Oral Statement Script to Deliver Testimony (§ 4.21)
7) Operating within Time Limits and Effective Use of the Clock (§ 4.22)
8) Operating with the Use of a Briefing Book (§ 4.23)
9) Use of Graphics and Visuals (§ 4.24)
10) Speaking Style, Demeanor, and Format (§ 4.25)
11) Preparation and Rehearsal by Federal Government Departments and Agencies (§ 4.26)
12) Example of Federal Departmental and Agency Congressional Committee Hearing Preparation and Rehearsal Approaches and Methods: National Aeronautics and Space Administration (NASA) (§ 4.27)
13) Example of Federal Departmental and Agency Congressional Committee Hearing Preparation and Rehearsal Approaches and Methods: United States Agency for International Development (USAID) Preparation of Testimony and Witnesses (§ 4.28)
14) Example of Federal Departmental and Agency Congressional Committee Hearing Preparation and Rehearsal Approaches and Methods: Internal Revenue Service (IRS) Preparation of Testimony and Witnesses (§ 4.29)
15) Example of Federal Departmental and Agency Congressional Committee Hearing Preparation and Rehearsal Approaches and Methods: Bonneville Power Administration (BPA) Preparation for Congressional Hearings (§ 4.30)
16) Example of Federal Departmental and Agency Congressional Committee Hearing Preparation and Rehearsal Approaches and Methods: National Science Foundation (NSF) Witness Preparation (§ 4.31)
17) Preparation and Rehearsal by Trade Associations (§ 4.32)
18) Preparation and Rehearsal by Business and Corporate Offices (§ 4.33)
19) Preparation and Rehearsal by Nonprofit, Non-Governmental (NGOs), Private and Voluntary (PVOs), and Public Interest Organizations (§ 4.34)

- Witness rehearsals provide an opportunity to make pre-hearing adjustments to statements and the presentation of a witness to a committee. (§ 4.35)
- To provide witness support at a hearing, many organizations and witnesses utilize a briefing team or a group of professional colleagues who accompany the witness to the hearing. (§ 4.36)
- During hearing rehearsals, a witness should practice using a microphone. (§ 4.37)
- On the day of the hearing, a witness should arrive early, get a feel for the hearing room, and attend to last-minute courtesies and details. (§ 4.38)
- During the preparation and rehearsal stage, a witness should get a “feel” for what will actually occur in the hearing room by considering a checklist of items regarding what a witness should expect and assess at the hearing. (§ 4.39)

- There are special considerations that executive, judicial, and legislative branch witnesses testifying before a congressional committee should understand and include in their preparation to testify. (§ 4.40)
- Witnesses often come into contact with the media before and after congressional committee hearings, and should be prepared to address the media and respond to questions. (§ 4.41)
- During the preparation phase prior to a congressional hearing, a witness should develop an understanding of the appropriate dress standard and personal demeanor in order to look and act the part of a professional and effective witness at the hearing. (§ 4.42)
- There are several important tips that can be helpful to a witness preparation team in assisting a witness to prepare for testimony. (§ 4.43)
- As a witness preparation checklist, there are several important touch points for a witness to consider during preparation for a hearing. (§ 4.44)
- A witness can be well-served by considering some established recommended general approaches to preparation for the question-and-answer phase. (§ 4.45)
- A Washington lawyer outlines some valuable pointers for preparation by those called to testify before a congressional committee. (§ 4.46)
- HITS: Humor in Testimony is evident even in mock congressional hearings, as demonstrated in a fabricated hearing on the subject of UFOs. (§ 4.47)

Chapter Five

Presentation and Delivery of Oral Testimony

Chapter Five

Section

Summary Table of Contents

§5.0 Introduction and Overview: Welcome to the "Show"

The hearing day is here! This is it. No more preparation. The day of reckoning has arrived. It is time for the witness to deliver the goods—the presentation of oral testimony at a hearing.

It is show time!

Just as the major leagues are the "show" or "the big show"—the pinnacle venue for players—in professional baseball, hearing day is the "show" within the congressional committee hearings process for the witness. Rehearsals are behind you, and it is time for the real thing. No second chances, no "do-overs." You have prepared. Now you have to produce, perform, and deliver.

For a witness, the presentation of oral testimony at a hearing is the first essential element of the "show," and it is similar to being on offense in a sport. (The question-and-answer phase is the second essential element. See Chapter 6, "Responding to Committee Questions.") When testifying, the witness "has the ball," and it is his or her "turn at bat." Presenting testimony is a witness's chance to act, to deliver, to demonstrate preparation, knowledge, and skills, and to score points in the form of delivering a stellar performance. Its singular purpose is the opportunity for a witness to deliver a message and make a case in an affirmative manner to a committee without interruption. The witness is in the spotlight, commands the microphone, and has the green light to advance the content and themes of the testimony in a proactive fashion to the committee through the use of one-way communication—from witness to committee.

The congressional committee hearing is the major event and moment for which a witness has prepared. Presentation and delivery of oral testimony is the second major role of a witness, following the submission of an official written statement. Reliance on personal communication skills and instincts, plus adequate rehearsal and other preparation, if done correctly and diligently, should get most witnesses through the exercise of oral testimony at a hearing with flying colors.

Through a witness's experience and careful preparation, the act of delivering oral congressional testimony can be raised to a near-art form, complete with superb oratory skill, persuasive communication, and dead-on personal connection that combine to provide a committee with a memorable experience and valuable input, and a witness with great success in communicating an important message to Congress on behalf of his or her organization

Or, in the alternative, testifying can be ineffective, bland, boring, routine, monotonous, and forgettable.

In terms of presentation, the choice of those outcomes is up to the witness whose job it is to deliver and perform at the hearing.

Without question, many witnesses, especially those who have considerable experience testifying, may not need a lot of preparation and rehearsal. Based on qualities such as experience, knowledge, well-established communications skills, a great personality, and good old-fashioned natural ability, many witnesses may be able to waltz into a hearing room and turn in a stellar performance, even on short notice.

However, there are also many witnesses, especially first-timers and those with little to no experience testifying or speaking in public, who may need some sort of preparation and rehearsal as outlined in Chapter 4, "Preparation of the Witness." Those individuals, and sometimes even more experienced witnesses, might also benefit from a review of several considerations and aspects of the hearing world just prior to testifying, including right up to the time of the hearing.

This chapter is intended to cover numerous aspects and perspectives of the hearing environment that can help a witness look ahead at the task at hand and turn in a top performance, whether the witness is a newcomer or a veteran of many hearings. It lays out the major concepts of superior witness performance in presenting and delivering congressional testimony. The chapter discusses speaking format and presentation style, use of supporting materials, and the order, format, and method of delivering a concise and compelling statement to a committee with the use of a well-prepared script. It helps guide a prospective witness through hearing day mental preparation and logistical matters, and outlines how to excel at the witness table. It instructs a witness on how to engage and interact with a committee in an effective manner, and also provides a number of special tips for a witness in delivering a stellar message.

It may be helpful for a witness to review live or taped hearings to have a more complete understanding of the flow and dynamics of a committee hearing. To review video recordings and webcasts of actual hearings, go to individual committee sites accessible through <*www.House.gov*> and <*www.Senate.gov*>, and proceed to the links for menus of webcasts. Committees in both the House and Senate utilize video broadcasting and taping technologies for their hearings on committee cable channels administered by their respective chambers. Many committees post live and archived webcasts of their hearings on their respective committee web sites. See the Back of the Book for more information on this source. Additionally, C-SPAN provides a full archive of hearings on the Web at <*www.c-spanvideo.org*>.

§5.1 Substance versus Theatre

Congressional committee hearings serve a number of important purposes, and they are considered substantive and valuable by the committees that hold them. Hearings provide Congress with information needed to carry out its legislative and oversight responsibilities. (For more information on the substantive importance of congressional hearings, see § 1.20, The Use, Importance, and Value of Congressional Hearings.)

However, a good case can be made that many congressional hearings are more theatre than substance, perhaps even grandstanding in nature. This sometimes cynical, sometimes realistic view of hearings is supported by a wide array of antics, including hearings that are overly politically partisan or one-sided on an issue or in the selection

§5.2 The Value, Importance, and Delivery of Effective and Powerful Oral Testimony: Tips from Two Seasoned Veterans

"Members of Congress and, as importantly, their staffs are presented with more written and electronic documents than they can reasonably be expected to analyze in the time typically available to them. It is thus one of the ironies of our electronic age that personal presentations at Congressional hearings assume even greater importance than perhaps they did before the onslaught of information now available in so many other mediums. And, because there will be oral presentations which run directly counter to each other, the witness who establishes him- or herself as personally believable, comprehensible, and responsive will be the one most likely to be consulted after the hearing itself has concluded. That access, resulting from the personal credibility established (or not) in a very few minutes during a hearing presentation, is even more valuable than the hearing time itself in advancing the interest of those that the speaker represents.

Source: Honorable Ed Pease, Former Member of the United States House of Representatives (R-IN), 1997-2001, and currently Senior Vice-President, Government Relations, Rolls-Royce North America.

"Do not read your statement. Summarize it in a few minutes, and try to present your one, two, or three important messages in a coherent fashion. Then sit back, relax and prepare to answer questions."

Source: Honorable Charles Bowsher, Former Comptroller General of the United States and an experienced witness with hundreds of appearances before Congressional committees.

of witnesses, or that allow certain outside interests to have too much or, alternatively, no say-so in a hearing. (For more information on the theatrical aspects of congressional hearings, see § 1.63, Showcasing, Publicity, Celebrity, and Grandstanding Hearings.)

On balance, many hearings are a blend of substance and theatre. For any given hearing, a witness should examine the hearing climate, issue, and purpose to understand fully the extent of the balance of these qualities, and how various situations might affect the atmosphere and mood of the hearing, as well as the role of the witness in testifying.

§5.3 The Role of the Witness

Remember that the four major roles of a witness in a nutshell are to:

- Prepare and submit written testimony to the committee;
- Deliver oral testimony to the committee;
- Respond to committee questions, and
- Follow-up in providing post-hearing information to the committee.

For more information, see Chapter 4, "Preparation of the Witness," especially § 4.0, Preparing the Witness: Introduction and Overview; and § 2.18 through § 2.20 regarding The Essential Elements of Effective Congressional Testimony.

§ 5.4 The Role of the Committee Hearing

For every witness appearing before a congressional committee to deliver testimony, it is important to remember that the primary importance of a committee hearing is that it provides Congress with information needed to carry out its legislative and oversight responsibilities. Regardless of your view of hearings from your own personal or institutional perspective, Members of Congress and their committees consider the hearings process important to their work, and the importance and value of hearings are also grounded in the fact that the proceedings make a public record.

Consequently, the hearings process and your preparation—right up to the moment you testify—deserve careful preparation, thoughtful analysis, and well-delivered oral testimony that is informative and helpful to the committee. Keeping these factors in mind at the hearing will help keep you grounded in the value and importance that hearings can have. Do not be disappointed if only a few members of a committee appear for the hearing at which you are testifying. Your delivery and performance should be the same whether there is a full house or just one member in the chair.

For more information and a refresher on the topics of the environment, context, purposes, goals and roles of congressional hearings, see Chapter 1, "The Context for Congressional Hearings and Testimony," especially § 1.0, Introduction and Overview: The Authority and Foundation for Congressional Hearings; § 1.20, The Use, Importance, and Value of Congressional Hearings; § 1.30, The Dynamics and Environment of Congressional Hearings; and Chapter 4, "Preparation of the Witness," especially § 4.0, Introduction and Overview.

§ 5.5 Making the Most of Witness Preparation

Delivering testimony at a hearing is the culmination of the preparation and experience of a witness. It is sometimes helpful to review a checklist of reminders, tips, and rehearsal activities that were used during the preparation phase. For a quick review of information covered in the chapter on preparing the witness, scan the summary of Chapter 4, "Preparation of the Witness," at § 4.999, Chapter Summary.

It might also be a valuable exercise to review the important points outlined in the following sections: § 4.4, What to Expect as a Witness; § 4.5, Tips for First-Time Witnesses; § 4.6, Threshold Questions for a Witness to Consider in Preparation for a Hearing; § 4.13, Delivering the Oral Statement: To Read or Not to Read; § 4.38, The Day of the Hearing: Thinking and Planning Ahead; § 4.39, What a Witness Should Expect and Assess at the Hearing; § 4.42, The Witness's Personal Appearance, Attire, and

Demeanor: Looking and Acting the Part; and, § 5.73, The Top Twenty Tips of the Trade for the Delivery of Oral Testimony by a Witness.

Recalling the steps and activities of preparation, as well as the key ingredients of an effective presentation, can help refresh your memory about the reasons and importance for delivering testimony in an engaging, effective, and dynamic manner.

§ 5.6 Going Up in the Stands: The Thirty-Thousand Foot Perspective—Keeping It All in Context

Relax. On hearing day especially, a witness should not become overwrought by the circumstances of the hearing and all the attendant activity. Rather, a witness should try to see the hearing for what it is—an exercise in communication between parties. Keeping a healthy perspective on the meaning and purpose of a hearing will allow a witness to see the event in its best context—the flow of information from the witness to the committee, followed by questions and answers. As they say in baseball, keep your eye on the ball, not on the crowd.

Behind all the ceremony, celebrity, and formality, the hearing is really nothing more than a means of communication, and it is a perfect opportunity for a witness to excel in presenting important information and making the best case for his or her organization. Adequate preparation and rehearsal should allow the witness to be a full player in the hearing room without being overly concerned about—or, even worse, intimidated by—the committee players and processes or the klieg lights and cameras of the broadcast journalists. What this really boils down to is taking a deep breath, and proceeding to the task at hand for which you have prepared—delivering testimony clearly and succinctly in a compelling way, and answering committee questions in a responsive and thorough manner—preferably without allowing distractions to interfere.

§ 5.7 Getting Down to Basics and Details

Despite all the preparation and rehearsal preceding a congressional committee hearing, it eventually all comes down to the moment when the hearing and the witness's testimony commence. At that moment, the job of the witness essentially is to bring all his or her preparation and information to bear on the event of the hearing itself. With an almost myopic view, a witness should approach that moment with organization, purpose, and resolve. It is time to get down to the basics of testimony delivery and the details of the information being presented and the case being advocated. The role of the witness at that point is to impart to the committee orally the content of the testimony in as clear, succinct, and convincing a manner as possible.

§ 5.8 Replicating the Witness's Best Rehearsal

During the hearing preparation phase and witness rehearsals, occasionally there are times when a witness feels like he or she has turned in a top performance, whether on the entire presentation or on a portion of it. In the final moments leading up to a hearing, a witness can be well-served by envisioning or recalling those "high" moments of successfully rehearsed testimony delivery, and mentally reinforcing the need and desire to replicate the best parts of rehearsals in the actual hearing.

A witness's thought process might work this way: "I nailed the opening and closing in the dress rehearsal, and gave my best performance on the key themes and messages during the taped critique. My presentation today will follow those successful models." "I made all the key points very clear in my responses to questions during the 'murder board,' so I will respond to questions today in similar fashion." Mental preparation and visioning of the presentation can be very helpful to a witness.

For more information on rehearsals and preparation, see Chapter 4, "Preparation of the Witness."

§5.9 Relying on Preparation, Best Instincts, and Good Communications Skills

To provide comfort and solace to a witness just prior to testifying, it may be helpful to recall that most speech coaches and trainers will remind you to rely on your good preparation, instincts, and communication skills, and to stick to the script, and you will do just fine in your presentation. That formula is certainly reasonable, and it seems to work most of the time.

Ed Barks, a noted professional presentation skills trainer and author of *The Truth About Public Speaking: The 3 Keys to Great Presentations*, describes the main ingredients of great presentations as preparation—"what you need to take into account before your presentation"; performance—"how you act during your remarks"; and assessing feedback—an honest "look-back" that "puts you on the road to improvement after you speak."

Typical speech 101 courses highlight the fact that a delivery or presentation can be considered successful only if it is interesting, clear, and compelling. Assuming the information and case in your presentation are substantive, your testimony should be of interest to the committee. That interest factor is important in gaining and holding the committee's attention, without which your presentation is not really being heard by your targeted audience.

The witness should not only have a clear concept in mind of what she or he wishes to convey and accomplish in the testimony, but the ideas being conveyed, the case being made, and the action being requested should also be clear to the committee.

Finally, the substance and merit of the case being made, along with the ability during delivery to make a convincing case, should provide the necessary advocacy and persuasion to constitute a compelling presentation.

For more information on rehearsals and preparation, see Chapter 4, "Preparation of the Witness."

For information about speaking in public and delivering effective presentations generally, see *The Truth About Public Speaking, The 3 Keys to Great Presentations*, Ed Barks, Ogmios Publishing, 2005.

§ 5.10 Getting a Handle on the Hearing Room Environment

A witness should "read" the hearing room upon entering it. To get a full perspective of the venue, she or he should get a feel for all the players and processes in play, and scan the room before sitting down at the witness table. "Soaking in the scene" helps allow a witness to grasp the moment, feel more comfortable proceeding, and avoid distractions caused by people or activities in the hearing room.

For a refresher on the layout and locations of hearing rooms, see § 2.10, Congressional Hearing Room Layout and Logistics: The "Playing Field," Forum, and Venue; § 2.11, Congressional Committee Hearing Room Locations; and § 2.12, Diagram of a Typical Committee Hearing Room Floor Plan.

§ 5.11 Recognizing and Understanding Partisanship

Members of Congress often have strong partisan viewpoints or positions on issues, programs, and legislative initiatives, and they frequently announce, discuss, and stake out those positions at a committee hearing. It is important for a witness to be as politically savvy as possible when going before a committee. This means seeing political and issue partisanship for what it is, and understanding how it affects members of the committee and their perspectives, as well as the dynamics of a hearing. Based on party politics or personal ideology, committee members often have solidly established positions and viewpoints on issues to the extent that they are unable or unwilling to hear or consider new or additional information or differing perspectives. If you happen to confront that type of situation at your hearing, do not let it deter you from the goal, purpose, and flow of your testimony and answers.

During preparation for a hearing, witnesses are encouraged to conduct a political analysis of the topic issue that will be the subject of a hearing, as well as to glean a complete understanding of the interests and issues near and dear to the committee and its members. If a witness has included those activities in preparation for a hearing, she or he can rely on that information in dealing with committee members who may have a different viewpoint or tend to speak or ask questions in an adversarial or even hostile manner. (For more information on the enterprises of political, issue and stakeholder analysis, see § 3.8, Issue Analysis and Topic Outline; § 3.9, Political Analysis and Landscape; and § 3.10, Issue Context and Stakeholders.)

During a hearing, particularly in introductory remarks by the chair and committee members, as well as during the question-and-answer period, individual viewpoints of committee members quite often emerge, and witnesses must often engage and interact with committee members on those topics. Understanding the partisan features and issues of a committee and its makeup will allow a witness to engage more productively, without either being overly concerned about trying to convert a member on his or her thinking about an entrenched policy or issue position, or marginalizing or disregarding a committee member's perspective. From the moment a hearing begins, a witness should be prepared for, and take notice of, any partisanship that may surface in the hearing's deliberations. This is a particularly true because Congress has evolved into a more partisan, and sometimes even contentious, institution, and much of the attendant drama plays out in the context of committee hearings.

If a witness has concerns or questions about a political or partisan matter, that matter should be discussed with committee staff prior to the hearing. A witness should not address partisan issues during a hearing, nor engage in taking sides on political or partisan issues beyond the subject of the hearing and the purpose of the testimony.

For more information on partisanship in committee hearings, see § 1.32, Partisanship and Political Analysis: Where Policy and Politics Converge; § 3.9, Political Analysis and Landscape; and § 6.25, Dealing with Partisanship and Political or Policy Agendas.

§ 5.20 Just before the Hearing . . .

As a hearing begins, a witness should relax and be ready to take the microphone. Some people like to be alone to think or relax just before a presentation. Others enjoy the social time with people in the hearing room. How one gears up just before "going into the game" is personal and stylistic. A witness should be as relaxed and natural as possible. It is wise not to do anything completely new or out of the ordinary that might upset a witness's routine, concentration, or train of thought. It is time to focus on the task at hand, and take care of last-minute matters so the witness is unencumbered to proceed with the delivery of testimony. Witnesses should be sure to attend to any personal matters such as a drink of water, restroom stops, clothing adjustments, medicines, reading glasses, hearing aid devices, and any circumstances that may require the assistance of the committee staff, especially for physically challenged witnesses.

§ 5.21 At the Hearing Table . . .

Once seated at the witness table, a witness should get comfortable, organize the oral statement script, briefing book, and any other papers directly in front of him or her on the table, and generally be prepared to proceed in the manner in which he or she typically proceeds when making a formal presentation. A witness should observe and take stock of who is in the hearing room, especially the committee members and other witnesses at the witness table, if there are others.

A witness should check the positioning and setting of the microphone to ensure ease in use when it is time to commence testifying, and be sure to have the timing device within easy view. If water is provided at the witness table, and a witness would like to have a glass ready, he or she should pour a glass (away from the table to avoid spillage) before the hearing or testimony starts.

A witness should locate and make eye contact with any briefing or support team members prior to commencing the presentation. Once settled into his or her seated position at the witness table, a witness should face the chair, maintain a comfortable and upright posture, with both hands on the witness table, and be prepared to begin testifying once the chair has completed a statement introducing the witness or witnesses.

For more information regarding use of a microphone, see § 4.37, Rehearsing the Use of a Microphone; and § 5.22, Effective Use of a Microphone.

§5.22 Effective Use of a Microphone

Once seated at the witness table, a witness should quickly become acquainted with the microphone and its use. In fact, it is preferable to "meet the mike" prior to the hearing, if possible. Many committees use either a single microphone for one witness, or a number of microphones for a panel of witnesses. Most microphones in use on Capitol Hill are attached to a long, flexible extension neck on a solid base that allows easy movement and maneuverability to suit the witness's position at the table and individual upper-body height.

Before beginning to testify, a witness should adjust the microphone so that it is placed directly in front of her or his position, in line with the chair of the committee, and with the microphone extension angled upward toward the witness so that the actual microphone itself is approximately 10–12 inches from her or his mouth. The goal is for the witness to be able to speak into the microphone in an easy and natural manner while also being able to look forward, refer to oral statement notes, and maintain eye contact with the committee while delivering the statement.

As a "mike test," some witnesses like to ask the chair if the microphone is working properly and the witness is being heard clearly. This approach is acceptable and sometimes helpful, but usually unnecessary because committee staff or sound technicians managing the sound system and the microphone's input/output will adjust the system as needed, and the chair will likely advise a witness if a microphone adjustment is necessary.

Speaking into a microphone requires only one's natural, full conversational voice directed at the microphone. In delivering testimony, a witness should lean slightly forward, attempt to project her or his voice *through*, not *at*, the microphone, and try to forget that the microphone is even there.

For information about microphone use rehearsal, see § 4.37, Rehearsing the Use of a Microphone.

§5.30 Organization and Use of Written Text to Deliver the Oral Testimony

One of the most important check-offs for a witness just prior to the beginning of a hearing and the presentation of testimony is to make sure that the written text, narrative, or script that will be used for reference to deliver the oral testimony, sometimes also called a message statement, is properly organized and ready for the witness's easy use during the presentation. That document, usually different from the written statement prepared for a committee, should be placed in front of the witness, and care should be taken that it is, in fact, the actual document that the witness has used in preparation for the hearing, including any marginalia, highlights, last-minute additions, notes, or reminders.

Certainly some witnesses, particularly those with lots of experience testifying or with their own workable style, may simply utilize an annotated version of the official written statement, or some combination or variation using highlighted portions of the official written statement and some side notes. The type of document used by a witness at the hearing as the oral testimony script is left to the discretion of the witness. However, many witnesses may need or want a separately prepared script that contains the precise wording or an outline of what they actually intend to say to the committee. Consequently, whatever form or style the oral statement document takes, it should be well-prepared, well-rehearsed, and ready to go at the hearing.

While it is generally too late at the hearing to write or rewrite the script to be used to testify (except for brief or small last-minute notations or additions), there are some basic pointers that are important to highlight that can help make the witness's testimony more effective, compelling, and well-received. These pointers should, of course, be considered and incorporated earlier during drafting and rehearsal of the narrative script for oral testimony, but it is prudent to review them again just before a hearing in the context of actually delivering the testimony. In fact, it is sometimes helpful to annotate the script utilizing the following pointers as guides and prompts during the delivery of the statement.

Since the written text used to deliver oral testimony will often differ from the official written statement submitted to the committee, and because the contents of the oral testimony script are spoken by the witness and not read by the committee, the witness should take care to deliver oral testimony utilizing as many verbal and other accentuating features and techniques as possible, including:

- Deliver oral testimony under the assumption that you are educating and informing the committee in the first instance, and that the official written testimony has not been read by the committee.
- During oral testimony, if references are made to the written testimony submitted to the committee, ensure that those references are strictly

made with respect to the written document itself, not to the assumption (whether true or false) that the statement has been read by the committee.

- Ensure that the script used to deliver oral testimony is formatted with the use of features that allow the document to be easily read and quickly referenced by the witness for use in delivering the testimony, including highlighted portions, special indentation, enumeration, and large-sized print.
- In the oral testimony script, especially highlight or underline all major themes and points, and verbally highlight them in oral delivery.
- To emphasize and underscore certain key points in the delivery of testimony, use intentional pauses, changes in voice pitch or volume, hand gestures, and a change in the pace of delivery.
- With the use of enumeration or listing, prioritize in order of importance what you want to convey in your message.
- Ensure that the basic thematic messages of the testimony, including the "bottom line" or key message, are stated upfront in headline statements utilizing "oral cues" such as "primary message" and "key theme" to underscore the significance of the messages. Sometimes it is preferable to open the substantive message portion with a statement such as, "Today, I would like to make several key points in support of the pending legislation," or something similar.
- To draw the committee's attention to the immediacy of an issue, lay down a marker of urgency, time sensitivity, or event relationships by using phrases such as "critical change is needed at this time"; "in response to the current crisis or recent events"; and "in relationship to the committee's bill on this subject."
- Relate the basic message or theme of the testimony to the timeliness of, and connection to, the committee's consideration of the issue or relevant legislation.
- Use enumeration to count off, organize, and highlight major points, and to demonstrate clarity of message and numerical priority, by using key phrases such as "first and foremost"; "the first priority is"; and "my initial point is . . . my second major point is . . . my fifth and final point is . . ."
- To support enumerated points, employ the use of specifics such as evidence, examples, vignettes, corroboration, brief analyses, data, anecdotes, quotes, cases-in-point, best and worse case scenarios, studies, and research results.
- Provide crisp and succinct explanations of context, connections, and rationale to support a key point with an eye toward demonstrating how the items of support prove, justify, or underpin the basic points, themes, and messages.
- Utilize the narrative or outlined message statement script as a reference. Speak to the committee directly as much as possible from memory and

first-hand knowledge, and then from reference to the script, but without actually reading the text. When using the reference script, glance down for the reference, wording, theme, or phrase, and then regain eye contact with the committee members as soon as possible when making a statement.

For more information on the importance and crafting of an oral statement script, see § 3.18, Important Documents: Drafting the Statement and Making the Record—Narrative, Outline, or Notes Used for Oral Presentation.

To review an actual operational document utilized as the narrative script for delivery of oral testimony, see § 3.34, Sample of Oral Statement—Written Document Used as Reference to Deliver Oral Testimony.

For more information regarding witness preparation and use of an oral witness statement, see § 4.11, Preparation and Use of Oral Statement Script or Outline.

For information on the preferred manner of delivering testimony with use of a prepared document, see § 4.13, Delivering the Oral Statement: To Read or Not to Read.

For information on rehearsing oral testimony by using a prepared script, see § 4.21, Witness Rehearsal of Oral Testimony and Answers to Questions—Relying on the Oral Statement Script to Deliver Testimony.

§5.31 Delivering the Goods—Presenting Effective Oral Testimony

In presenting oral testimony to a congressional committee, a witness should utilize and rely upon his or her best instincts, speaking skills, preparation, and the script in front of the witness to deliver the statement and make an effective case. A witness should attempt to be conversational, succinct, straightforward, and direct, and speak to the committee as an educator, advocate, and helpful resource.

A witness should present testimony in a manner that is interesting, clear, and compelling, while always directing the testimony to the key targeted audience—the members of the committee. A witness should be as confident and relaxed as possible, should stick to the script of the testimony to stay on track, and should remain calm, professional, and in control while presenting the testimony.

As outlined in § 5.30, Organization and Use of Written Text to Deliver the Oral Testimony, reliance on a written narrative or script specifically designed to assist a witness in delivering oral testimony is highly recommended.

For additional and related information, see § 4.4, What to Expect as a Witness; § 4.5, Tips for First-Time Witnesses; § 4.6, Threshold Questions for a Witness to Consider in Preparation for a Hearing; § 4.13, Delivering the Oral Statement: To Read or Not to Read; § 4.38, The Day of the Hearing: Thinking and Planning Ahead; § 4.39, What a Witness Should Expect and Assess at the Hearing; and § 5.73, The Top Twenty Tips of the Trade for the Delivery of Oral Testimony by a Witness.

§ 5.32 Sample of Oral Testimony Format Outline

GAO Testimony Outline

It is a good idea to offer no more than three reasons in a five-minute opening statement. Persuasive oral testimony is often arranged as follows:

Introduction

- Greet Chair and committee members
- Identify the topic of the hearing
- State the request made of GAO
- Present labeled statement of the main message of the testimony

Body of Testimony

1. Enumerated POINT (Reason)
   Support & Explanation
2. Enumerated POINT (Reason)
   Support & Explanation
3. Enumerated POINT (Reason)
   Support & Explanation

Conclusion

- Summary
  Restated enumerated reasons
- Close-off
  (possible reference to significance)

Source: GAO Performance and Learning Instructor Manual, Delivering Testimony, September 2001, United States General Accounting Office (now Government Accountability Office).

§ 5.33 Organization and Use of Prepared Written Support Materials

In addition to the testimony script that should be placed directly in front of the witness for use and reference, the briefing book, and any other written materials such as charts, graphs, or other visuals (if used at all) should likewise be organized methodically on the table for easy use and access by the witness during the hearing. These collateral materials should be organized in a manner that reflects the order or nature of their use or reference by the witness during the hearing, whether during the testimony phase or the question-and-answer period.

For more information, see Important Documents, § 3.13 through § 3.22; § 3.28, Use of Graphics and Visuals; § 4.23, Witness Rehearsal of Oral Testimony and Answers to Questions—Use of Graphics and Visuals; § 5.70, Effective Use of Visual Aids, Charts, and Graphics; and § 6.34, Witness Use of a Briefing Book to Answer Committee Questions.

§5.34 Keeping Notes and Score on a Writing Pad

It is a good idea to have a readily available note pad or blank sheet of paper on the witness table in front of the witness next to the oral testimony script for use in jotting notes or comments about various items that might be helpful during or after the hearing. For example, if the chair refers to a paragraph or point included in the written testimony, the witness might want to make a note of that comment for use or reference later in the testimony. When a committee member arrives or departs, a witness may wish to make a note to ensure the inclusion or exclusion of that member in any relevant references during the testimony.

If a committee member expresses special interest or concern about a certain matter during opening statements, a witness may wish to note that issue so it can be properly addressed, emphasized, or refuted later during testimony. Similarly, there are occasions when committee members raise a subject matter that is more appropriately addressed during the question-and-answer period, or even after the hearing as a follow-up action item. These items are perfectly suited as additions to the note pad.

In short, the note pad is for the personal use of the witness in whatever way it can be helpful. While certainly not a requirement, it is wise to have a pad on the table just in case it is needed by the witness.

For information on the use of a note pad during the question-and-answer phase of a hearing, see § 6.41, Use of Note Pad during Questions and Answers.

§5.35 Utilizing a Briefing or Support Team

Prior to commencing the delivery of testimony, if it is in the witness's hearing plan to use or rely upon a briefing or support team for any reason, the witness should know precisely where the team is sitting, if not at the witness table, and should have easy access to those individuals. It is highly preferable that the witness has rehearsed calling on colleagues for assistance, in whatever form that might take, to ensure a smooth flow during the testimony or question period. The witness should have a plan for referring to colleagues when in need of information or assistance during the hearing. Typically a support team sits directly behind a witness at a hearing.

For more information about a briefing or support team, see § 2.67, Congressional Hearing Participants: The "Players"—Witness Support Teams; § 4.36, Witness Support: Use of Briefing Staff or Team; and § 6.36, Witness Use of Briefing or Support Team.

§5.36 Establishing the Witness's Own Comfort Zone

As soon as you take your seat at the witness table, get comfortable and settle in, take a deep breath, organize your notes and materials, and remember why you are there to testify. Try to feel and act comfortable, and you will convey to the committee in a professional sense that you are in your comfort zone as a witness and as a spokesperson for your organization and viewpoint. Establishing a comfort zone and relaxing before beginning to testify will help enhance the ease and flow of a witness's delivery.

§5.37 Demonstrate a Commanding Presentation Style and Demeanor

Establish your presence at the witness table immediately and a commanding presentation style in your very first words to the committee. Greet the committee with a forceful opening line such as "Good morning, Mr. Chairman and members of the committee. I am pleased to be here today to discuss the merits of S. 432." Let the committee see and hear that you have taken the stage and that you mean business. Your presentation style and demeanor should be relaxed and conversational, but nonetheless professional, direct, and business-like. Committees appreciate a witness with a commanding presentation style and demeanor that is balanced—not overbearing or too solicitous.

§5.38 Nailing the Introduction and Setting the Tone

It is important for a witness to open his or her remarks with a strong introduction. Nailing the introduction announces that you are ready to deliver an important message, and sets the tone for the rest of your remarks. Highlight the introductory portions of your script to ensure ease in referring to them as you begin your remarks to the committee.

§5.39 Submitting the Written Statement for the Record

Most committee chairs will usually announce that a witness's official written statement will be made part of the hearing record. However, should such a statement from the chair not be made prior to a witness's testimony, it is standard practice for the witness to request respectfully that his or her written statement be included in the hearing record in full.

§5.40 Sticking to the Script in Delivering Testimony

Assuming that a well-prepared script document is in place at the witness table and being utilized by a witness, it is important for the witness to stick to that script to convey organization, ensure succinctness and clarity, and guarantee that the entire statement and its important messages are delivered in the time allotted by the committee. On some occasions a witness may feel a need to vary from the script, but this type of digression should be the exception, and used only when a last-minute thought occurs to the witness. Even on those occasions, an unrehearsed or unprepared comment that is not well-thought-out in advance may prove to be an unwise addition to the presentation. The old adage is generally true most of the time: Stick to the script!

For information on sticking to the script during committee questioning of a witness, see § 6.32, Sticking to the Script in Response to Committee Questions.

§5.41 Speak to the Committee Members—Don't Read to Them

To the extent possible, a witness should attempt to speak to the committee—to talk to the committee members in a conversational manner—without reading the statement if possible. If a witness must read part or all of the statement, it should be done in a delivery style with such familiarity and easy flow that it is the next best thing to speaking directly to the committee without notes. In such cases, the statement should be conversational in nature so that the written words on the script reflect the witness's style of oral delivery and speaking. By all means, avoid a monotonous reading of a statement that neither captures the committee's attention nor conveys the message of the statement in a compelling manner.

For more information on presentation style and preparation, see § 3.18, Important Documents: Drafting the Statement and Making the Record—Narrative, Outline or Notes Used for Oral Presentation; § 3.34, Sample of Oral Statement—Written Document Used as Reference to Deliver Oral Testimony; § 4.11, Preparation and Use of Oral Statement Script or Outline; § 4.13, Delivering the Oral Statement: To Read or Not to Read; § 4.21, Witness Rehearsal of Oral Testimony and Answers to Questions—Relying on the Oral Statement Script to Deliver Testimony; and § 5.30, Organization and Use of Written Text to Deliver the Oral Testimony.

§5.42 Focus on the Primary Targeted Audience—the Committee

A cardinal principle of congressional hearings is that it is the committee and its members who are the primary audience for a witness's testimony. At the hearing, a witness should direct the testimony to the committee, through the chair, and to all the members of the committee. Prudent audience analysis means knowing which members of the committee are likely to attend the hearing, and then, at the actual hearing, sizing up the attendance to determine who, in fact, is present. Knowing the actual audience and their positions on the issues will help instruct the witness on how to focus, express, and frame remarks during testimony and, later, during questions.

For more information on targeted audiences at a hearing, see § 2.80, The Targeted Audiences of a Witness's Testimony; § 3.12, Analysis and Targeting of the Committee and Audiences; § 4.14, Focusing the Witness on Targeted Audiences; and § 6.33, Focusing on the Questioner during Questions and Answers.

§5.43 Make a Personal Connection with the Committee

From his or her very first words uttered to a committee when delivering testimony, a witness should attempt to make as much of a brief and genuine personal connection with the committee as possible. If nothing else, the witness self-introduction can include comments such as welcoming the opportunity to testify, thanking the committee for a chance to provide information, or highlighting the importance of the committee's attention to the issue of the hearing.

Witness connection to a committee might also be conveyed in the form of a personal comment about appearing before the committee previously, working on the hearing issue on other occasions, or focusing on the special interest of one or more committee members. The point is for a witness to relate to the committee in more of a personal manner than just relying on the institutional reason for appearing to testify. It is a matter of human nature and interest that committee members will be more engaged in the testimony of a witness if they feel some sort of connection to the witness, however remote. Warming up the committee members with a personal comment or connection is always a good idea.

§ 5.44 Importance of Voice Variation, Inflection, Projection, Clarity, Quality, Tone, and Tenor

The effectiveness and success of a witness's testimony are often measured by the substance and content of his or her oral statement, as well as by the way the message is delivered. To help make the delivery of testimony more interesting and dynamic, a witness should consider the use of several speaking techniques to liven up the presentation and avoid monotony. Varying one's voice patterns, pitch, and inflection in the presentation of material is a good way to hold the committee's interest, emphasize key issues, and differentiate between and among points being made. The use of pauses in speaking can provide emphasis and draw special attention to an important point.

It is also important for a witness to project his or her voice effectively so that the committee hears the full thrust of the oral testimony, can detect various forms of emphasis, and is able to understand clearly what is being said. Similarly, a witness should speak with great clarity in delivering testimony, including enunciating words and phrases carefully so that they are clearly understood by the committee and for the record, and with a pace of delivery that is not too fast or too slow. Careful and clear articulation is especially important when employing long, unusual, or difficult words or complex phrases in the delivery of testimony.

The sound, quality, and character of a witness's voice and vocal variations used in delivering testimony should also accurately reflect the tone and tenor of speaking that are appropriate and desirable for a hearing setting, and that depict the witness's demeanor. Through normal speech patterns, the witness should attempt to convey a professional and relatively serious approach and delivery that is presented in a comfortable, relaxed, and conversational manner.

For more information, see § 4.25, Witness Rehearsal of Oral Testimony and Answers to Questions—Speaking Style, Demeanor, and Format.

§5.45 Importance of Eye Contact, Body Language, and the Use of Gestures

To complement substantive content and well-spoken delivery in presenting oral testimony, a witness should use good eye contact, body language, and gestures as effective communication tools.

One of the most effective delivery techniques that a witness can utilize to connect with a committee is proper eye contact. In many cases, good eye contact can have more of an impact on the delivery than the content of the testimony itself. Proper eye contact entails looking members of the committee straight-on, eye to eye, not looking over their heads, only at the chair, or scanning the hearing room like an oscillating fan. Good eye contact should bring a response in the form of an expression from committee members that they are listening and hopefully interested. A witness should attempt to look each committee member in the eye on occasion throughout delivery of testimony, and especially when addressing a question asked by that member.

Good positive body language can also add to the professionalism and easy flow of testimony, and demonstrate the confidence of a witness. A witness should be relaxed at the witness table, but seated upright and squarely facing the dais, with full attention to the committee. The witness's hands should be placed on the witness table.

Just as with proper eye contact and good body language, gestures should be considered as part of a witness's tool box of techniques for effective communication and persuasion. The use of hand gestures, made in a natural and reasonable manner, can especially be helpful in supporting statements that suggest a thought or issue, or to accentuate, highlight, or enumerate a point or theme in the message being delivered. The use of a hand gesture as if cutting the air or with the palm facing downward is effective in making emphatic points. A gesture with the palm facing upward is effective to support a comment that proposes, suggests, or offers an idea or recommendation.

When using verbal enumeration of points to highlight a series of messages or key points, it is helpful to hold up the appropriate number of fingers or use a simple hand gesture. An occasional nod of the head to emphasize a point can also be useful, and "yes" or "no" nods can sometimes be used in conjunction with statements that are positive or supportive, or negative or in disagreement, respectively.

§5.50 Presentation Format and Order

While there is no perfect or uniform format and order of presentation of testimony by a witness, there are several common elements that contribute to effective and well-organized oral testimony, ranging from the introduction, substance and content, to emphasis, details and the closing. Sections 5.51 through 5.59 provide a checklist and explanation of the elements of typical format and order.

§5.51 Presentation Format and Order— Opening with Self-Introduction by Witness and Summary of Issue Position and Hearing Topic

Once the chair has introduced the witness and asked him or her to proceed, the witness should open by making any comments of self-introduction that may be appropriate, and thanking or acknowledging the committee for inviting the witness to testify and participate in the hearing. The witness should then state the purpose or mission of the testimony about to be given, and offer a summary of the testimony's content and the organization's position on the issues as they relate to the hearing and its purpose. This type of opening addresses the issues: "Here is who I am and why I am here to testify."

§5.52 Presentation Format and Order—Presenting Major Thematic Statement and Layout of Case

At the beginning of the delivery of testimony just following the self-introduction, a witness should present the essential or major thematic statement that sums up the message and content of the testimony. This practice allows for an early and upfront announcement of the major theme in order to attract the committee's attention and interest, and to lay the foundation for the content presentation that will follow. It also has the benefit of demonstrating to the committee that the witness is organized, prepared, and ready to deliver a powerful statement. It is the witness's announcement to the committee, "Here is what I am going to tell you."

§5.53 Presentation Format and Order—Making the Basic Case and Outlining the Main Messages

Following the self-introductory and thematic statements, a witness should move directly into making the principal case and its basic ingredients or components, preferably no more than three to five in number. These main or basic messages should be highlighted and distinguished by the witness through enumeration and other forms of emphasis, especially since they represent the core content of the information being presented to the committee. This portion of the oral testimony says to the committee: "Here are my case and basic messages."

§5.54 Presentation Format and Order—Providing Supporting Data, Rationale, Analyses, Studies and Research Results, Evidence, Explanations, Anecdotes, Examples, Vignettes, Corroboration, Quotes, Cases-in-Point, Best and Worse Case Scenarios, Comparisons, and Contrasts

To support the basic case and main messages being presented to the committee, a witness should consider variously utilizing a number of reinforcing features and techniques, including, for example, data, rationale, analyses, studies and research results, evidence, explanations, anecdotes, examples, vignettes, corroboration, quotes, cases-in-point, best and worse case scenarios, comparisons, and contrasts.

Data can take the form of any information and special details, such as facts, figures, and statistics, that substantively support the basic premise of the case or message. A rationale provides the reasoning, principle, or basis for some aspect of the message, including perhaps its need or benefit. Analyses demonstrate thoughtful consideration and examination of an issue, and provide back-up information that helps justify a point being made. Studies and research results show a committee that an organization has exercised diligence in arriving at conclusions, and they provide good data and support for a message. Evidence provides supportive information that helps prove a point or underpin an issue or assertion. Explanations, preferably brief, help elucidate a point or issue more clearly so it can be better understood by the committee.

Anecdotes provide real-world stories and examples that reinforce or support a point, contention, or need. Examples and vignettes provide details to show or demonstrate the application of a point being made and lend a sense of reality to an issue. Corroboration is information that bolsters an assertion and strengthens its credibility. Quotes can be used to put a human face and real-world application on an issue or point being made, as well as to boost the credibility of a statement. Cases-in-point are specific and precise "spot-on" examples of an assertion. Describing best and worse case scenarios allows a committee to hear the "book ends" of the impact, results or outcome of an issue or discussion topic. Comparisons demonstrate similarity and like features of issues, programs or assertions. Contrasts point out differences in these items.

Each of these methods can provide helpful support that serves as a foundation for the primary case and messages being advocated by a witness, and, therefore, they should be employed throughout the testimony by the witness. They help answer the question in the minds of the committee members: "Why should we accept or agree with your case and messages?"

§5.55 Presentation Format and Order—Highlighting Recommendations, Requested Remedies, and Calls to Action

Just as the major themes and messages of testimony should be spotlighted in the main portion of the testimony, so should any resulting recommendations to the committee, requested remedies such as legislation or oversight, and calls to action such as further hearings or legislative measures, likewise be highlighted next by a witness in delivering testimony to a committee. This "action" portion of the testimony, in fact, is a stellar moment and opportunity for a witness to contribute his or her organization's suggestions about what should be done about a problem, issue, or concern. Consequently, the presentation of these elements should be as carefully planned and delivered as the major themes.

Committees often look to this portion of the testimony as the most helpful and useful information because it provides them with new and creative ideas that can assist them in their various roles as legislators. For a witness, this portion of the testimony is often the gold standard, because it presents to the committee the basic case, goal, or message of the organization. It is the chance for a witness to say to a committee: "This is what you should do." The use of enumeration is especially effective when used by a witness to list suggested courses of actions, recommendations for change or improvement, and remedies that address a particular issue or need.

§5.56 Presentation Format and Order—Projecting Outcomes, Expectations, and Alternatives

After the major messages and themes have been presented, and particularly following the presentation of any recommendations, requested remedies or calls to action, a witness may wish to engage in the exercise of projecting various outcomes, laying out expectations, and outlining alternatives for the committee's consideration. Similar to recommendations that are made by a witness, these projections or forecasts help allow the committee to see, through the eyes of the witness, the various possibilities and permutations related to a particular issue and certain courses of action.

For example, a witness might project an outcome or results for a federal program if it were to be provided more federal funding. A witness might set up an array of expectations for the committee to consider if a federal program does not receive increased funding. And a witness might describe various alternatives that the committee might consider in approaching the revisions or reforms needed in the reauthorization of a federal program. These tactics, when used properly, can be very helpful to a committee in seeing the complete picture with respect to a program, issue or policy, and they are also valuable tools for use by a witness is presenting a compelling case on behalf of his or her organization. They also send the message to the committee: "Here's what can happen if you don't act, or if you act a certain way."

§5.57 Presentation Format and Order—Summarizing: Restatement of Case and Position

Once the major themes, messages, supporting information, recommendations, and projections have been presented, a witness should begin bringing closure to the testimony by summarizing the essential elements of the case being made and the position of the organization being represented. This is the opportunity for the witness to tell the committee in a reinforcing manner: "Here is what I just told you and why it's important." In this case, repetition—brief, succinct, and to the point—is a good ploy, but it should be presented truly in summary style.

§5.58 Presentation Format and Order—Winding Up: The Grand Conclusion

A witness's testimony should end on a high note—with enthusiasm, promise, commitment, confidence, and competence as key words and characteristics in the minds of the committee members as they consider the testimony they have just heard. The purpose of winding up is to announce to the committee that a witness is at the end of the testimony, as well as to induce the committee's interest and attention to the finale.

A witness's role at this point is to highlight, one last time, the importance and significance of the issues and the organization's positions; to demonstrate any sense of urgency and timeliness that might impact on the committee's action and the issue at hand; to substantiate the legitimate need for, and value of, any requests, recommendations, or calls to actions—all key characteristics and rationale for the committee as it considers the reasons for any change, reform, response or other action. A witness should deliver this grand conclusion in a powerful and sincere manner to cap the performance of testifying, and should highlight these closing words on the written script so that they are especially useable in the presentation. The grand conclusion is the final chance to say to the committee: "Here's the case in a nutshell for your consideration and action."

§5.59 Presentation Format and Order—Inviting Questions from the Committee

After winding up and concluding the testimony, and as final comments before giving up the microphone, a witness should thank the committee for the opportunity to appear and testify, and invite questions from the committee by indicating that the witness would be pleased to answer any questions the members of the committee might care to ask. In short, this close-out tells the committee: "Thanks again for including me, and please consider me a reliable and engaged resource."

§5.60 Examples of Presentation Format and Order: The Anatomy of an Oral Witness Statement

In the four representative oral testimony statements below, taken from actual congressional hearing transcripts, note the bracketed editorial comments and notations regarding the association of certain aspects and content of the statements with many of the best practices outlined in this chapter, especially § 5.51 through § 5.59. Each of the four statements is representative of typical witness oral testimony before congressional committees, and provides examples of stylistic approaches, content usage, and message bolstering that can serve as models for oral testimony by witnesses.

To review a series of questions and answers associated with these four statements, see § 6.48, Sample Question-and-Answer Dialogues: The Anatomy of an Effective Response.

1) **Testimony of Ted Danson**, representing OCEANA, at an oversight hearing of the House Committee on Natural Resources on the subject of "Offshore Drilling: Environmental and Commercial Perspectives."

STATEMENT OF TED DANSON, OCEANA

[*Note the opening and introduction; greeting to committee; and statement of credentials and standing.*]

Mr. Danson. Thank you very much. Good morning. My name is Ted Danson. I am a longtime ocean activist and a member of the Board of Directors of Oceana. We are a global ocean conservation organization based here in Washington, D.C. And I would like to thank you, Mr. Chairman, and members of the Committee for giving me the opportunity to speak to you today.

[*Note the issue background; major theme statement/thesis; and summary of issue position.*]

In the late 1980s, Occidental Petroleum proposed slant drilling off the coast of Santa Monica. I was very concerned about the impact this would have on the ocean environment, so I teamed up with an environmental lawyer to fight it. I am happy to report that we won. After that, to make sure our oceans would continue to be protected, we co-founded American Oceans Campaign, which worked for 15 years to protect the oceans from oil drilling and other threats. We later decided to expand the capacity of the American Oceans Campaign by joining with Oceana, which is now the largest international organization focused solely on protecting the oceans. And so today I am here to testify against the opening up of the Outer Continental Shelf of our oceans to oil and gas development.

[*Note the delivery of major messages and basic case, and the use of supporting data including evidence, rationale, vignettes, and research results.*]

The same reasons that made more offshore drilling a bad idea when I founded the American Oceans Campaign are still valid today. I am encouraged by the administration's announcement yesterday that they will be taking additional time to examine the offshore drilling issue.

Oil and water don't mix. Our oceans give essential protein to nearly half the world's population. In the U.S., recreational and commercial fisheries combined supply over 2 million jobs. On top of that, coastal tourism provides 28.3 million jobs, and annually generates $54 billion in goods and services.

Ecosystems are disrupted, top to bottom, by the short- and long-term effects of oil. More oil spills mean less abundant oceans; more oil spills mean fewer wonderful, pristine beaches; more oil spills mean fewer jobs.

While not intentional, spills do happen. And according to the National Academy of Sciences, no current cleanup methods remove more than a small fraction of oil spilled in the marine waters, especially in the presence of broken ice.

Approximately 120 million gallons of oil end up in the world's oceans every year from oil platforms, marine transportation, vessel discharges, and accidents.

The impacts of oil on fish and other wildlife are numerous and well own. Ingesting oil is usually lethal, and long-term exposures can result in serious problems, such as reduced reproduction and organ damage.

Each offshore oil platform generates approximately 214,000 pounds of air pollutants a year. These pollutants include precursors to smog, acid rain, and contribute to global warming. Pollution released from rigs can affect people and animals living within 180 miles of that platform.

[*Note the return to, and highlighting of, the major theme, and the use of supportive examples and details.*]

For all these reasons, offshore oil drilling is such a bad idea that for more than 25 years our leaders put an end to it. Today it is still a terrible idea. In fact, with today's science, we have even more reason to keep the oil companies out of our oceans. That is because we now know that burning fossil fuels contributes to climate change.

Climate change is potentially catastrophic for the oceans due to something scientists call acidification. As our oceans absorb carbon dioxide from the air, they become more acidic. Coral reefs, essential to ocean life, are already in trouble. If emissions continue to increase, there is likely to be mass extinctions of coral by the middle of the end of the century.

Acidification also threatens the very base of the entire ocean food chain. Scientists estimate that the southern ocean could reach the tipping point as early as 2030. This means that in only 20 years, it is likely that creatures at the base of the food web, such as krill and sea snails, will be unable to create their shells. If the base of the ocean food web collapses, it would be catastrophic for the oceans, especially for our fisheries and everyone that depends on them for food and for jobs.

[*Note the statement of facts and position; use of evidence and vignettes; and statement of problems and challenges.*]

Despite all of these problems, oil companies still want to invest billions of dollars in continuing our dependence on oil instead of creating a sustainable plan for the future. The argument for increased offshore drilling is essentially that it will get gas prices to come way down. That is simply not true. The oil companies are making us a sucker's offer. They are asking Americans to take 100 percent of the risk of ocean drilling for just a fraction of any potential benefits. In fact, even at peak production, increased drilling offshore would account for less than 1 percent of current energy demand in the U.S., and that is if in this global market the oil would stay in the U.S., which is unlikely. It would only amount to mere pennies in savings at the pump.

The high gas prices from this summer were not due to a lack of oil drilling in American oceans, they were a result of high demand in a worldwide oil market. As we have seen, prices came way down in just a few months, which is a clear demonstration of that fact.

[*Note the summary, highlighting and conclusion of the theme and key messages; call to action, recommendations, and requested remedies; and the use of enumeration.*]

The bottom line is this: Offshore oil drilling may be a good deal from the perspective of an oil executive's office, but it is a bad deal for a citizen looking at it from a California or a New Jersey beach. And so today I ask you to take three important steps that would steer our country in the right direction toward affordable energy and healthy oceans.

First, I believe Congress should quickly reinstate the moratorium on new oil leasing in the Outer Continental Shelf and Bristol Bay.

Second, the threats to the Arctic demand a separate and distinct planning process. Ongoing oil development activities must be suspended until that is completed.

Finally, clean, carbon-free ocean energy, such as wind, tidal, wave and current power, must be a piece of our sustainable energy future. The Natural Resources Committee should hold hearings on the renewable resources that our oceans offer. Stimulating these energy sources creates jobs.

[*Note the additional call to action and outline of challenges; concluding summary; restatement of position and case; and winding up and "thanks" to the committee.*]

Let's work with the oceans, not against them. Let's use their abundant wind and water energy to do things that will be good for the planet and good for America. Let's give future generations oil-free beaches and oceans that are an abundant source of food, wildlife and clean energy.

Thank you for this opportunity.

The Chairman. Thank you, Ted.

Source: H. Hrg. 111-1, Committee on Natural Resources, U.S. House of Representatives, Feb. 11, 2009.

For the entire record of the hearing online, perform an Internet search for "f:47302.wais", including the quotation marks.

To review select questions and answers associated with this testimony, see § 6.48, Sample Question-and-Answer Dialogues: The Anatomy of an Effective Response.

2) **Testimony of Philippe Cousteau**, representing Ocean Conservancy, at an oversight hearing of the House Committee on Natural Resources on the subject of "Offshore Drilling: Environmental and Commercial Perspectives."

STATEMENT OF PHILIPPE COUSTEAU, OCEAN CONSERVANCY

[*Note the simple opening and introduction that establish credibility and standing.*]

Mr. Cousteau. Thank you, Chairman Rahall, Ranking Member Hastings and the Committee, both for holding this series of hearings and for inviting me to speak here today. It is certainly an honor to speak on behalf of the oceans.

I am CEO of EarthEcho International, as the Chairman said earlier, where we work to empower individuals to take action to restore and protect our oceans. And

I also serve on the board of trustees of the Ocean Conservancy, the country's oldest and largest ocean nonprofit, harnessing over 35 years of policy and scientific expertise to anticipate ecological threats to the ocean.

[*Note the statement of background, basic theme, outline of challenges, and recommendations.*]

As many of you know, I have grown up around the ocean, and marine conservation has been part of my family's legacy for decades. Indeed, I remember hearing tales about my grandfather and his adventures, diving for the first time off the southern coast of France. But I also remember stories about how devastated he was by the changes that he saw over his lifetime, over a relatively short period of time, on those very reefs which are more or less a dead zone today. And I think that it is an irony that in the last 50 years we have seen not only the greatest amount of exploration of the oceans, but also the greatest amount of exploitation and destruction of them at the same time.

Now, what is so critical about the Outer Continental Shelf is that almost all of the nonfisheries-based, not to mention much of the fisheries-based, exploitation occurs there.

We face great hardship in this country at this time, and the ocean and coastal communities are a critical part of our economy. Over 50 percent of our GDP is generated in coastal counties where approximately 50 percent of our population resides, with blue jobs and marine industries contributing greatly.

I am not advocating that we do not develop the Outer Continental Shelf, but if we are to realize the full benefit of our oceans, if they are to continue to provide us with the opportunities for economic development, it must be done in a way that is planned and that takes into consideration the health of the environment, or we will merely reap short-term gains at the expense of future generations.

[*Note restatement of major theme, position and basic messages; and the use of requests and recommendations, a call to action, enumeration, projected outcomes, and supportive detail such as alternatives and examples.*]

Specifically, speaking on behalf of Ocean Conservancy, we seek three things. First, Congress must act where it failed last fall. As Ted said, we must fully reinstate the moratorium on new oil leasing in the Outer Continental Shelf. Now, I strongly maintain that the reinstatement of that moratorium is absolutely critical to the health of the ocean. But if there is to be new drilling, at the very least—and again, I am against it—but at the very least, if there is to be new drilling, we must make sure and legislate that the process of new drilling siting and the conditions applied to exploration and production minimize their impacts. Science should guide any activity that occurs in the OCS, and where science is not adequate, it is absolutely crucial that studies should be conducted before any leasing occurs for any uses.

And contrary to popular belief, not all ocean floors are created equal. There are a myriad of different types of habitat, from deep coral reefs to rich rocky habitats, to some relatively barren terrain, but the current process does not sufficiently consider these variables.

Similarly, some regions are especially vulnerable, and Congress must ensure they are protected. In the Arctic, for example, as Ted said, we lack the baseline scientific information necessary to make informed decisions, and there is no capacity to handle accidents and oil spills in its ice-filled seas.

Rather than oil, I believe we must vigorously enhance our efforts to develop ocean renewable energy. That is the future. From wind, solar, wave, tidal, and even ocean thermal energy conversion, there is an endless potential to responsibly develop new and clean sources of energy and provide new jobs and economic development for this country.

The second specific recommendation is for a comprehensive plan to put order in the ocean and stop the anarchy of fractionalized development. In late 20th century America, urban sprawl saw suburbs creep across the landscape in ever-widening mazes of highways and strip malls. In the ocean, the situation is similar, only worse. We need comprehensive planning, with conservation as a central deciding factor, so that the multiple competing industrial uses work together in a way that is sustainable for our shared ocean future. Indeed, it is not only critical for the environment that we plan, but also for industry, so that they can anticipate more accurately the outcome of permitting and development.

And the third specific recommendation is the creation of an ocean investment fund. This would set aside a small portion of the revenue generated off these uses to pay for activities and projects that maintain and restore marine ecosystem health, such as comprehensive environmental-based spatial planning of the Outer Continental Shelf.

[*Note the concluding summary and the restatement of position.*]

Now, just as I said earlier that the last 50 years have seen the greatest amount of change and damage to our oceans, I believe it is the next 50 years that are the most crucial, the next 50 years that are our years, years that we will decide the fate of the world, and we have no time to lose. We must have the courage and conviction and foresight to make the decisions now that will set the course for our future forever.

[*Note the closing, use of a powerful quotation, and wrap-up thank-you to committee.*]

Let me close my time with you by sharing some final words from my grandfather, one of my favorite quotes: "We can find happiness in protecting the world around us not only because we cherish it for its awesome beauty, power and mystery, but because we cherish our fellow humans, those who live today, and those who will live tomorrow, living beings who, like ourselves, will increasingly depend on the environment for happiness, and even for life itself."

Thank you for giving me this opportunity, and on behalf of EarthEcho International, as well as the half-million members in support of Ocean Conservancy, thank you for allowing their voices to be heard as well.

Source: H. Hrg. 111-1, Committee on Natural Resources, U.S. House of Representatives, Feb. 11, 2009.

For the entire record of the hearing online, perform an Internet search for "f:47302.wais", including the quotation marks.

To review select questions and answers associated with this testimony, see § 6.48, Sample Question-and-Answer Dialogues: The Anatomy of an Effective Response.

3) **Testimony of Honorable Thomas Graham** before a hearing of the House Foreign Affairs Committee on the subject of "The July Summit and Beyond: Prospects for U.S.-Russia Nuclear Arms Reductions."

STATEMENT OF THE HONORABLE THOMAS GRAHAM, JR., EXECUTIVE CHAIRMAN OF THE BOARD, THORIUM POWER LTD.

(FORMER SPECIAL REPRESENTATIVE TO THE PRESIDENT FOR ARMS CONTROL, NON–PROLIFERATION, AND DISARMAMENT, AND LEGAL ADVISOR TO SALT II, START I AND II)

[*Note the opening and introduction, connection to the committee, and reference to time limit.*]

Ambassador GRAHAM. Thank you, Mr. Chairman. It is an honor to appear before you and the members of this very important committee. I have been here a number of times in the past, and it is always a pleasure to return. I will try hard to keep my comments to 5 minutes as I have been advised, so I will summarize the statement that I have already submitted.

[*Note the statement of background and importance of issue, and emphasis on the basic theme.*]

The Nuclear Non-Proliferation Treaty is the most important international security instrument that we have. President Kennedy was convinced that nuclear weapons were going to sweep all over the world. There were predictions during his time that there could be as many as 25 nuclear weapon states with nuclear weapons integrated into their arsenals by the end of the 1970s.

If that had happened, likely there would be more than 40 today. If that had in fact happened, the security situation would have been far, far different from what we face now, but it didn't happen. It didn't happen largely because of the entry into force of the Nuclear Non-Proliferation Treaty in 1970 and the associated extended deterrence policies of the United States and the Soviet Union. In actuality, there have only been four additional countries beyond the original five that have acquired nuclear weapons.

Two were virtually there in 1970, Pakistan came later and North Korea, well, they did whatever they did, but apparently they do have some weapon capability. But the treaty is based on a central bargain, a basic bargain, which is that most of the world agrees not to have nuclear weapons, and the nuclear weapon states agree that they will share peaceful nuclear technology and that they will pursue disarmament measures aimed at the eventual elimination of their nuclear stockpiles, most importantly a nuclear weapon test ban and reductions in nuclear weapons.

[*Note the outline of issue extremes and the use of projected outcomes and message-supporting information such as evidence and examples.*]

The nuclear weapon states unfortunately have never truly lived up to their side of this bargain, that is the disarmament obligations, and now the other side of the bargain is starting to fall apart with the Iranian nuclear weapon program, the apparent objective of North Korea to become a nuclear weapon state and expanding nuclear weapon arsenals in India and Pakistan. So the NPT is in crisis, and it is our most important agreement as I said. Some believe that soon there could be a new wave of proliferation seriously damaging the NPT even further.

If these experts are correct, United States and Russian close cooperation is essential to stopping it. There is no other way it can happen. Between these two states, we have 95 percent of the nuclear weapons in the world. We have cooperated in the past for many years with Russia, and it is important that this cooperation resume, which it really does not right now. But some say, is such cooperation possible?

A Russian official might say well, after 9/11, we gave you support. President Putin was the first international leader to call President Bush. We opened our bases in Central Asia. We provided logistical support to the Northern Alliance, and what happened? The United States withdrew from the ABM Treaty. That was a treaty that was important, as we saw it, to our strategic stability, and now there is proposed deployment of U.S. missile defenses near our border. NATO continues to expand into the Baltics. There are efforts to bring Ukraine into NATO apparently against a majority of their population. Then, there was the war in Georgia last summer, competing narratives. Russia is seen as the aggressor by some. Georgia is seen as recklessly trying to convert Ossetia into part of Georgia contrary to negotiations and a standstill had been in existence for a long time.

In any case, the truth may be somewhere between those two extremes, but the result of that has been to cancel the U.S.-Russia nuclear cooperation agreement, which was many years in the development.

[*Note the statement of challenges to be met and a call to action.*]

Russia is the most important international relationship that we have, and we must try to understand the world from the Russian point of view. The START treaty expires by its terms in December unless renewed, but there is a strong view that the levels should be reduced, and the new counting rules negotiated and the treaty verification system modified to reflect the effect of the new counting rules.

From the very beginning of the START process, the Russians have linked the START process to antiballistic missile defense. When START I, the current treaty was negotiated, the Russian negotiator made a statement that said in effect we will only observe this treaty as long as the ABM Treaty exists. The follow-on treaty, START II, which never came into force. When the U.S. withdrew from the ABM Treaty, Russia withdrew its ratification of START II that would have reduced the START I levels by 50 percent. Just the day before yesterday, President Medvedev said that there will be no new START treaty unless U.S. deployments in Europe are canceled, and then he went on to say in any case, the relation between strategic offensive arms and defensive weapons needs to be spelled out in the treaty.

[*Note the use of projected potential outcomes and expectations, and an additional call to action.*]

It may be the case, I am not saying that it is, but I am saying it might be the case that the Russians will not go ahead with a new START treaty unless they believe in some way, whether it is a comment at the negotiations or whether it is in writing, that there will be no further NATO expansion in the foreseeable future, and that the U.S. will not deploy ABM systems in Eastern Europe.

If we want this agreement with the Russians, and if we want to have the kind of cooperation with Russia that is essential to preventing further nuclear weapon proliferation, then we are going to have to think very seriously about the proposed ABM deployments in Eastern Europe.

[*Note the conclusive statements, the call to action, the use of supporting information such as statistics and examples, the use of reference to experts to provide issue credibility, the statement of perspectives and forecasts, and the quick close and thank-you.*]

Then, I might add that President Obama said in Prague that first we would have a START agreement, and then we, the United States and others, would move on to multilateral nuclear weapon negotiations ultimately aimed at zero nuclear weapons, but 1,500 strategic nuclear weapons under a follow-on START treaty are a long way from the levels that the other nuclear weapon states have. There is no other nuclear weapon possessing state, I believe, that has more than 500 total weapons, so their reserve weapons of the United States and Russia and the Russian tactical weapons, so, it looks to me as though we are going to have to have many years of the bilateral START process before we can get to the multilateral phase. And that phase itself, once we get there years in future, will be very complicated because it will involve the British, French and Chinese as well as Israel, Pakistan and India. North Korea, one would assume, would give up their program, but we need to proceed that way because time is not on our side. If the objective of zero nuclear weapons is every to be seriously contemplated as advocated by the four statesmen, one of whom is here, former Secretaries of State George Schultz and Henry Kissinger, former Secretary of Defense William Perry and former Senator Sam Nunn, this multilateral phase must begin not too far off in the future. So a long road toward zero lies ahead, and we need to proceed because time is not on our side. Thank you, Mr. Chairman.

Source: H. Hrg. 111-21, Committee on Foreign Affairs, U.S. House of Representatives, June 24, 2009.

For the entire record of the hearing online, perform an Internet search for "f:50635.wais", including the quotation marks.

To review select questions and answers associated with this testimony, see § 6.48, Sample Question-and-Answer Dialogues: The Anatomy of an Effective Response.

4) **Testimony of Dr. Keith B. Payne** before a hearing of the House Foreign Affairs Committee on the subject of "The July Summit and Beyond: Prospects for U.S.-Russia Nuclear Arms Reductions."

STATEMENT OF KEITH B. PAYNE, PH.D.,
CEO AND PRESIDENT, NATIONAL INSTITUTE OF PUBLIC POLICY

(FORMER DEPUTY ASSISTANT SECRETARY OF DEFENSE FOR FORCES POLICY AND COMMISSIONER ON THE CONGRESSIONAL STRATEGIC POSTURE COMMISSION)

[*Note the opening, introduction, and connection and reference to colleagues on the witness panel.*]

Mr. PAYNE. Thank you, Mr. Chairman. It is an honor and privilege to testify here today, particularly alongside of Secretary Perry and Ambassador Graham, gentlemen for whom we all have great esteem.

[*Note the immediate announcement of the theme and messages, connoting, "Here's what I am going to tell you."; the use of six crisp, concise, enumerated messages; the use of observations and recommendations; and the informative and instructive nature of the remarks.*]

President Obama has announced that the United State will seek a new post-START agreement by the end of this year. I would like to take a few minutes to make six short points about the apparent direction of this engagement because some of the early indications are somewhat troubling.

[*Note the use of supportive detail and data, and additional information to support a complex message.*]

First, Russian officials have already said that the new agreed number of warheads should be 1,500 deployed warheads. Yet, the discussion of specific numeric limitations of an agreement should only follow the conclusions of the nuclear posture review that is just underway in the Pentagon. Identifying specific arms control ceilings now prior to the conclusions of this study would be putting the cart before the horse.

Second, the Russian and United States sides have agreed that the post-START treaty will include reductions in the number of strategic force launchers, i.e. the number of deployed ICBMs, SLBMs, Submarine Launched Ballistic Missiles, and strategic bombers. Russian President Medvedev has said that Russia would like the number of these launchers to be reduced several times below the 1,600 permitted now under START.

That is a smart position for Russia. It is a very bad position for us. Why so? Because the number of deployed Russian strategic ICBMs, SLBMs and bombers will drop dramatically with or without a new arms control agreement. Based solely on Russian sources, it is possible to anticipate that within the next 8 to 9 years the number of Russian strategic launchers will have dropped from approximately 680 today to fewer than half that number simply as a result of the aging of their system and the pace of their modernization program.

The Russians would like to make lemonade out of this lemon of their aging launchers by getting reductions in real U.S. systems without eliminating anything that they would not withdraw in any event. That is not simply my conclusion. It is the conclusion of Russian officials and Russian commentators as expressed in Russian publications.

[*Note the use of a projected outcome and the use of examples.*]

Beyond the bad negotiating principle of giving up something for nothing, there will be serious downsides for the United States in moving to low numbers of strategic launchers. For example, it would encourage placing more warheads on the remaining launchers, i.e. MIRVing, which is precisely what the Russians are doing.

Moving away from heavily MIRVed strategic launchers has long been considered highly stabilizing and a key U.S. START goal. Why should we now start encouraging MIRVing by going down to low launcher levels?

[*Note the use of analysis and the projection of outcomes.*]

Third, the forthcoming negotiations appear to exclude the entire arena of non-strategic nuclear weapons, i.e. tactical nuclear weapons, yet this is where Russia maintains most of its nuclear arsenal. According to open sources, Russia has approximately 4,000 deployed tactical nuclear weapons. That is an astonishing 10 to 1 numeric advantage over the United States. These Russian tactical nuclear weapons are of greatest concern with regard to the potential for nuclear war and the potential for nuclear proliferation. They should be our focus.

Yet, the administration appears to have already agreed to negotiate only on strategic forces at this point. If that position holds, it will be a serious mistake.

[*Note the use of an example to support the main message.*]

Fourth, the Russian side has demanded numerous additional limits on other United States capabilities as the price to be paid for an early agreement on strategic nuclear forces. For example, President Medvedev recently said that strategic reductions are only possible if the United States alleviates Russian concerns about "U.S. plans to create a global missile defense."

In fact, no limits on United States missile defense are necessary for significant reductions in Russian strategic force launchers and warheads. No limits are necessary on missile defense. The need for U.S. BMD capabilities could not be clearer given recent North Korean nuclear missile rattling and Iranian political upheaval. United States ballistic missile defense is not about Russia. Yet, the Russians are demanding this linkage.

It would seem self-evidently a mistake to include limits on United States ballistic missile defense as a price to be paid for an agreement that requires nothing of the Russians beyond discarding the aged systems they plan to eliminate in any event and will not touch the real problem, i.e. Russian tactical nuclear weapons.

[*Note the use of a recommendation for order of action, the use of a professional opinion, and the succinctness of the message being conveyed.*]

Fifth, before establishing new nuclear arms control limits, it would seem reasonable to resolve Russian violations of existing arms control agreements. In my opinion, the most important of these violations has been discussed openly in Russian publications. It is the Russian testing of the SS–27 ICBM with MIRVs in direct violation of START. Confidence in Russian compliance needs to be established prior to or at least part of any new efforts to negotiate limitations.

[*Note the wrap-up and conclusive enumeration with the use of "finally."*]

Sixth and finally, President Obama has endorsed the goal of nuclear disarmament, and some have suggested that the post-START re-engagement with Russia should be seen as a useful step toward nuclear zero.

[*Note the use of analysis to support a statement of position.*]

The Congressional Posture Commission rightly concluded that for nuclear zero to be plausible, there would have to be a fundamental transformation of the world order. That a dramatic transformation would be necessary for nuclear zero to be plausible suggests that taking any steps now not to be predicated on that elusive goal. Any new agreement should be judged on its own merit, not on its potential for moving toward nuclear zero; not on the hope that it constitutes a step toward nuclear zero.

[*Note the summary and conclusion that connote, "Here is what I told you."; the highlighting and importance of action; and the quick closing and thank-you.*]

These are the six major concerns I have with regard to the apparent early direction of the administration's effort to re-establish START-like negotiations as a centerpiece of United States-Russian engagement. It is important to establish the right agenda at the beginning of negotiations. If not, the results can be unacceptable no matter how well our team negotiates. I appreciate this opportunity to share my concerns with you. Thank you.

Source: H. Hrg. 111-21, Committee on Foreign Affairs, U.S. House of Representatives, June 24, 2009.

For the entire record of the hearing online, perform an Internet search for "f:50635.wais", including the quotation marks.

To review select questions and answers associated with this testimony, see § 6.48, Sample Question-and-Answer Dialogues: The Anatomy of an Effective Response.

§ 5.70 Effective Use of Visual Aids, Charts, and Graphics

A witness should carefully coordinate and plan the presentation of, and referral to, various forms of graphics and visual or demonstration aids with the oral presentation of the witness testimony. It is a good idea to include cues in the text of the script to ensure timely usage of props and proper reference to them. A witness should ensure that all parts of the visuals work well and as intended, and that the witness is able to maneuver them with ease as needed. A witness should request that any visual aids be included in the record along with the written testimony.

§5.71 Sample of Design and Use Guidelines to Ensure Visual Aids Have Their Desired Impact

Use of Visual Aids

For visual aids to have their desired impact, certain guidelines need to be followed in their design and use.

1) Approval. Make sure Committee staff know and approve of the nature of the visual aid that you intend to use. Arrangements need to be made for easels, slide projectors, VCRs, and monitors. Make sure there will be no objection to dimming the lights, if necessary.
2) Design. Keep it simple. Include only vital information. Follow the "glance rule." The viewer need only glance at the visual aid to understand its meaning. Complicated tables and graphs defeat the purpose of visual aids. Simplify them.
3) Preparation. Allow sufficient time for graphics preparation. Coordinate graphic development with publishing advisors.
4) Preview. Arrange with Committee staff to do a practice set up of your visual aid in the Committee room. Where will you put your easel(s)? What furniture needs to be moved. Where are the convenient electrical sockets, how are the lights dimmed? Will opening a door create a draft that blows over your foam board chart?
5) Presentation. Plan the actual introduction of the visual aid. Will it be displayed throughout your testimony? If you are using more than one chart, this can lead to confusion. Instead it is best to have charts mounted in their order of presentation on an easel with a cover, or blank sheet, over each graphic. As you speak, an assistant will uncover each chart at a pre-planned verbal cue.
6) Self-explanatory. The charts should be virtually self-explanatory. One of the most common faults of visual aids is explanations of charts that take longer than making the point in simple oral testimony.
7) Departure. Plan to have the chart removed from sight when it is no longer being referenced.

Make sure not to overload your testimony with statistics, and make sure not to present more than a couple, three at the most, charts. Over-use of visual aids, particularly slides, is another common mistake. Other points to consider when using visual aids are as follows:

- make sure they are large enough to be seen by all;
- don't pass around visual aids, its distracting;
- be sure to include a copy of the visual aid in your testimony submitted for the record; and
- don't talk to your visual aid.

Source: GAO Performance and Learning Instructor Manual, Delivering Testimony, September 2001, United States General Accounting Office (now Government Accountability Office) (GAO).

A witness should use visual aids to:

- Underscore and support points in the script that the witness is making orally;
- Draw the attention of the committee and stimulate its interest in the presentation;
- Drive home a major point or theme by demonstrating that a picture, chart or other form of visual aid is worth a thousand words; and
- Create a visual source for discussion, questions and answers in the hearing for the committee members to return to for consideration.

For more information on the use and rehearsal of graphics and visual aids, see § 3.28, Use of Graphics and Visuals; § 4.24, Witness Rehearsal of Oral Testimony and Answers to Questions—Use of Graphics and Visuals; and § 5.71, Sample of Design and Use Guidelines to Ensure Visual Aids Have Their Desired Impact.

§5.72 Don't Leave an Elephant in the Room or Money on the Table

These tongue-in-cheek admonitions are meant only to sensitize a witness to the need to ensure that the witness's and organization's task, mission, and agenda for a hearing are complete, and that no large looming issue or message goes unstated or unaddressed. For example, if it appears to a witness that a committee member just did not understand a certain point being made in the witness's testimony, the witness should consider repeating or clarifying that point later in the testimony.

Other examples may include a change in circumstances or an unanticipated turn of events. If breaking news just before a hearing has some bearing on the topic of the hearing, a witness may wish to address that matter even if there are no prepared remarks in the script. If the chair or a committee member makes a comment that needs addressing or correcting, a witness should consider respectfully adding remarks or offering a rebuttal during the testimony at some point or in answering questions posed by the committee later in the hearing. If the availability of a remedy or a particular course of action becomes evident during a hearing, a witness should certainly comment on that matter if it makes sense to do so, even if no prepared remarks are available.

The idea is to do a quick mental survey of what a witness hopes to accomplish in the testimony, and then to address anything that was omitted or that needs more emphasis before the end of the testimony, or, at least, during the question-and-answer period.

§5.73 The Top Twenty Tips of the Trade for the Delivery of Oral Testimony by a Witness

In summary fashion, this listing of substantive and stylistic tips can be helpful to a witness in delivering oral testimony on hearing day:

- **Tip 1**—Committee State of Mind: Try to determine the committee's, and its respective members', state of mind concerning the hearing topic and your case.
- **Tip 2**—Witness State of Mind: Try to convey to the committee, through your testimony and body language, your own state of mind in making your case and advocating your position.
- **Tip 3**—Know and understand the committee, its processes, its priorities, the purpose of the hearing, and all relevant issues.
- **Tip 4**—Master the issues. Remember that you are the expert. The committee is depending on you to deliver a message that will be informative, compelling, and helpful.
- **Tip 5**—Stay the course and stick to the script by keeping your message and testimony simple, clear, and direct.
- **Tip 6**—Nail the big points early in your remarks. Come out swinging and make a strong first impression.
- **Tip 7**—Use powerful introductions and closings.
- **Tip 8**—Highlight and annotate the script to remind yourself to add extra emphasis for the opening and closing sections, as well as for key messages within the text.
- **Tip 9**—In presenting your major themes, exhibit knowledge, understanding, and passion about the issues, your case, and your position.
- **Tip 10**—Limit your testimony presentation to three-five main points. Hit the major points clearly and succinctly, and then move to the next item after demonstrating support and rationale.
- **Tip 11**—Summarize your message in headline fashion. Think "sound bites." After making your basic case to the committee members, remind them in highlight fashion what you just told them.
- **Tip 12**—Be sure to submit the full text of your written statement for the record.
- **Tip 13**—Be respectful, but be a peer of the panel. Communicate on the committee's level. Avoid speaking "up" or "down" to the committee.
- **Tip 14**—Exude confidence in your presentation and command of your subject.
- **Tip 15**—Remain cool, collected, and even-keeled throughout the hearing.
- **Tip 16**—Project your voice in a conversational manner. Speak to the committee. Don't lecture or read.
- **Tip 17**—Be attentive to all remarks and responsive to all questions from the committee.

- **Tip 18**—Engage the committee with your statement, responses, and demeanor. Try to persuade the members of the committee that they should embrace and discuss your message.
- **Tip 19**—Use descriptive and engaging highlighting and enumeration phrases to emphasize points clearly, including major themes, sub-themes, reasons, explanations, and other support factors. For example, incorporate phrases such as: "Our first goal is . . . my second point is . . . the paramount piece of evidence is . . . the final accounting will be . . . our primary challenge is . . . our major hurdle is . . . our chief purpose is . . . our key conclusion is . . ."
- **Tip 20**—Leave the committee with the impression that you are well-prepared, that you have a strong and persuasive message and good ideas, that you are adding value to their quest for information, and that you are willing to be helpful in contributing valuable ideas for use in their decisionmaking process.

§5.74 Characteristics of Effective, Well-Delivered Testimony

From the standpoint of evaluating or critiquing a witness's performance in presenting testimony, these common characteristics of effective well-delivered testimony represent a menu or checklist of what a witness should attempt to accomplish at a hearing:

- Accentuate the best elements of strong, effective testimony, and avoid weak or ineffective testimony;
- Execute a smooth, concise, and clear delivery of oral testimony, preferably not read;
- Present testimony at a moderate rate or pace—not too fast or too slow;
- Deliver a purposeful and dynamic message directed toward the committee members;
- Connect with committee members, including using good eye contact and body language; and
- Make a commanding delivery with strong voice projection and energized speech to engage and maintain the interest and attention of the committee.

§5.75 HITS: Humor in Testimony— John Boehner's April Fool's Day Parody Testimony

Sometimes humor in congressional testimony is used in fictional and facetious ways—to prove or make a point, to jab the opposition, or to create a parody. So goes the bantering between and among members of Congress. U.S. House of Representatives Republican Leader John Boehner (R-OH) penned a 2008 April Fool's fabricated statement that he suggested, tongue-in-cheek, might be representative of what Venezuelan President Hugo Chavez might provide as written testimony for the House Select Committee for Energy Independence and Global Warming.

Washington, Apr 1, 2008—On this April Fool's Day, House Republican Leader John Boehner (R-OH) today released written testimony of Venezuelan President Hugo Chavez, who was not invited to today's Select Committee for Energy Independence and Global Warming hearing on the oil industry. Chavez, whose state-owned CITGO is the world's sixth largest oil supplier, would enjoy significant tax breaks under energy legislation recently passed by the Democrat-led House, in spite of the socialist dictator's threats to cut off energy supplies to the United States and ongoing anti-American rhetoric and policies. President Chavez's testimony follows:

TESTIMONY OF HUGO CHAVEZ, PRESIDENT OF VENEZUELA
Select Committee for Energy Independence and Global Warming
Hearing on "Drilling for Answers: Oil Company Profits, Runaway Prices and the Pursuit of Alternatives"
April 1, 2008

Chairman Markey, though I was unable to attend today's hearing in person, I hope you will accept this written testimony. More importantly, I hope you will accept my sincere 'thank you' for the tax breaks the new Democratic Majority provided to my state-owned oil giant, CITGO, in recent 'energy' legislation passed by the House of Representatives.

It is especially relieving to know that while CITGO receives these tax breaks, five other major oil companies—including American-owned companies employing thousands of working Americans—will be forced to pay higher taxes, raising energy costs on consumers in your country and endangering scores of jobs as well. Please extend my gratitude to Speaker Pelosi, Majority Leader Hoyer, Whip Clyburn, Chairman Emanuel, and everyone who played a role in scheduling this legislation for a vote in the House of Representatives.

Being a socialist dictator is a difficult—and often lonely—burden these days. As more nations move toward democracy, the number of socialist dictators in our world is declining, and we can use all the help we can get. As I seek to keep our socialist movement afloat in South America, it is comforting to know that I have such strong allies in the House Democratic Majority.

Though the American economy is struggling and families in your country are feeling the strain from rising costs for everything from food to fuel, I'm pleased the House Majority did not allow these realities to stand in the way of your admirable efforts to raise taxes on them in order to pay for more government spending and, more importantly, my own tax breaks.

Moreover, I am so grateful that you have overlooked my repeated threats to cut off Venezuelan energy supplies to your nation and my consistently cozy relationship with the Castro regime in Cuba—regardless of which Castro is in charge. To know that I will receive tax breaks not provided to my global competitors, even in spite of my radical Left-wing, authoritarian ideology, gives me great confidence in my future relationship with this Congress.

Before I conclude, I hope you will permit me to make two additional pitches for policy actions out of this Congress. First, Chairman Markey, I want to applaud the ongoing support that has reportedly been provided by at least one of your House

Democratic colleagues for my Marxist brothers in the Colombian FARC—a terrorist organization I have been working closely with to expand my influence in that nation. News reports recently detailed a trip one senior House Democrat made to Colombia to force Colombian President Alvaro Uribe—an American ally—to position me as a mediator between Colombia and the FARC. As you might expect, I wholeheartedly supported that effort and strongly encourage similar meetings in the future as well.

Likewise, Mr. Chairman, I strongly encourage you to impress upon your Democratic colleagues how vital it is to my influence in South America that the Majority continues bottling up the so-called U.S.-Colombia free trade agreement. As you might expect, free trade between your nation and my neighbors in Colombia would be a sharp blow to my efforts to expand my reach throughout South America, and any assistance you can provide me in derailing the agreement would be most appreciated.

In conclusion, Mr. Chairman, though I understand not being invited to today's politically motivated, made-for-TV hearing on the oil industry, please know that I am ready and willing to provide whatever assistance I can to advance the House Majority's policy goals, on energy and otherwise. I hope you will relay that message to your Democratic leadership team, and I appreciate the opportunity to thank you for your ongoing assistance to my socialist regime.

Source: Reprinted with permission of U.S. House of Representatives Republican Leader John Boehner (R-OH); <*http://republicanleader.house.gov/News/DocumentSingle.aspx?DocumentID=87494*>.

§5.999 Chapter Summary

- A congressional committee hearing is a major event for both the committee and the witness, and it is particularly a "big show" or pinnacle moment for the witness. (§ 5.0)
- Witnesses may encounter hearings that are either substantive or more theatrical in nature, or a combination of the two. (§ 5.1)
- Congressional experts with considerable experience with committee hearings expound on the value and importance of effective and powerful oral testimony. (§ 5.2)
- Anyone testifying should keep in mind the four major roles of a witness. (§ 5.3)
- Witnesses should be mindful of the overall role of a committee hearing, including its importance in providing Congress with information needed to carry out its legislative and oversight responsibilities. (§ 5.4)
- Delivering testimony at a hearing is the culmination of the preparation and experience of the witness, and, consequently, the witness should make the most of his or her preparation, including reflecting on rehearsals. (§ 5.5)

- A witness should keep a healthy perspective on a hearing, including the purpose of the hearing and the witness's role, and avoid distractions to the extent possible. (§ 5.6)
- As a hearing commences, a witness should bring his or her preparation and information to bear on the oral testimony, and should approach that moment with organization, purpose, and resolve. (§ 5.7)
- To achieve top performance in a hearing, a witness should attempt to replicate the best elements of preparation and rehearsal. (§ 5.8)
- A witness should rely on her or his preparation, best instincts and good communications skills in delivering testimony that is interesting, clear, and compelling. (§ 5.9)
- Upon entering a hearing room, a witness should take stock of the venue, and glean a full perspective of the surroundings. (§ 5.10)
- A witness should recognize and understand political and issue partisanship, as well as how it affects the dynamics of a committee and a hearing. (§ 5.11)
- Just before a hearing begins, a witness should relax, focus on the task at hand, and attend to any personal matters. (§ 5.20)
- Once seated at the witness table, a witness should get comfortable, organize his or her hearing materials, and prepare to proceed when the chair raps the gavel. (§ 5.21)
- Prior to beginning to testify, a witness should become acquainted with the microphone and its use, and make any necessary adjustments. (§ 5.22)
- One of the most important check-offs for a witness just prior to the presentation of testimony is to make sure that the written script that will be used to deliver the oral testimony is properly organized and ready for use. That script should be structured for easy reference and use by the witness, and should facilitate the utilization of verbal features and techniques that highlight key elements of the testimony. (§ 5.30)
- In delivering effective oral testimony, a witness should rely on effective preparation, use of his or her best instincts and speaking skills, and a well-crafted script to present an interesting, clear, and compelling statement. (§ 5.31)
- An effective model outline for oral testimony presentation demonstrates how persuasive testimony should be arranged, including a powerful introduction, substantive content in the body of the statement, and an effective conclusion. (§ 5.32)
- If a witness plans to use a briefing book or other written documents during a hearing, those materials should be organized on the witness table for easy reference and use. (§ 5.33)

- It can be helpful for a witness to have a readily available note pad or blank sheet of paper on the witness table for use in jotting notes or comments for reference during or after the hearing. (§ 5.34)
- If a witness intends to utilize a briefing team, it is important that the individuals on the team be located near the witness, and that a plan be in place for convenient and easy consultation. (§ 5.35)
- A witness should establish his or her own comfort zone at the witness table by relaxing, organizing materials, and focusing on the reason for testifying. (§ 5.36)
- A witness should demonstrate a commanding presentation style and demeanor in the very first words spoken. (§ 5.37)
- It is important for a witness to make a strong introduction to set the tone for the testimony to follow. (§ 5.38)
- While most committees will include a witness's written statement in the record as a matter of practice, a witness should request the statement's inclusion in the record if there is doubt. (§ 5.39)
- It is important for a witness to stick to the prepared script to convey a sense of organization, ensure succinctness and clarity, and guarantee that the entire statement is delivered in the time allowed. (§ 5.40)
- A witness should preferably speak to the committee, as opposed to reading a statement. If a witness chooses to read a statement, the text should be conversational and reflective of the witness's oral delivery style. (§ 5.41)
- Focusing on the committee as the primary targeted audience should be a cardinal rule for every witness. (§ 5.42)
- Whenever possible, it is helpful for a witness to make some semblance of a personal connection with the committee to warm up the audience. (§ 5.43)
- To make oral testimony more interesting, a witness should consider using several speaking techniques, such as voice variation and projection, to enliven the presentation. (§ 5.44)
- To complement the substantive content and well-spoken delivery of a witness's oral statement, good eye contact, body language, and gestures are effective tools. (§ 5.45)
- There are several common elements of presentation format and order that contribute to effective and well-organized oral testimony. (§ 5.50)
  1) Opening with Self-Introduction by Witness and Summary of Issue Position and Hearing Topic (§ 5.51)
  2) Presenting Major Thematic Statement and Layout of Case (§ 5.52)
  3) Making the Basic Case and Outlining the Main Messages (§ 5.53)
  4) Providing Supporting Data, Rationale, Analyses, Studies and Research Results, Evidence, Explanations, Anecdotes, Examples,

   Vignettes, Corroboration, Quotes, Cases-in-Point, Best and Worse Case Scenarios, Comparisons, and Contrasts (§ 5.54)
   5) Highlighting Recommendations, Requested Remedies and Calls to Action (§ 5.55)
   6) Projecting Outcomes, Expectations, and Alternatives (§ 5.56)
   7) Summarizing—Restatement of Case and Position (§ 5.57)
   8) Winding Up: The Grand Conclusion (§ 5.58)
   9) Inviting Questions from the Committee (§ 5.59)

- It can be helpful for a witness to be familiar with effective presentation format and order by reviewing actual oral witness statements from congressional hearing records, complete with notations about best practices. (§ 5.60)
- A witness should coordinate, rehearse, and plan the presentation of any visual aids or graphics to ensure their timely and effective use and easy reference during the hearing. (§ 5.70)
- An effective example of design and use guidelines for visual aids can help inform a witness how to ensure the desired impact of visual aids used during a hearing. (§ 5.71)
- During a hearing, a witness should be alert to ensure that all points in the oral statement have been articulated, and that no opportunity to reinforce the case or address a looming issue goes unattended. (§ 5.72)
- Review of a summary listing of The Top Twenty Tips of the Trade for the Delivery of Oral Testimony by a Witness can be helpful to a witness on hearing day. (§ 5.73)
- Review of a listing of key common characteristics of effective, well-delivered oral testimony can help a witness turn in a stellar performance on hearing day. (§ 5.74)
- HITS: Humor in Testimony can be used in fictional or facetious ways to make a special point, jab the opposition, or create a parody, as evidenced by an April Fool's fabricated statement written by U.S. House of Representatives Republican Leader John Boehner (R-OH). (§ 5.75)

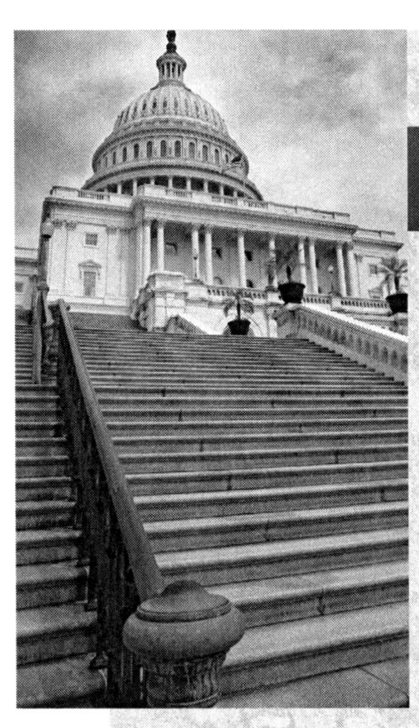

Chapter Six

Responding to Committee Questions

Chapter Six

Section

Summary Table of Contents

§6.0 Introduction and Overview

The question-and-answer phase of a congressional committee hearing is an important component of the hearing process for both a committee and a witness. It is often said to be more important in many respects than the presentation of testimony itself. After submission of written testimony and the delivery of oral testimony, responding to questions posed by members of a congressional committee is the third major role of a witness in a congressional committee hearing.

The question-and-answer portion of a hearing typically follows the testimony of one or more witnesses, and it entails a true exchange, dialogue, discussion, and form of two-way communication between the committee and a witness. There are occasions when a committee will variously ask a witness no questions, one or two perfunctory questions, or an entire line of probative questions, depending on the subject matter of the hearing, the testimony and professional affiliation of the witness, and the interest of committee members.

For a witness, responding to committee questions is also the second essential element of the "show"—the pinnacle event that comes in the form of a hearing for witnesses, much as the major leagues are the "show" or pinnacle for professional baseball players. (Delivering oral testimony is the first essential element. See Chapter 5, "Presentation and Delivery of Oral Testimony.")

A witness's role in responding to a committee's questions is somewhat akin to being on defense in a sport, with the committee being on offense, because the question-and-answer phase of a hearing returns the spotlight to the committee, following witness testimony, to allow its members to ask a witness any questions they wish to ask. However, the offense-defense analogy is not totally accurate, because (continuing the sports metaphor) there is also an element of offense for a witness during questions and answers.

In responding to committee questions, a witness has an opportunity to make any statements that are reasonable, relevant, and within the scope of the hearing topic and the bounds of propriety—all ostensibly while primarily being responsive to the questions being asked by the committee. Essentially then, a witness "plays" offense and defense during the question-and-answer period, as opposed to playing only offense during the testimony phase of a hearing. The witness shares the spotlight with the committee in a back-and-forth, give-and-take scenario.

This chapter discusses the best practices for witnesses' handling and being responsive to committee questions after the testimony is complete. It describes how to field and respond to different types of questions, and how to engage the committee to enhance the witness's presentation. It describes the role of the witness in responding to questions, the use of support materials, and how to anticipate questions from a committee. It also provides numerous tips and hints for an excellent performance, as well

§6.1 Importance of Answering Committee Questions in an Effective and Responsive Manner: Perspectives of a Congressional Expert

"After your testimony, use your answers to questions to highlight your key points, not summarize them. Answering questions can be much more intimidating than simply providing testimony. So be confident, even though you don't have much time to think, let alone answer. The first question posed to you might either be on point to the subject at hand, or could be totally unimportant to you as a witness, but could be of utmost importance to Congressman X. Thus, it's important to know the committee members and where their interests lie. Eye contact is important. Look directly at the member asking the question. If you know your answer will strike a chord with another member, focus some attention there too, while being mindful of who asked the question. Know your subject matter. That's why you're there. Know your stuff, but avoid giving political answers. That's not your job. If you cannot answer a substantive question, it makes you more credible to say so, and offer to research and respond later. The follow-up contacts with staff in providing those answers can be of great benefit to your cause. Finally, be confident and make sure that your facts are valid. Your word is your bond, and thus your credibility and that of the group you are representing is at stake."

Source: Douglas Todd, Director, Government Affairs, Siemens Corporation; formerly: Deputy Assistant Secretary for Congressional Affairs at the U.S. Department of Energy; Manager of Government Affairs at Battelle Memorial Institute and Northrop-Grumman Corporation; and a Congressional staff member.

as samples of actual hearing transcripts of real-world congressional committee hearing questions and answers.

To observe the "give-and-take" of the committee question-and-answer phase, a witness preparing to testify may wish to review real-life examples by watching webcasts of congressional hearings. Committees in both the House and Senate utilize video broadcasting and taping technologies for their hearings on committee cable channels administered by their respective chambers. Many committees post live and archived webcasts of their hearings on their respective committee web sites. To see the webcasts of numerous hearings available for viewing, go to the individual committee sites accessible through <*www.House.gov*> and <*www.Senate.gov*>, and proceed to the links for menus of webcasts. See Appendix 4 and Appendix 5 for more information on this source. Additionally, C-SPAN provides a full archive of hearings on the Web at <*www.c-spanvideo.org*>.

§6.2 Questions and Answers from a Committee's Perspective

Members of a congressional committee consider the question-and-answer portion of a hearing an opportunity to probe the hearing topic and the witness's testimony for a wide array of additional information, including clarifications, refinement of position, recommendations, perspectives, and additional details that may vary depending on the topic, the witness, and the questioner. Committees engage a witness with questions to explore further the case and messages outlined and advanced in the testimony delivered by the witness, and to elicit from the witness information that might be helpful to the committee and relevant to the purpose of the hearing.

Committee members also widely utilize the question-and-answer period in hearings as a forum to express themselves on the subject of the hearing, and to articulate their own perspectives, concerns, and conclusions. Committee members will often regale their committee colleagues, the witness, the hearing record, the media, and the general public with speeches, lectures, and sometimes even diatribes on virtually any subject of their choosing, as long as it is, in most cases, remotely related to the subject of the hearing or the statements or organizational relationship of the witness. Consequently, members of a committee are well-known to inject their own perspectives, positions, commentaries and agenda into a hearing situation, and to stake out political, partisan and policy positions near and dear to their hearts.

§6.3 Questions and Answers from a Witness's Perspective

For a witness, the question-and-answer phase of a congressional committee hearing is both an opportunity to be responsive to the inquiries and questions of committee members, and to continue to advance the major themes of the witness's testimony within the context of the answers given to questions. In many respects, the witness is "on the hot seat" to answer virtually any question posed by the committee. However, the witness is also in the position to return to, and highlight, the key messages of the testimony, to agree or disagree respectfully with the committee over issues and positions when necessary, and to provide additional information that helps reinforce the purpose of the witness's appearance.

For information on witness rehearsal in preparation for answering committee questions, see § 4.15 through § 4.34, Witness Rehearsal of Oral Testimony and Answers to Questions.

§6.4 It's All about Being Responsive

In one special sense, a witness's answers to questions asked by committee members in a congressional hearing are primarily about being responsive to the members, their questions and their interests. Responsiveness is the first goal of answering committee questions. Many questions, for example, are essentially asking "why," and beg for a responsive answer that provides reasons, rationale, and explanations. Other questions ask "who," "what," "where," "when," and "how," and should be answered with direct factual responses. Committees appreciate and expect candor, straightforwardness, thoroughness, and honesty in responses by witnesses to their questions. However, in fairness to the witness, responsiveness does not necessarily mean providing an answer the questioner wants or the witness believes the questioner wants. It principally means answering questions with accuracy, a factual basis, sincere perspectives, and honest positions and opinions, regardless of the expectations of the questioner or committee.

§6.5 Segue from Testimony

In the order and format of a congressional committee hearing, a committee's questioning of witnesses occurs after the witness or witnesses have testified. It is typically a natural flow and segue from the affirmative testimony of witnesses to the "give-and-take" of the question-and-answer phase of a hearing. Questions begin when the chair announces it is time for the question-and-answer phase to commence. That moment might occur immediately following the testimony of a single witness or after a panel of several witnesses has testified.

§6.6 Role, Format, and Dynamics of a Congressional Committee in Asking Questions

The role of congressional committee members during the question-and-answer phase of a hearing is essentially to lead with questions they wish to pose to a witness, including follow-up questions. The dynamics between and among various members of a committee, as well as between a questioner and a witness, are often unique.

With respect to format and order of business, the committee chair will typically begin with questions personally or designate a colleague to begin questioning. Then the ranking member of the committee will be recognized to ask questions. The order of business and questioning from then on usually follows seniority, with alternating recognition by the chair of majority and minority members, and with some deference to those committee members who are actually present at the time in the hearing room, as well as to those who must come and go due to other scheduling priorities. Committees generally operate with a time limit for each committee member to ask questions.

Committee members are well-known for delivering sometimes long, detailed speeches about an issue before actually posing a question to the witness. Their speeches are sometimes aimed at committee colleagues, and can involve political jockeying regarding certain policy or political positions. Committee members' remarks toward a witness or a witness's organization are often directed in the form of challenges, questions, requests, expectations, or admonitions related to the activities and mission of the witness's organization, especially if the witness represents an executive branch entity. In some instances when an issue is particularly contentious, committee members and witnesses may actually engage in sparring, and occasionally the drama can become fairly intense.

Questions asked by committee members can variously be friendly, neutral, or hostile in nature. However, committees should allow witnesses the time and opportunity to respond to questions in an orderly and courteous manner, and there are times when a committee chair must remind his or her committee colleagues to honor that commitment.

§6.7 Role of the Witness in Answering Questions

During the question-and-answer phase of a congressional committee hearing, a witness's chief role is to answer questions that are asked by committee members. A witness should be fully prepared to answer questions about the hearing topic, the content of the witness's formal written statement, the elements of the witness's oral testimony to the committee, testimony and answers from other witnesses, statements by members of the committee, and virtually anything else even remotely associated with the witness's organization and reason for appearing before the committee.

Preparation for the question-and-answer phase of a hearing is very important, especially because a witness must be prepared for just about anything, including questions that are off-subject from the hearing topic, or that are related to a recent event or media report. Questions may also be unfriendly or hostile, including accusatory and inflammatory remarks on occasion, and political and partisan overtones can sometimes seem overbearing. However, a witness should deal with each and every question in a direct, fair, and reasonable way, try to side-step political and partisan jousting, and attempt to respond to questions professionally and calmly, regardless of the nature of the inquiry.

In order to be able to answer committee questions effectively and responsively, it is vital for a witness to be prepared thoroughly on the hearing topic, the details of his or her own testimony, and every aspect of the case and message being advocated by the witness at the hearing. A witness should stick to the script of the testimony and preparation for answers to questions, and try to avoid venturing beyond his or her own knowledge base or expertise in responding to inquiries. All questions should be answered in a responsive manner. However, if a witness does not know or forgets an answer to a particular question, it is perfectly acceptable to respond that the witness will provide the answer to the inquiring committee member following the hearing.

At all times, a witness should attempt to maintain a professional, courteous, respectful, deferential, and helpful demeanor. However, there are times when a witness, in good faith and with due cause, should respectfully stand his or her ground, and not tolerate a committee member's badgering or belittling, if that should occur. Professionalism, courtesy, deference, and simple common decency are a two-way street.

For a refresher on preparing the witness for committee questions, see Chapter 4, especially § 4.19, Witness Rehearsal of Oral Testimony and Answers to Questions—"Murder Boards" and Question-and-Answer "Dry Runs"; and § 4.45, Recommended General Approaches to Preparation for the Question-and-Answer Phase.

§ 6.10 Scope of Subject Matter for Congressional Hearings: To Answer or Not

The scope and "fair game" nature of issues and topics that may be the subject of committee members' questions of a witness are generally and preferably limited or related to the focus of the hearing itself and the content of a witness's written and oral testimony. However, committee members have and utilize wide latitude in addressing almost any issue they choose in questioning witnesses, with only a rare or occasional interruption or admonition from the chair. Essentially, witnesses are subject to virtually any question about any topic, and, consequently, should be prepared to field any question that might be asked.

That is not to say, however, that a witness must absolutely answer any and every question. If a question is beyond a witness's scope of knowledge or expertise, if it is far afield from the focus of the hearing or the witness's testimony or organizational affiliation, or if it is otherwise an inappropriate or unanswerable question in the mind of a witness, the witness should politely defer, and indicate his or her inability to answer on whatever relevant grounds fit the circumstance.

Committee members are also often prone to digress or stray from the hearing topic or the subject matter and focus of a witness's testimony. In some cases, committee members have little interest in, or regard for, the statement or position of a particular witness, and only want the opportunity to interrogate the witness during the question-and-answer phase of the hearing for their own sometimes unstated or unknown reasons. A committee member's reason for that approach may be to probe an issue, even if it is unrelated to the hearing topic, that is connected to the witness or to his or her organization. Occasionally that type of inquiry can become outright hostile, and may even be intended to embarrass the witness or to expose a finding, fact, or problem.

When any of these types of questioning occur, a witness must decide how far to go in being responsive, helpful, and engaged. There are times when a witness might just have to indicate an unwillingness to pursue an issue because of the nature of the question or apparent motives of the questioner. To the greatest extent possible, a witness who faces that type of situation should respond in a professional and respectful, yet firm, manner. If a witness must disagree with a statement or decline to answer a question, it should be done in a congenial fashion, with some accompanying reasonable explanation. A witness should never respond with "no comment."

Witnesses should otherwise make a reasonable effort to respond to committee questions, and, when an answer is not readily available or known, indicate to the committee that a written response will be provided to the committee as a follow-up to the hearing.

For information on preparing a witness to respond to committee questions, see Chapter 4, especially § 4.19, Witness Rehearsal of Oral Testimony and Answers to Questions—"Murder Boards" and Question-and-Answer "Dry Runs." For more information on activities in follow-up to a hearing, see Chapter 7.

§6.11 Anticipating Questions: Being Prepared

A cardinal rule in the preparation of a congressional committee hearing witness is to be fully prepared to respond to a wide array of anticipated questions posed by committee members. While there is no certain method for knowing precisely what questions a committee will ask, witnesses can glean ideas for possible questions that might be asked by committee members from numerous sources and circumstances:

- ongoing committee concerns raised in previous hearings or with the organization directly;
- media reports and other forms of industry and government communications;
- problems and questions associated with the hearing topic;
- the witness's organization, its history, and any relationships to the hearing topic;
- advice and information from congressional committee staff and congressional documents; and
- issue, stakeholder, and political analyses of the hearing topic and committee members.

The better a witness can anticipate hearing questions, the more likely it is that the witness will have the ability to respond effectively to questions when appearing before a congressional committee.

Adequate research and rehearsal (especially "murder boards" and question-and-answer practice sessions or "dry runs") in preparation for a hearing appearance, combined with the use of FAQs, question modules, and other support materials, should be helpful to a witness in being able to anticipate most of the questions likely to be asked at a hearing.

For information on preparing a witness to respond to committee questions, see Chapter 4, especially § 4.19, Witness Rehearsal of Oral Testimony and Answers to Questions—"Murder Boards" and Question-and-Answer "Dry Runs"; and § 4.45, Recommended General Approaches to Preparation for the Question-and-Answer Phase.

For information on FAQs and question modules, see § 3.22, Important Documents: Drafting the Statement and Making the Record—FAQs and Question Modules.

For information on issue, stakeholder, and political analyses, see, respectively, § 3.8, Issue Analysis and Topic Outline; § 3.10, Issue Context and Stakeholders; and § 3.9, Political Analysis and Landscape.

§6.12 Friendly and "Softball" Questions

Often in a hearing setting, a congressional committee will ask a witness easy or friendly questions, sometimes called "softball" questions. These questions essentially provide the opportunity for a witness to answer and elaborate regarding an issue that is important to his or her organization, that is not problematic or controversial, or that reinforces a policy or political position.

Sometimes the inquiry might simply seek a little more information or detail about something mentioned in a witness's testimony. Questions such as these allow a witness to continue to advance the major theme and messages in the witness's testimony, and to elaborate on related points. In some cases, with executive branch witnesses especially, friendly questions are asked by committee members of the same party as the administration to demonstrate support for the witness, the organization and its programs, and to indicate for the record and all concerned that the questioner and the organization are of like minds on a particular issue.

Consider this example in which a Democratic House committee member engages an Obama administration witness with a fairly easy and straightforward question that opens the door for the witness to expound on major positions of administration policy.

> *Chairman Spratt.* Mr. Doggett.
>
> *Mr. Doggett.* Thank you very much. Thank you so much for your testimony and your important work, Dr. Romer.
>
> With reference to the revenues that will be necessary to finance health care reform, after we have gotten the most that can be had in terms of savings and have tried to assure as efficient a program as possible, I know the President has suggested some ways of providing those revenues.
>
> Is it important in an economic sense that the financing for any health care plan be progressive in its effect on our population?
>
> *Ms. Romer.* You are absolutely right that the President has, as he has been proposing, how are we going to pay for what we have been proposing, he absolutely has said that this needs to be paid for. That is why he is done (sic) more than $600 billion in hard spending savings. But he has suggested a particular tax increase. Limiting the itemized deduction for high-income Americans.
>
> The President has looked at the trends over the last decade, where we do know that middle-class families have taken a hit. And he feels it is incredibly important that we not raise taxes on middle-class families. He has made a very strong commitment to that promise. And we think it is important for the economy that it take the form that he has described.

Source: House Hearing, Committee on the Budget, U.S. House of Representatives, June 19, 2009, Serial No. 111-12.

Available online by performing an Internet search for "f:50542.wais", including the quotation marks.

For information on preparing a witness to respond to committee questions, see Chapter 4, especially § 4.19, Witness Rehearsal of Oral Testimony and Answers to Questions—"Murder Boards" and Question-and-Answer "Dry Runs"; and § 4.45, Recommended General Approaches to Preparation for the Question-and-Answer Phase.

§6.13 Unfriendly and Hostile Questions

Unfriendly and hostile questions asked of a witness by committee members are those inquiries that witnesses dread most, but for which extra witness preparation should be a priority, to the extent possible. These questions tend to be very direct, sometimes difficult to answer, and usually part of the intent of the questioner to put the witness on the spot or to elicit an answer that is not helpful to the witness's cause or interests. In the case of administration witnesses appearing before congressional committees, the questions often emanate from a member of the opposing political party. However, tough questions can come from any quarter, policy position, or committee member. Committee members will often ask hard-hitting, probative questions that might include challenges to a fact or position, accusations of mismanagement or poor performance, intense inquiries about organizational operations, motives, and results, and out-and out sparring with a witness about priorities and perspectives.

These lines of questioning can be very unfriendly, hostile, and unsettling to a witness because they usually go to the heart of challenges, problems, difficulties, or professional judgment associated with a witness's organization, activities, views, and positions. Furthermore, committee members usually demonstrate by the tone and tenor used to ask such questions that they mean business and are being tough on the witness. Consequently, witnesses should be fully prepared to field unfriendly and hostile questions through the use of sufficient preparation and rehearsal, appropriate supporting information and documents in a briefing book or folder, and a responsive demeanor that tolerates the type of question being asked without losing one's professionalism, respectfulness, and even-keeled approach. The use of prepared answers in documents such as FAQs and question modules can be especially helpful to a witness in addressing unfriendly or hostile questions posed by a committee.

Consider this example of a rather tense question-and-answer exchange between a Republican Senate committee member and an Obama administration witness.

> *Senator Shelby.* Senator Dodd, I would just like to ask the Inspector General one last question. You have been generous with your time here. Do you believe that the TARP money has been wisely expended thus far, from what you have seen?
>
> *Mr. Barofsky.* Are you asking me?
>
> *Senator Shelby.* Yes, sir, I am addressing you.
>
> *Mr. Barofsky.* I don't know.

Senator Shelby. You don't know? You don't know that, and you are the Inspector General?

Mr. Barofsky. I think it is too early to tell whether it has been wisely spent.

Senator Shelby. Do you believe that where a lot of these banks have benefited, loaned no money, paid huge bonuses and so forth, like Merrill Lynch and others, do you believe that is the right message and the right thing for the American people at this time of great challenges?

Mr. Barofsky. Senator Shelby, I think your question asks a number of questions. Obviously, I think that any institution—

****

Senator Shelby. You are not evading the question, are you?

Mr. Barofsky. No, no. I think any institution that has violated the terms of its agreement, obviously that is very much a wrong thing. Banks that misuse the funds, that is a wrong thing. And I think that is why we are pushing for this accountability, not only within the TARP but outside the TARP through our survey, and I look forward to being able to report back to you and give you an answer to your question after I have acquired the necessary data to answer it.

Senator Shelby. Thank you.

Source: S. Hrg. 111-40, Committee on Banking, Housing and Urban Affairs, United States Senate, Feb. 5, 2009.

Available online by performing an Internet search for "senate hearing 111-40", including the quotation marks.

For information on preparing a witness to respond to committee questions, see Chapter 4, especially § 4.19, Witness Rehearsal of Oral Testimony and Answers to Questions—"Murder Boards" and Question-and-Answer "Dry Runs"; and § 4.45, Recommended General Approaches to Preparation for the Question-and-Answer Phase. For information on FAQs and question modules, see § 3.22, Important Documents: Drafting the Statement and Making the Record—FAQs and Question Modules.

§6.14 Pre-Scripted and "Planted" Questions

On some occasions, congressional committees will ask hearing witnesses questions that have been provided to the committee by the witness or another party. These questions alternatively may be friendly or hostile to the witness. This situation opens the door for "gaming" and political and policy brinksmanship by witnesses and others. On occasion, executive branch agencies will provide scripted questions to a committee prior to a hearing, either upon request or on their own initiative. This scenario occurs with some regularity, especially between executive branch departments or agencies and committee members of the same party as the administration. Committees, however, are under no obligation to utilize scripted questions, although they may use the questions either per se, or consider them in the formulation of their own questions.

Many committees will not or do not engage in this practice at all, but some will, either openly or privately. Those wishing to ask for planted or pre-scripted questions should contact the appropriate committee staff, but be prepared for a "no" answer. Those committees that do allow planted questions are usually predisposed to support or favor the requesting party or organization, as well as their issues or priorities, or, they might just be friendly, engaging, and willing to be open to a variety of questions.

The moral of the story is that a witness might have some luck working with committee staff to ensure that key desirable questions are, in fact, asked at a hearing, either orally by a committee member, or in writing for follow-up answering after the hearing. See § 6.15 for an example of planted questions.

§6.15 Samples of Pre-Scripted or "Planted" Questions

The following line of questioning was submitted to a Senate Appropriations subcommittee prior to a hearing focusing on the funding requests of a federal agency, USDA's Animal and Plant Health Inspection Agency (APHIS). The agency's administrator testified and answered questions at the hearing. In preparation for the hearing, the subcommittee staff utilized these questions to formulate their own questions for the agency witness and to inform subsequent discussions with the agency.

The language for the questions was submitted to the subcommittee by a lobbyist (who happens to be the author of this book) for an organization that opposed certain proposed regulatory actions under consideration by the agency. The intention in submitting the questions was to focus the subcommittee's attention on the rulemaking process and these potential actions, and to influence the subcommittee to expose not only the agency's consideration of such regulatory actions, but also the organization that was promoting the regulatory change and agency action. APHIS is responsible for enforcement of the Animal Welfare Act, under which those actions would be considered.

Ultimately, the goal was to persuade the subcommittee to restrict the agency's use of federal funds for the purpose of rulemaking and implementing the actions under consideration. The hearing strategy worked, and that goal was accomplished, as noted in the strong committee report language that accompanied the funding bill. That language follows the scripted questions.

SENATE APPROPRIATIONS SUBCOMMITTEE ON AGRICULTURE, RURAL DEVELOPMENT, AND RELATED AGENCIES

Hearing Questions for APHIS March 2, 1999
Expansion of APHIS' Regulation of Dog and Cat Dealers
to Cover Residential Breeders

The Committee understands that, in response to a petition for rulemaking filed by the Doris Day Animal League (DDAL) and a subsequent lawsuit on that issue, USDA/APHIS is currently discussing and writing a proposed rule that could substantially alter the regulatory climate for the commercial pet industry and for hobby and show breeders of dogs and cats who breed and raise puppies and kittens in their own homes and then sell them directly at retail. We have been advised that, while the agency is currently reviewing and evaluating comments submitted in response to an Advanced Notice of Proposed Rulemaking (ANPR) in the fall of 1998, recent informal discussions with agency officials have resulted in the perception that APHIS is moving ahead with the formulation of expanded rules in this area.

1) Is APHIS, in fact, actively pursuing a regulatory change in this area? If so, what public policy rationale are you advancing to support your decision to expand or alter current regulations?

2) How would APHIS' proposed changes in regulatory policy affect hobby and show breeders of dogs and cats, and breeders of hunting, breeding and security dogs, who breed and raise puppies and kittens in their own residential property and sell them only at retail?

3) What would be the additional cost of APHIS' proposed expansion in regulatory authority, and is the agency requesting any funding for this purpose in the fiscal year 2000 budget request? Specifically, what portion, if any, of the $515,000 increase requested in the APHIS budget justification for Animal Welfare Act/Animal Care would be used for expanded activities? Do you anticipate future requests for appropriated dollars for related regulatory changes?

4) Who in the pet industry precisely would be the target of new or additional licensing and regulation under the proposed changes, and what would be the justification for such a change?

5) Would any entities currently regulated under the Animal Welfare Act, such as commercial breeders who sell their stock at wholesale, be deregulated or treated differently if the proposed regulations are adopted?

6) Among retail breeders of dogs and cats, what number and percentage are hobby and show breeders who maintain and breed their animals on residential premises?

7) If the agency's proposed rule were to be adopted, what would be the total regulated population in the dog and cat industries, and what would be the attendant increases in licensees and registrants, as well as APHIS inspection sites annually?

8) What are the current status of, and the timetable for, the rulemaking process on this issue?

Source: Personal and Professional Files of William N. LaForge.

Resulting Report Language:

"The Committee directs the agency not to increase funding and not to expand the licensing and regulations for Animal Care to license and regulate persons currently exempt from its licensing and regulatory requirements who breed and raise dogs

> and/or cats on their own residential property and sell these dogs and/or cats at retail directly to personas (sic) who purchase them for their own use and enjoyment. The Committee does not believe that such an expansion in regulation is necessary to protect the welfare of the animals involved, nor that APHIS has the capacity to carry out such an expansion in regulation without undermining the effectiveness of its regulation of current licenses."

Source: S. Rept. 106-80, Agriculture, Rural Development, Food and Drug Administration, and Related Agencies Bill, 2000, p. 53, *<http://thomas.loc.gov/cgi-bin/cpquery/?&dbname=cp106&sid=cp106312HH&refer=&r_n=sr080.106&item=&sel=TOC_175625&>.*

§6.20 The Sources of Committee Hearing Questions

From where do the questions come that congressional committee members ask witnesses during a hearing?

The answer is: from a wide array of sources. Questions posed to congressional committee hearing witnesses may stem from many different origins, and may have their genesis in any number of documents, experiences, and circumstances. In preparation for a hearing, and to brief the committee chair and members, congressional committee and personal staff typically prepare written questions for their bosses' use during the hearing.

Staff members draw ideas for questions from the written statements submitted by witnesses prior to a hearing. Testimony and questions from previous hearings often serve as reminders or suggestions for contemporary hearing questions. The special interests of members of the committee holding the hearing can spark a line of questions on a certain topic. Current events and media-generated interest in certain topics can provide readily available information on which to base hearing questions.

Vignettes and cases emanating from government and private sector sources that illustrate a problem with a certain policy or law also provide fodder for hearing questions. Issue stakeholders and program or policy constituents are additional sources of information that might help a committee formulate questions to ask witnesses at a hearing. Some questions are even pre-scripted or "planted" by entities inside or outside government who have a particular interest in a hearing topic and the witnesses testifying. (See § 6.14, Pre-Scripted and "Planted" Questions.)

Other questions may flow directly and naturally from the oral testimony that is presented to a committee, as committee members ponder the issue and have a chance to explore issues with a witness in more detail during the question-and-answer phase of a hearing. There is also often a natural "give-and-take" during the question-and-answer period in which committee members and witnesses sometimes engage in long, protracted discussions that involve a particular line of questioning and responses.

§6.21 Preparing Answers in Advance to Expected or Anticipated Questions

A witness should make every effort in advance of a congressional hearing to prepare answers to expected or anticipated questions that are likely to be asked by a committee. Many experienced witnesses actually prepare scripted answers to questions they know or believe will be asked at a hearing.

Two excellent means of preparation are the use of question modules and FAQs, both of which provide prepared, scripted, ready-to-use answers that are available to the witness as a reference during the question-and-answer period of a committee hearing.

A question module typically entails a brief two-to-three sentence scripted answer that responds to a particular question, followed by one or more paragraphs of additional information that can provide supportive details and explanations as may be needed by the witness. This additional supportive data is often included in descending order of importance and priority of use. This presentation flow and format of information allow a witness to respond optimally with a crisp two-to-three sentence answer that maximizes effectiveness and responsiveness, while also providing supplementary information that can be used as needed to complete the answer or respond to follow-up questions.

FAQs, or frequently asked questions, are a composite listing of answers to several questions that are anticipated on the hearing topic, the content of the testimony, the witness and his or her organization, and other related matters. FAQs tend to be shorter than question modules, and have other applications and uses beyond congressional hearings, such as distribution to the media, congressional offices, and the public. FAQs provide a readily accessible and easy-to-use script of answers for use by a witness in answering questions. Both FAQs and question modules may be included in briefing books or folders used by a witness at a hearing.

For information on FAQs and question modules, see § 3.22, Important Documents: Drafting the Statement and Making the Record—FAQs and Question Modules; and § 6.35, Witness Use of Answer Modules and FAQs in Responding to Committee Questions. For more information on briefing books, see § 3.19, Important Documents: Drafting the Statement and Making the Record—The Briefing Book.

In many cases, a witness may also simply turn to the text of the written statement or oral testimony script for information to use in responding to a question, whether it is anticipated or not. Referring to the basic documents for information to provide answers is easy and simple. In the context of an answer provided in response to a committee question, a basic restatement of information already provided to the committee in the testimony can reinforce a theme or message that goes to the heart of a witness's appearance before the committee. It is similar to the concept of sticking to the script. Repetition of a point, through its inclusion in an answer to a question, is a good technique to underscore the importance of a basic message included in the testimony.

§6.22 Anatomy of the Ideal Answer: Techniques on How to Answer Questions Effectively

Admittedly, there is no ideal or perfect answer for a witness to provide to any given question in a congressional committee hearing setting. But adequate preparation, solid information, and the right approach and demeanor can go a long way in helping a witness construct and deliver an answer that is the next best thing to ideal. If there were perfection in a witness's answer, it would certainly include these features, formats, techniques, and best practices:

- **Listen thoughtfully and carefully.** A witness should formulate and provide an answer after carefully listening to and understanding the question.
- **Pause.** A witness should respond only after a brief pause to ponder the question, consider context, formulate the answer, and consult any relevant materials (or the briefing team).
- **Consider context.** A witness should make a judgment about the type of answer to be given, including its appropriateness, complexity, and relevance, and whether to answer at that moment, if at all, or later in writing. A witness should refrain from answering if he or she feels unable or unqualified to respond.
- **Clarify.** A witness should correct or clarify any mistaken, incorrect, or inaccurate statements or underlying assumptions or premises included in a question by the committee or an answer by another witness, as well as ask for clarification from the committee if a question is confusing or ambiguous.
- **Consult materials.** When needed as resources in the formulation of an answer, a witness should employ information from FAQs, questions modules, the text of the written testimony or the script of the oral testimony, and any other available materials.
- **Be responsive.** To answer questions asking "who," "what," "where," "when," "why," and "how," provide basic responsive replies that include facts, data, reasons, rationale, explanations, evidence, anecdotes, research results, and other supporting information and details.
- **Be positive.** A witness should deliver answers to questions in an affirmative manner, without repeating a negative premise or dwelling on negative aspects of an issue.
- **Be brief.** A witness should deliver a response that is a concise, succinct, well-planned two- or three-sentence answer, with no speeches or digressions, and should utilize verbal cues and enumeration to highlight major points in an answer.
- **Be sure and candid.** A witness should take great care to provide accurate and relevant information in an answer that is directly responsive to the question, factual in content, and devoid of exaggeration.

- **Return to the script.** In answers to questions, a witness should restate, underscore, and refer to major themes and messages in the testimony.
- **Amplify if necessary.** A witness should provide additional information, support, and explanation if requested by the committee, if the answer's issue is complex, or if the witness deems more detail to be necessary and important under the circumstances.

§6.23 Use of Question-and-Answer Phase to Underscore Testimony: Strategies for Boosting Answer Content and Approach

In the context of responding to committee questions in a congressional hearing, a witness should attempt to utilize that phase of the hearing to underscore and highlight the major themes outlined in the testimony presented earlier to the committee. While it is important to be as responsive to a question as possible, witnesses are also in a position to incorporate or repeat key messages and points, from the oral testimony statement, in the answers given to committee questions.

Often this technique or strategy flows naturally from the question that is asked by a committee member, and that results in a witness's clear and obvious answer that includes key points made earlier. In other situations, a witness may have to look carefully for an opening in the "give-and-take" with the committee to inject a key point that is at least somewhat related to the questions asked and the answers given.

The question-and-answer phase of a congressional committee hearing affords a witness a chance to revisit themes and messages, previously articulated in the oral testimony statement, that are responsive to the questions "who," "what," "where," "when," "why," and "how," by offering relevant and targeted reasons, rationale explanations, facts, data, and other message-supporting information.

One effective approach is to identify and focus on the issue or theme that is posited by the question, and then include in the answer the relevant basic talking points or content from the testimony. The use of FAQs and question modules can be helpful with this approach. (For information on FAQs and question modules and their use in answering questions, see § 3.22, Important Documents: Drafting the Statement and Making the Record—FAQs and Question Modules; and § 6.21, Preparing Answers in Advance to Expected or Anticipated Questions.)

Another technique involves "bridging" or connecting the question's thrust or issue with an answer that includes key message points or statements that are then connected to and supported by spot-on examples, explanations, reasons, rationale, data, factual evidence, research, analogies, and anecdotes.

Consider the following hypothetical answer utilizing "bridging" that includes a concise and succinct responsive answer that is grounded in sound public policy, and that is supported by reasons, an explanation, facts, evidence, examples, and an anecdote.

Senator: "Why should this subcommittee support funding for a proposal that takes dollars away from the Food Stamp program that feeds people, and then invests those dollars in the application of a pesticide to help farmers?"

Witness: "Senator, the dollars are all serving the same basic public policy purpose and goal—helping to feed the people of the State of Bliss, while also helping their agricultural industry control a pest that is an obstacle to the self-sustained food production of that very state. Redirection of a small portion of the Food Stamp budget, to provide funding for a tiny but important pesticide program, will go a long way in providing a more stable, productive and profitable meat, hide and dairy industry for the state. We have evidence that two out of every three farmers in the state are suffering from an infestation of this pest. One recent case reported to us by a farmer demonstrated a near-total loss of his farm last year, while his neighbor's herd was almost pest-free due to the application of an effective pesticide. Ultimately, the outcomes of sustainable agriculture and food production will help save federal spending on Food Stamp outlays, and the people will still have plenty to eat."

§6.24 Witness Panels: Interaction and Dynamics

When an individual witness is included in a panel at the witness table, as opposed to being the sole witness, the witness should be especially aware of, and responsive to, the interaction of the panel members and the dynamics of the panel format.

The dynamics, freedom, and ease of a witness's role in answering questions as part of a panel can be quite different from the experience of a witness who appears solo. With a panel format, questions from a committee may be directed to one particular witness, to the entire panel, or even to no one in particular, and, consequently, confusion may result. Additionally, on some occasions, panel witnesses may have differing perspectives or positions on the hearing topic or issue under discussion.

Each witness should attempt to be respectful and deferential toward the other witnesses, but not at the expense of his or her own individual answer and the need to be responsive to the questioner in an effective and responsible manner. A witness should be sensitive to the actions and issue positions of other witnesses as they inject themselves into the discussion, as well as to the desire by others to ensure that they have an opportunity to respond to a question.

In some situations, fellow witnesses can be too anxious to respond in an attempt to put their respective position or message on the table early. Nevertheless, a witness should be careful not to interrupt or interfere with the answer or comments of another witness, and should wait his or her turn to respond if another witness has begun to answer a question. It is perfectly permissible to request clarification from the committee or individual questioner about the intended target of a question.

Additionally, in cases in which other witnesses have answered a general question posed to the panel at large, a witness is well within his or her rights to request the committee's permission to respond as well. As an example, a witness might inquire of the chair as follows: "Mr. Chairman, would the committee allow me an opportunity to respond to that question as well?" As a strategy and best practice, many witnesses allow or prefer other witnesses to respond to a question first, in order to have a little extra time to consider the question thoughtfully, to reflect on the other witnesses' answers, and to have the last word or final say on the issue.

For more information on witness panels, see § 2.93, Regular Order and Format of Proceedings: The Normal Procedural Conduct of a Hearing—Introduction and Order of Witnesses: Format for Witness Testimony; and § 2.94, Regular Order and Format of Proceedings: The Normal Procedural Conduct of a Hearing—Use of Witness Panels.

For more information on the order and format of committee questions, see § 2.97, Regular Order and Format of Proceedings: The Normal Procedural Conduct of a Hearing—Committee Members' Questions and Witnesses' Responses; and § 2.98, Regular Order and Format of Proceedings: The Normal Procedural Conduct of a Hearing—Order of Questioning of Witnesses.

§6.25 Dealing with Partisanship and Political or Policy Agendas

Political and partisan speeches, diatribes, questions, bantering, and discussion are common in the context of the question-and-answer period of congressional committee hearings, and a witness should make every attempt to steer clear of engaging in these types of exchange. Committee members will sometimes use their "bully pulpit" to expound on an issue in a political or partisan way, sometimes in an excitable and shrill manner. It behooves a witness to avoid delving into a debate or give-and-take about pointedly political and partisan policy agendas, actions, perspectives, and viewpoints, and a witness should strive not to take sides or champion one political or partisan view over another.

A witness should attempt to answer questions of any nature in a professional and even-keeled manner, using words and phrases that are carefully chosen to impart a balanced, nonpartisan, nonpolitical, constructive, and helpful response to a question. If a question is politically charged or overtly partisan in nature, a witness should stick to the facts in delivering an answer, and may on occasion even defer if the subject matter or thrust of the question is beyond the scope of the witness's purview or area of expertise.

A witness should provide answers that minimize or eliminate the chance that the response will be used, interpreted, or distorted by a committee member for political gain or to bolster a particular partisan perspective. The bottom line for a witness is to avoid being dragged into a partisan discussion or political controversy, or worse, sparring with a committee member over a political or partisan point.

§6.30 Handling Questions and Answers: Points to Remember

- Be prepared. Anticipate questions.
- Pause before you answer.
- Don't echo the negative words.
- Don't go full circle to the negative question premise.
- Always answer the question. Don't over-answer.
- Find the issue that encompasses the question.
- Bridge to specific, positive information—facts, evidence, and anecdotes that support your selling points.

Source: United States Government Accountability Office, Participant Manual, Delivering Testimony, GAO Learning Center, January 2007.

§6.31 Mistakes to Avoid: Witness "Don'ts" in Responding to Committee Questions

- Interrupting the questioner.
- Trying to be cute or clever.
- Evaluating the question.
- Giving a second speech.
- Guessing or bluffing an answer.
- Being disrespectful.
- Answering a hypothetical question.

Source: United States Government Accountability Office, Participant Manual, Delivering Testimony, GAO Learning Center, January 2007.

For more information on the political and partisan aspects of a congressional committee hearing, see § 1.32, Partisanship and Political Analysis: Where Policy and Politics Converge; § 3.9, Political Analysis and Landscape; and § 5.11, Recognizing and Understanding Partisanship.

§6.32 Sticking to the Script in Response to Committee Questions

During the question-and-answer phase of a hearing, just as during the presentation of testimony, it usually serves a witness well to stick to the script as much as possible. In formulating an answer to a question, a witness should draw from personal memory and knowledge, the testimony statement, and prepared materials to stay on message and respond directly to a question. It is ideal to respond with two or three sentences that are on point, and then to provide additional information as requested in follow-up questions or as may seem necessary. Responses that include variances from the major themes and messages can be troublesome. For more information on sticking to the script, see § 5.40, Sticking to the Script in Delivering Testimony.

§6.33 Focusing on the Questioner during Questions and Answers

A witness should direct an answer to a question primarily to the committee member asking it, while also ensuring that the entire committee is receiving the response and is being included in the answer by the witness. This delivery combination can be achieved by focusing initially, and primarily throughout the response, on the questioner per se, including the use of direct eye contact, and also by addressing other committee members from time to time during the answer by using a pivot of the head and effective eye contact.

For more information on targeted audiences at a hearing, see § 2.80, The Targeted Audiences of a Witness's Testimony; § 3.12, Analysis and Targeting of the Committee and Audiences; § 4.14, Focusing the Witness on Targeted Audiences; and § 5.42, Focus on the Primary Targeted Audience—the Committee.

For information on eye contact and other forms of body language, see § 5.45, Importance of Eye Contact, Body Language, and the Use of Gestures.

§6.34 Witness Use of a Briefing Book to Answer Committee Questions

Having a well-prepared and well-organized briefing book can be an excellent resource for a witness during the question-and-answer phase of a congressional committee hearing. A briefing book typically consists of any documents, research materials, and other information that may be helpful to a witness during a hearing, including the witness statement, FAQS, and question modules. Located on the witness table in front of, or to the side of, the witness, a briefing book is especially helpful to a witness as an easy-to-use and easy-to-access reference tool during questioning by a committee.

For basic information on the development, contents and use of a briefing book, see § 3.19, Important Documents: Drafting the Statement and Making the Record—The Briefing Book.

For information on rehearsing the use of a briefing book, see § 4.23, Witness Rehearsal of Oral Testimony and Answers to Questions—Operating with the Use of a Briefing Book.

For information on the organization and use of prepared materials, see § 5.33, Organization and Use of Prepared Written Support Materials.

For information on the use and application of a briefing book during the question-

and-answer phase of a hearing, see § 6.11, Anticipating Questions: Being Prepared; and § 6.21, Preparing Answers in Advance to Expected or Anticipated Questions.

For more information on FAQs and question modules, see § 3.22, Important Documents: Drafting the Statement and Making the Record—FAQs and Question Modules; § 6.21, Preparing Answers in Advance to Expected or Anticipated Questions; and § 6.35, Witness Use of Answer Modules and FAQs in Responding to Committee Questions.

§6.35 Witness Use of Answer Modules and FAQs in Responding to Committee Questions

Prepared and pre-scripted answers to questions in the form of FAQs (frequently asked questions) or question modules can be great assets to a witness in formulating answers during the question-and-answer phase of a committee hearing. These documents should be well-prepared, well-organized in a briefing book or folder, well-rehearsed, and easily accessible and used by a witness.

For information on the preparation and use of FAQs and question modules, see § 3.22, Important Documents: Drafting the Statement and Making the Record—FAQs and Question Modules; and § 6.21, Preparing Answers in Advance to Expected or Anticipated Questions.

§6.36 Witness Use of Briefing or Support Team

Witnesses occasionally utilize briefing or support teams that can be especially helpful during the question-and-answer phase of a hearing to help identify and formulate answers to questions, and to assist with the location of resource materials needed by the witness to deliver an answer. These individuals, typically colleagues from an agency or outside organization, usually sit right behind the witness in the first row of seats, although they might also be allowed to sit at the witness table with the witness to be in ready-mode to answer questions or help locate resources in a briefing book or elsewhere. If a witness uses a briefing team, their combined efforts should be planned and rehearsed for ease and convenience of use on the hearing day.

For more information about a briefing or support teams, see § 2.67, Congressional Hearing Participants: The "Players"—Witness Support Teams; § 4.36, Witness Support: Use of Briefing Staff or Team; and § 5.35, Utilizing a Briefing or Support Team.

§6.40 Witness's Use of Legal Counsel during Questions and Answers

On some occasions, a witness may wish to have accompanying legal counsel at the witness table. For example, legal counsel frequently appears with witnesses at investigative hearings. House and Senate rules, as well as some committee rules, provide witnesses with legal protections such as the right to legal counsel and the right to have counsel present to provide legal advice at a hearing.

If a witness needs or intends to engage legal counsel for an appearance at a congressional committee hearing, the witness should take great care in discussing protocol with the relevant committee staff to ensure compliance with chamber and committee rules. Frequent consultation with, or reliance upon, legal counsel in a committee hearing by a witness is generally not well-received by a committee, but it is the prerogative of a witness, in most cases, whether to have and utilize counsel at a hearing.

For more information, contact the relevant congressional committee staff (U.S. Capitol Switchboard telephone number is 202-224-3121), and also see § 2.53, A Witness's Right to Legal Counsel, as well as the rules for the House (<*rules.House.gov*>) and Senate (<*rules.Senate.gov*>), and rules for each individual committee, accessed through committee links available at <*www.Senate.gov*> and <*www.House.gov*>.

§6.41 Use of Note Pad during Questions and Answers

Use of a note or scratch pad can be particularly helpful to a witness during the question-and-answer phase of a congressional committee hearing. Many witnesses actually write down the question that has been posed in order to have it in front of them in writing, as well as to buy a little time to formulate an answer. A note pad or sheet of blank paper can be a handy tool to jot down the essence of a question for instantaneous review or later consideration, to note a reminder of a fact or comment to be added for the record, or to pen a comment about a committee member's interest in a particular issue or aspect of the hearing topic.

When notations of questions are kept on a pad, a witness can also refer to them later as needed in the question-and-answer period, as well as later after the hearing. Sometimes an issue may also be raised by a committee member in his or her opening statement, or by another witness during testimony or answers, that might merit a quick notation for reference later in answering questions. Availability of a note pad can also facilitate the need to write a note to a colleague or member of the briefing team.

For more information, see § 5.34, Keeping Notes and Score on a Writing Pad.

§6.42 Top 25 Tips, Techniques, and Tactics for a Witness in Answering Committee Questions

- **Tip 1**—Listen carefully to question, and write it down if helpful.
- **Tip 2**—Pause, if necessary, to formulate thoughts. Avoid being in a hurry.
- **Tip 3**—Be responsive and succinct.
- **Tip 4**—Renew and review major themes.
- **Tip 5**—Answer the question or offer to provide a written response later.
- **Tip 6**—Defer, deflect, or qualify when answering hypothetical questions. Try not to refuse to answer.

- **Tip 7**—Be candid. Do not bluff, blur, or mislead. Admit the admissible. If an answer is unknown, admit it, and provide a written response later.
- **Tip 8**—Use prepared FAQs and question modules.
- **Tip 9**—Focus on the questioner, but address the entire committee.
- **Tip 10**—Be open, engaging, cooperative, and creative.
- **Tip 11**—Know and play your role effectively.
- **Tip 12**—Anticipate questions—supportive and hostile.
- **Tip 13**—Prepare pre-scripted" or "planted" friendly questions provided to committee.
- **Tip 14**—Rehearse responses and know them well.
- **Tip 15**—Avoid sounding defensive or defiant.
- **Tip 16**—Expound with detail only when asked. Don't say too much.
- **Tip 17**—Disagree agreeably, respectfully, and deferentially.
- **Tip 18**—Use answers to correct or clarify misstatements or incorrect facts stated by committee, another witness, or the media.
- **Tip 19**—Provide measured, factual, and even-keeled responses.
- **Tip 20**—Avoid exaggeration and hyperbole.
- **Tip 21**—Employ examples, statistics, reasons, rationale, numbers, vignettes, and anecdotes.
- **Tip 22**—Use answers to underscore and highlight key messages and major theses.
- **Tip 23**—Beware of the hostile or "ambush" question.
- **Tip 24**—Use responses to questions to restate, highlight, and summarize whenever possible and appropriate.
- **Tip 25**—Avoid giving speeches or lectures.

§6.43 Expressions that Take the Edge Off an Answer in Disagreement

During the question-and-answer phase of a congressional hearing, when confronted with the need to disagree or take issue with a committee member, or to offer a different perspective or conclusion, a witness may wish to employ some key proven words and phrases that connote disagreement, albeit within the context of an agreeable and respectful style of response. These and similarly crafted responses can help soften the blow of a difficult or contrary answer.

- Respectfully, I/we must disagree.
- With great respect for the committee's intentions and deliberation, I must take issue with that position.

- With deference to the committee, our agency/organization has come to a different conclusion.
- I understand and respect the committee's position, but we have a different perspective on this matter.
- I acknowledge the committee's established position on this issue, but I would hope that you will carefully consider a differing view point as well.
- Understanding the committee's viewpoint, I must say that we assess the situation a little differently.
- Mr. Chairman, we are offering a remedy or solution to the problem that is very different from those under consideration by the committee.
- We realize the committee has spoken on this issue previously, but have you considered this alternative?
- We must disagree with that position, Senator, but please understand that we do so respectfully, yet with complete confidence in our position.
- Our experience and expertise lead us to a different outcome and decision.

§6.44 A Note on Candor and Transparency

During the question-and-answer phase of a hearing, a committee should get the feeling—in substance and in style—that a witness is being helpful, informative, candid, and transparent to the greatest extent possible in providing answers to questions. Sticking to the script and responding in two to three concise sentences are good tactics for starters, but some questions may require answers that are more detailed or explanatory to satisfy the questioner.

A witness should attempt to provide a committee member with a complete, candid, and transparent response that will help meet the committee's expectations, and provide information and understanding regarding the question topic. Any signal from a witness that he or she is not being candid provides a quick target for further committee questions, perhaps even hostile in nature, and may even lead to further scrutiny by the committee, including possible accusations of untruthfulness, especially if the witness is under oath. The best practice for a witness is to be straightforward and honest in dealing with the committee and its questions.

§6.45 Answers, Responses, and Information to Be Provided for the Record by a Witness

At the conclusion of a congressional committee hearing, a witness is often requested or expected to submit written answers to written questions, written responses to questions that were unanswered or partially answered during the hearing, and other information. This information is provided to a committee for the hearing record and to fulfill an obligation to a requesting committee member.

On many occasions, that follow-up information to be provided to a committee after a hearing may variously emanate from a specific request of a committee member during or following the hearing, a list of written questions provided by a committee member for the witness's written response, an oral response to a question for which the witness does not have an answer at the hearing, or other materials or information that the witness is requested to submit, or might have agreed to submit, to the committee for its consideration and for the record. There are many instances, for example, when a witness cannot answer a question completely or at all, and it is perfectly permissible to indicate that the answer or information requested is not known or available at the hearing, but, instead, will be provided to the committee as soon as possible after the hearing or by a date certain. A large percentage of post-hearing follow-up involves witnesses' answers to written questions provided by a committee to the witnesses after a hearing. (See Chapter 7, "Post-Hearing Activities and Follow-Up.")

Committees tend to keep the hearing record open for a period of time after the conclusion of the actual hearing in order to provide time and opportunity for important follow-up items, such as answers to questions and promised additional materials, to be included in the record. Committees usually provide a due date for these materials.

For an example of follow-up answers to be provided after the hearing, see § 6.46, Sample Answers for the Record Provided after a Hearing.

For more information on hearing follow-up activities regarding written questions, see § 7.4, Committee Follow-Up Activities and Responsibilities: Preparation of Follow-Up Written Questions for Witnesses; and § 7.22, Follow-Up Activities and Responsibilities of a Witness: Written Committee Questions for a Witness.

§6.46 Sample Answers for the Record Provided after a Hearing

Consider the following typical example in which Congressman Paul Ryan (R-WI), ranking minority member on the House Committee on the Budget, proffers written questions to Peter Orszag, Director of the Office of Management and Budget, and a witness appearing at a committee hearing, for follow-up answers to be provided after the hearing.

Following Congressman Ryan's comments making the request are five follow-up questions he posed to Director Orszag, accompanied by the Director's written responses.

> *Mr. Ryan.* But I am assuming we are going to have a markup in this committee on the budget before April. So that means there are lots of questions that we would like to get answers to before we start moving a budget resolution going to the floor.
>
> So, in the interest of time, I have some questions I would like to submit to you for the record to get more details to what you are planning on rolling out in April so that we can make better decisions when this committee begins to mark up the budget resolution. And if you could respond to me on these in a prompt way before we actually consider our budget resolution, I sure would appreciate that.

Director Orszag's Responses to Questions for the Record From Representative Ryan

1. Discretionary Outyears

The previous Administration did not provide account level detail for discretionary accounts beyond the budget year. Some Members of Congress and the Washington Post viewed this as hiding key details about the President's budget. In the interest of transparency and long-term budgeting, please provide account level detail through 2019.

Response

The FY 2010 Budget transmitted to the Congress on February 26 was an overview. The full details of the Budget are under development, and information on the discretionary outyears will be provided as part of that transmittal.

2. Federal Employment Levels

Please provide the federal employment levels for FY 2008, 2009, and 2010. These are traditionally part of the budget submission.

Response

The FY 2010 Budget transmitted to the Congress on February 26 was an overview. The full details of the Budget are under development, and information on federal employment will be provided as part of that transmittal.

3. Employment and Unemployment Assumptions

What are your employment and unemployment assumptions used in the budget? Please provide your estimate of the impact that the stimulus bill had upon these assumptions.

Response

As described in Table S-8 of the FY 2010 Budget, the Administration assumes that the unemployment rate will average 8.1 percent in 2009 and decline from there as the economy recovers. Over the next four years, it declines steadily and levels off at 5.0 percent in 2014. The Chair of the Council of Economic Advisers has estimated that the American Recovery and Reinvestment Act will add approximately three and half million jobs to the U.S. workforce by the end of 2010. This estimate is reflected in the Administration's forecast.

4. Concurrent Receipt Proposal

Please explain your concurrent receipt proposal for DoD and VA. Does your proposal do away with the phase-in of concurrent receipt?

Response

No. This proposal expands concurrent receipt to a previously ineligible population—veterans who are medically retired from DoD with fewer than 20 years of service. The proposal phases in concurrent receipt of VA disability and DoD retirement benefits for this group of veterans over a five-year period.

5. Financing for Surface Transportation

In your budget, how much surface transportation funding comes from the dedicated user taxes that have funded this program since its inception in 1956? How

§6.47 Helpful Hints for a Witness

- Be sure to make the most of simple courtesies such as thanking the committee for its work and for the invitation to testify.
- If you are unsure if you have provided a responsive answer, ask the questioner.
- Be aware of the time clock and stay within the time limit prescribed for your testimony and answers to questions.
- If there is additional written material you wish to have placed in the record to supplement your testimony, respectfully make the request of the chair.
- Politely defer to other witnesses to allow them the opportunity to respond, but ask the chair for the opportunity to respond if you have not been given the opportunity to address a particular question because another witness is monopolizing the discussion.
- If it appears that other witnesses are receiving more attention, questions and time, politely request of the chair that you be allowed an opportunity to respond to a question.
- If you need a little extra time to formulate an answer to a question, time-buying tactics such as repeating the question or commenting on its importance might help. If needed, simply ask the chair for a moment's indulgence to consult your briefing book, statement, or briefing team.
- If you or your organization can legitimately assist the committee with an issue or problem, offer that assistance and provide contact information.
- Offer to assist the committee with further input or work on a legislative or oversight matter beyond the hearing day.

much comes from appropriations of general revenue? How much comes from non-traditional financing mechanisms?

Response

The FY 2010 Budget presents baseline funding levels for surface transportation programs and does not include information about funding sources. The Administration recognizes that current law receipts are not sufficient to fund current law spending and looks forward to working with Congress to developing a sustainable surface transportation funding system—one that responds to our nation's changing needs.

Source: H. Hrg. 111-4, Committee on the Budget, U.S. House of Representatives, March 3, 2009.

Available online by performing an Internet search for "f:47729.wais", including the quotation marks.

§6.48 Sample Question-and-Answer Dialogues: The Anatomy of an Effective Response

In the four representative question-and-answer dialogues excerpted below, taken from actual hearing transcripts, note the bracketed editorial comments and notations regarding the association of certain aspects and content of the answers with many of the best practices outlined in this chapter, especially § 6.22, Anatomy of the Ideal Answer: Techniques on How to Answer Questions Effectively; and § 6.23, Use of Question-and-Answer Phase to Underscore Testimony: Strategies for Boosting Answer Content and Approach. Each of the four exchanges is representative of typical question-and-answer dialogues between a congressional committee and hearing witnesses, and provides examples of styles, approaches, and techniques that can serve as models for a witness's responses to committee hearing questions.

To consider these four sets of questions and answers in the context of the actual hearings from which they come, and to check the dialogue against the respective oral testimony statements, see § 5.60, Examples of Presentation Format and Order: The Anatomy of an Oral Witness Statement.

1) **Questions and answers** from an oversight hearing of the House Committee on Natural Resources on the subject of "Offshore Drilling: Environmental and Commercial Perspectives," involving exchanges between Chairman Nick Rahall (D-WV) and two witnesses, Ted Danson and Philippe Cousteau.

(To consider these questions and answers in the context of the actual hearing from which they come, and to check the dialogue against the respective oral testimony statements, see items 1 and 2 of § 5.60, Examples of Presentation Format and Order: The Anatomy of an Oral Witness Statement.)

[*Note the chair's preliminary comments prior to the initial question, and the four-prong question posed to both witnesses.*]

The Chairman. Gentlemen, I thank you both for your testimony; it has been superb. And I appreciate what you said and understand your desire to see the moratoria reinstated. However, we may be in a situation where the ship has already sailed, and the political reality may be that the moratoria, as we knew it, will not be reimposed. You both have alluded to that.

If that is the case—and I know, Philippe, you have said that science should be our guide—but if that is the case, what environmental safeguards would you both suggest be incorporated into any leasing program beyond what is in current law? For instance, do we need buffer areas? Or do we need certain areas with unique resources and features set-off limits? Do we need environmental and safety safeguards imposed before we allow drilling to continue?

[*Note the concise, three-paragraph direct response, and the use of comparison and contrast, disagreement with an idea, and an analogy.*]

Mr. Cousteau. Well, I think we do indeed need as much protection as possible and as much research and knowledge as possible. We know so little about our oceans. I think people look at space and think "the final frontier," when, in fact, we have explored less than 10 percent of our oceans.

One of the challenges with the idea of a buffer zone, I would say 50 miles off the shore, is that ecosystems don't respect a straight, direct line around the continental United States. They vary in size and space where they are. So, I think a buffer zone, while a good idea, is probably not the best way to proceed.

I think we need as much to understand and explore as much about the various ecosystems that exist in the ocean and then site appropriately. There are some places that are just not appropriate for any kind of development, very fragile marine ecosystems, deep sea coral reefs, et cetera, and I think all of that needs to be taken into consideration. Siting (sic) is the first and foremost, and knowledge, science. We need to know what exists before we exploit it. You would not put a coal-fired power plant in the middle of a pristine national forest. It is the same in the oceans. We must at least, at the very first, know what exists there before we exploit it.

The Chairman. Ted.

[*Note the reference to the chair's use of a metaphor; the underscoring of the basic theme and messages; the return to the script of the testimony; the use of amplification and explanation, including data, evidence and statistics; the application of research results and analysis; the predication of results and outcomes; the bridging and connection of the answer to the original statement; the use of a time line to amplify; the use of statistics and figures; the underscoring and highlighting of the main points; and the summary used to bridge the answer to the testimony statement's theme and messages.*]

Mr. Danson. My hope would be that you would sail the ship back into port, because I think we are flirting with disaster by drilling and opening up the Outer Continental Shelf, period.

We don't talk a great deal about what is happening to the fisheries of the world, and a lot of times when we talk, it sounds like we are talking about an environmental sweet, thoughtful, let's take care of the fishes and the beauty, but we are talking about economy and jobs and food.

Our fisheries around the world are an $80-billion-a-year landed industry. One-third of the world's fisheries have totally collapsed, which means that they are below the 10 percent level, which means they may not come back. The U.N. says that 75 percent of our fisheries are either fully or over-fished.

If we continue to harvest our fisheries the way we are by destroying habitat with bottom-trawling and wasteful by-catch being thrown overboard, science tells us we could literally fish out our oceans commercially in the next 40 to 50 years if the trends continue.

So, you have an incredibly delicate balance in our fisheries already. Now you add acidification to the ocean, which would destroy, literally make it impossible for the bottom of the food chain to create shells that allow them to survive.

The animals and creatures that eat the bottom of the food chain would also disappear.

So, you have insults to the ocean from all different sides, besides the pollution of oil spills in areas—the Outer Continental Shelf, which is the nurseries for most of our fisheries, so that all of the added insults could literally have an impact on our oceans in our children's lifetime or our grandchildren's lifetime where we could fish out or destroy our fisheries completely. That is $80 billion a year, that is a billion people a year around the world that depend on that food. That is, you know, 200 million people who have jobs that they depend on to go out and be able to fish. So, this is about the economy, and it is about jobs.

So, my answer is, absolutely do not open it up. You are pulling your finger out of the dike, and all sorts of bad things, I do believe, will happen. And we take the risks for very little benefit.

Source: H. Hrg. 111-1, Committee on Natural Resources, U.S. House of Representatives, Feb. 11, 2009.

For the entire record of the hearing online, perform an Internet search for "f:47302.wais", including the quotation marks.

To review testimony associated with these questions and answers, see § 5.60, Examples of Presentation Format and Order: The Anatomy of an Oral Witness Statement.

2) **Questions and answers** from an oversight hearing of the House Committee on Natural Resources on the subject of "Offshore Drilling: Environmental and Commercial Perspectives," involving exchanges between Representative Niki Tsongas (D-MA) and two witnesses, Ted Danson and Philippe Cousteau.

(To consider these questions and answers in the context of the actual hearing from which they come, and to check the dialogue against the respective oral testimony statements, see items 1 and 2 of § 5.60, Examples of Presentation Format and Order: The Anatomy of an Oral Witness Statement.)

The Chairman. The gentlelady from Massachusetts, Ms. Tsongas.

[*Note the questioner's long statement prior to the actual three-prong question.*]

Ms. Tsongas. Thank you very much for your testimony and your great passion around protecting the oceans. And also, Mr. Cousteau, I was moved and reminded again by your grandfather's quote how we have only one Earth, and how it is our obligation to protect it.

As you have both testified, our oceans contain unique ecosystems that support diverse species and many of our national treasures. One of these national treasures is the Georges Bank off the coast of Massachusetts, a mass of sand and gravel underwater plateau. Nearly the entire bank is less than 200 feet deep, in some places only 10 feet deep. And as you can imagine, it plays an important role in the Gulf of Maine by accelerating the tidal waves as they race across the bank toward and away from New England. This cycle distributes nutrients which support an abundance of marine life, including 259 different species of animals. Congressman Ed Markey from Massachusetts has introduced legislation, which I support, that would protect this area, and I hope that we are successful in passing this important bill.

But as you know, and as you both mentioned, waters and ecosystems are not contained within State or national boundaries. How would you suggest we work with our neighbor, Canada, here on the east coast, and our neighbor, Mexico, on the west coast as we begin to address the importance of protecting these natural resources? Have you given it any thought? Have you worked with partners there? I am curious to hear your comments.

[*Note the witness's admission to not knowing the answer, followed by a commitment to provide information and an answer after the hearing.*]

Mr. Danson. For Oceana, do you mind if I get back? Because I know there is a great answer, I am not aware of it. But I know we do work and think about that a great deal. So, do you mind if we get back to you with that answer?

Ms. Tsongas. Absolutely.

Ms. Tsongas. Mr. Cousteau.

[*Note this witness's similar deflection and commitment to provide information subsequently, his bridge to the oral testimony statement messages, a further all to action, and a return to the testimony script.*]

Mr. Cousteau. I think certainly, as well, that any specific work that Ocean Conservancy has done with Mexico and Canada I would have to get back to you, and we certainly can do that.

Mr. Cousteau. But I think, again, that this is such an outstanding country, and we have such an opportunity for leadership, we must focus on our own back yard first and provide the protections and the responsible management of those systems first to then be able to walk the walk and not just talk the talk. And I think that is absolutely critical, and it is going to be a difficult process, but since when has the United States, this great country, turned its back on a difficult challenge? We have always embraced them and overcome them. And I think we must start now, because it will be difficult to map and to understand the Outer Continental Shelf as much as we need to, and we must start now.

Source: H. Hrg. 111-1, Committee on Natural Resources, U.S. House of Representatives, Feb. 11, 2009.

For the entire record of the hearing online, perform an Internet search for "f:47302.wais", including the quotation marks.

To review testimony associated with these questions and answers, see § 5.60, Examples of Presentation Format and Order: The Anatomy of an Oral Witness Statement.

3) **Questions and answers** from a hearing of the House Foreign Affairs Committee on the subject of "The July Summit and Beyond: Prospects for U.S.-Russia Nuclear Arms Reductions," involving exchanges between Chairman Howard Berman (D-CA) and three witnesses, Honorable William Perry, Dr. Keith Payne and Honorable Thomas Graham, Jr.

(To consider these questions and answers in the context of the actual hearing from which they come, and to check the dialogue against the respective oral testimony statements [with respect to witnesses Payne and Graham only, not Perry], see items 3 and 4 of § 5.60, Examples of Presentation Format and Order: The Anatomy of an Oral Witness Statement.)

[*Note the chair's segue to question-and-answer phase of the hearing, and his first question posed to all three witnesses on the panel. Also note the genuine dialogue and discussion between the committee and three like-minded witnesses on the panel.*]

Chairman BERMAN. Because no one else is here, I am going to yield myself as much time as it takes before someone else returns. The ranking member, in her opening statement, raised a number of—I thought—interesting questions which should be dealt with. Dr. Payne raised some of those and a number of other ones as well. So it would seem to me good to get a little dialogue going among the panelists on a few of those issues. First, on the issue of the urgency of doing it. As I understand it, because START expires in December, all of the verification provisions at that point, if there is not a new treaty, will disappear. The SORT limits will still apply, but there are no verification procedures under SORT. Isn't that in and of itself a reason from our national security interests to want a new treaty in place—that either continues or revises, but maintains some level of inspection and verification? I ask that for starters for anyone who would want to address it.

[*Note the witness's willingness to answer first, his concise two-point response, and his use of enumeration and explanation.*]

Secretary PERRY. If I could make two comments on that, please? I think there are two reasons for proceeding promptly with the START follow on. The first one is the one you mention, which is the START treaty does expire in December and that is the only treaty that has the verification procedures, which I think are quite important. I would add to that it is possible if we reach that point and still do not have the treaty, it is possible that we could get an extension of the old START treaty. I think a much better solution is actually having the new START follow-on treaty ready at that time. That is what I would recommend. Beyond that point, and not directly related, but importantly indirectly related is that this START follow-on treaty will be the touchstone I think of the new strategic relationship, which we are trying to develop with the Russians. That is going to be useful for other areas in which we need cooperation with the Russians, not the least of which is cooperation with Russia in containing the Iranian nuclear program, so that is an indirect, but I think very important, reason for moving ahead. Thank you.

[*Note the chair's question to the second and third witnesses on the topic of the remarks of the first witness.*]

Chairman BERMAN. Dr. Payne, let me just hear your thoughts on both of Dr. Perry's points. And on the first point, for the purpose of maintaining a verification process, you either are going to need a new treaty, or you are going to need a mutual agreement to extend the current treaty. I think by its terms, it can only be extended for 5-year blocks. I guess the parties could agree to something different than that, but it requires the parties to agree. Otherwise, this all disappears. But, Dr. Payne, and then Ambassador Graham, you could arbitrate.

[*Note the use of explanation, clarification, and amplification; the use of bridging to the script of the testimony; the highlighting of the main messages; the use of example, anecdote, and personal experience; and agreement with first witness's position.*]

Mr. PAYNE. Thank you, Mr. Chairman. I agree with Secretary Perry's comments. We should do everything we can to extend the verification provisions of START beyond the end date for START. The Moscow Treaty is legally binding. It will extend out to 2012, but the verification provisions of START were part of why we could negotiate the Moscow Treaty the way we did; because we knew we had the verification provisions of START. I very much would like to see those extended, sir.

The point I was making is that we don't need to identify new reductions beyond those in the Moscow Treaty at this point well before the nuclear posture review has completed its effort and identified the kind of requirements we need. I have some very personal experience with doing nuclear posture reviews inside the Pentagon. It is a long, arduous, very complex task, and the numbers that we agree upon should come out of that, not lead it. We should have strategy drive our numbers, not numbers drive our strategy. I also agree with Dr. Perry that we need to work closely with the Russians on nonproliferation, on counterproliferation and on counterterrorism. It seems to me that these ought to be the focus of where we work with the Russians at this point, in addition to extending the START verification procedures, because that is where we and the Russians have compelling overlapping interests.

Chairman BERMAN. Well, Ambassador Graham?

[*Note the use of underscoring, highlighting, and bridging to accentuate the main theme and messages of the testimony statement, and the use of the prediction of results.*]

Ambassador GRAHAM. I think it is very important to conclude a START treaty as soon as that can be accomplished. The relationship that we have had with Russia has been so bad for so many years, and they are essential to our success in containing nuclear proliferation, which appears right now to be a greater threat than it was a few years ago. The Russians regard this as very important to them.

As a practical matter, given the changes that are being contemplated, not just the reduction to 1,500, but the counting rules and the verification changes, I think it is unlikely that it will be in force by end of the year. It may be completed by the end of the year, but still ratification in our Senate will be required. I might just mention there is an organization, Partnership for a Secure America, which has as members just about everybody all of us have ever heard and is a very prestigious organization that is very much in favor of moving forward on START.

Chairman BERMAN. I take Dr. Payne is not a member of that?

Ambassador GRAHAM. Well, I don't see him on the list, but he should be, but Dr. Perry is a member.

Mr. PAYNE. I will look at that.

[*Note the use of a direct bridge to the witness's testimony statement, as well as a recommendation and a call to action.*]

Ambassador GRAHAM. We will get you on. We have to go so far to make real progress to make this world more secure. As I said in my opening comments, we have this phase and then probably another phase and then what to do about reserve weapons and tactical weapons and get all those to a low level before we can start the multilateral phase, which itself will take, who knows? A decade or so, and so I think that we need to proceed expeditiously.

[*Note the chair's time for questioning has expired, and his calling upon a Republican member of the committee for the next series of questions.*]

Chairman BERMAN. My time has expired. Other members have returned, so I will not be able to ask my other 10 questions right now. And I am very pleased to yield to the gentleman from California, Mr. Rohrabacher for comments or questions for 5 minutes.

Source: H. Hrg. 111-21, Committee on Foreign Affairs, U.S. House of Representatives, June 24, 2009.

For the entire record of the hearing online, perform an Internet search for "f:50635.wais", including the quotation marks.

To review testimony associated with these questions and answers, see § 5.60, Examples of Presentation Format and Order: The Anatomy of an Oral Witness Statement.

4) **Questions and answers** from a hearing of the House Foreign Affairs Committee on the subject of "The July Summit and Beyond: Prospects for U.S.-Russia Nuclear Arms Reductions," involving exchanges between Representative Dana Rohrabacher (R-CA) and three witnesses, Honorable William Perry, Dr. Keith Payne and Honorable Thomas Graham, Jr.

(To consider these questions and answers in the context of the actual hearing from which they come, and to check the dialogue against the respective oral testimony statements [with respect to witnesses Payne and Graham only, not Perry], see items 3 and 4 of § 5.60, Examples of Presentation Format and Order: The Anatomy of an Oral Witness Statement.)

[*Note the introductory remarks and speech-like statement by the questioner prior to the actual question.*]

Mr. ROHRABACHER. Thank you very much, Mr. Chairman. We are rushing back and forth obviously to activities on the floor, so I missed Dr. Payne's testimony, and I will follow up by reading it. Thank you very much. A few questions and thoughts about what I heard before I left a few minutes ago. This talk about a world without nuclear weapons, let me just for the record, Mr. Chairman, suggest that talk about a world without weapons is nonsense as long as we live in a world with tyrants who murder their own people and threaten others.

These tyrants and these gangsters that have been with humankind in all of recorded history, I don't think they are affected in a positive way by such moral proclamations of how we need to disarm. Ronald Reagan once said that those who turn their swords into plowshares will soon be plowing for those who didn't, and we live in a world where there are tyrants, not just disagreements between morally equal societies, but tyrants and gangsters that rule countries that are capable of producing nuclear weapons.

Question No. 1: This talk about the ideal of a world without nuclear weapons, is this not encouraging countries like North Korea, should I say rogue governments and wacko despots like the ones that control North Korea and Tehran and other such counties, does this not encourage them to move forward with their nuclear program thinking that the more stable democracies in the world may well decide to disarm nuclear weapons? That is my first question for the panel.

[*Note the witness's offer to answer first, and the use of a presidential quotation.*]

Secretary PERRY. If I may make two comments or points?

Mr. ROHRABACHER. Yes, sir.

Secretary PERRY. First of all, you have quoted Ronald Reagan very appropriately. I would like to also quote Ronald Reagan in which he said, "We seek a world without nuclear weapons." This is a direct quote from Ronald Reagan.

[*Note the committee member's use of humor.*]

Mr. ROHRABACHER. Yes. I may have written that, so I better know it.

[*Note the witness's connection with the questioner.*]

Secretary PERRY. Indeed, it was the Reagan initiative at Reykjavik which inspired George Schultz and Henry Kissinger, Sam Nunn and myself to make the proposal we made.

Mr. ROHRABACHER. Yes. Let me just be the first to admit, Dr. Perry, that Ronald Reagan's goal was a reduction of nuclear weapons. It was a world that was safer with a reduced level, but I do not believe that he was every serious about thinking that we could have a world without nuclear weapons. Maybe you are suggesting that talk today is along that very same line, just philosophical.

[*Note the use of clarification; direct responsive answer that is on-point; the return to enumeration and answering the question; and the use of personal experience, anecdote and time line.*]

Secretary PERRY. Well, he did say that, and I assume that he was serious when he said it, but I also believe he understood, and I understand, that this is not going to happen anytime soon or with the present geopolitical situation. The second point I want to make, which is whether this talk would encourage North Korea, I have had many years of dealing with North Korea, and my impression is they do not need any encouragement to seek nuclear weapons. They have all their own reasons for wanting to seek nuclear weapons, and they have proceeded on this long before anybody ever mentioned this proposal. Their program goes back at least 20 years.

Mr. ROHRABACHER. Ambassador Graham, go right ahead.

[*Note the use of clarification and explanation.*]

Ambassador GRAHAM. Well, Congressman, I agree with what Dr. Perry just said, and I would just add a few further comments. In the world in which we live, which is exceedingly dangerous and growing more so by the day, nuclear weapons really have no utility for us. Their only role is to deter weapons held by others. We are not going to stop al-Qaeda with nuclear weapons. We are not going to correct a situation anywhere in the world with nuclear weapons.

Mr. ROHRABACHER. What about China, Mr. Ambassador? Do you think that our possession of nuclear weapons, the fact that we have a potential enemy in China that has millions of people more at their disposal to be part of their military? You don't think our nuclear arsenal may have some effect on China?

[*Note the use of explanation with supportive data and evidence.*]

Ambassador GRAHAM. Well, the concept of zero worldwide weapons means that nobody has them, including the Chinese, and I don't think America would use nuclear weapons against countries that don't have them, nor do I think we have need to do that. The situation, Congressman, is that nuclear weapons in the fractured world in which we live with 50 to 70 failed or failing states, nuclear weapons are becoming a threat even to their possessors. If I may presume to say so, I think that is one of the motivations of Dr. Perry and Secretary Schultz and their colleagues to undertake their efforts to pursue zero nuclear weapons.

[*Note the dialogue and concern regarding time limits and a second round of questions.*]

Mr. ROHRABACHER. Thank you very much, Mr. Ambassador. I am afraid I am being gaveled now.

Ambassador GRAHAM. Can I just add one thing?

Chairman BERMAN. Can you fit it in?

Mr. ROHRABACHER. Are we going to have a second round of questions?

Chairman BERMAN. Yes. I am here as long as you are willing to be here.

Mr. ROHRABACHER. 30 seconds.

Chairman BERMAN. All right. Everybody okay with 30 seconds?

Mr. ROHRABACHER. Yes.

Chairman BERMAN. Take it away, but after that, we go back to the 5-minute rule.

[*Note use of clarification and amplification; return to witness statement script; underscoring of major theme and messages; and use of supporting evidence and examples.*]

Ambassador GRAHAM. I just wanted to confirm the danger of nuclear weapons. The head of al-Qaeda in Afghanistan gave an interview yesterday to Al-jazeera, and he said, "God willing, the nuclear weapons will not fall into the hands of the Americans," he is talking about the Pakistani weapons, "and the Mujahidin will take them and use them against the Americans." That is one reason why having them around is not a good idea.

Source: H. Hrg. 111-21, Committee on Foreign Affairs, U.S. House of Representatives, June 24, 2009.

For the entire record of the hearing online, perform an Internet search for "f:50635.wais", including the quotation marks.

To review testimony associated with these questions and answers, see § 5.60, Examples of Presentation Format and Order: The Anatomy of an Oral Witness Statement.

§6.50 HITS: Humor in Testimony— Federal Reserve Chairman Ben Bernanke

In the following exchange during the question-and-answer phase of a hearing conducted by the House Budget Committee on "The Near-Term Outlook For The U.S. Economy," a committee member confuses the professional backgrounds of witnesses. The incident itself is sufficiently humorous, and the witness's reply only adds to the humor. Representative Marcy Kaptur (D-Ohio) is the committee member, and Federal Reserve Chairman Ben Bernanke is the witness.

For at least one brief moment, humor prevailed and laughter was abundant in the committee room in the midst of what was otherwise a very serious and somber hearing. The Chairman of the Federal Reserve demonstrated once again that it pays to have a sense of humor when dealing with the U.S. Congress.

Ms. Kaptur. Number three, seeing as how you were the former CEO of Goldman Sachs, what percentage—

Mr. Bernanke. No. You are confusing me with the Treasury Secretary.

Ms. Kaptur. I have got the wrong firm? Paulson. Oh, okay. Where were you, sir?

Mr. Bernanke. I was the CEO of the Princeton Economics Department.

Ms. Kaptur. Oh, Princeton. Oh, all right. Sorry. Sorry. I got you confused with the other one. I am sorry. Well, I am glad you clarified that for the record.

Source: H. Hrg. (110-27), Committee on the Budget, U.S. House of Representatives, Jan. 17, 2008.

For the complete transcript of the hearing online, perform an Internet search for "f:40338.wais", including the quotation marks.

§6.999 Chapter Summary

- The question-and-answer phase of a congressional committee hearing, which typically follows the presentation of testimony, is an important component of the hearing process for both a committee and a witness. (§ 6.0)
- A veteran congressional expert explains the importance of a witness's answering committee hearing questions in an effective and responsive manner. (§ 6.1)
- From a committee's perspective, committee members consider the question-and-answer portion of a hearing an opportunity to probe the hearing topic and a witness's testimony for a wide array of additional information, as well as a forum to articulate their own views, findings, and concerns. (§ 6.2)
- For a witness, the question-and-answer phase of a congressional hearing is an opportunity to be responsive to the questions of committee members, and to reinforce the essential messages of the testimony. (§ 6.3)
- A witness's answers to questions asked by committee members in a congressional hearing are primarily about being responsive to the members, their questions and their interests. (§ 6.4)
- The question-and-answer phase of a congressional committee hearing is a natural segue from the presentation of testimony by witnesses. (§ 6.5)
- The role, format, and dynamics of a congressional committee during the question-and-answer portion of a hearing include posing questions to witnesses, a certain order and time limitation for questioning witnesses by the committee, and oral statements by committee members that sometimes morph into lectures and political jockeying. (§ 6.6)
- During the question-and-answer phase of a congressional committee hearing, a witness's chief role is to answer questions that are asked by committee members concerning the hearing topic, the content of the witness's written and oral statements, testimony and answers from other witnesses, and other matters associated with the witness's organization and reason for appearing before the committee. (§ 6.7)
- The scope of subject matter for questions that are asked at congressional committee hearings is usually focused on the topic of the hearing itself and witnesses' testimony, but it may be expanded at will by the committee to cover almost any issue. Consequently, witnesses should be prepared to field any question that might be asked. (§ 6.10)
- In preparation to respond to a wide array of anticipated questions posed by committee members, witnesses can glean ideas for possible questions that might be asked by committee members from numerous sources and circumstances. (§ 6.11)
- In the course of a congressional hearing, committee members may

alternatively ask friendly and easy questions, as well as unfriendly or hostile questions. (§ 6.12 and § 6.13)

- Committee members may occasionally ask hearing witnesses questions that have be pre-scripted or "planted." (§ 6.14 and § 6.15)
- Committee members use a wide array of sources for the questions they ask witnesses, including numerous documents, experiences and circumstances such as prior hearing records, written statements of witnesses, oral testimony given by witnesses, and vignettes from government or private sector activities. (§ 6.20)
- A witness would be wise to prepare answers to expected or anticipated hearing questions that are likely to be asked by a committee, including the use of FAQs and question modules. (§ 6.21)
- There are several important best practices and techniques that can be utilized by a witness in answering committee hearing questions effectively and responsively, beginning with carefully listening to and thoughtfully considering the question itself. (§ 6.22)
- A witness should attempt to utilize the question-and-answer phase of a hearing to underscore and highlight the major themes outlined in the testimony presented earlier to the committee by incorporating or repeating key messages and points in the answers given to committee questions. (§ 6.23)
- When witness panels are used in a congressional committee hearing, an individual witness should be especially aware of, and responsive to, the interaction of the panel members and the dynamics of the panel format. (§ 6.24)
- A witness should avoid engaging in exchanges with a committee on matters of a partisan or political nature. (§ 6.25)
- There are several key points a witness should remember when considering how to handle questions during a congressional committee hearing. (§ 6.30)
- Congressional committee witnesses are wise to avoid making some common mistakes such as interrupting the questioner and answering hypothetical questions. (§ 6.31)
- Just as with congressional testimony per se, it behooves a witness to stick to the script in answering committee questions. (§ 6.32)
- A witness should focus on the questioner in providing an answer to the committee, but also direct the response toward the entire committee. (§ 6.33)
- Use of a well-prepared and well-organized briefing book by a witness to answer committee questions provides an excellent resource for a witness during the question-and-answer phase of a congressional committee hearing. (§ 6.34)
- Prepared and pre-scripted answers to questions in the form of FAQs (frequently asked questions) or question modules can be great assets to a witness in formulating answers during the question-and-answer phase of a committee hearing. (§ 6.35)

- The use of briefing or support teams by a witness can be helpful during the question-and-answer phase of a hearing to help identify and formulate answers to questions, and to assist with the location of resource materials needed by the witness to deliver an answer. (§ 6.36)
- While there are occasions when a witness may wish to have accompanying legal counsel at the witness table, a witness should pay careful attention to committee rules and protocols about the use of legal counsel. (§ 6.40)
- The use of a simple note pad or scratch sheet can be a valuable tool for a witness during the question-and-answer phase of a hearing. (§ 6.41)
- A witness can be well-served by considering a list of tips, techniques, tactics, and best practices that can be helpful in answering questions posed by a congressional committee. (§ 6.42)
- On those occasions when a witness is confronted with the need to disagree with a committee member in answering a question, there are some proven words and phrases that can help take the edge off the response. (§ 6.43)
- In providing responses to committee questions, a witness should make every effort to be candid, transparent, helpful, and informative. (§ 6.44)
- At the conclusion of a congressional committee hearing, a witness is often expected to submit written answers to written or otherwise unanswered questions to a committee for the hearing record and to fulfill an obligation to a requesting committee member. (§ 6.45 and § 6.46)
- A witness can be well-served by considering a list of helpful hints ranging from simple courtesies and time limitation awareness to deferring to other witnesses and offering additional assistance to a committee. (§ 6.47)
- To get a feel for live committee hearing question-and-answer sessions, a witness may wish to review four samples of actual question-and-answer dialogues, complete with editorial comments and notations regarding best practices. (§ 6.48)
- HITS: Humor in Testimony—In the world of congressional committee hearing questions and answers, humor occasionally raises its curious head, as it does in an exchange involving Federal Reserve Chairman Ben Bernanke. (§ 6.50)

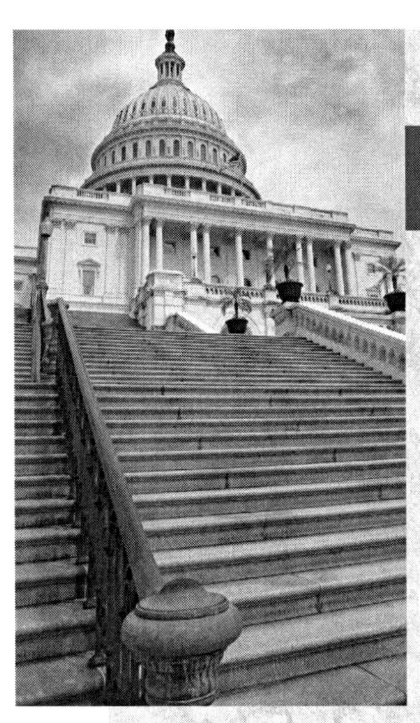

Chapter Seven

Post-Hearing Activities and Follow-Up

Chapter Seven

Section

§7.0 Introduction and Summary

When the smoke clears at the conclusion of a congressional committee hearing—when the preparation, testifying, and question-and-answer session are all history—there is frequently still work to be done on the part of both the committee staff and a witness. Numerous sources—the hearing itself, the testimony, requests from committee members, a witness's obligation to respond to unanswered and supplemental written questions, and the occasional need to provide additional information for committee members and for the record—all give rise to an array of post-hearing activities and follow-up that are the joint responsibility of committee staff, witnesses, and their organizations.

For a committee and a witness, effective and timely post-hearing follow-up helps to ensure the success of the overall hearings process and to reinforce the impact of a witness's testimony. This chapter outlines and discusses the committee's and the witness's basic activities, obligations, and responsibilities after a hearing has concluded.

§7.2 Committee Follow-Up Activities and Responsibilities

At the conclusion of a hearing, committee staff are generally responsible for bringing closure to all aspects of the hearing. By virtue of requests from committee leadership or under the general scope of responsibilities as staff professionals, committee staff may be expected to prepare various documents and reports, written questions for witnesses, and correspondence. Staff also attend to administrative matters, including the coordination of the editing, printing, and publishing of committee hearings transcripts. Sections § 7.3 through § 7.10 discuss several important activities and responsibilities of committees and their staffs once a hearing has been concluded.

§7.3 Committee Follow-Up Activities and Responsibilities—Preparation of Post-Hearing Documents

In some cases, a committee may request that its staff prepare a summary document that includes all the hearing testimony and related materials. This document may, in turn, be distributed to committee members, the media, and interested parties, may be made available to the public for review, and will likely be included in the officially published hearing volume.

Staff are also requested to prepare reports, written questions for witnesses, transmittals of information, and correspondence, depending on the type of hearing and its outcome. See § 7.4 and § 7.5 below for more information on these specific categories.

For more information on a committee's preparation of hearing documents, see § 2.8, Committee Preparation of Hearing Documents—Briefing Materials.

§7.1 Perspectives of a Former Congressional Committee Staff Director on the Importance of Timely and Effective Post-Hearing Follow-up

"Few opportunities present themselves where an individual has simultaneous direct access to multiple Members of Congress. Congressional hearings provide that 'perfect storm.' While testimony is usually of a formal nature, it still allows a witness to have an audience with decision-makers and the staff who will actually write and implement the wishes of those Members. As a result, an issue may be presented, debated and decided upon in one occasion—that being the hearing. While the subsequent mark-up process officially decides many issues in the legislative process, a hearing, if correctly executed, can many times obviate the need for further consideration of a particular issue.

"In a post-hearing scenario, a witness may have several unique and important responsibilities, beyond the usual responses to follow-up questions, including:

- Helping the committee staff or members' offices draft legislation;
- Making himself or herself available for further sharing of information;
- Providing names of, and opening doors to, other experts in the witness's field;
- Suggesting other hearing topics that are pertinent to the current issues;
- Serving as a source of information to the Administration in promoting the committee's views; and,
- Serving as an independent source of information to those who oppose the committee's views.

"With these and all post-hearing follow-up activities, it is critical that a witness respond to the committee in a timely and effective manner."

Source: Jim Morhard, Morhard & Associates, LLC; formerly Chief Clerk and Staff Director, Committee on Appropriations, United States Senate.

§7.4 Committee Follow-Up Activities and Responsibilities—Preparation of Follow-Up Written Questions for Witnesses

On behalf of the committee leadership and members, committee staff members prepare follow-up written questions for witnesses that might alternatively be given to the witnesses immediately after the hearing adjourns, or distributed to them later in print form or through electronic mail. These questions tend to expand on a witness's testimony and on questions posed to a witness orally at a hearing by committee members. They are intended to elicit answers that will amplify, clarify, and complete the hearing record and be responsive to the committee's inquiries. Witnesses are expected to reply in writing to these questions within a time frame established by the committee.

§7.5 Committee Follow-Up Activities and Responsibilities—Special Follow-Up and Actions Based on Type of Committee Hearing

Depending on the type of hearing, there may be specific and required targeted follow-up by committees and their staff. For example, Senate confirmation hearings typically lead to a report to the full Senate in preparation for a floor vote. In the case of investigative hearings, a committee may choose to prepare and issue a report, with accompanying findings and recommendations that occasionally may entail a referral to federal or state courts or agencies for possible further investigation and adjudication.

For authorization or legislative hearings, a committee may use hearing information as the basis for the introduction of a bill and the development of amendments, and the conduct of a hearing often opens the way for a committee to proceed to marking up a bill and reporting it to the respective chamber for floor consideration. Budget and appropriations hearings serve as the bases for committee decisions and recommendations regarding the federal government's requests and justification for virtually every government program.

The results of oversight hearings often include correspondence and other follow-up with executive branch departments and agencies, as well as the possibility of corrective legislation introduced and sponsored by the committee. Committee staff professionals are engaged in all these follow-up activities on behalf of their committee leadership and members.

§7.6 Committee Follow-Up Activities and Responsibilities—Administrative Matters

In a post-hearing setting, committee staff attend to various administrative and logistical matters such as clearing the hearing room, coordinating with administrative, security, and other congressional staff, following up with media representatives, and responding to inquiries from witnesses and interested outside parties. Staff also coordinate follow-up correspondence with witnesses and others as may be necessary or requested by the committee, including requests for additional information, written questions for the record, and thank-you notes.

§7.7 Committee Follow-Up Activities and Responsibilities—Review and Editing of the Hearings Transcript

Committee staff members coordinate with the official reporter to have the transcript of a congressional hearing prepared, and subsequently reviewed by committee members and staff and by witnesses. Each committee is given wide latitude in determining its own procedure for reviewing and correcting hearing transcripts. Typically, members of Congress and their staff correct and edit members' statements in a hearing transcript, and witnesses review and edit their own respective portions of the transcript. Committee staff ensure that the editing is completed in timely fashion as directed by the committee leadership and policy.

For information on a witness's role in reviewing and editing a hearing transcript, see § 7.26, Follow-Up Activities and Responsibilities of a Witness: A Witness's Review and Editing of Hearings Transcripts.

For more information on published hearing records, see § 1.81, Results and Outcomes of Hearings: Legislative and Regulatory Actions and Remedies—Published for Public Record; and § 1.82, Results and Outcomes of Hearings: Legislative and Regulatory Actions and Remedies—Committee Hearing Transcripts as Published Documents for the Committee and Public Record.

§7.8 Committee Follow-Up Activities and Responsibilities—Printing and Publishing of Congressional Hearings Transcripts

The printing of hearings is determined by each committee, but not always required, depending on the subject, relevance, and importance of a hearing. Many committees direct that their hearings be printed, and some committees put hearing transcripts on their web sites. The original of each hearing transcript is maintained in a committee's archives, and may be available for inspection and review by the public. Committees are generally free to publish hearing transcripts as they wish. They are encouraged to post their proceedings, including hearing information and transcripts, on their web sites.

The U.S. Senate and the U.S. House of Representatives both encourage their committees to publish and make available hearings transcripts before floor consideration of a measure that was the subject of a hearing. The Appropriations Committees require printed hearings to be available three days before floor consideration. Committees in both the House and Senate also have access to video broadcasting and taping technologies for their hearings on committee cable channels administered by their respective chambers. Many committees post live and archived webcasts of their hearings on their respective committee web sites.

To see the webcasts of numerous hearings available for viewing, go to the individual committee sites accessible through <*www.House.gov*> and <*www.Senate.gov*>, and proceed to the links for menus of webcasts. See the Back of the Book for more information on this source. Additionally, C-SPAN provides a full archive of hearings on the Web at <*www.c-spanvideo.org*>.

Supplementary materials and documents are also subject to printing by a committee, are usually incorporated into the hearing transcript document, and can include written statements of witnesses, visual aids such as charts and graphs, research materials and results of studies, outside witness statements from individuals who did not appear at a hearing, and various forms of questions posed to a witness by a committee during or after a hearing.

For specific information on the printing and publishing of hearings transcripts, see House, Senate, and respective committee rules for details. House rules can be found at <*rules.House.gov*>. Senate rules can be found at <*rules.Senate.gov*>. House and Senate committee rules may be accessed through committee links provided at <*www.House.gov*> and <*www.Senate.gov*>.

Once printed, congressional hearings transcripts are posted on various government and private web sites, including individual committee web sites and the Government Printing Office's (GPO's) web site at <*www.gpoaccess.gov/chearings/index.html*>. At the end of each congressional session, each committee's printed hearings are organized and bound together by the Library of Congress.

For more information on published hearing records, see § 1.81, Results and Outcomes of Hearings: Legislative and Regulatory Actions and Remedies—Published for Public Record; and § 1.82, Results and Outcomes of Hearings: Legislative and Regulatory Actions and Remedies—Committee Hearing Transcripts as Published Documents for the Committee and Public Record.

§7.9 Committee Follow-Up Activities and Responsibilities—Keeping the Committee Hearing Record Open

After the conclusion of a congressional hearing, committees have the authority to keep a hearing record open for a period of time in order that additional information may be included in the formal hearing record. Witnesses should be aware of that open record period of time in order to fulfill any commitments or obligations to provide written answers to questions or other information offered to the committee by the witness or requested by the committee itself.

§7.10 Committee Follow-Up Activities and Responsibilities—Committee Requests for Assistance from a Witness and Other Action Items

Committees may request from a witness, or suggest to a witness the production of, any number of written documents, such as reports, data, statistics, research results, correspondence, graphs, charts, and special responses or information for the committee at large or for a particular member of the committee.

Committees may also request a witness to be available for further consultation and advice, to identify and refer other experts and resources, to suggest other hearing topics, and to serve as an informational source for the executive branch and for supporters or opponents of the committee's position on certain issues.

Committees expect timely responses from witnesses, including the use of interim reports or updates if the document or prescribed assistance cannot be produced in a short period of time. Similarly, committees expect timely responses from, and engagement by, witnesses who have offered or been requested to provide information or special assistance to the committee, such as supplying legislative analysis and drafting, research and technical data, and follow-up consultations.

§7.20 Follow-Up Activities and Responsibilities of a Witness

At the conclusion of a congressional hearing, a witness must often engage in a number of follow-up activities with the committee that staged the hearing. A witness will usually need to maintain contact with committee staff, be responsive to questions and other committee requests, and generally assist the committee in completing the hearing record and bringing closure to the hearings process. The keys to a witness's post-hearing involvement with a committee are to be diligent, responsive, and timely in concluding all matters concerning the witness's appearance before the committee. Sections § 7.21 through § 7.26 discuss several important activities and responsibilities of witnesses and their organizations once a hearing has been concluded.

§7.21 Follow-Up Activities and Responsibilities of a Witness—Witness Communications with Committee Staff

At the conclusion of a congressional committee hearing, a witness should contact the committee staff member who had responsibility for the hearing, or who was the witness's original committee contact, to ensure that the witness knows and understands any obligations for post-hearing follow-up. If nothing else, that contact provides a final opportunity for a witness to express appreciation to the committee for the invitation to testify. If there are follow-up responsibilities for a witness, committee staff will usually advise the witness immediately after a hearing concerning any responses, information, or other materials that are due to the committee, as well as the deadline for the witness to comply.

The committee staff contact can be a valuable resource to a witness during the fulfillment of any post-hearing obligations, such as responses to questions, delivery of materials or information, and any other assistance requested by the committee. Additionally, beyond the hearing scenario, a committee staff contact can prove valuable to a witness and his or her organization in other matters such as being notified of committee activities and having a known point-person for the purpose of future issue advocacy.

§7.22 Follow-Up Activities and Responsibilities of a Witness—Written Committee Questions for a Witness

Committees frequently provide witnesses with lists of additional or follow-up questions when a hearing is concluded. During many congressional hearings, committee members are often unable to ask a witness all the questions they wish to ask due to time limits and sometimes lengthy lines of questioning. So they provide the unasked questions to witnesses for post-hearing follow-up answers that are to be provided in writing for the committee hearing record.

Similarly, committee members and staff will sometimes develop additional questions for witnesses as a result of discussion, statements, or general questions and answers that take place during a hearing. These questions may actually be prepared after a hearing, but nonetheless are provided to a witness for post-hearing follow-up written responses. Witness should strive to answer post-hearing questions in a responsive manner and within the deadline prescribed the committee.

§ 7.23 Follow-Up Activities and Responsibilities of a Witness—Responses to Unanswered or Partially Answered Questions during the Hearing

Occasionally, members of a committee will ask questions during a hearing to which witnesses do not have answers either totally or partially. In such instances, witnesses should offer to provide, and committees will expect, more complete answers or information in writing at a later date that will respond to unanswered or partially answered questions, that will allow the witness to expand on oral answers or testimony already provided at the hearing, and that will allow a witness to provide written comments on issues raised at the hearing that were not included in his or her testimony or answers to oral questions. These questions should be answered separately from those discussed in § 7.22, Written Committee Questions for a Witness, and should likewise be answered responsively in writing and in a timely manner.

§ 7.24 Follow-Up Activities and Responsibilities of a Witness—Responses to Committee Requests for Information and Assistance from Witnesses

In response to a congressional committee's post-hearing requests for written documents, such as reports, data, statistics, research results, correspondence, graphics, and charts, witnesses should be prepared to produce the requested information in a timely manner. Additionally, witnesses should respond diligently to requests for special information for the committee at large and for a particular committee member.

During the course of a congressional hearing, in addition to questions asked orally of a witness, committees will also sometimes suggest or request that a witness work with the committee's staff on follow-up matters, such as the drafting and analysis of legislation, ensuring a complete hearing record, double-checking the accuracy of information provided to the committee, providing industry and other pertinent contact information, delivering research, technical, and other data for the committee's use and consideration, referring the committee to other experts and resources, suggesting other hearing topics, serving as an informational source to the executive branch, the media and to supporters or opponents of the committee's positions, and providing general consultation and advice.

Witnesses should attempt to work cooperatively and in a timely fashion with committee staff during post-hearing discussions and deliberations, especially as a committee is crafting legislation, drafting a report, or preparing for markup of a bill.

§7.25 Follow-Up Activities and Responsibilities of a Witness—Documents, Information, and Assistance Offered or Promised to a Committee by a Witness

Occasionally during a hearing, especially in response to questions, a witness may affirmatively offer to provide a committee with supplemental materials, relevant documents, special information, and other assistance and advice. A witness may also wish to be available to a committee on an ongoing basis for further consultation and sharing of information. In circumstances involving such commitments, a witness should take great care to be responsive in a thorough and timely manner, and to deliver on the witness's offer or promise diligently and completely.

§7.26 Follow-Up Activities and Responsibilities of a Witness—A Witness's Review and Editing of Hearings Transcripts

Witnesses should expect the opportunity to review the hearing record, to provide additional or corrected information for the record, and to receive a copy of the hearing transcript in most cases, although printed copies are often not available for lengthy periods of time.

Virtually all committees allow witnesses to review their testimony, before it is included in the final hearing transcript, for the purpose of editing grammatical, transcription, and obvious factual errors or omissions. However, permission to make basic or substantive changes to witness testimony, statements, and answers in a transcript may require committee approval. Consequently, witnesses wishing to make substantive changes to their portion of a committee hearing transcript should first consult with the relevant committee staff.

For information on a committee's role in reviewing and editing hearings transcripts, see § 7.7, Committee Follow-Up Activities and Responsibilities—Review and Editing of the Hearings Transcript.

For more information on published hearing records, see § 1.81, Results and Outcomes of Hearings: Legislative and Regulatory Actions and Remedies—Published for Public Record; and § 1.82, Results and Outcomes of Hearings: Legislative and Regulatory Actions and Remedies—Committee Hearing Transcripts as Published Documents for the Committee and Public Record.

§7.27 Follow-Up Activities and Responsibilities of a Witness—A Witness's Use of Hearings Transcripts

After congressional hearings transcripts have been printed and published, there are numerous uses and applications available to witnesses and their organizations. Immediate use may include references and citations in organizational publications and on web sites, internal organization information and education, and collaterals for media, governmental, and public requests and responses. Organizations often file, catalogue, and archive hearings transcripts that involve their enterprise in some way, and may include them in reference, library, or resource files for use by the organization, researchers and the public.

For more information on published hearing records, see § 1.81, Results and Outcomes of Hearings: Legislative and Regulatory Actions and Remedies—Published for Public Record; and § 1.82, Results and Outcomes of Hearings: Legislative and Regulatory Actions and Remedies—Committee Hearing Transcripts as Published Documents for the Committee and Public Record.

§7.40 HITS: Humor in Testimony—"Agency vs. Committee"

What could possibly be humorous about typically mundane post-hearing follow-up activities? Generally speaking, the answer is "nothing." However, in one memorable situation, involving a Senate committee and a federal agency, humor surrounded a post-hearing incident, even if neither party saw anything funny about the episode at the time.

It seems that a certain federal agency had developed a reputation over the years for its abysmally poor financial recordkeeping. When the agency's director appeared before the Senate Appropriations subcommittee for the annual hearing concerning the agency's funding request, the subcommittee chair, at the prompting of his staff director, inquired about the disarray of the agency's financial records and the status of hopefully improving management practices. The director assured the subcommittee that matters were improving. Subsequent to the hearing, the subcommittee requested that agency officials follow-up by meeting with the subcommittee staff, at which time they were also to produce the agency's financial records and files.

The result: Agency officials met with the subcommittee staff, and brought along the agency's totally disheveled financial records, including thousands of receipts from around the world, in a cardboard box!

So much for effective follow-up!

Source: Author's memory.

§7.999 Chapter Summary

- After a congressional committee hearing concludes, there are often important follow-up activities and responsibilities required of both committee staff and witnesses. (§ 7.0)
- A former United States Senate committee staff director underscores the importance of timely and effective post-hearing follow-up by a witness. (§ 7.1)
- From a committee's perspective, committee staff are responsible for post-hearing follow-up activities that bring closure to a hearing by attending to a variety of document preparation and administrative tasks, including the following responsibilities: (§ 7.2)
  1) Preparation of Post-Hearing Documents (§ 7.3)
  2) Preparation of Follow-Up Written Questions for Witnesses (§ 7.4)
  3) Special Follow-Up and Actions Based on Type of Committee Hearing (§ 7.5)
  4) Administrative Matters (§ 7.6)
  5) Review and Editing of the Hearings Transcript (§ 7.7)
  6) Printing and Publishing of Congressional Hearings Transcripts (§ 7.8)
  7) Keeping the Committee Hearing Record Open (§ 7.9)
  8) Committee Requests for Assistance from a Witness and Other Action Items (§ 7.10)
- From a witness's perspective, a witness is responsible for a number of post-hearing follow-up activities requiring close cooperation with committee staff, responsiveness to follow-up questions, and general assistance to the committee in bringing closure to a hearing, including responsibilities in the following areas: (§ 7.20)
  1) Witness Communications with Committee Staff (§ 7.21)
  2) Written Committee Questions for a Witness (§ 7.22)
  3) Responses to Unanswered or Partially Answered Questions during the Hearing (§ 7.23)
  4) Responses to Committee Requests for Information and Assistance from Witnesses (§ 7.24)
  5) Documents, Information, and Assistance Offered or Promised to a Committee by a Witness (§ 7.25)
  6) A Witness's Review and Editing of Hearings Transcripts (§ 7.26)
  7) After congressional hearings transcripts have been printed and published, there are numerous uses and applications available to witnesses and their organizations. (§ 7.27)
- HITS: Humor in Testimony—Even in the midst of post-hearing follow-up activities, there is an occasional nugget of humor. (§ 7.40)

Back of the Book

Back of the Book

Appendix One
Useful Web Sites

1) Congressional Hearing Rules and Guidelines—For congressional committee hearing rules and guidelines, consult the rules of the U.S. Senate, the rules of the U.S. House of Representatives, and the rules of individual Senate and House committees.

   - Rules of the U.S. Senate: <*rules.Senate.gov*>
     To review several excerpted portions of Rule XXVI of the Standing Rules of the U.S. Senate relating to committee hearings, see § 2.5, Selected Excerpts Pertaining to Committee Hearings from Rule XXVI of the Standing Rules of the Senate—Committee Procedure.
   - Rules of the U.S. House of Representatives: <*rules.House.gov*>
     To review several excerpted portions of Rule XI of the Rules of the House of Representatives relating to committee hearings, see § 2.4, Selected Excerpts Pertaining to Committee Hearings from Rule XI of the Rules of the House of Representatives—Procedures of Committees and Unfinished Business.
   - Rules of Senate committees: accessed through links by committee name at <*www.Senate.gov*>
   - Rules of House committees: accessed through links by committee name at <*www.House.gov*>

   For a sample of congressional committee rules, directives, and guidelines, see § 2.6, Sample of Committee Rules, Directives, and Guidelines.

   For information on congressional committee rules, policies, and guidelines, see § 2.3, Committee Rules, Policies, and Guidelines.

2) Transcripts and Records of Congressional Hearings

   - <*www.gpoaccess.gov/chearings/index.html*>
   - <*www.Thomas.gov*>
   - Individual committee web sites accessed through committee name links at <*www.Senate.gov*> and <*www.House.gov*>

   For more information on hearing transcripts and records, see § 1.5, Congressional Hearing Information Sources: Web Sites and Links; and § 1.6, Access to Congressional Committee Hearing Transcripts.

3) Congressional Hearing Information and Records

   - <*www.Thomas.gov*> (Library of Congress legislative information source)

- *<www.capitolhearings.org>* (provided as a public service by C-SPAN)
- *<www.loc.gov/law/find/hearings.html>* (Library of Congress Law Library site)
- *<www.lexisnexis.com/infopro/zimmerman/disp.aspx?z=1324>* (LexisNexis)
- *<www.gpoaccess.gov/congress/index.html>* (GPO Access—Government Printing Office)
- *<www.gao.gov>* (Government Accountability Office—GAO)
- Individual committee web sites accessed through committee name links at *<www.Senate.gov>* and *<www.House.gov>*

  For more information, see § 1.5, Congressional Hearing Information Sources: Web Sites and Links; and § 1.6, Access to Congressional Committee Hearing Transcripts.

4) Training

- *Preparing and Delivering Congressional Testimony*, from TheCapitol.Net *<www.CongressionalTestimony.com>*

Appendix Two
Congressional Committees and Contact Information

Contact congressional committees by telephone through the Capitol switchboard at 202-224-3121, or via electronic mail at addresses listed on committee web sites accessible through committee links found at <*www.Senate.gov*> and <*www.House.gov*>.

- Standing Committees of the U.S. Senate
  - Agriculture, Nutrition, and Forestry
  - Appropriations
  - Armed Services
  - Banking, Housing, and Urban Affairs
  - Budget
  - Commerce, Science, and Transportation
  - Energy and Natural Resources
  - Environment and Public Works
  - Finance
  - Foreign Relations
  - Health, Education, Labor, and Pensions
  - Homeland Security and Governmental Affairs
  - Judiciary
  - Rules and Administration
  - Small Business and Entrepreneurship
  - Veterans' Affairs
- Special, Select, and Other Committees
  - Indian Affairs
  - Select Committee on Ethics
  - Select Committee on Intelligence
  - Special Committee on Aging
- Joint Committees
  - Joint Committee on Printing
  - Joint Committee on Taxation
  - Joint Committee on the Library
  - Joint Economic Committee

(For United States Senate committee links, go to <*www.Senate.gov*>, and click on the relevant committee.)

- U.S. House of Representatives
  - Committee on Agriculture
  - Committee on Appropriations
  - Committee on Armed Services
  - Committee on the Budget
  - Committee on Education and Labor
  - Committee on Energy and Commerce
  - Committee on Financial Services
  - Committee on Foreign Affairs
  - Committee on Homeland Security
  - Committee on House Administration
  - Committee on the Judiciary
  - Committee on Natural Resources
  - Committee on Oversight and Government Reform
  - Committee on Rules
  - Committee on Science and Technology
  - Committee on Small Business
  - Committee on Standards of Official Conduct
  - Committee on Transportation and Infrastructure
  - Committee on Veterans' Affairs
  - Committee on Ways and Means
  - Joint Economic Committee
  - Joint Committee on Printing
  - Joint Committee on Taxation
  - House Permanent Select Committee on Intelligence
  - House Select Committee on Energy Independence and Global Warming

  (For United States House of Representatives committee links, go to <*www.House.gov*>, and click on the relevant committee.)

Appendix Three
How to Find Congressional Committee Hearing Schedules

To determine the schedule, topic, date, time, and location of congressional hearings in the U.S. Senate and U.S. House of Representatives, contact the relevant committee directly by telephone via the U.S. Capitol switchboard at 202-224-3121, or via the committee's web site, which can be found as an electronic link by committee name at <*www.Senate.gov*> and <*www. House.gov*>.

Schedules of committee hearings are usually available through these resources:

- <*www.Senate.gov*> (Click on "Committees," and then on "Hearings and Meetings" to access the Daily Digest Committee Meetings/Hearings Schedule.)
- <*www.House.gov*> (Click on "committee hearings" under "Currently on the House Floor.")
- Individual committee web sites accessed through committee name links at <*www.Senate.gov*> and <*www.House.gov*>
- Individual committee offices by telephone via the U.S. Capitol switchboard at 202-224-3121
- <*www.Thomas.gov*> (Library of Congress legislative information source; see Senate and House hearing schedules under Congressional Schedules, Calendars)
- <*www.capitolhearings.org*> (provided as a public service by C-SPAN)
- <*www.gpoaccess.gov/congress/index.html*> (GPO Access—Government Printing Office)
- *CQ Today*, the Legislative News-Daily from *Congressional Quarterly*
- *Congressional Daily*, a *National Journal* Group Publication
- *The Washington Post*
- *The Washington Times*

Appendix Four
Live Broadcast Coverage of Congressional Committee Hearings

Live media broadcasts of congressional hearings are provided routinely by C-SPAN and occasionally by other cable and major television networks on a selective basis. Contact the selected media source or the relevant congressional committee for schedules, times, and dates of hearings to be broadcast. For a schedule of upcoming hearings to be televised by C-SPAN, go to the C-SPAN web site at <*www.c-span.org*>. To access copies of hearings going back to 1986, call the C-SPAN Archives (800-277-2698). To contact a congressional committee, call the U.S. Capitol switchboard at 202-224-3121, and ask for the committee by name.

Appendix Five
Webcasts and Videotaped Congressional Committee Hearings

To access a sizeable menu of webcast and videotaped congressional committee hearings for viewing, go to the individual committee sites accessible at <*www.House.gov*> and <*www.Senate.gov*>, and proceed to the links for menus of webcasts. Committees in both the House and Senate utilize video broadcasting and taping technologies for their hearings on committee cable channels administered by their respective chambers. Many committees post live and archived webcasts of their hearings on their respective committee web sites. Additionally, C-SPAN provides a full archive of hearings on the Web at <*www.c-spanvideo.org*>.

Appendix Six
Samples of Congressional Committee Hearing Written Testimony

To review samples of written testimony prepared for congressional hearings, go to the following sections in the body of the book:

§ 3.29—Samples of Written Statements

§ 3.30—Statement Prepared for House Judiciary Subcommittee on Courts and Intellectual Property in Opposition to the Split of the 9th Circuit Court of Appeals

§ 3.31—Statement Prepared for House Appropriations Subcommittee on Transportation in Support of Federal Funding for Clean Air Research

§ 3.32—Statement Prepared for Senate Appropriations Subcommittee on Agriculture, Rural Development, and Related Agencies in Support of Federal Funding for Turfgrass Research

§ 3.33—Statement Prepared for Senate Appropriations Subcommittee on Labor, Health and Human Services, Education, and Related Agencies in Support of Hospital Funding

Appendix Seven
Samples of Transcripts of Congressional Committee Hearing Oral Testimony

To review four excerpts of transcripts of congressional committee hearing oral testimony, see § 5.60, Examples of Presentation Format and Order: The Anatomy of an Oral Witness Statement, in the body of the book.

Appendix Eight
Samples of Transcripts of Congressional Committee Hearing Questions and Answers

To review four excerpts of transcripts of congressional committee hearing questions and answers, see § 6.48, Sample Question-and-Answer Dialogues: The Anatomy of an Effective Response, in the body of the book.

Appendix Nine
FAQs (Frequently Asked Questions)

Do you have a question about congressional hearings? Consider the following FAQs. (For more information, consult the referenced section in the main body of the book noted in parentheses after each answer.)

1) *What is a congressional hearing?*
A congressional hearing is a formal meeting of a committee of the U.S. Senate or U.S. House of Representatives organized and conducted to receive testimony from witnesses who appear before the committee to provide information that is helpful to the committee in the execution of its responsibilities. (Introduction and Chapter 1)

2) *Why does Congress hold hearings?*
The major overall purpose of any congressional hearing is to elicit information from witnesses that will be helpful to the committee in its work on legislation and other matters that come before the committee. There are several different types of congressional hearings categorized and defined either by their specific purpose or committee venue or both. Congressional hearings are important early steps in the legislative process and in the path of a bill on its way to congressional passage and ultimately becoming law. In many cases, hearings are one of the first major steps in the formation of a consensus in support of a measure and can be considered one of Congress's primary fact-gathering systems, somewhat akin to the scientific process of gathering data prior to making assumptions or decisions. (§ 1.10, § 1.20, and § 1.50)

3) *What is the legal authority for congressional hearings?*
The basic authority for conducting hearings and calling witnesses to testify before committees of Congress lies in the official rules and guidelines of the United States House of Representatives and of the United States Senate and their various committees. (§ 1.0)

4) *Where are congressional hearings held?*
Congressional committee hearings are usually held in specially designated committee hearing rooms in the various buildings that house the committees of the U.S. Senate and U.S. House of Representatives. (§ 2.10 and § 2.11) Field hearings may be conducted in various other locations around the country at a committee's discretion. (§ 1.60)

5) *When are congressional hearings held?*
Congressional committees are empowered to conduct committee hearings whenever they wish. Most hearings occur during the normal business hours of the House and Senate when they are in session, but hearings may be authorized at other times as well. (§ 1.30)

6) *Who organizes congressional hearings?*

Congressional committees organize hearings under the direction of the committee chair; designated committee professional staff carry out most of the organizational duties. (§ 2.1)

7) *Are there rules and guidelines regarding congressional committee hearings?*

Yes, rules and guidelines regarding congressional committee hearings are set out in the officials rules of the U.S. Senate, the U.S. House of Representatives, and the individual committees of each chamber. (§ 2.3)

8) *Who decides the topics or subject matter of hearings?*

The committee sponsoring a congressional hearing determines the topic or subject matter for a hearing; the committee chair plays a major role in the decision-making. (§ 1.10 and § 1.30)

9) *Who decides who testifies?*

The committee sponsoring a congressional hearing determines who will testify at a hearing. The chair, ranking minority member, and members of the committee contribute to the decision-making on the selection of witnesses. (§ 2.21 through § 2.27)

10) *How do committees decide which witnesses will be invited to testify?*

Witness selection is one of a committee's most important roles in preparing for a hearing, and thoughtful consideration goes into determining the witnesses to be invited, the order and format of their appearance, and the perspectives and viewpoints they will bring to the committee. Invited witnesses are usually experts or knowledgeable authorities such as members of Congress not on the committee holding the hearing, federal and state officials, representatives of private or public interest groups, and private citizens. (§ 2.21)

11) *How does someone secure an invitation to testify at a congressional hearing?*

Witnesses must be invited by a congressional committee in order to able to appear and testify at a hearing. A congressional committee basically has wide latitude and authority to invite whomever it wishes to testify before a hearing of the committee, and, in some instances, can even compel a witness to appear by using the power of a subpoena. Witnesses may be chosen based on their institutional or professional role or position, as a result of a request or recommendation, or for any reason deemed important by the committee issuing the invitation. (§ 2.21)

12) *How do I contact congressional committees?*

Congressional committees may be contacted telephonically through the U.S. Capitol switchboard at 202-224-3121, or via their respective web sites found as links on their respective chamber's web sites at <*www.Senate.gov*> and <*www.House.gov*>. For appointments and meeting locations, committee offices are located throughout the Capitol complex on Capitol Hill, and their room numbers are indicated on directories inside the entrance of each House and Senate building and the U.S. Capitol, as well as on directories located adjacent to each bank of elevators in each building. (§ 2.11)

13) *Who are the "players" involved in a hearing?*

A wide array of individuals are involved with operations and conduct of a congressional committee hearing, including the committee chair, ranking minority member, committee members, non-committee members and personal staff, witnesses, witness support teams, federal departments and agencies, the media, interest groups, nonprofit organizations, the general public, the audience, an official hearing reporter, and other official and administrative personnel. (§ 2.60 through § 2.72)

14) *Why would someone want to testify at a hearing of a congressional committee? What are the benefits of testifying?*

From the perspective of a witness and organizations that testify, hearings provide a valuable means to communicate viewpoints on a matter of public policy directly to congressional decision-makers. Hearings are important to both private and public institutions in communicating their policy positions on issues of importance to them. Organizations, ranging from federal executive and judicial branch officials and national associations to state and local governments and private businesses, use congressional hearings to "have their say" in the national debate and formulation of federal laws, and to make the record clear on policy subjects near and dear to their hearts. (§ 1.20)

15) *What is a witness?*

A witness is an individual who testifies at a congressional committee hearing. (§ 1.10, § 1.30, § 2.16, § 2.20, and § 2.66)

16) *What is testimony?*

Testimony is both the written and oral statements presented to a committee by a witness at a congressional hearing. In a broad sense, it also includes comments made by a witness during the question-and-answer period of a hearing. (§ 1.10, § 1.20, § 2.18, § 2.19, § 2.20, § 3.1, and § 5.2)

17) *What are the roles and responsibilities of a witness who testifies at a hearing?*

Witnesses appearing before a committee to deliver testimony play a key role in the hearing process. Witnesses are called to provide information, education, and advocacy to assist the committee in making decisions on legislative and other measures under the committee's jurisdiction. They represent various perspectives on the topic of the hearing and play the role of an expert bringing vital information to the attention of the committee. Witnesses are responsible for providing a committee with a written statement, delivering oral testimony at the hearing, responding to questions asked by the committee during the hearing, and following up with various post-hearing activities. (§ 2.14 through § 2.20, § 2.66, § 3.1, § 4.3, § 4.4, § 5.3, § 5.73, § 5.74, § 6.1, and § 6.3)

18) *Can a witness be compelled to appear before a congressional committee to testify?*

Yes, in some instances, a congressional committee can compel a witness to appear to testify by using the power of a subpoena. (§ 2.27 and § 2.39)

19) *Can anyone attend a congressional hearing?*

Generally, yes, anyone may attend a congressional committee hearing as long as it is an open hearing, and not closed due to the nature of the hearing topic. (§ 1.65 and § 1.66)

20) *Why are some hearings open to the public, and others closed?*

Congressional hearings must be open to anyone, unless specifically deemed a closed hearing by the committee, in open session, under the rules of the Senate or House and the relevant committee. Hearings that are closed to the public include those concerning certain aspects of national security and defense, select foreign policy and energy policy matters, sensitive homeland security and law enforcement information, and intelligence matters, as well as when a rule of the House or Senate might otherwise be violated. (§ 1.65)

21) *How long do committee hearings last?*

The duration of a congressional committee hearing is totally within the discretion of a committee and its chair. Some hearings are relatively short and can be completed within an hour or two. Others may extend throughout an entire day and even over to additional days. Protracted confirmation hearings and hearings on major public policy issues or legislation may run several days in duration. (§ 2.112)

22) *How many congressional hearings are conducted each year?*

Congressional committees conduct hundreds of hearings each year. For the years 2006–2008, unofficial reports indicate the average number of Senate hearings at 782 and of House hearings at 1,266. (§ 1.30)

23) *What written documents are involved in being a congressional hearing witness?*

The primary document is the written witness statement that is provided to a committee for inclusion in the hearing record. There may also be post-hearing written answers to questions posed to a witness by a committee. During the process of developing and preparing a witness statement, there are several additional documents that can be helpful to a witness. (§ 3.0, § 3.13 through § 3.22, § 7.4, § 7.22 through § 7.25)

24) *What is the difference between written and oral testimony?*

Written testimony is the prepared document that is usually submitted to a committee by a witness prior to a hearing and included in the hearing record itself. Oral testimony is the verbal presentation by a witness of an abbreviated version of the written testimony. (§ 3.1, § 3.13, § 3.39, and § 5.2)

25) *What is the difference between delivering testimony and answering questions at a hearing?*

Delivering testimony and answering committee questions at a congressional hearing are two of the key roles and responsibilities of a witness. The delivery of oral testimony is an affirmative, scripted presentation to a committee by a witness that contains the witness's major messages and basic case, usually delivered within a limited period of time. Answering questions posed to a witness by a committee is more of a responsive exercise that elucidates and expands on the topic of the hearing and the witness's earlier statement. (§ 5.0, § 5.3, § 6.0, and § 6.3)

26) *How does a witness prepare or rehearse to testify before Congress?*
A witness typically prepares to testify by studying the written witness statement and other resources, rehearsing the delivery of testimony through a variety of activities, and practicing answers to anticipated questions. (Chapter 4)

27) *Is a written record made of a congressional hearing?*
Yes, an official reporter usually transcribes the entire content of a hearing to make a complete record of the statements, testimony, discussion, and questions and answers. Witnesses have an opportunity to review and edit the transcripts before the report of the hearings is published. Published hearings are excellent resources for a witness and his or her organization. (§ 1.31, § 2.72, § 7.7, § 7.8, § 7.26, and § 7.30)

28) *How can someone access the records of congressional hearings?*
There are a number of sources available to access the records of congressional hearings, including congressional committees themselves, the Government Printing Office, and the Library of Congress. (Appendix One, item 2; § 1.5 and § 1.6)

29) *Are congressional hearings broadcast live?*
Yes, many congressional committee hearings are broadcast live, but on a selective basis. Live media broadcasts of congressional hearings are provided routinely by C-SPAN (<*www.c-span.org*>) and occasionally by other cable and major television networks. Many committees also post live and archived webcasts of their hearings on their respective committee web sites. Contact the selected media source or the relevant congressional committee for schedules, times, and dates of hearings to be broadcast or webcast. (Appendix Four and § 2.69)

30) *Are there video recordings of congressional hearings available for viewing?*
Yes, committees in both the House and Senate utilize video broadcasting and taping technologies for their hearings on committee cable channels administered by their respective chambers. Many committees post live and archived webcasts of their hearings on their respective committee web sites. To access a sizeable menu of webcast and videotaped congressional committee hearings for viewing, go to the individual committee sites accessible at <*www.House.gov*> and <*www.Senate.gov*>, and proceed to the links for menus of webcasts. Additionally, C-SPAN provides a full archive of hearings on the Web at <*www.c-spanvideo.org*>. (Appendix Five; § 1.5, § 4.15, § 5.0, and § 6.0)

31) *Do witnesses testify alone or in groups?*
A witness may be scheduled as a solo witness or as part of a group called a witness panel. Committees have the discretion to utilize either format in any combination they choose. (§ 2.90 and § 2.94)

32) *Who are typical witnesses at congressional committee hearings?*
Committees have the authority to invite whomever they wish to testify. Typical witnesses at congressional hearings include government officials, business and industry representatives, experts from various fields of endeavor, state and local governmental officials, researchers and academics, nonprofit and non-governmental entities, and sometimes just ordinary citizens. (§ 2.30 through § 2.39)

33) *Who presides over a congressional hearing?*
The committee chair or his or her designee presides over a congressional committee hearing. (§ 2.61)

34) *How do committee members participate in a hearing?*
Committee members participate in a hearing by making statements on the topic of the hearing, listening to the testimony of witnesses, and asking questions of witnesses. (§ 1.10, § 2.63, § 2.92, and § 2.97)

35) *How are congressional hearings conducted? Is there an order of business?*
Congressional committee hearings are conducted in concert with the agenda and order of business as determined by the sponsoring committee. Each committee hearing operates from an agenda prepared for the chair and members by staff, in accordance with the stated purpose and mission of the hearing. Each individual committee decides the order of business and format of witness appearance and testimony. (§ 1.10, § 2.90 through § 2.110)

36) *How can someone learn more about a particular committee or hearing?*
To access information about a congressional committee, contact the committee by telephone through the Capitol switchboard at 202-224-3121, or check out the committee's web site, accessible through committee links found at <*www.Senate.gov*> and <*www.House.gov*>.

To learn about scheduled hearings, go to one of these sources: <*www.Senate.gov*> (Click on "Committees," and then on "Hearings & Meetings" to access the Daily Digest Committee Meetings/Hearings Schedule.); <*www.House.gov*> (Click on "committee hearings" under "Currently on the House Floor."); individual committee web sites accessed through committee name links at <*www.Senate.gov*> and <*www.House.gov*>; individual committee offices by telephone via the U.S. Capitol switchboard at 202-224-3121; <*www.Thomas.gov*> (Library of Congress legislative information source; see Senate and House hearing schedules under Congressional Schedules, Calendars); <*www.capitolhearings.org*> (provided as a public service by C-SPAN); <*www.gpoaccess.gov/congress/index.html*> (GPO Access—Government Printing Office). (Appendix Three, § 1.4, and § 1.5)

37) *Does someone have to be an expert to testify before a congressional committee?*
No, a witness does not necessarily have to be an expert per se on a certain subject to testify, but a witness is generally considered to be a valuable and credible source of information, and often is, in fact, an expert in his or her particular field of endeavor. (§ 2.21, § 2.66, and § 5.3)

38) *Are there time limits on testimony presented by a witness?*
Yes, committees usually limit a witness to a specific amount of time for presentation of oral testimony. Committee rules often provide time restrictions for a witness's testimony and usually limit witnesses to a brief summary statement. The time limit ranges from five minutes to ten minutes, or more, in the discretion of the chair. (§ 2.96)

39) *How do witnesses know what questions will be asked by a committee during a hearing?*
In most cases, witnesses do not know in advance what, if any, questions they might be asked during a congressional committee hearing. However, prudent and diligent preparation, rehearsal and research, plus consultation with committee staff, can help prepare a witness for anticipated or expected questions. (§ 6.11 through § 6.21)

40) *Are there training programs for witnesses and those helping to prepare a witness for a hearing?*
Yes, several private organizations and institutions of higher learning offer private or commercial training programs for those who wish to learn about testifying before a congressional committee hearing. Within the federal government, the Government Accountability Office (GAO) offers its professionals one of the best training programs available in preparing and delivering congressional testimony. The publisher of this book, TheCapitol.Net, is a leader in this field of training. (<*www.TheCapitol.Net*>)

41) *What are the results or outcomes of a congressional hearing?*
Hearings can produce a wide array of results, intended or unintended, and are used broadly in support of various outcomes, including making a complete record of the hearing proceedings, educating and informing the committee and the public, adding value and advocacy to a public policy debate, influencing legislation or executive branch actions, and fueling public interest and discussion. (§ 1.80 through § 1.88)

42) *Do all congressional committees conduct hearings?*
Most congressional committees conduct hearings because of their legislative, oversight, budget, investigative, or appropriations responsibilities. Hearings are a primary method used by committees to gather data and become informed about important issues. A few committees in the House and Senate are primarily concerned with "in-house" procedural matters, and, consequently, may not hold many hearings. (§ 1.0, § 1.20, § 1.30, and § 1.40)

43) *What do committees do with the information gathered at a congressional hearing?*
Congressional hearings are one of the first major steps in the formation of a consensus in support of a measure and can be considered one of Congress's primary fact-gathering systems. Hearings can produce a wide array of results that are used broadly in support of various outcomes, including making a complete record of the hearing proceedings, educating and informing the committee and the public, adding

value and advocacy to a public policy debate, influencing legislation or executive branch actions, and fueling public interest and discussion. Procedurally, committees typically edit and revise the transcripts of the information gathered during a congressional hearing, and have that information printed and published. (§ 1.20 and § 1.80 through § 1.92)

44) *Can anyone testify before a congressional committee?*
Yes, anyone is eligible to testify before a congressional committee, but it is necessary to be invited or subpoenaed to testify by the committee. (§ 2.21 through § 2.27)

45) *Are witnesses paid or reimbursed for testifying?*
It is considered an honor and a privilege, and a duty and obligation in some cases, for a witness to testify before a congressional committee. Testifying is part and parcel of a congressional function that includes many witnesses from outside government who are, more or less, expected to participate at their own expense. Consequently there are no provisions for payment of witnesses. In some instances, witnesses may be entitled to reimbursement for per diem expenses and transportation, although these payments are generally used only in hardship cases. (§ 2.52)

46) *What does a hearing room look like, and how is it set up?*
There are many different sizes, shapes, and styles of congressional committee hearing rooms on Capitol Hill. The typical hearing room is an auditorium-styled room with a dais or raised bench at one end of the room, with the bench or dais often semi-circular in style from one end to the other. This platform serves as the staging and seating area for members of the committee who face outward toward the witness table, audience, and committee room. The committee chair presides from the center seat position on the dais, with the ranking minority member in an adjacent chair and their committee colleagues flanking the center, usually with majority party members on one side and minority party members on the other, seated in order of their seniority on the committee.

On the main floor of the committee room is a desk for a reporter or recorder of the proceedings who transcribes or tapes the hearing as it occurs. To one side of the room along the wall is usually a press table with chairs for print and broadcast journalists. There is also often a table for the personal staff of both members and non-members of the committee. Directly in front of the chair is the witness table where witnesses appearing before the committee sit and deliver their testimony. Most hearing rooms are typical auditorium-style with several rows of chairs for those in attendance. (§ 2.10, § 2.11, and § 2.12)

47) *How does a committee prepare for a hearing?*
A congressional committee's decision to conduct a hearing triggers an array of administrative and substantive activities required to organize, plan, and prepare for the hearing on the parts of both the committee and any witnesses. For the committee's part, most of this work is undertaken by committee staff, who attend to all administrative, logistical, and substantive aspects of hearing preparation. They schedule a date, a hearing room, and the appropriate technical and

administrative assistance to support the hearing. The staff ensure proper notice of the hearing is given, issue invitations and subpoenas to witnesses, and provide briefings for committee members.

Committee staff prepare written materials for the committee members, and handle communication with witnesses. They provide information to witnesses, including committee rules and guidelines, stylistic and formatting requirements for the prepared statement, and scheduling and logistical information such as time, place, room, layout, order of appearance, and hearing schedule.

Other administrative duties performed by committee staff include setting up the hearing room; laying out briefing materials and other documents; reserving seating areas for the media, congressional staff, and witnesses; arranging for security and technology requirements; and providing committee liaison with all hearing participants. (§ 2.1)

48) *What advice should a first-time witness consider?*

A first-time witness should focus on understanding the congressional committee's agenda, becoming familiar with the topic of the hearing and the subject matter of the testimony, and rehearsing the oral testimony and answers to questions. It would also be prudent to review the sections in the book on the roles and expectations of a witness (including tips for first-time witnesses), and on how to be an effective witness. (§ 2.2, § 4.3 through § 4.5, § 2.16, § 2.20, § 5.3, and § 5.73)

49) *How does a witness prepare to answer questions asked at a committee hearing?*

For a witness, the question-and-answer phase of a congressional committee hearing is both an opportunity to be responsive to the questions of committee members, and to continue to advance the major themes of the witness's testimony within the context of the answers given to questions. The core activity of witness preparation is a witness's rehearsal of the oral testimony and answers to expected or possible committee questions. Rehearsals can take many forms and utilize many methods, including "murder boards" and question-and-answer "dry runs." (§ 4.15 through § 4.25 and § 6.3)

50) *How is a witness expected to dress for a hearing?*

Business attire is generally considered appropriate for an appearance as a witness before a congressional committee. Business suits or at least coat and tie for gentlemen, and business suits or dress ensembles for ladies, are preferable. "Business dress" is a common standard. (§ 4.42)

51) *Do witnesses rehearse or practice their testimony?*

Yes, most witnesses prepare and rehearse their testimony and their answers to potential questions that might be asked at a hearing. There are numerous methods for effectively preparing and rehearsing for a congressional hearing. A critical ingredient of a successful hearing and high-quality oral testimony from the perspective of both the committee and the witness is a well-prepared witness. (Chapter 4)

52) *What rehearsal methods are used by witnesses to prepare for a hearing?*
Witnesses use a number of methods to prepare for a congressional committee hearing, including hearing simulation or mock hearings, practice "runs" and live peer review, "murder boards" and question-and-answer "dry runs," videotaped and critiqued drills, and reliance on the oral statement script. (§ 4.15 through § 4.25)

53) *What are the key elements of effective testimony?*
To deliver effective testimony, a witness should execute a smooth, concise, and clear delivery of oral testimony; present the testimony at a moderate rate or pace; deliver a purposeful and dynamic message directed toward the committee members; connect with committee members, including using good eye contact and body language; and make a commanding delivery with strong voice projection and energized speech to engage and maintain the interest and attention of the committee. Both written and oral testimony should focus on building an effective and compelling case for the position or issue being presented to a committee, as well as on the development of sound and persuasive arguments and rationale that support the position or issue. (§ 2.18 through § 2.20, § 3.40 and § 5.74)

54) *What information should be included in a witness's testimony?*
A witness's testimony should include the basic case being presented to a committee, complete with supporting data. The essential components of building the case and developing the arguments for congressional testimony or statements include education, persuasion, and argumentation; explanation of issues, facts, and remedies sought; witness standing and credibility; a succinct position outline; and sound public policy rationale, support, and reasoning. (§ 3.40 through § 3.45, and § 3.51)

55) *Are there different types of congressional hearings?*
Yes, there are several different types of congressional hearings categorized and defined either by their specific purpose or committee venue or both, including legislative hearings, budget and appropriation hearings, oversight and investigative hearings, Senate confirmation hearings, field hearings, showcasing and grandstanding hearings, and public or open and closed or classified hearings. (§ 1.50 through § 1.65)

Appendix Ten
Contact Information Regarding Questions about Congressional Committee Hearings, Testimony, and Witnesses

For any questions or inquiries about any aspect of congressional hearings, testimony or witnesses, contact the relevant congressional committee.

- Committee web sites accessed through links found at <*www.Senate.gov*> and <*www.House.gov*>
- Senate and House committees telephonically via U.S. Capitol switchboard at 202-224-3121

Appendix Eleven
Sample Cover Page and Excerpts of Printed Congressional Committee Hearing Transcript

To see the entire printed transcript as a PDF, perform an Internet search for "f:50180" pdf, including the quotation marks.

S. HRG. 111–31

NOMINATION OF HON. RAY LAHOOD TO BE SECRETARY OF THE U.S. DEPARTMENT OF TRANSPORTATION

HEARING

BEFORE THE

COMMITTEE ON COMMERCE, SCIENCE, AND TRANSPORTATION UNITED STATES SENATE

ONE HUNDRED ELEVENTH CONGRESS

FIRST SESSION

JANUARY 21, 2009

Printed for the use of the Committee on Commerce, Science, and Transportation

(Continued on page 384)

SENATE COMMITTEE ON COMMERCE, SCIENCE, AND TRANSPORTATION

ONE HUNDRED ELEVENTH CONGRESS

FIRST SESSION

JOHN D. ROCKEFELLER IV, West Virginia, *Chairman*

DANIEL K. INOUYE, Hawaii
JOHN F. KERRY, Massachusetts
BYRON L. DORGAN, North Dakota
BARBARA BOXER, California
BILL NELSON, Florida
MARIA CANTWELL, Washington
FRANK R. LAUTENBERG, New Jersey
MARK PRYOR, Arkansas
CLAIRE McCASKILL, Missouri
AMY KLOBUCHAR, Minnesota
TOM UDALL, New Mexico
MARK WARNER, Virginia
MARK BEGICH, Alaska

KAY BAILEY HUTCHISON, Texas, *Ranking*
OLYMPIA J. SNOWE, Maine
JOHN ENSIGN, Nevada
JIM DEMINT, South Carolina
JOHN THUNE, South Dakota
ROGER F. WICKER, Mississippi
JOHNNY ISAKSON, Georgia
DAVID VITTER, Louisiana
SAM BROWNBACK, Kansas
MEL MARTINEZ, Florida
MIKE JOHANNS, Nebraska

ELLEN L. DONESKI, *Chief of Staff*
JAMES REID, *Deputy Chief of Staff*
CHRISTINE D. KURTH, *Republican Staff Director and General Counsel*
PAUL NAGLE, *Republican Chief Counsel*

(II)

(Continued on page 385)

CONTENTS

(III)

(Continued on page 386)

NOMINATION OF HON. RAY LaHOOD TO BE SECRETARY OF THE U.S. DEPARTMENT OF TRANSPORTATION

WEDNESDAY, JANUARY 21, 2009,

U.S. SENATE,
COMMITTEE ON COMMERCE, SCIENCE, AND TRANSPORTATION,
Washington, DC.

The Committee met, pursuant to notice, at 2:05 p.m. in room SR–253, Russell Senate Office Building, Hon. Senator John D. Rockefeller, Chairman of the Committee, presiding.

OPENING STATEMENT OF HON. JOHN D. ROCKEFELLER IV, U.S. SENATOR FROM WEST VIRGINIA

The CHAIRMAN. The meeting will come to—the hearing will come to order. I want to start out my chairmanship by yielding to John Kerry who has a 30-minute, maybe 30-hour or 30-second announcement he wants to make.

STATEMENT OF HON. JOHN F. KERRY, U.S. SENATOR FROM MASSACHUSETTS

Senator KERRY. Thank you very much, Mr. Chairman. I appreciate the privilege. I'm managing the nomination on the floor so I need to leave.

I just wanted to welcome you as Chairman. We're delighted that you're going to be taking the helm of this Committee. We know your passion for all of the issues in front of the Committee.

And just personally, as somebody who's shared this journey with you on the Committee, I'm delighted that you've taken on the gavel. And I look forward to your leadership. It's good to be here with you.

I want to welcome our new Senators also. It's great to have all them here. And I would ask unanimous consent that my full statement be placed in the record as if read in full.

[The prepared statement of Senator Kerry follows:]

PREPARED STATEMENT OF HON. JOHN KERRY, U.S. SENATOR FROM MASSACHUSETTS

Thank you Mr. Chairman, and welcome Congressman LaHood. In your fourteen years serving the constituents of Illinois' 18th District, you built a record that has won you the respect of colleagues across party lines for your commitment to pursuing the best policy solutions regardless of party affiliation.

At a time when our physical infrastructure is in desperate need of repair, our crowded skies are in need of a navigation system fit for 21st century air travel, and our collective thinking on transportation policy must account for the increasing effects of global climate changing, I am hopeful that you will bring a breath of fresh

(1)

(Continued on page 387)

2

air to an agency that will be at the center of an infrastructure revolution in this country.

Despite the onslaught of bad financial news, we all have the privilege to live and work and travel in the most prosperous nation in the world. But travel by train in this country, you'd never know it.

Meanwhile, traffic congestion continues to worsen in American cities of all sizes, creating a $78 billion drain on the U.S. economy in the form of 4.2 billion lost hours and 2.8 billion gallons of wasted fuel. In 2007, domestic flight delays cost the U.S. economy $41 billion and consumed about 740 million additional gallons of jet fuel according to the Joint Economic Committee.

As part of the upcoming debate on economic stimulus, we're preparing to make a massive investment in this country's infrastructure. In my mind, that investment has to come with a commitment to the transportation infrastructure that will help us become cleaner and more efficient travelers in this next American century. I look forward to hearing your thoughts on what that commitment should look like.

I also look forward to hearing your view on the Administration's commitment to implementing the CAFE standards adopted as part of the Energy Independence and Security Act. I originally introduced fuel economy legislation in 2002, and this Committee has been fighting for years to improve the efficiency of our Nation's passenger fleet. This bill is one of the most important pieces of energy legislation that we have passed during my time in the Senate—one which was sorely overdue.

This legislation is a key element of our efforts to ensure that the advanced cars and trucks of the future are built here in America. Unfortunately, the Bush Administration has not yet promulgated a final rule implementing the 2007 fuel economy legislation. I hope that you view this as an opportunity to write a standard that will support our climate change and energy security goals by moving the domestic auto industry as quickly as practicable toward the goal of achieving at least 35 miles per gallon by 2020.

The CHAIRMAN. And so be it.

Senator KERRY. And I look forward to supporting your nomination Congressman. We'd reached our agreements over lunch yesterday and after the Inauguration, but I really look forward to your stewardship there. Thank you.

The CHAIRMAN. Thank you. Thank you, Senator Kerry. And obviously I want to welcome everyone to the first session.

Not everybody is here. But it's two. Nobody expected it would be that early.

And I wanted, with the forbearance of the three distinguished people at the witness table, I want to just say a word about the Committee. I'm not Chairman. I'm still Chairman of the Intelligence committee, so you can pitch me right out of the room if you want.

[Laughter.]

The CHAIRMAN. But Danny actually isn't big enough to do that, you see. So, I'm OK.

[Laughter.]

The CHAIRMAN. This is a very exciting thing to me. I'm deeply proud to be Chairman of this Committee or to be able to get into that position. I've been on this Committee for 24 years, and have specialized in certain areas.

I had no idea until I started to do preparation the unbelievable scope of what it is that we have to do, everything from putting ten extra runways at O'Hare Airport if Dick Durbin wants it.

[Laughter.]

The CHAIRMAN. I mean, there's just no end to our capacity of affecting climate change, transportation, telecommunications, the FCC. We've got control of sports. Unfortunately, it's only college sports, not professional sports, but——

[Laughter.]

(Continued on page 388)

3

The CHAIRMAN. We'll take what we can get. And I'm very proud that Senator Inouye, who I think is going to come today, is now doing Appropriations. And I'm very proud that I've been able to work with him.

I look forward, I think we all do, to working very, very hard for Americans, setting forth a very aggressive agenda on this Committee. I think this Committee over the years has had its ups and downs, but we have not been always at our best. And I think our challenge now is to be at our best all the time on all subcommittees, all subcommittees. Everything rises in importance to the level of anything else, not just what catches the moment or what seems to be the most intractable.

I'm also looking very much forward to working with Kay Bailey Hutchison, who will be Ranking, and all members as we move things through the Committee. On the Democratic side we're welcoming Senator Mark Begich, who evidently walks everywhere in this city. Walked home from the last ball last night. Was that the three o'clock one?

Senator BEGICH. I don't know what time it ended, but it was late.

The CHAIRMAN. It was late. OK.

[Laughter.]

Senator BEGICH. But I'm here for you.

The CHAIRMAN. And Tom Udall. And Mark Warner. All of them are distinguished people who are going to be on the Commerce Committee when the resolution passes, which could very well before the end of the day I would think.

We're not organized, you know. We don't know who the new Republican members are going to be. And I hope Kay Bailey comes and tells us so that we know. But we are not able at this point to really have a subcommittee structure fully worked out as to who's going to be on what subcommittee until we know who all the members are going to be. And that makes sense. And it's frustrating. But it's the way things should work if they have to work that way.

I'm very excited by the talent on both sides of the aisle here. I think when you really look at the scope of the Commerce Committee you see it's endless. And it's one of the original committees created. And its work is really wherever we want it to go.

I think we can be a big part of climate change legislation, a big part of economic recovery. I look forward to working with members on a bipartisan basis, and I expect that we'll get a lot done.

I want us to have a very aggressive agenda. That doesn't mean that we meet three times a day, but it means that we meet on a regular basis. We'll try to systemize that so people can put that on their calendars, whether that's going to be a couple times a week, whatever. I promise that I'll share that kind of news with my colleagues very shortly.

Now we have to begin the business of this day, which is a very good day, because we have before us the confirmation hearing of Congressman Ray LaHood to be Secretary of Transportation. I'm for him anyway, but my wife Sharon said that even if I weren't I would have to be because she's from Illinois too. And so, that's that.

[Laughter.]

(Continued on page 389)

4

So I'd like to congratulate Representative LaHood on his nomination. And if you have any family members here we would be very proud to meet them.

Mr. LAHOOD. Thank you, Senator. Thank you very much for holding this hearing. My wife and three of my children are here. And I would like to introduce them, if they would stand.

My wife of 42 years, Kathy. Sitting next to Kathy is my son, Sam. Behind Sam is my oldest son, Darren, and his wife, Kristen. And my daughter, Amy, and her husband, Kevin are here. Kevin, are you here? Stand up.

[Laughter.]

Mr. LAHOOD. That is the LaHood army. It doesn't get any better than that, Mr. Chairman. So, thank you.

The CHAIRMAN. Thank you very much. Now we also have another great opportunity because we have former Congressman Bob Michel, who I've always been a great fan of. I'll never forget that garage story you told me, Congressman Michel. It remains deep in my heart and part of my affection and respect for you.

And then my fellow White Sox fan, Dick Durbin. Well that was embarrassing last night. I mean there was only one White Sox fan in the entire crew out there in Afghanistan. And I kept thinking about you.

So they are going to introduce Congressman LaHood. And I cannot think of two finer human beings, more experienced people, to be able to do that. And so, please do so.

STATEMENT OF HON. RICHARD J. DURBIN, U.S. SENATOR FROM ILLINOIS

Senator DURBIN. Thank you very much, Mr. Chairman. Let me also acknowledge Senator Hutchison. Glad you're with us here today at the kick-off of this newly-formed Commerce Committee.

I want to personally thank the Chairman for who now is assuming this responsibility. It was my good fortune to serve on the Intelligence Committee for 4 years where you served as Ranking Member and as Chairman. And I know the fine work you did there. Much like the minister who shoots a hole in one on Sunday morning, you couldn't talk to us about your best work.

And I just want to say publicly that you have dedicated yourself to the assignments you've been given whether it's on the Intelligence Committee or on the Commerce Committee and call on your staff to really perform at the highest level. I'm glad to hear it will be an active committee. And under your leadership it will be a very effective committee. So I congratulate you on that score.

You know, a lot of us here wax poetic about the good old days around Capitol Hill. And for a few members on this committee, including Senator Wicker, who've had the good fortune to serve in the House of Representatives, that's where many of us got started. And there were great old days.

And I can recall coming to the Congress and meeting right off the bat, not only the Speaker of the House, Tip O'Neill, but one of his closest friends, the Republican leader, Bob Michel from my State of Illinois. Those were days when we fought like cats and dogs on the floor all day and then managed to find some time to be together in the evenings and get to know one another on a bi-

(Continued on page 390)

5

partisan basis. And that really made for a much more pleasant and productive environment. I think what President Obama had to say yesterday and what's he's been saying throughout his campaign is the hope that we will return to that environment.

I just want to say that the nominee for Secretary of Transportation is a person who follows in that tradition. Ray LaHood distinguished himself in many ways, first as Chief of Staff to the Minority Republican Leader, Bob Michel and then in his own right as Congressman from that same district. He led the effort in the House of Representatives during some of the most divisive and contentious times to find civility and decorum. And to try to have bipartisan retreats where members would come together with their families and really come to know one another on a personal basis.

As you come to know Ray you'll understand why his leadership in this area was genuine and personal. It's been my good fortune to know him for many years. Born and bred in the City of Peoria, Illinois, he's been a schoolteacher before he got involved in government work. And I will tell you as a member of the only Congressional delegation, a good bipartisan delegation, I didn't have a closer friend than Ray LaHood, who was on the opposite side of the aisle and represented my hometown of Springfield.

We worked on so many things together, transportation projects, economic development projects. I trusted him completely. His word was good. And I knew that we could work together in a positive and productive way and show some results at the end of the day. We also co-chair the Abraham Lincoln Bicentennial Commission which will celebrate the 200th anniversary of Abraham Lincoln's birth in February of this year. So we've worked together in a lot of different capacities.

I know that President Obama started off in forming his Cabinet wanted to make sure that it was bipartisan and to show that there were leading Republicans who could serve in his Cabinet and do so effectively. I'll be honest with you. I went to him and I said I think Ray LaHood is that person. I hope you'll consider him. And he said he would.

I know that Rahm Emmanuel as the President's Chief of Staff knows Ray as closely as I do, as well as I do. And he felt the same way. And this opportunity came along and it was a great one.

Because Ray LaHood has shown his understanding of transportation issues as a Member of Congress and has worked for these issues during the time that he served. We have this traditional rivalry that many of you have in your states between downstate and Chicago. And some politicians make a career out of poking the wounds between those two areas and trying to keep everybody fighting with one another.

Now Ray and I come from the downstate side of that equation. Neither of us has ever tried to capitalize on that geographical distinction. If we had an important meeting of the Illinois delegation about a major mass transit issue in the City of Chicago, Ray LaHood of Peoria would be there because of his genuine interest in our state and its transportation. And whether it was highways for downstate, whether it was mass transit for the City of Chicago, the development of one of the nation's most important airports in O'Hare or looking forward to the vision of how we can use smart

(Continued on page 391)

6

transportation modes to reduce the use of energy and to try to protect our environment, Ray LaHood has been a leader in that regard.

Now if he is graced with the approval of the Senate and I hope that he will be, to be our next Secretary of Transportation, he will have an awesome, immediate responsibility. This new Recovery and Reinvestment bill focuses a lot on our nation's bridges, highways, the infrastructure, the airports, realizing that's critical to economic growth. I can't think of a better person to be given that assignment. And that's why I come here today to completely support his nomination.

A former DOT official was recently quoted as saying, "the most important part of the DOT Secretary's job is knowing how to work with other people." Well I can tell you, Mr. Chairman, Ray LaHood has the most important part of that job covered if he becomes our next Secretary of Transportation. I'm pleased and proud as a fellow Illinoisan to wholeheartedly recommend him and encourage the confirmation of my friend, Ray LaHood. Thank you very much.

The CHAIRMAN. Thank you, Senator Durbin. Yes, sir.

STATEMENT OF HON. ROBERT H. MICHEL, FORMER U.S. REPRESENTATIVE, ILLINOIS

Mr. MICHEL. Mr. Chairman and Members of the Committee, I appreciate the opportunity to piggyback on the great introduction of our Senator Dick Durbin. I've known the LaHood family for over 25 years. And I know that when Ray grew up it was in the climate of work ethic and certainly being frugal about how you spent your money.

Before his election to the Congress to succeed me as my Chief of Staff, he was for 10 years in that position just prior to his being elected to the Congress. It was my last 10 years out of 14 years as leader on the minority side of the aisle in the House. And during that time our relationship became much more than employee/employer relationship. Over that period of time we became the best of friends. I think, quite frankly, both families would say that we were family with one another.

He's a very quick study on the issues of the day. Always careful in his decision-making process. And has a special gift for dealing fairly with his contemporaries. I tell you he's guided with a wonderful, moral compass. He knows right from wrong. He's an honest, forthright individual. I could trust him, as Senator Durbin said, without any reservation whatsoever.

And as a Congressman he was no ideologue, a conservative Republican, always a gentleman and respectful of his contemporaries and willing to work for a consensus. His special efforts to improve the relationship in the House which is at times—I'd enjoyed the wonderful days earlier on. And then it became worse and worse and the rancorous exchanges; it was just rather nauseating at times.

Ray had the good experience of having experienced it really kind of under both conditions. And when he came then to the Congress he wanted to do whatever he could to let's get back to the days when we could talk with one another and counsel with one another. And as Dick Durbin has said, he did a marvelous job trying to or-

(Continued on page 392)

7

ganize, I think, three or four of those retreats with so many whatever Republicans wanted to come, whatever number of Democrats wanted.

And as a matter of fact it led to Tom Foley and I, the then Speaker, former Speaker of the House, to visit and counsel with some of those freshman members to try and encourage them to take advantage of that opportunity to get to know one another. And do away with these acrimonious exchanges. Well, after a while it dissipated and but I always have to give Ray the credit for trying to make the most of it.

And then finally, Mr. Chairman, and I appreciate your conceding to my asking for just a minute or two to buttress Dick Durbin's introduction. I have to applaud the President for seeing the qualities in Ray LaHood that will serve his Administration well. I think there's no question but that every member of this committee when all is said and done, will be mighty proud of his service as the Secretary of Transportation. And I'm sure Ray will always keep in mind too, that he has an obligation, certainly to please the President who is the benefactor in this case. And thank you, Mr. Chairman and the members of the Committee for the opportunity to speak on behalf of my dear friend and compatriot, Ray LaHood.

The CHAIRMAN. Thank you, Congressman. Thank you very, very much.

Mr. MICHEL. Thank you.

The CHAIRMAN. Thank you. Let me just say before I call on Kay Bailey Hutchison, the Ranking Member to make any comments that she may want to make, that we had to postpone this hearing. And it's one of those infuriating things called paperwork.

People have to answer so many questions now. And so the word was well they hadn't finished the paperwork, so that's why we had to cancel the meeting and then people said it was the FBI that does the paperwork so we removed the word FBI because otherwise everybody would think something was going on, Ray. We didn't want that because, you know, the Ranking Member and I read your FBI report and it's just sparkling clean and I wanted to say that.

Before we actually proceed, my opening statement will come before my opening questions. And I'd now like to say that I'm very honored to have as the Ranking Member Kay Bailey Hutchison. We've served on this committee together for years. We've done aviation together successfully for a number of years. It's a very strong working relationship. She's an extraordinarily talented person, as everybody knows. And I would like to call on you, Senator Hutchison for whatever comments you might want to make.

STATEMENT OF HON. KAY BAILEY HUTCHISON, U.S. SENATOR FROM TEXAS

Senator HUTCHISON. Thank you, Mr. Chairman. Since this is our first real hearing as Chairman and Ranking Member I appreciate your remarks and do look forward to having this relationship continue. We've done some great work in aviation. We had and agreed to FAA reauthorization through our committee last year.

I look forward to working on that again this year. And I hope that our committee will be very active. And I look forward to working with you.

(Continued on page 393)

8

I also wanted to welcome the new members on our side of the committee. Johnny Isakson, Sam Brownback, Mel Martinez, Mike Johanns, our new members that will be joining our committee this year.

Congressman LaHood, we welcome you. And certainly you have had two outstanding endorsements already. And many of us who've worked with you do agree with your integrity and the ability to come together and do things in a bipartisan way. And I think your appointment shows that we are going to have input that will be very important in this Administration.

There are three areas that I am concerned with, that I think are a priority. Certainly this year the Highway Trust Fund, the Highway Reauthorization will be before us. And it is my hope that we can timely pass a Highway Authorization bill.

I say that with almost tongue in cheek because it usually takes us three or four years to pass that five-year bill. And then we pass it and a year later, we have to do it again. But it is important that we work together and you will be a key leader here.

One of my great concerns is the Highway Trust Fund. I think it does not meet today's test of relevance. Certainly the highway system, the Federal system has been built out. We have the skeleton.

And I think today, unlike when President Eisenhower started the system, every state has its own priorities and its own capability to fund. So I think the old donor/donee concept really needs to be looked at carefully. We would always have to have some small percentage of the gasoline taxes for the maintenance of the highway system. I think we would all agree on that.

But I do think now that states have such great needs that especially growing states like mine, that are also donor states, need some relief from the huge amount that we send to Washington and never get back. We're now looking at more toll roads, more taxes to fund our highways when we're sending billions to Washington and going to other states. So I hope that we can start looking at a concept where states would be able to have their own money, their own priorities in the Highway Trust Fund with some smaller amount that would be kept for maintenance. That is something that the Secretary of Transportation has suggested in the last 6 months or so. And I think it's something that is very, very important for us to start discussing.

Second, FAA Reauthorization, which as we have noted, this committee passed in a very bipartisan way because it is so important. And our bill passed through the Senate and was generally supported. It did not get through conference so we still don't have one. And in March the FAA extension runs out.

We know that NextGen for our air traffic control system is essential for us to be able to use our air space in the most efficient way, in the most safe way and also our ground space. And because our NextGen has not been able to go forward in a comprehensive way, we do still have many delays, especially in the New York airspace which then affects the whole country.

So I hope that it will be one of your major priorities that we pass an FAA Reauthorization bill and that we get it signed by the President and that we really focus on our air traffic control system becoming more efficient and certainly with safety as a priority. I

(Continued on page 394)

think we can do that. And we will certainly need the help of this Administration.

Third, is Amtrak and high-speed rail. I believe that this Administration that has just taken the oath of office yesterday will be more favorable to Amtrak. And one of the things that Senator Lautenberg and I have done on this committee is made a pact that Amtrak is Amtrak, that our national system is important for our country and for the future. And I support the Northeast Corridor and he and others that are in the Northeast support the national system.

But the national system has been a stepchild. And if we are going to continue to have very bad service, it's going to exacerbate the problem with the funding. So I hope that you will look at Amtrak and high-speed rail as a priority in this Administration. Because I think if we're going to have a transportation system that serves all the people of our country, it's going to mean we have aviation, we have high-speed rail and Amtrak from which states can form compacts and add to the efficiencies as well as of course, our highway system.

And I think with that kind of priority focus we can do so much better. And I look forward to working with you to that end. Thank you.

[The prepared statement of Senator Hutchison follows:]

PREPARED STATEMENT OF HON. KAY BAILEY HUTCHISON, U.S. SENATOR FROM TEXAS

Thank you Senator Rockefeller, it is always a pleasure to work with you and I look forward to a prosperous session in our new roles. Senator Rockefeller and I have worked together for a number of years, most recently as respective Chair and Ranking Member of the Aviation Subcommittee. We have always worked in a bipartisan manner and I look forward to the challenges ahead of us.

Many of the Committee's most difficult challenges will also test today's nominee. I am pleased that this Committee is moving expeditiously on the nomination of the Honorable Raymond LaHood for the position of Secretary of Transportation. I think this is very appropriate since the range of problems confronting the next Secretary is amongst the most difficult that any new Secretary has faced in quite some time.

As Rep. LaHood is keenly aware, we are all looking for ways to revive our economy and many have suggested infrastructure and other transportation related projects can play a long term role in moving our country forward.

It is important our next Transportation Secretary provides the stable leadership and strong voice needed to ensure transportation is a priority within the new Administration.

I expect Rep. LaHood will need to hit the ground running. While I reserve final judgment and although the specific details of a stimulus package are not yet clear, transportation infrastructure programs are likely to receive an increase in funding. If enacted, the quick and efficient delivery of those funds to high priority projects will be challenging, but it is very important they are spent appropriately and efficiently.

One prerequisite and commitment I would like from Rep. LaHood, is to create some short-term stability in our transportation programs. Many States have good ready-to-go highway projects that will improve surface infrastructure and bolster the economy; not just through the addition of construction jobs, but also through the improved movement of goods and people.

Unfortunately, the existing highway program expires at the end of September, however. So Congress and the new Administration will have to work very hard on a reauthorization. This will be very difficult because of the current fiscal state of the Highway Trust Fund and also because the current formula's disparate treatment between the states. But we must reauthorize the program and stop passing short-term extensions that send out dribbles of money to the states, preventing states ability to plan and undertake large transportation projects. Many projects could grind to a halt if we don't act.

(Continued on page 395)

We have already seen this scenario play out with the FAA reauthorization bill, creating a dire situation with the airport grants program. We all know that our aviation system is facing significant capacity constraints. The problem is that the current extension for the program and the taxes that support the aviation trust fund expire at the end of March. The airports have only received half a year's funding.

I hope that Rep. LaHood, if confirmed, would support a full Fiscal Year extension of the current FAA Reauthorization bill, through September 30, 2009. This Committee will work hard to pass a new FAA Reauthorization bill, but we will need the Secretary's support and coordination to do so in a timely manner.

As Secretary, you will also need to keep a close managerial eye on the FAA's air traffic control modernization program, known as NextGen. The funding, implementation, and transition management of NextGen needs to be a priority for the Department. We are currently operating outdated equipment with ever increasing congestion issues in the air and on the ground. These congestion issues are causing problems throughout the aviation system, particularly in the New York airspace. A near-term focus is necessary on our national air transportation system if we expect to meet the future travel demands and eliminate gridlock in our skies and at our airports.

I also look forward to hearing your views on Amtrak and high speed rail. I believe this is an area we have neglected too long. The Amtrak reauthorization that has just been signed into law is an important step, but now we need strong leadership at the Department to ensure that we have a national passenger rail system that works.

I look forward to your testimony.

The CHAIRMAN. Thank you, Senator Hutchison.

What I'm going to do now and I'm still working it over in my mind if I want to make this a regular practice. I think sometimes if every single member gives an opening statement, when you have people who have flown in from all kinds of places to testify, and if you have a full committee, which I hope we're going to have because it's going to be an exciting committee and people are going to want to be here no matter what the subcommittee or in some cases the full committee meeting might be about, that opening statements take time.

The other side of that is that members have other meetings. And I have to recognize that, and that they have things they want to say.

So today we're going to have opening statements from each member. I should say incidentally that our three new members, one of whom has already defected——

[Laughter.]

The CHAIRMAN. Are to be treated today as members of the Senate and because we don't have our actual ratios worked out yet. So just members of the Senate, I mean you're just going to have to live with that, hopefully just for one day.

[Laughter.]

The CHAIRMAN. Is that OK? Alright.

And also I'd like to say that from now on I want to call on people according to the order in which they arrived at the Committee. This is not going to be, like most everything in the Senate, based on seniority. I think having people speak other than on the basis in which they arrived. If they arrived early, they should speak earlier.

And I just happen to believe in that. But today we'll also use the seniority system for that. We'll start with Senator Cantwell, then we'll go to Senator Snowe and then back and forth.

Appendix Twelve
Selected Bibliography and Suggested Reading

Links to the sources below, where available online, are on this book's website at <*www.TCNTBC.com*>

- *Congressional Deskbook, The Practical and Comprehensive Guide to Congress*, Michael L. Koempel and Judy Schneider, TheCapitol.Net
- *Delivering Testimony, GAO Performance and Learning Instructor Manual*, United States Government Accountability Office, September 2001
- *Delivering Testimony, Participant Manual*, United States Government Accountability Office, January 2007
- *Lobbying and Advocacy*, Deanna Gelak, TheCapitol.Net
- *Making Their Minutes on the Hill Count: Congressional Witnesses Play Roles in a Carefully Scripted Drama*, Maureen Fan, The Washington Post, August 5, 2004
- *Media Relations Handbook for Agencies, Associations, Nonprofits and Congress*, Bradford Fitch, TheCapitol.Net
- *Persuading Congress*, Joseph Gibson, TheCapitol.Net
- *Preparing for Congressional Testimony, Participant Manual*, United States Government Accountability Office, November 2005
- *Rules of the United States House of Representatives*, <*rules.House.gov*>
- *Rules of the United States Senate*, <*rules.Senate.gov*>
- *The Truth About Public Speaking, The 3 Keys to Great Presentations*, Ed Barks, Ogmios Publishing, 2005

CRS Reports

- "Field Hearings: Fact Sheet on Purposes, Rules, Regulations, and Guidelines," by Valerie Heitshusen, CRS Report for Congress RS20928
- "Hearings in the House of Representatives: A Guide for Preparation and Conduct," by Richard C. Sachs and Carol Hardy, CRS Report for Congress 96-623
- "Hearings in the House of Representatives: A Guide for Preparation and Procedure," by Thomas P. Carr, CRS Report for Congress RL30539
- "Hearings in the U.S. Senate: A Guide for Preparation and Conduct," by Richard C. Sachs and Carol P. Hardy, CRS Report for Congress 96-822
- "Hearings in the U.S. Senate: A Guide for Preparation and Procedure," by Betsy Palmer, CRS Report for Congress RL30548
- "House Committee Hearings: Arranging Witnesses," by Christopher Davis, CRS Report for Congress 98-304
- "House Committee Hearings: Preparation," by Christopher Davis, CRS Report for Congress 98-488
- "House Committee Hearings: Scheduling and Notification," by Christopher Davis, CRS Report for Congress 98-339
- "House Committee Hearings: The 'Minority Witness Rule,'" by Christopher Davis, CRS Report for Congress RS22637
- "House Committee Hearings: Witness Testimony," by Christopher Davis, CRS Report for Congress 98-338
- "Senate Committee Hearings: Arranging Witnesses," by Betsy Palmer, CRS Report for Congress 98-336
- "Senate Committee Hearings: Preparation," by Betsy Palmer, CRS Report for Congress 98-489
- "Senate Committee Hearings: Scheduling and Notification," by Betsy Palmer, CRS Report for Congress 98-337
- "Senate Committee Hearings: The 'Minority Witness Rule,'" by Christopher Davis, CRS Report for Congress RS22649
- "Senate Committee Hearings: Witness Testimony," by Betsy Palmer, CRS Report for Congress 98-392
- "Senate Confirmation Process: A Brief Overview," by Lorraine H. Tong, CRS Report for Congress RS20986
- "Types of Committee Hearings," by Valerie Heitshusen, CRS Report for Congress 98-317

Appendix Thirteen
Further Contact Regarding *Testifying Before Congress*

Let Us Hear from You.

To comment on the contents of *Testifying Before Congress*, or to offer suggestions for possible inclusion in future editions, contact the book's web site at <*www.TestifyingBeforeCongress.com*> or <*www.TCNTBC.com*>.

TheCapitol.Net
PO Box 25706
Alexandria, VA 22313-5706

Or send your suggestions to:
publisher@thecapitol.net

Keep Up-to-Date.

To see periodic updates, revisions and additions to the content of *Testifying Before Congress* online, please see the book's web site at <*www.TCNTBC.com*>.

Index

References are to chapters (Ch.), sections, and appendices (App.).

D

E

F

G

H

Q

R

S

T

U

V

W

Final HITS: Humor in Testimony

"When witnesses come before Congress, I can ask them leading questions. There's no one to object and no judge to rule against me. It's great."

Source: U.S. Representative Michael Arcuri (D-NY), on making the transition from being a prosecutor to being a Member of Congress

About TheCapitol.Net

We help you understand Washington and Congress.™

For over 30 years, TheCapitol.Net and its predecessor, Congressional Quarterly Executive Conferences, have been training professionals from government, military, business, and NGOs on the dynamics and operations of the legislative and executive branches and how to work with them.

Instruction includes topics on the legislative and budget process, congressional operations, public and foreign policy development, advocacy and media training, business etiquette and writing. All training includes course materials.

TheCapitol.Net encompasses a dynamic team of more than 150 faculty members and authors, all of whom are independent subject matter experts and veterans in their fields. Faculty and authors include senior government executives, former Members of Congress, Hill and agency staff, editors and journalists, lobbyists, lawyers, nonprofit executives and scholars.

We've worked with hundreds of clients across the country to develop and produce a wide variety of custom, on-site training. All courses, seminars and workshops can be tailored to align with your organization's educational objectives and presented on-site at your location.

Our practitioner books and publications are written by leading subject matter experts.

TheCapitol.Net has more than 2,000 clients representing congressional offices, federal and state agencies, military branches, corporations, associations, news media and NGOs nationwide.

Our blog: Hobnob Blog—hit or miss ... give or take ... this or that ...

Our recommended provider of government training in Brazil is PATRI/EDUCARE <www.patri.com>

TheCapitol.Net supports the T.C. Williams Debate Society, Scholarship Fund of Alexandria, and Sunlight Foundation

TheCapitol.Net

Non-partisan training and publications that show how Washington works.™

PO Box 25706, Alexandria, VA 22313-5706 703-739-3790 www.TheCapitol.Net

Breinigsville, PA USA
19 August 2010
243814BV00006B/7/P

9 781587 331725